INDEX

TO

PRINTED

VIRGINIA
GENEALOGIES

INCLUDING

KEY and BIBLIOGRAPHY

[Compiled by ROBERT ARMISTEAD STEWART]

WITH AN ADDED

FOREWORD

By

JOHN FREDERICK DORMAN
Editor, *The Virginia Genealogist*

CLEARFIELD

Originally Published
Richmond, 1930

Reprinted
Genealogical Publishing Company
Baltimore, 1965

Reprinted with an added Foreword
Genealogical Publishing Company
Baltimore, 1970

Reprinted for
Clearfield Company, Inc. by
Genealogical Publishing Co., Inc.
Baltimore, Maryland
1991, 1997, 2003

Library of Congress Catalogue Card Number 73-119445

International Standard Book Number: 0-8063-0418-9

FOREWORD

By

JOHN FREDERICK DORMAN

The location of information about Virginia families was made relatively easy by two publications of the early 1930s. The first of these was Robert Armistead Stewart's *Index to Printed Virginia Genealogies*. The other was Dr. Earl Gregg Swem's *Virginia Historical Index*. While the latter covered every personal and place name and subject mentioned in the 120 volumes of eight periodical and serial works dealing with Virginia, a monumental project which has never been .duplicated in any other state, the Stewart *Index* drew citations from more than eight hundred titles, representing over one thousand individual volumes containing genealogical data.

Under some 6000 family name entries there are more than 18,000 individual references. The *Index* covers most of the genealogies of Virginia families published before 1930, histories of Virginia and West Virginia counties, biographical encyclopedias and Virginia periodicals. In addition, Virginia references were drawn from numerous other publications such as the genealogical columns of the *Baltimore Sun* and the Louisville, Ky., *Courier-Journal*, the *New England Historical and Genealogical Register*, county histories of Ohio, Illinois, Missouri and other states, and *Lineage Books* of the Daughters of the American Revolution, the entries in these cases being selective.

As Dr. Stewart pointed out in his Preface, the *Index* was begun by William Glover Stanard, for thirty-five years editor of *The Virginia Magazine of History and Biography*, and Mrs. Rebecca Johnston of the Virginia Historical Society staff and was completed by him when other duties prevented their continuing the work.

In the forty years since first publication of *Index to Printed Virginia Genealogies* much additional information about Virginia families has been printed. Location of data in genealogies, both of individual families and in collected series, was greatly facilitated by the publication in 1967 of Stuart Brown's *Virginia Genealogies, A Trial List of Printed Books and Pamphlets*. The several indexes of Donald Lines Jacobus and more recently the *Genealogical Newsletter* edited by Inez Waldenmaier (1955-63) and *Genealogical Periodical Annual Index* edited by Ellen Stanley Rogers and George Ely Russell (1962-   ) serve as guides to articles in magazines. There is, however, no satisfactory guide to sketches of Virginia families which have appeared in county histories since 1930.

As a basic reference source for the location of information about Virginians, Dr. Stewart's *Index* stands as his monument. In completing the work of William G. Stanard and seeing it printed he placed future generations of historians and genealogists forever in his debt.

Robert Armistead Stewart was born in Portsmouth, Va., March 9, 1877, the only child of Colonel William H. and Annie Wright (Stubbs) Stewart. His father, who had served as lieutenant colonel of the 61st Virginia Regiment, C.S.A., from April 1861 until the surrender at Appomattox, was for almost twenty years Commonwealth's Attorney of Norfolk County and from 1878 until 1880 editor of the *Daily Times* of Portsmouth. R. A. Stewart was educated at Portsmouth Academy, Portsmouth English and Classical School and Col. Hillary P. Jones' School in Norfolk, and in 1894 matriculated at the University of Virginia where he received his B.A. and M.A. degrees in 1898.

For two years, while an undergraduate, he was assistant to Major Horace Jones, principal of the University High School at Charlottesville. In 1899-1900 he filled the chair of French and German at Wofford College, Spartanburg, S.C., but then returned to the University of Virginia for postgraduate study. When he received the degree of Doctor of Philosophy in 1901 he was the youngest man ever to receive that honor from the University. During that session he was also assistant in Teutonic Languages at the University and with James A. Harrison was associate editor of a sixteen volume edition of the works of Edgar Allan Poe.

In 1901-02 he was Assistant Professor of Modern Languages at Tulane University in New Orleans and while there published *Textual Notes for the Tales of Edgar Allan Poe*, a detailed study of the variations among the earliest printed versions of those prose works. He returned to Virginia in 1903 to become Assistant Professor of Modern Languages at Richmond College. He became Professor of Romance Languages in 1912 and continued to fill that chair until 1917. During these years he published a volume of verse, *Knights of the Golden Horseshoe and Other Lays* (1909), which dealt with various events in Virginia's history and contained an appendix giving background references, continued his writings on Poe's works with *The Case of Edgar Allan Poe, Pathological Study Based on the Investigation of Lauvriere* (1910), and edited two volumes in the *Graded Classics Series, Poems and Tales of Edgar Allan Poe* (1911) and *Carlyle's Essay on Burns* (1912).

iv

From 1917 to 1919 Dr. Stewart taught at Johns Hopkins University in Baltimore and then for several years devoted his time to writing. In this period he issued three adventure books for boys under the pseudonym Gordon Stuart, *The Boy Scouts of the Air in the Dismal Swamp* (1920), *The Boy Scouts of the Air at Cape Peril* (1921) and *The Boy Scouts of the Air on Baldcrest* (1922). In 1923 he published *Goldin Stairs*, a volume of verse in Negro dialect.

In 1924 he returned to the University of Richmond where he was Assistant Professor of Romance Languages until 1931. His genealogical publications date from this period. In October, 1926, he began a quarterly magazine, *The Researcher; a Magazine of History and Genealogical Exchange.* Before it terminated publication in July, 1928, he had made available through its pages such diverse materials as extracts from the Revolutionary War naval records, tax lists of various Virginia counties, early land patents and sketches of families. In 1929 he succeeded The Rev. Clayton Torrence as editor of the *Sons of the Revolution in the State of Virginia Semi-Annual Magazine* which he continued until 1932, printing various historical and genealogical articles. His detailed study of "The First William Byrd of Charles City County, Virginia," based on early court records, was published in *The Virginia Magazine of History and Biography* in five installments during 1933-34 and was followed in 1934-35 by "Excerpts from the Charles City County Records, (1655-1666)" which discussed various historical events gleaned from the court order books of that period.

Dr. Stewart's Introduction to Mrs. Nell M. Nugent's *Cavaliers and Pioneers, Abstracts of Virginia Land Patents and Grants* (1934) is a brief but comprehensive presentation of the history of Virginia during its first fifty years and of the policies in effect relating to the granting of land. To this he appended a list of "Ancient Planters" who were in Virginia by 1616.

The same year (1934) he published *The History of Virginia's Navy of the Revolution* which still remains the standard account in print of that subject. The roster of naval personnel appearing therein contains much information about descendants of Revolutionary War sailors.

In the late 1930's and early 1940's Dr. Stewart was a frequent reviewer of books for *The Virginia Magazine of History and Biography*. He had become a member of the Society of the Cincinnati in 1907, representing Second Lieutenant Charles Stewart, 11th Regiment, Virginia Continental Line, and in October, 1938, was elected Genealogist of the Virginia Cincinnati. He held that office until shortly before his death. He was also examining genealogist for the National Society of Colonial Dames of America in the Commonwealth of Virginia. Almost two hundred pages of *Genealogy of Members, Sons of Revolution in the State of Virginia* (1939) contain lineages prepared by him for that society.

As Dr. Stewart's health declined he retired from active participation in most historical and genealogical affairs. At the time of his death, however, he had completed a mystery novel dealing with Williamsburg in 1711 and was preparing a companion novel on the early Jamestown settlement.

He died on January 18, 1950, at the home of his uncle Charles Stewart in Falls Church, Va.

John Frederick Dorman
Editor, *The Virginia Genealogist*

Washington, D. C.
February, 1970

PREFACE

―――――o―――――

This "Index to Printed Virginia Genealogies" was begun, some years ago, by Dr. William G. Stanard, aided by Mrs. Rebecca Johnston, on the initiative of a member of the Virginia Historical Society. When the compilers had completed upwards of twelve thousand index cards urgency of other duties constrained them to resign the work. The undertaking was then assigned to the present writer, who has added many thousand references and assembled the material in the form in which it herewith appears. Dr. Stanard's comprehensive knowledge of Virginia genealogy, however, made his successor's task merely a routine of enlarging what had been efficiently planned and carried so far towards its goal.

The Bibliography and Key preceding the Index proper include all works on Virginia genealogy discoverable by the compilers up to the period of going to press. Reference abbreviations are found in bold face type, followed by the title of the book or newspaper in question printed in full.

Numerous county histories, etc., pertaining to states formed from the original Old Dominion contain pedigrees of families derived from the Mother State. Of these volumes many have been searched and Virginia lineages duly indexed, though an exploration of the ground in its entirety was obviously precluded by limitations of time and of space.

ROBERT ARMISTEAD STEWART.

Richmond, Va., October, 1930.

KEY AND BIBLIOGRAPHY

Key and Bibliography

(An abbreviated title used in the Index is printed below in **bold face type** and followed by the title of the work in full.)

A

ADAMS—Biographical Genealogy of the Virginia Adams Families, etc., by Thomas Tunstall Adams, 1928. William Byrd Press, Inc.

Adams Co., Ohio—A History of Adams County, Ohio, etc., by Nelson W. Evans and Emmons B. Hivers. West Union, Ohio, 1910.

Albemarle—Albemarle County in Virginia, etc., by Edgar Woods, Charlottesville, Va. The Michie Co., 1901.

ALEXANDER (*Augusta*)—Alexander Family Chart, July, 1914.

ALEXANDER—The Alexander Family; Virginia, Princeton-New York branch. Second edition, New York, July, 1914.

ALEXANDER—Alexander Family Records. First American Settlers and Early Colonial Families. New England and Virginia Records.

ALEXANDER—The Alexander Family, by W. M. Clemens, New York, 1914.

ALEXANDER—Life of Archibald Alexander, D. D., by J. W. Alexander, New York, 1854.

Alleghany—A Centennial History of Alleghany County, Virginia, by Oren F. Morton, Dayton, Va. J. K. Ruebush Co., 1923.

ALLERTON—A History of the Allerton Family in the U. S., 1585-1885, etc., by W. S. Allerton, New York, 1888.

ALLERTON—Allertons of New England and Virginia, by Isaac J. Greenwood, 1890. Reprint from New Eng. His. and Gen. Register, vol. 44, 1890.

Alstons and Allstons—The Alstons and Allstons of North and South Carolina, etc., by Jos. A. Groves, M. D., Selma, Ala. The Franklin Printing and Publishing Company, Atlanta, Ga., 1901.

AMERICA HERALDICA—A compilation of coats of arms, crests and mottoes of prominent American families settled in this country before 1800. Ed. by L. deV. Vermont, New York. Brentano Brothers, 1886.

AMERICAN FAMILY ANTIQUITY, Vol. I, by Albert Wells, New York, 1880. Page 125-170.

AMMONET—Jacob Ammonet of Virginia and part of his descendants.

ANCESTRY AND DESCENDANTS OF THOMAS GREENWOOD OF NEWTON, MASS., AND JOHN GREENWOOD OF VIRGINIA. See "Greenwood".

ANDERSON—Andersons of Gold Mine, Hanover Co., Va., by Edward Anderson, Chicago, Ill.

ANDERSON—A Monograph of the Anderson, Clark, Marshall and McArthur Connection.

ANDREWS—Genealogical Tree of the descendants of Isham Andrews who went from Virginia to Georgia about 1760, by L. W. Andrews.

Antiquary—The Lower Norfolk County, Virginia, Antiquary, Vols. I-VI, edited by Edward Wilson James. Baltimore. The Fredinwald Co., Printers, 1895-1906.

ARDERY—Kentucky Records, etc., by Mrs. Julia Spencer Ardery, Lexington, Ky. Daughters of the American Revolution of Kentucky, 1926.

Aris Sonis Focisque, being a memoir of an American Family, the Harrisons of Skimino. Edited by Fairfax Harrison from material collected by Francis Burton Harrison and privately printed for them. New York. The DeVinne Press, 1910.

Arkansas—Pioneers and Makers of Arkansas, by J. H. Shinn, Little Rock, 1908.

Armistead—The Family of Armistead of Virginia. Printed for W. S. Appleton, Boston, 1899.

Armistead—The Armistead Family, 1635-1910, by Mrs. Virginia Armistead Garber, Richmond, Va. Whittet & Shepperson, Printers, 1910.

Armstrong—Notable Southern Families, by Zella Armstrong, Chattanooga, Tenn. The Lookout Publishing Co., 1918.

ARP—Ancestral Records and Portraits. A Compilation from the Archives of Chapter I of the Colonial Dames of America. The Grafton Press, Publishers, New York, 1910.

Auglaize Co., Ohio—History of Western Ohio and Auglaize County, by G. W. Williamson, Columbus, Ohio, 1905.

Augusta—History of Augusta Church, from 1737 to 1900, by Rev. J. N. Vandeventer, Staunton, Virginia. The Ross Printing Co., 1900.

Augusta Co.—[Waddell's Annals of Augusta Co.] Annals of Augusta County, Virginia, from 1746 to 1871, by Jos. A. Waddell, 2d ed., revised and enlarged. Staunton, Va., C. R. Caldwell, 1902.

Avery, I, II—Genealogical Records—gathered from graveyards, public monuments and family papers, etc., by Carrie White Avery, 2 vols. Washington, 1925.

Bacons of Virginia and Their English Ancestry, by C. H. Townsend.

B

Bagby—King and Queen County, Va., by Rev. Alfred Bagby, D. D. New York and Washington, 1908.

Bagby—Bagby Family Tree. by Rev. Alfred Bagby, D. D., Richmond, 1897.

Ball—Colonel William Ball of Virginia, etc., by Earl L. W. Heck. Sydney William Dutton, 103 Newgate St., London, E. C. 1, MCDMXXVIII.

Barbour Co., W. Va.—History of Barbour County, Western Virginia, Morgantown, W. Va. Acme Publishing Co.

Barksdale—Genealogy of Part of the Barksdale Family in America, by Sarah H. Hubert, Atlanta, Ga., 1895.

Barnes—Barnes Family in West Virginia, by Rev. I. A. Barnes, D. D., 1920. Mennonite Publishing House, Scottsdale, Pa.

Baron Christoph von Grafenreid's account of the founding of New Bern. See de Graffenried.

Baronetage—A New Baronetage of England, etc., 1769.

Barret—The Rev. Robert Barret of Virginia and his descendants, compiled by Edward A. Claypool, Chicago, Ill. (1907), blue print.

Barton's Virginia Colonial Decisions, edited by R. T. Barton, 2 vols., 1909.

Baskerville—Genealogy of the Baskerville Family and some allied families, etc., by Patrick Hamilton Baskervill, Richmond, Va. W. E. Jones' Sons, Inc., 1912.

Baskerville—Additional Baskerville genealogy, etc., by P. Hamilton Baskerville, Richmond, Va. William Ellis Jones' Sons, Inc., 1917.

BASYE AND TAPP FAMILIES OF AMERICA (Omaha), 1912.
Bates, et al of Virginia and Missouri, by Onward Bates. Privately printed, Chicago, 1914.
Bath Co.—Annals of Bath County, Virginia, by Oren F. Morton, Staunton, Va. The McClure Co., Inc., 1917.
BEAN—The Bean Family of Hardy Co., Va. (now W. Va.), compiled by Josephine Bean Wilson, Athens, Ohio, Aug., 1917 (14 pp.).
BEDINGER—George Michael Bedinger, a Kentucky Pioneer, by Danske Dandridge, 1909.
BEAU MONDE (weekly), edited by W. Cabell Trueman. Genealogies by W. G. Stanard.
BECKHAM—Beckham Family in Virginia and the Branches thereof in Ky., Tenn., Pa., and Va., by J. M. Beckham, Richmond, 1910.
BECKWITH—The Beckwiths, by Paul Beckwith, Albany, N. Y., 1891.
BEDFORD COUNTY—"Our Kin", being historical and genealogical sketches of old Families of Bedford County, Virginia", etc. Including Ackerly, Bolling, Buford, Burks, Calloway, David, Douglas, Gwatkin, Hatcher, Jeter, Johnson, Joplin, Logwood, Moorman, Otey, Parker, Phillips, Poindexter, Robertson, Robinson, Slaughter, Sledd, Snead, Spencer, Talbot, Turpin, Wallace, White, Wright. By Mary Denman Ackerly, of Lexington, Va., and Lula Eastman Jeter Parker, Bedford, Va.
BEDINGER—George Michael Bedinger—A Kentucky Pioneer.
BEGGS—The Book o' Beggs.
BELL (*Augusta*)—Bell Family in America, by W. M. Clemens, New York, 1913.
Bell—Our Quaker Friends of Ye Olden Time, by James Pinkney Bell. J. P. Bell Company, Lynchburg, Va., 1905.
BERKELEY OF BARN ELMS—Chart by William Clayton Torrence in Va. State Library.
Berkeley Co., W. Va.—History of Berkeley County, West Virginia, by Willis F. Evans, Wheeling, 1928.
BEVERLEY—Major Robert Beverley and his descendants, by W. G. Stanard, in VHS.
BEVILLE—The Beville Family of Virginia, Georgia, and Florida, etc., by Agnes Beville Vaughan Todcastle. Boston, privately printed, 1917.
BHNC—Biographical History of North Carolina, 8 vols. Charles L. Van Noppen, publisher, Greensboro, N. C.
BINFORD—Binford Family Genealogy. Compiled and arranged by Mary L. Bruner. Wm. Mitchell Printing Co., Greenfield, Indiana.
Biog. Cyc. of Ky.—Biographical Cyclopedia of the Commonwealth of Kentucky. John M. Gresham Company, Chicago-Phila., 1896.
Biog. Encyc. of Ohio—Biographical Encyclopedia of Ohio.
BIRD—Bird Genealogy, by W. B. Wiley, St. Louis, 1903.
BITTINGER AND BEDINGER FAMILIES, by Lucy F. Bittenger [n. p.], 1904.
BLAIR—Hon. John Blair, Jr., An Address, by H. F. Wickham, 1913.
Blair, etc.—The History of the Blair, Banister and Braxton Families, by Frederick Horner, Philadelphia, 1898.
BLUNTS OF ISLE OF WIGHT CO., VA., by James Francis Crocker, Portsmouth, Va., 1914.
Boddie—Boddie and Allied Families, by J. T. and J. B. Boddie. Privately printed, 1918.
BOLAND PAPERS.
BOLLING—Memoirs of the Bolling family written by Robert Bolling of Chellowe, Buckingham Co., Va., etc., 1803. Translated from the original French manuscript by John Robertson, Jr., son of Wm.

BOLLING—A Memoir of a portion of the Bolling Family in England and Virginia, by T. H. Wynne. Printed for private distribution, Richmond, Va. W. H. Wade & Co., 1868.

BOLLING—The Genealogy of the Descendants of Thomas Tabb Bolling and Seignora Peyton. Compiled by Mary Carter Thurber. Published by Roberta Bolling Blake, MDCCCIX, n. p. (privately printed).

Boogher—Gleanings of Virginia History. Compiled by Wm. F. Boogher, Washington, D. C., 1903.

BOONE—The Boone-Bryan History, by Dr. J. D. Bryan, Frankfort, Ky.

Border Settlers—The Border Settlers of Northwestern Virginia from 1768 to 1795, etc. Published by Judge J. C. McWhorter, Hamilton, Ohio. The Republican Publishing Co., Hamilton, Ohio, 1915.

BOWDOIN—Some Account of the Bowdoin Family, by Temple Prince, 2d and 3d editions, New York, 1894 and 1900.

BOWIE—The Bowies and their kindred, by W. W. Bowie, Washington, 1899.

BOWLES—History of the Bowles Family, by T. A. Farquhar, Phila., 1907.

BOWMAN (Amherst)—Fragmentary Annals of a Branch of the Bowman Family, by Charles W. Bowman, Washington, D. C., 1912.

BOYD FAMILY JOURNAL, March, 1925. Wm. M. Boyd, Editor, Adairsville, Ga. Tribune Publishing Company, Cartersville, Ga.

BOYER—The American Boyers, 2d ed., by Rev. Charles C. Boyer, Kutztown, Pa. Press of Kutztown Publishing Co., 1915.

BRANCHIANA—Being a partial account of The Branch Family in Virginia, by James Branch Cabell. Printed by Whittet & Shepperson, Richmond, Va. [n. d.]

BRANCH OF ABINGDON—Being a partial account of the ancestry of Christopher Branch of "Arrowhattocks" and "Kingsland", in Henrico County, and the founder of the Branch family in Virginia, by James Branch Cabell. Printed by William Ellis Jones' Sons, Inc., Richmond, Va. (Pub. Dec., 1911).

BRAND—The Brand Family of Monongalia Co., Virginia (now West Virginia), by Franklin Marion Brand, of Morgantown, W. Va.

BRANNER—Casper Branner of Virginia and his descendants.

Braxton Co., W. Va.—History of Braxton County and Central West Virginia, by John Davison Sutton, Sutton, W. Va., 1919.

BRECKINRIDGE—Joseph C. Breckinridge, Jr., by E. D. Warfield, New York, 1898.

Bristol Parish—A History of Bristol Parish, etc., by Rev. Philip Slaughter, D. D. (2d ed.) J. W. Randolph & English, Richmond, Va., 1879.

BROADDUS—A History of the Broaddus Family, by A. Broaddus, Louisville, 1888.

BROADUS—Life and Letters of John A. Broadus, by A. T. Robertson, 1901.

Brock, I, II—Virginia and Virginians, etc., by Dr. R. A. Brock, 2 vols. H. H. Hardesty, Publisher, Richmond, Va., 1888.

BROUN—Dr. Wm. Leroy Broun, by T. L. Broun, N. Y., 1912.

BROUN—The Broun Family and their Kindred. Chart of the descendants of William Broun the Immigrant to Virginia, by Virginia M. Broun.

BROWN—Brown of Scotland and Virginia.

BROWN—Genealogy of the Brown Family of Prince William Co., Va., by James E. Brown, Chicago, 1898.

Browning, C. D.—Some Colonial Dames of Royal Descent, by C. H. Browning, Phila., 1900.

Browning, R. D., 3d (III)—Americans of Royal Descent, by C. H. Browning, 3d edition, Phila., 1894.

Bruce IV, V, VI—History of Virginia, edited by Philip Alexander Bruce (and others). Chicago and New York. The American Historical Society, 1924, 6 vols.

BRUMBACH—Genealogy of the Brumbach Families, etc., by Gaius Marius Brumbaugh, M. S., M. D., Frederick H. Hitchcock, Genealogical Publishing Co., 105 W. Fortieth St., New York.

Bruton Church—Historical Sketch of Bruton Church, Williamsburg, Va., 1903, by William A. R. Goodwin.

BRYAN—The Memoirs of William Jennings Bryan, by himself and his wife Mary Baird Bryan, Philadelphia, Chicago. The John C Winston Company, 1915.

BRYAN (*Valley of Virginia*)—The Boone-Bryan History. By Dr. J. D. Bryan, Frankfort, Ky.

BUCHANAN FAMILY RECORDS, by W. M. Clemens, New York [n. d.]

BS—Baltimore Sun. Genealogical column.

BUCKNER—Reminescences of the Buckner Family, by Mrs. Priscilla A. Riordan, edited by Katherine E. Tuley, Chicago, 1901.

Buckners of Va.—The Buckners of Virginia and the Allied Families of Strother and Ashby, edited by W. A. Crozier (New York, 1907. By the Genealogical Association.)

Buford—A Genealogy of the Buford Family in America, with records of a number of Allied Families, by Marcus Bainbridge Buford, San Francisco, 1901.

BULLINGTON *CHART*—by Arthur B. Clarke, blue print. Va. State Library.

BURFORD—The Burford Genealogy, by M. W. and N. J. Burford, Indianapolis, 1914. Privately printed.

Burgess—Virginia Soldiers of 1776. Compiled and edited by Louis A. Burgess, 3 vols. Richmond Press, Inc., Richmond, Va., 1927 and 1929.

BURWELL GENEALOGY, by Mrs. Anna Gleaves Rich. Printed chart [n. p., n. d.]

BURWELL FAMILY—Record of the Burwell Family, copied in part from the manuscript by the Rev. Robt. Burwell. Revised 1908 by George H. Burwell and others, of Millwood, Clarke County, Va. [n. d.] Whittet & Shepperson, Printers.

BYRD—The Writings of Colonel William Byrd of Westover in Virginia, Esqr. Edited by J. D. Bassett, New York, 1901.

C

Cabells, etc.—The Cabells and their Kin, by Alexander Brown, Boston and New York, MDCCCXCV.

CAMPBELL (*Augusta*)—"Stony Mead", by Katherine Green.

CAMPBELL FAMILY MAGAZINE, January, 1916, Vol. I, No. 1, edited by Wm. Montgomery Clemens, N. Y.

Campbell Co.—Campbell Chronicles and Family Sketches embracing the History of Campbell Co., Va., 1782-1926. R. H. Early, Lynchburg, 1927.

Campbell, Pilcher, etc.—Historical Sketches of the Campbell, Pilcher and Kindred Families, by Margaret Campbell Pilcher, Nashville, Tenn., 1911. Press of Marshall & Bruce Co.

CAMPBELL'S HISTORY OF VIRGINIA—History of the Colony and Ancient Dominion of Virginia. Philadelphia, J. B. Lippincott & Co., 1850.

Cantrill-Cantrell—The Cantrill-Cantrell Genealogy, by Susan Cantrill Christie. The Grafton Press, Fifth Ave., New York, 1908.

Caperton—The Killing of Adam Caperton, etc., by J. H. Caperton and W. H. Gordon, Jr. [n. p.], 1918.

Carlyle-Whiting—Descendants of John and Sarah (Fairfax) Carlyle, by Richard Henry Spencer, Richmond, Va. Whittet & Shepperson, 1910.

Caroline County—A History of Caroline County, Va., etc., by Marshall Wingfield. Press of Trevvett-Christian & Co., Inc., Richmond, Va., 1924.

Carolinians II—Cyclopedia of Eminent and Representative Men of the Carolinas of the Nineteenth Century, Vol. II, Madison, Wis. Brant & Fuller, 1892.

Carter Family Tree—Va. State Library.

Carter Henry Harrison—A Memoir.

Carter [Thomas Carter]—The Descendants of Capt. Thomas Carter of "Barford", Lancaster Co., Va., etc., by J. L. Miller, Thomas, W. Va., n. p., 1912.

Carter—Giles Carter of Virginia—Genealogical Memoir by General William Giles Harding Carter, U. S. A. The Lord Baltimore Press, Baltimore, Md., 1909.

Cartmell—Shenandoah Valley Pioneers and their descendants, A History of Frederick County, Va., by T. K. Cartmell, Winchester, Va. Eddy Press Corporation, 1909.

Cary—The Devon Carys. New York, privately printed. The De Vinne Press, 1920.

Cary—The Virginia Carys. An Essay in Genealogy. Privately printed. The DeVinne Press, New York, 1919.

Cary—Sally Cary, by W. M. Cary. Privately printed, New York, 1916.

Cary—Cary Family in America, by Henry Grosvenor Cary, Boston, 1907.

Caskie—The Caskie Family of Virginia, by Jacquelin A. Caskie, 1928.

Cauthorn—Record of the Cauthorn Family, compiled by R. C. Phillips. Edited by Lucy Albion Luxford, Richmond, Va. The Dietz Printing Co., 1909.

Chaplines from Va. and Md., by Maria J. L. Dare, Washington, 1902.

Chappell—A Genealogical History of Chappell, Dickie and other Kindred Families of Virginia, 1635-1900, by Philip E. Chappell, revised edition. Hudson Kimberley Publishing Company, Kansas City, Mo., 1900.

Chaumiere Papers—Containing Matter of interest to descendants of David Meade of Nansemond County, Va. Edited by Henry J. Peet, Chicago.

Chenoweth—History of the Chenoweth Family, Address of Captain William F. Cobb [n. p.], 1912.

Chester—Genealogical Memoirs of the Family of Chester of Chicheley, by Robert Edmond Chester Waters, Esq., B. A., London, 20 Pancras Road, N. W., 1878.

Chichester—History of the Family of Chichester from A. D. 1088 to 1870, by Sir Alex. Palmer Bruce Chichester, Bart., London. John Carden Hotten, 74 and 75 Piccadilly, W., 1871.

Christ Church Parish—Vestry Book of Christ Church Parish, Middlesex County, Virginia, 1663-1767, transcribed, etc., by C. G. Chamberlayne, Richmond, Va. Old Dominion Press, 1927.

Cisco—Historic Sumner County, Tennessee, with genealogies of the Bledsoe, Cage and Douglass Families, etc., by J. G. Cisco, Nashville, 1909.

CLAIBORNE—A Genealogical Table of the Descendants of Secretary William Claiborne, by G. M. Claiborne, Lynchburg, Va. J. P. Bell Company, 1900.

CLAIBORNE—William Claiborne of Virginia, with some account of his pedigree, by John Herbert Claiborne, New York and London, 1917. G. P. Putnam Sons.

CLAN GREGOR YEAR BOOK.

CLAN EWING OF SCOTLAND, ETC., by Elbert William R. Ewing. Cobden Publishing Co., Ballston, Va., 1922.

Clemens' Wills—Virginia Wills before 1790. A complete abstract of all names mentioned in over six hundred recorded wills from courthouse records of Amherst, Bedford, Campbell, Loudoun, Prince William and Rockbridge counties, by William Montgomery Clemens. Pompton Lakes, N. J. The Biblio Co., Inc., 1924.

Cloyd, Basye, etc.—Genealogy of the Cloyd, Basye, etc., Families of America, by A. D. Cloyd, M. D., Omaha, Nebraska, 1912.

COCKE—Memoir of the Cocke Family (articles published in the VHM), republished by James Cocke Southall, 1898.

Coghill—The Family of Coghill, 1377-1879, by James Henry Coghill. Cambridge, Riverside Press, 1879.

COKE OF TRUSLEY—In the county of Derby, and branches therefrom; a family history compiled by Maj. John Talbot Coke. Printed for private circulation. London. Printed by W. H. and L. Collingridge. City Press, 1889.

COLES—Gov. Edward Coles, edited by C. W. Alford, Illinois State Historical Library, Springfield, 1920.

COLES—Sketch of Edward Coles, by E. B. Washburne, Chicago, 1882.

Colonial Church—The Colonial Church in Virginia, etc., by the Rev. Edward Lewis Goodwin, Milwaukee. Morehouse Publishing Company. London, A. R. Mowbray & Co., 1927.

CONFEDERATE VETERAN (monthly).

CONNELLY—Eastern Kentucky Papers, edited by William Elsey Connelly.

CONQUEST OF THE COUNTRY NORTHWEST OF THE RIVER OHIO, 1778-1783, AND LIFE OF G. R. CLARKE, by W. H. English, Indianapolis, 1896. [*English's Conquest of the Northwest.*]

Convention 1788—The History of the Virginia Federal Convention of 1788, etc., by H. B. Grigsby. Virginia Historical Society, 2 vols., Richmond, Va., 1890-1891.

COOKE—John Esten Cooke, Virginian, by John O. Beatty, Columbia University Press, N. Y., 1922.

Cooke-Booth—Descendants of Mordecai Cooke, of "Mordecai's Mount", Gloucester Co., Va., 1650, and Thomas Booth, of Ware Neck, Gloucester Co., Va., 1685, by Dr. and Mrs. Wm. Carter Stubbs, New Orleans, 1923.

COOPER AND ALLIED FAMILIES, by W. F. Cooper, 1906.

CORBIN—Chart Pedigree of the Corbin Family.

Coshocton Co., Ohio—Historical Collections of Coshocton County, Ohio, etc., 1764-1876. Cincinnati, R. Clarke & Co., 1876.

COUNTY COURT NOTE BOOK, edited by Mrs. Milnor Ljungstedt, Bethesda, Md.

COWAN—Chronological Genealogy of James Cowan, Sr., etc., by Julia E. Sellers, London. O. Bell Press, 1911-1919.

COWDEN—Ancestry of the Cowden and Welch Families, by Rev. James Martin Welch, Indiana, Pa., January, 1904.

COWLES—Branches of Virginia Cowles Family, compiled by Eugene Cowles, 1903-1904.

Cox—The Cox Family in America, by Rev. Henry Miller Cox, A. M., New York, 1912. Printed for the author by the Unionist Gazette Association, Somerville, N. J.

Cox—The Cox Family in America, by Rev. Henry Miller Cox, A. M., New York, 1912. Printed for the author by the Unionist Gazette Association, Somerville, N. J.

Crawford—Crawford Family Record, etc., by William N. Clemens. Limited, New York, 1914.

Crawfurdiana—Laures Crawfurdiana—Descendants of John Crawford of Virginia, New York, 1883.

Crocker—Our Crocker Ancestors, by James F. Crocker. Whitson & Shepherd, Printers, Portsmouth, Va., 1914.

Crocker—The maternal ancestors and kindred of Margaret Jane Crocker. Portsmouth, Va., W. A. Stokes, Printers, 1914.

Crockett—The Crockett family and connecting lines (Vol. V of *Notable Southern Families*), edited by Janie Preston Collup French (Mrs. J. Stewart French), and Zella Armstrong. Press of the King Printing Company, Bristol, Tenn.

Crozier—Virginia County Records, edited by W. A. Crozier, Vol. VII. Hasbrouck Heights, N. J., 1910.

Culbertson—Genealogy of the Culbertson and Culberson Familiees. Revised edition. By Lewis R. Culbertson, M. D. The Courier Co., Printers and Binders, Zanesville, Ohio, 1923.

Culpeper—The Proprietors of the Northern Neck. Chapters of Culpeper Genealogy. Privately printed. The Old Dominion Press, Richmond, Va., 1926.

Culpeper—Notes on Culpeper County, Va., embracing a revised and enlarged edition of Dr. Philip Slaughter's History of St. Mark's Parish, by Raleigh T. Green, Culpeper, Va., 1900.

Cumberland Parish—Lunenburg Co., 1746-1816. By Landon C. Bell. The William Byrd Press, Inc., Printers, Richmond, Va., 1930. Contains genealogies of Cameron (Rev. John), Bacon, Ballard, Betts, Billups, Bouldin, Blagrove, Brodnax, Buford, Caldwell, Chappell, Claiborne, Clay, Cureton, Cox, Delony, Dixon, Edloe, Ellidge, Embry, Farmer, Ferth, Fontaine, Garland, Davis, Gee, Hall, Hardy, Hawkins, Hobson, Howard, Jackson, Macfarland, Marrable, Martin, Nash, Neblett, Parrish, Pettus, Phillips, Ragsdale, Read, Robertson, Smith, Speed, Stevenson, Stokes, Street, Tabb, Talbott, Taylor, Tomlinson, Tucker, Twitty, Winn.

Curio—The Curio I. Richmond, Va.

Custer—The Custer Family, by Milo Custer, Bloomington, Ill., 1912.

Custis Reminiscences.

Cyc. Va. Biog., I-V—Cyclopaedia of Virginia Biography, under the editorial supervision of Lyon Gardner Tyler, LL. D. Lewis Historical Publishing Co., New York, 1915.

D

Dabney—Sketch of the Dabneys of Virginia, etc., by William H. Dabney. Press of S. D. Chiles & Co., Chicago, 1888.

Dabney—Life and Letters of Robert Lewis Dabney, by Thomas Cary Johnson, Richmond. The Presbyterian Committee of Publication, 1903.

Daingerfield—Descendants of John Daingerfield and his wife, New Kent Co., Va., 1640. Edited by Lawrence McRae (typed copy).

DAR—Lineage Book. National Society of the Daughters of the American Revolution.

DASHIELL—Dashiell Family Records, by Benjamin L. Dashiell, Baltimore, Md., 1929 (2 vols.).

DAVIS—The Life of John W. Davis, by Theodore A. Huntley. New York, Duffield and Co., 1924.

DAVIS—Genealogy of Jefferson Davis. Address by Wm. H. Whitsett, 1908.

DAVIS—Genealogy of Jefferson Davis and of Samuel Davies, by William H. Whitsett, A. M., D. D., LL. D. New York and Washington. The Neale Publishing Co., 1910.

Davis—Davis (Davies and David) Family in Wales and America, etc., by Harry Alexander Davis, Washington, D. C. H. A. Davis, 1927.

DAWSON—Family Record—A Collection of Family Records, with biographical sketches and other memoranda, of various families bearing the name of Dawson, or allied families of that name and individuals. Compiled by Charles C. Dawson, Albany, N. Y., J. Munsell, 1874.

De Graffenried—History of the de Graffenried Family, 1191 A. D. to 1925, by Thomas P. de Graffenried, of New York City. Published by the Author, 1925.

DE GRAFFENREID (de Graffenried)—Christoph von Graffenried's Account of the Founding of New Bern, etc. N. C. Historical Commission, Raleigh, 1920.

DESCENDANTS OF JOHN STUBBS OF CAPPAHOSIC, Gloucester Co., Va., by W. C. Stubbs, New Orleans, 1902.

DESCENDANTS OF GEORGE PARKER AND HIS WIFE... See Parker.

DESCENDANTS OF SAMUEL HUNTER OF AUGUSTA Co., VA.

DESCENDANTS OF VALENTINE HOLLINGSWORTH. See Hollingsworth.

Des Cognets—William Russell and his Descendants, by Anne R. Des Cognets, Louisville, Ky., 1884.

Dinwiddie Papers—The Official Records of Robert Dinwiddie, Lt. Governor of the Colony of Virginia, 1751-1758, etc. Virginia Historical Society, 2 vols., Richmond, Va., 1883.

DOUGLAS FAMILY (*Loudoun*)—Genealogical Chart of the Douglas Family, compiled by John S. Wise. New York, 1894.

Douglas—The Douglas Register, Being a detailed record of Births, Marriages and Deaths, together with other interesting notes as kept by the Rev. William Douglas, from 1750 to 1797. Transcribed and edited by W. Mac. Jones. J. W. Fergusson & Sons, Printers and Publishers, Richmond, Va., 1928.

Draper Series V—Frontier Retreat on the Upper Ohio, 1779-1781. Draper Series V (Wisconsin Historical Society, 1917).

Du Bellet—Some Prominent Virginia Families. By Louise Pecquet Du Bellet. 4 vols. Lynchburg, Va., 1907.

Duke, etc.—A Genealogy of the Duke-Shepherd-Van Metre Family, by S. G. Smythe. Press of the New Era Printing Co., Lancaster, Pa., 1909.

DULANY (Dulaney)—Something about the Dulaney (Dulany) Family and the Southern Cobb Family, by B. L. Dulaney, Washington D. C. [n. d.]

Dunmore's War—Documentary History of Dunmore's War. Edited by R. G. Thwaite and Louise P. Kellogg. Western Historical Society, Madison, 1905.

Dupuy—The Huguenot Bartholomew Dupuy and his Descendants. By Rev. B. H. Dupuy. Louisville, Ky. Courier-Journal Job Printing Co., 1908.

E

EARLE—History and Genealogy of the Earles of Secausus, etc., by Rev. Isaac Newton Earle, Marquette, Mich. Guelff Printing Co., 1925.

Early—A History of the Family of Early in America, by Samuel Stockwell Early, Albany, N. Y. Joel Munsell's Sons, Publishers, 1896.

EARLY—The Family of Early which settled on the Eastern Shore of Virginia. By R. H. Early. Lynchburg, Va., 1920.

EDWARDS (*Northern Neck*)—Historical Sketch of the Edwards and Todd Families. By G. H. Edwards. Springfield, Ill., 1894.

Ellis—A Memorandum of the Ellis Family, by Thomas H. Ellis, Richmond, 1849.

EMMET—The Emmet Family, etc., by Thos. Addis Emmet, New York. Privately printed (Bradstreet Press), 1898.

English's Conquest of the Northwest—The Conquest of the country Northwest of the River Ohio, 1778-1783, etc., by William Hayden English. Indianapolis and Kansas City, Mo. The Bowen Merrill Company, 1896.

Essex Co.—History of Essex County, Virginia, 1607-1692. F. F. V. Series, by Pauline Pearce Warner and Thomas Hoskins Warner. Published at Dunnsville, Essex Co., Va.

EVERARD—Sir Richard Everard, Kt., by Marshall Delancey Heyward. Augusta, Illinois.

EWING—D. A. R. Family Chart. Compiled by Jean Booker.

EWING—Ewing Family with Cognate Branches, etc., by Presley Kittredge Ewing and Mary Ellen (Williams) Ewing. Houston, 1919.

EWING—Clan Ewing of Scotland. Early History and Contribution to America. By Elbert William R. Ewing. A. M., LL. B., LL. D. Cobden Publishing Co., Ballston, Va.

F

FAIRFAX—The Proprietors of the Northern Neck. Chapters of Culpeper Genealogy. Privately printed. The Old Dominion Press, Richmond, Va., 1926.

FAIRFAX—The Fairfaxes of England and America in the Seventeenth and Eighteenth Centuries, etc., by Edward D. Neill. Albany, N. Y. Joel Munsell, 1868.

FAIRFAX—Randolph Fairfax. Sketch of his Life, by Philip Slaughter, 2nd ed., 1878.

FAIRFAX—An Historical Sketch of the Two Fairfax Families of Virginia. New York. The Knickerbocker Press, 1913.

FAMILIAE MINORUM GENTIUM (Harleian Society).

FAMILY OF HOGE. See "Hoge".

FAMILY RECORDS OF THE MOREHEADS. See "Morehead".

FAUNTLEROY—Blue print charts, etc., of Powell, Fauntleroy, Holmes, Magill, Conrad (Winchester), together with those families with which they are connected, by Col. P. C. Fauntleroy. Virginia State Library.

Fauquier Bulletin—Bulletin of the Fauquier Historical Society. Richmond, Va., 1924.

Fayette Co., W. Va.—History of Fayette County, West Virginia, by J. T. Peters and H. B. Corden, Charleston, W. Va. Jarrett Printing Company, 1926.

FENWICK ALLIED ANCESTRY, by Edwin Jackett Sellers, Philadelphia, 1916.

FICKLIN—The Ficklin Family from the first of the name in America to the recent time, with some account of the family in England, by W. H. Ficklin, Denver, 1912.

FIELD (Feild)—Record of all the Field Family in America whose ancestors were in this country prior to 1700, by F. C. Pierce, 2 vols. Chicago, 1901.

Fishback—Genealogy of the Fishback Family in America, etc., compiled and edited by Willis Miller Kemper. New York, T. M. Taylor, 1914.

FISHBACK—Genealogy of the Fishback Family. The Descendants of Harman Fishback, the Emigrant, with additional data, compiled and edited by Reuben Dewitt Fishback, Cincinnati, 1926.

Floyd—Biographical genealogies of the Virginia-Kentucky Floyd Families, etc., by N. J. Floyd. Williams and Wilkins Company, Baltimore, 1912.

FLOYD—Life and Diary of John Floyd, by C. H. Ambler, Richmond, 1918.

Foote—Sketches of Virginia, by W. H. Foote (1st and 2nd series), Philadelphia, 1850, 1856.

FOOTE—The Foote Family, by A. W. Foote. Vol. I, Rutland, Vt., Marble City Press, The Tuttle Publishing Co., 1907.

Forrest's History of Norfolk, Va.—Historical and Descriptive Sketches of Norfolk and Vicinity, etc., by William Forrest. Philadelphia, Lindsay and Blackiston, 1853.

FORSYTH OF NYDIE, ETC., by Forsyth de Fronsac, New Market, Va., 1888.

Fothergill—Wills of Westmoreland County, Virginia, 1654-1800, by Augusta B. Fothergill. Appeals Press, Richmond, Va., 1925.

FOWLER—Annals of the Fowler Family, etc., compiled and edited by Mrs. James Joyce Arthur, Austin, Texas. Ben. C. Jones & Co., Publishers, 1901.

Francis Morgan, etc., by Annie M. Sims, Savannah, Ga., 1920.

FRY—Memoir of Col. Joshua Fry, etc., by the Rev. J. P. Slaughter. Randolph & English, Richmond, Va., 1880.

FRYE—Frye Genealogy, by Ellen Frye Barker, New York. Tobias A. Wright, Printer, 1920.

Funk—A brief history of Bishop Henry Funck and other Funk pioneers, etc., by Rev. A. J. Frietz of Milton, N. J. Elkhart, Ind., Mennonite Publishing Co., 1899.

Funsten-Meade—The ancestors and descendants of Colonel David Funsten and his wife Susan Everard Meade, compiled for Hortense Funsten Durand, by Howard S. F. Randolph, New York, The Knickerbocker Press, 1926.

G

GAINES—The Gaines Genealogy. Our Line from 1620 to 1918, by L. P. Gaines, Calhoun, Ga., 1918.

Garrard—Governor Garrard of Kentucky, His Descendants and Relatives, by Anne R. des Cognets, Lexington, Ky., 1896.

GENEALOGICAL RECORDS, MANUSCRIPTS, ENTRIES OF BIRTHS, MARRIAGES AND DEATHS IN FAMILY BIBLES. Colonial Dames in State of New York. New York, MCMXVII.

GENEALOGICAL RECORD OF THE DESCENDANTS OF HENRY MAUZY AND JACOB KISLING, by Richard Mauzy, Harrisonburg, Va., 1911.

GENEALOGICAL STATEMENT, by Capt. C. T. Allen.

GENEALOGY OF THE CLOYD, BASYE, ETC., FAMILIES OF AMERICA.

GENEALOGY OF THE MERCER-GARNETT FAMILY OF ESSEX COUNTY, VIRGINIA, ETC., by James Mercer Garnet, Richmond, Va. Whittet & Shepperson, Printers, 1910.

GENEALOGY—Records, etc., Colonial Dames in State of New York, New York, MXCXXVII.

GENEALOGY (Weekes' ed.).

Gentry—Gentry Family in America, including Notes on Claiborne, Harris, Hawkins, Robinson, Smith, Wyatt, Sharp, Fulkerson, and others, by Richard Gentry, New York, 1909.

GIBBENS—The Gibbens-Butcher Genealogy, by A. F. Gibbens, Parkersburg, 1894.

GILES—William Branch Giles, by D. R. Anderson, Menasha, Wis., 1914.

Gilmer's Georgians—Sketches of some of the first settlers of Upper Georgia, etc., by George R. Gilmer, New York. D. Appleton & Co., 1855.

Glengarry McDonalds—The Glengarry McDonalds of Virginia, by Mrs. Flora McDonald Williams, Louisville. George G. Fetter Company, 1911.

GLENN GENEALOGY (MS.), by Robert S. Phifer.

GLOVER MEMORIAL: AND GENEALOGIES, by Annie Glover. Boston, 1887.

GODDIN—Genealogy of the Goddin Family, by Arnette Goddin Vaughan, Richmond, Va., 1923.

Goode—Virginia Cousins—A Study of the Ancestry and Posterity of John Goode of Whitby, by G. Browne Goode. Richmond, Va., MDCCCXXXXVII.

Goodwin—Goodwin Families of America. By John S. Goodwin. Supplement William and Mary College Quarterly, October, 1899, Williamsburg, Va.

GORDON (*Lancaster*)—William Fitzhugh Gordon, etc., by Armistead C. Gordon. The Neale Publishing Co., New York and Washington, 1909.

GORDON—Col. James Gordon of Lancaster (1714-1768), etc., by Armistead C. Gordon, Staunton, Va., 1913.

Gordon—Gordons in Virginia, etc., by Armistead C. Gordon. Limited ed. Hackensack, N. J., C. M. Clemens, 1918.

GOSNOLD AND BACON—The Ancestry of Bartholomew Gosnold. A Collection. By J. Henry Lea. Boston Press of D. Clapp & Son, 1904.

Grayson Co—Pioneer Settler of Grayson County, Virginia, by Benjamin Floyd Nuckolls, Bristol, Tenn. The King Printing Co., 1914.

Green's Ky. Families—Historic Families of Kentucky, by Thomas Marshall Green, 1st series. P. Clarke & Co., Cincinnati, 1889.

GREENWOOD—Ancestry and Descendants of Thomas Greenwood, of Newton, Mass. . . . . John Greenwood of Va. By Frederick Greenwood, New York, 1914.

GREGOR (Clan Gregor)—Year Book, 1913.

GRESHAM FAMILY FROM EDWARD GRESHAM, ENGLAND, 1312-1400, TO THOMAS GRESHAM, VIRGINIA, 1923, by W. Macfarlane Jones. Brown-Neill Printing Co., Richmond, Va., 1923.

Griffith-Meriwether—The Record of Nicholas Meriwether of Wales and descendants in Virginia and Maryland, by W. R. Griffith, St. Louis, 1899.

GRIGGS FAMILY—Genealogy of the Griggs Family, by Walter S. Griggs. Limited Edition. Pompton Lakes, N. J. The Biblio Company, Inc., 1926.

GUNN—The Gunns, by Robert B. Gunn, Crawfordsville, Ga. C. G. Moore's Print Shop, 1925.

GUTHRIE FAMILY IN PENNSYLVANIA, CONNECTICUT AND VIRGINIA, by
H. M. and E. G. Dunn, Chicago, 1898.

H

HABERSHAM—History and Genealogy of the Habersham Family. By
J. G. B. Bulloch, Columbia, S. C., 1901.
Habersham Chap. II—Historical Collections of the Joseph Habersham
Chapter, D. A. R., Vol. II, Atlanta, 1903. Blosser Printing Co.,
1902.
HAKES—Hakes Genealogy. By Harvey Hakes, 2nd ed., with additions
and corrections. Wilkes-Barre, Pa. Press of R. Baur & Son,
1889.
HALE—Hale Family Chart. By Anna Gleaves Rich, Wytheville, Va.
(n. d.)
Halifax Co., N. C.—History of Halifax County. By W. C. Allen.
Boston. The Cornhill Company, 1918.
Halifax—A History of Halifax County, Virginia. By Mrs. Wirt
Johnson Carrington. Appeals Press, Inc., Richmond, Va., 1924.
HAMILTON—The Hamiltons of Burnside, North Carolina, and their an-
cestors and descendants, by Patrick Hamilton Baskervill, Rich-
mond, Va., W. E. Jones' Sons, Inc., 1916.
Hampden-Sydney—College of Hampden-Sydney. Dictionary of Bi-
ography, 1776-1825. By A. J. Morrison, Hampden-Sydney, Va.
n. d.
Hampshire—History of Hampshire County, W. Va. By Hu Maxwell
and H. L. Swisher, Morgantown, W. Va. A. B. Boughner, 1897.
HARDAWAY—Thomas Hardaway of Chesterfield County, Va., and his
Descendants, by Sarah E. Hubert. Whittet & Shepperson, Rich-
mond, 1906.
Hardesty—Hardesty's Historical and Geographical Encyclopedia.
New York, Richmond, etc. H. H. Hardesty & Co., 1884.
Hardin Co., Ohio—History of Hardin County, Ohio. Chicago, War-
ner Beers and Co., 1883.
Hardy—Colonial Families of the Southern States of America. By
Stella P. Hardy, New York, 1911.
HARMAN—Harman Genealogy (Southern Branch), with Biographical
Sketches, 1700-1924, by John Newton Harman, Senior, Tazewell,
Va. Richmond, Va., W. C. Hill Printing Co., 1925.
HARMAN—Harman-Harmon Genealogy and Biography, with Historical
Notes, 19 B. C. to 1928 A. D. Compiled and edited by John
William Harman, of Parsons, W. Va., 1928.
HARRIS (Albemarle)—Harris Genealogy, by G. D. Harris, Columbus,
Miss., 1914.
HARRIS (Henrico)—A Chart of Some of the Descendants of Capt.
Thomas Harris of Henrico Co., Va., who came to Virginia in
1611, etc. Richmond, Va., W. E. Jones, Printer, 1893.
HARRIS—The Harris Family of Virginia from 1611 to 1914. Data gath-
ered and printed by Thomas Henry Harris of Fredericksburg,
Va., 1914.
Harrison Co., W. Va.—The History of Harrison County, West Vir-
ginia. By Henry Haymond, Morgantown, W. Va. Acme Pub-
lishing Co., 1910.
HARRISON (Skimino)—Aris Sonis Focisque—The Harrisons of Skimino.
Being a Memoir of an American Family. Edited by Fairfax and
Francis B. Harrison. Privately printed, 1910.

HARRISON—Carter Henry Harrison—A Memoir. By W. J. Abbot. New York, 1895.

HARRISON(H. T. Harrison)—A Brief History of the First Harrisons of Virginia of the Cuthbert Harrison Line. By Henry Tazewell Harrison, April 2, 1915.

Harrison, Waples, Etc.—Harrison, Waples, and Allied Families. By William Welsh Harrison. Philadelphia, 1910.

HART—Genealogical Narrative of the Hart Family in the United States, compiled by Mrs. Sarah S. Young. Printed for private distribution. Memphis, Tenn. S. C. Toof & Co., Steam Printers, 1882.

HARVIE FAMILY. By L. E. and J. S. Harvie and Mrs. Carter W. Wormeley, Richmond, Va.

HAWKINS—Memoranda Concerning some Branches of the Hawkins Family and Connections. By Genl. John Parker Hawkins. Indianapolis, Ind., 1913.

Hayden—Virginia Genealogies, etc. By Horace E. Hayden, Wilkes-Barre, Pennsylvania, 1891.

HAYMOND—The Haymond Family. By Henry Haymond, Clarksburg, W. Va., 1903.

HEATWOLE—History of the Heatwole Family. By Cornelius J. Heatwole. New York. The Author, 1907.

HEATWOLE—A History of the Heatwole Family. By E. A. Heatwole. Dale Enterprise, Va., 1882.

HENDERSON—Ancestry and Descendants of Lieut. John Henderson of Greenbrier County, 1650-1901. By John Lyon Miller. Richmond, Va., Whittet & Shepperson, 1902.

HENDERSON (*Alexandria*)—Henderson Chronicles. By J. N. McCue, n. p., 1913.

Hening—Hening's Statutes at Large of Virginia.

HENRICO—The Vestry Book of Henrico Parish. By R. A. Brock (Annals of Henrico Co., etc., by Rt. Rev. L. M. Burton). Richmond, Va., Williams Printing Co., 1904.

HENRY—Henry, Ruffin and other genealogies (broadside), by Reginald Buchanan Ruffin (published by the author), 1911. Contains Addison, Anderson, Beverley, Bland, Bolling, Buchanan, Burke, Byrd, Carter, Corbin, De Jarnette, Everard, Goodwin, Henry, Meade, Randolph, Ruffin, Shippen, Skipwith, Tayloe, Taylor, Willing, Wormeley of "Rosegill".

HENRY—A History of the Henry Family. By John F. Henry. Louisville, 1900.

HENRY (*Hanover*)—Patrick Henry—Life, Correspondence and Speeches. By William Wirt Henry. New York, Charles Scribner's Sons, 1891.

HENRY (*Hanover*)—The True Patrick Henry. By George Morgan. Philadelphia and London, 1904.

Henry Co.—A History of Henry County, Va., etc. By Judith Parks America Hill. Martinsville, Va., 1925.

HERALDIC JOURNAL.

HIGGINSONS OF ENGLAND AND AMERICA, Part I, English Ancestry of N. E. and Va. Families. By Eben Putnam, 1903.

Highland Co.—A History of Highland County, Va. By Oren F. Morton, B. L., Monterey, Va.

HINES—Descendants of Henry Hines, Sr. (1732-1810), Louisville, 1925.

His. Ency. of Ill.—Historical Encyclopedia of Illinois. Edited by Newton Bateman, LL. D. (Paul Shelby, joint ed.). Chicago, Munsell Pub. Co.

HISTORY OF THE BATTLE OF PT. PLEASANT. By V. A. Lewis, Charles-
town, W. Va., 1909.
HISTORY OF CAMDEN CO., GA. By J. T. Vocelle, 1914.
HISTORY OF AUGUSTA CHURCH, ETC. By Rev. J. W. Van Deventer,
Staunton, Va., 1900.
HOGE—The Family of Hoge. A Genealogy compiled by James Hoge
Tyler. Edited and published by James Fulton Hoge. Rich-
mond, 1927.
HOGE—Life and Labors of Moses D. Hoge, D. D., LL. D., Richmond,
1899.
HOLLINGSWORTH—Descendants of Valentine Hollingsworth, Sr. By J.
A. Stewart. Louisville, Ky. John P. Morton & Company, In-
corporated, 1925.
HOLLINGSWORTH—Genealogical Memoranda. By W. B. Hollingsworth.
HOPKINS GENEALOGY.
HORD—Genealogy of the Hord Family. By Rev. Arnold Harris Hord.
J. P. Lippincott Co., Philadelphia, 1898.
HORD—Thomas Hord, Gentleman. A Supplement to the Genealogy of
the Hord Family. By Rev. Arnold Harris Hord, 1903.
HORD—The Hord Family of Virginia. A Supplement to the Genealogy
of the Hord Family. Compiled by Rev. Arnold Harris Hord,
1915. Philadelphia, Ferris & Leach.
HORD—Photostat Copy of the History of the Hord Family. By Robert
Hord.
HORTON, ETC.—See Hughes, etc., below.
HOUSTON GENEALOGY—Brief Biographical Accounts of Many Members
of the Houston Family, accompanied by a Genealogical Table.
By Rev. Sam'l Rutherford Houston, D. D. Elm St. Printing
Co., Cincinnati, 1882.
HOWARD—The Howard Lineage (Claypool, etc.), by Gustine Courson
Weaver. Powell & White, Cincinnati, Ohio.
HUDDLESTON—The Huddleston Family. By Clarissa S. Loving. Deep-
water, W. Va., 1924.
HUGHES—My Family Memoirs. By Thomas Hughes. Printed by
King Brothers, Baltimore, 1918.
HUGHES—The Hughes Family of Virginia and Kentucky. By Lydia
A. Hughes and R. H. Sullivan. Columbia, S. C., 1921.
Hughes, Etc.—Family History, including Hughes, Dalton, Martin,
Henderson, all originally of Virginia, and many Kindred
Branches. By Lucy Henderson Horton. Franklin, Tenn., 1922.
HUGHES—The Hughes Family and Connections. By W. L. Hughes.
Owensboro, Ky., 1911.
HUGUENOT—The Huguenot. Published by the Huguenot Society Found-
ers of Manakin in the Colony of Virginia (pedigrees of Reamy,
Cabaniss, Pasteur, Witt, Michaux, Marye, Maupin, etc.).
Huguenot Emigration—Documents, chiefly Unpublished, Relating to
the Huguenot Emigration to Virginia. With an Appendix of
Genealogies, etc. Edited by R. A. Brock, Va. His. Society,
Richmond, Va., MDCCCLXXXVI.
HUME—History of the Hume, Kennedy and Brockman Families. By
W. E. Brockman, Washington, D. C., 1916.
HUME—Statement of Francis Charles Hume of Galveston, Texas. Bound
with Pamphlets of Va. Genealogy, Va. His. Society. F. L. Finck
& Co., Stationers and Printers, Galveston, Texas (n. d.).
HUNTER FAMILY REGISTER—Descendants of Samuel Hunter of Augusta
Co., Va. Dubuque, Iowa, 1895.
HUNTER FAMILY RECORDS, ETC., by William M. Clemens, New York.
Limited ed. W. M. Clemens, 1914.

HUNTER (*Essex*)—Memoir of R. M. T. Hunter. By Martin T. Hunter, Washington, 1913.
HUNTER—Records of Hunter of Hunterston, Abbot's Hill and Park, Ayreshire, and Ayrehill, Fairfax Co., Va. By Mary A. H. Ball, Washington, D. C.

I

Irvins, Doaks, Etc.—The Irvins, Doaks, Logans, and McCampbells of Virginia and Kentucky. By Margaret Logan Morris. Indianapolis. Printed by C. E. Pauley & Co., 1916.
IVEY—Notes on the Ivey Family. By W. Mac. Jones. A. E. Ivey. Postoffice, Etbrick, Va., 1929.

J

JACKSON—Early Life and Letters of General Thomas J. Jackson, "Stonewall" Jackson. By Thomas Jackson Arnold. New York, Chicago, etc. Fleming H. Revell Co., 1916.
JEFFERSON—The True Thomas Jefferson. By W. E. Curtis, Philadelphia, 1901.
John Price—See Price.
Johnson Co., Ind.—History of Johnson Co., Ind. Chicago, Brant and Fuller, Publishers, 1888.
Johnson Co., Ky., Etc., by Mitchell Hall. Louisville, Ky., The Standard Press, 1928.
JOHNSON—See R. W. Johnson.
JOHNSON—Ancestry of Grafton Johnson. By Damaris Knobe. 1924, Hollenbeck Press, Indianapolis, Ind.
JOHNSTON (*Prince Edward*)—General Johnston. By Robert M. Hughes. T. Appleton & Co., New York, 1893.
Johnstons of Salisbury, with a brief supplement concerning the Harvey, Strother and Preston Families. Compiled by William Preston Johnston. New Orleans, Press of L. Graham & Son, Ltd., 1897.
JOHNSTON's OLD VA. CLERKS—Memorials of Old Virginia Clerks, etc. By Frederick Johnston, Lynchburg. Lynchburg, Va., J. P. Bell Co., 1888.
John Wise—Col. John Wise of England and Virginia, 1617-1695, His Ancestors and Descendants. By J. C. Wise. n. p. n. d.
Jolliffe—Historical, Genealogical and Biographical Account of the Jolliffe Family of Virginia, 1652 to 1693. By William Jolliffe. Philadelphia, Printed by J. B. Lippincott Company, 1893.
Jones—Peter Jones and Richard Jones genealogies compiled by Augusta B. Fothergill. Richmond, Va., Old Dominion Press, Inc., 1924.
JONES (*Brunswick*)—John Burgwin Carolinian * * * John Jones Virginian, etc. By Walter B. Jones of Montgomery, Ala. Privately printed, 1913.
JONES—Major Thomas ap Thomas Jones of Bathurst, Va. By Lewis H. Jones, n. p. n. d.
Jones, Roger Jones—Captain Roger Jones of London and Virginia, etc. By Judge L. H. Jones, Albany, N. Y., 1891. Repub. with additions, 1907.
JOURNAL OF THE HOUSE OF BURGESSES.

K

Kanawha—History of Charleston and Kanawha Co., West Va. By Wm. Sydney Laidley, Chicago, Ill. Richmond, Arnold Pub. Co., 1911.

Kanawha Co.—History of Kanawha County from its Origin in 1789 until the present time, etc. Charleston, W. Va., 1876.

KANAWHA Co.—History of Kanawha Co., W. Va., etc. Charleston. Office of West Virginia Journal, 1876.

KEIM AND ALLIED FAMILIES. A Bi-Centennial Commemoration. DeB. Randolph Keim, Editor. 1898, Harrisburg, Pa., Publishing Co.

Keith—The Ancestry of Benjamin Harrison, President of the United States of America, 1889-1893 and in chart form showing also the Descendants of William Henry Harrison, President of the United States of America in 1841. By Charles P. Keith, Philadelphia, 1893.

KEMP AND KEMPE—A General History of the Kemp and Kempe Families, etc. By F. H. Kemp. London, 1902.

Kemper—Family Genealogy of the Kemper Family in the United States, etc. Compiled and edited by Willis Miller Kemper and Harry Linn Wright. G. K. Haxlett & Co., Printers, Chicago, 1899.

Kennedy—Seldens of Virginia and Allied Families. By Mary Selden Kennedy. Frank Allabon Genealogical Co., 2 vols. New York, 1911.

KEY AND ALLIED FAMILIES (in preparation). By Mrs. Julian C. Lane. Statesboro, Ga.

Kilby, Etc.—Genealogy of Kilby, Tynes, etc. By C. M. Kilby, Lynchburg, Va., 1924.

KILLING OF ADAM CAPERTON, ETC.—Published Sept., 1918, for Mr. John Hays Caperton and William Alexander Gordon, Jr. Louisville, Press of J. P. Morton & Company, 1918.

King's Mountain—King's Mountain and its Heroes. By Lyman C. Draper. Cincinnati, 1881.

Kith and Kin, by Mrs. John Russell Sampson. The William Byrd Press, Inc., 1922.

KITH AND KIN—Addenda to Kith and Kin.

KLEINADT—See "Koiner".

Knox County, Ill.—History of Knox County, Illinois. By Charles C. Chapman and Co., Chicago. Blakeley, Brown and Marsh, Printers, 1878.

KNOXVILLE, TENN., SENTINEL.

KOINER—History and Genealogy. An Historical Sketch of Michael Klenadt and Margaret Diller, his wife. Prepared by a Committee, etc. Staunton, Va. Stoneburner & Prufer, Publishers, 1893.

L

LACY—The Walter Garner Lacy Branch of the Lacy Family of Colonial Virginia. Compiled by Harriet E. N. Chace.

LADD FAMILY—John Ladd of Charles City Co., Va. By Warren Ladd, New Bedford, Mass., 1890.

LANIER BIOGRAPHY—Sketch of the Life of J. F. D. Lanier. Printed for the family, 1877.

Lancaster—Historic Virginia Homes and Churches. By Robert A. Lancaster, Jr. J. B. Lippincott Company, Philadelphia and London, MCMXV.

La Rue—Six Generations of La Rues and allied families. By Otis M. Mather, Hodgenville, Ky., 1921.

LCJ—Louisville (Ky.) Courier-Journal.

Lee—Lee of Virginia, 1642-1892. Biographical and Genealogical Sketches of the Descendants of Col. Richard Lee, etc. By Edmund Jennings Lee. Philadelphia, 1895.

Lee—Stratford Hall and the Lees. By F. W. Alexander. Oak Grove, Va., 1912.

Lee—Genealogical History of the Lee Family of Virginia and Maryland. By E. C. Mead. New York, 1871.

Lee—A Record of the Descendants of Col. Richard Lee of Virginia. By C. F. Lee, Jr., and J. Packard, Jr. Reprint, Boston, 1872.

Lee—Lee of Virginia. By J. Henry Lea. Reprint, Boston, 1892.

Lester Family of Virginia—By Owen Bryant Lester, 1897.

Lewis and Kindred Families—See "McAllister".

Lewis—Genealogy of the Lewis Family in America from the Middle of the Seventeenth Century down to the present time. By Wm. Terrill Lewis. Louisville, Ky., 1893. Courier-Journal Job Printing Co.

Lewis (*Augusta*)—A Brief Narrative. By L. L. Lewis. Richmond, Va., 1915.

Lewis (*Gloucester*)—Family Record of Lawrence Lewis and Nelly Parke Custis. From Martha Washington's Bible. Philadelphia, 1890.

Lichtenstein—The Virginia Lichtenstein Family. By Gaston Lichtenstein. Richmond, Va., H. T. Ezekiel, Printer, 1912.

Licking Co., Ohio—History of Licking Co., Ohio. By Norman Newell Hill, Jr. Newark, O., A. A. Granham and Co., 1881.

Lillard—A Family of Colonial Virginia. By Jacques Ephraim Stout Lillard. Williams Printing Co., Richmond, Va., 1928.

Lincoln—History of the Lincoln Family, etc. By Waldo Lincoln. Worcester, Mass., Commonwealth Press, 1923.

Lindsay—The Lindsays of America. By Margaret I. Lindsay. Joel Munsell's Sons, Publishers, Albany, N. Y., 1889.

Lindsay—Annual Report of the Lindsay Family Association, 1910.

Lineage Book, Order of Washington—By J. G. B. Bulloch.

Lomax—Genealogy of the Virginia Family of Lomax, etc. Chicago, 1913.

Lomax—Genealogical and Historical Sketches of the Lomax Family. By Joseph Lomax. The Rookus Printing House, Grand Rapids, Mich., 1894.

Louisville's First Families—A Series of Genealogical Sketches. By Kathleen Jennings, Louisville, Ky. The Standard Printing Co., 1920.

Lower Shenandoah—History of the Lower Shenandoah Valley (Counties of Frederick, Berkeley, Jefferson and Clarke, etc.). Edited by J. E. Norris, Chicago, Illinois. A Warner & Co., Publishers, 1890.

Lumpkin Lore—By L. L. Cody. Macon, Ga., 1928.

Lyle Family—The Ancestry and Posterity of Matthew, John, Daniel, and Samuel Lyle, Pioneer Settlers in Virginia. By Oscar K. Lyle. Lecouver Press, New York, 1912.

M

McAllister—Genealogies of the Lewis and Kindred Families. Edited by J. M. McAllister and Laura B. Tandy. Columbus, Mo., 1906.

McAllister—Family Records of Abraham Addams McAllister and his Wife Ellen (Stratton) McAllister. Compiled for the Descendants by J. Gray McAllister, 1912.

McCarthys in Early American History—By Michael J. O'Brien. New York, Dodd, Mead & Co., 1921.

McClung—The McClung Genealogy. By Rev. Wm. McClung, Pittsburg, Pa., 1904.

McClure—The McClure Family. By J. A. McClure. Petersburg, Va., 1914.

McClure—McClure Family Records. By William M. Clemens. Limited edition, 1914. William M. Clemens, Publisher, 45 and 49 William St., New York.

McConnell—The McConnell Marriage Genealogy, etc. By Hugh M. Addington and Mattie E. Addington. Nickelsville, Va., Service Printery, Publisher, 1929.

McCormick—Family Record and Biography of the McCormick Family. By L. J. McCormick. Chicago, 1896.

McCormick—Family Trees accompanying the Genealogy of the McCormick Family. By Leander James McCormick. Chicago, Ill., 1896.

McCormick—Genealogies and Reminiscences. Compiled by Henrietta H. McCormick. Revised edition. Chicago, 1897.

McCue—The McCues of the Old Dominion. By John N. McCue. Mexico, Mo., 1912.

McDaniel—Life of George White McDaniel, D. D.

MacDonald—Genealogy of the MacDonald Family. Edition B, comprising all names obtained up to February, 1876. By F. V. McDonald, Yale College, New Haven, Conn.

McDonald—The Glengarry McDonalds of Virginia. By Mrs. Flora McDonald Williams. Louisville, George C. Fetter Company, 1911.

McDowell—Letter on the McDowell Family. By Major General Wm. Bering (n. p., n. d.).

McDowell (McDowells, Erwins, etc.)—History of the McDowells, Erwins, Irvines and Connections. By J. H. McDowell. Memphis, 1918.

McElroys of Kentucky.

McGavock—The McGavock Famiy. A Genealogical History of James McGavock and his Descendants from 1760 to 1903. By Rev. Robert Gray. Richmond, Wm. Ellis Jones, 1903.

McGuire—The McGuire Family in Virginia. By William F. Stanard. Old Dominion Press, Richmond, Va., 1926.

McIlwaine—Memories of Three Score Years and Ten. By Richard McIlwaine. New York and Washington, 1908.

McIlhany—Some Virginia Families. By H. M. McIlhany, Jr. Staunton, Va., 1903.

McIntosh I, and II—Brief Abstracts of Lower Norfolk County and Norfolk County Wills, by Charles Fleming McIntosh [Richmond]. The Colonial Dames of America in the State of Virginia, 1914-1922.

Mackenzie—Colonial Families of the United States of America, etc. By George N. Mackenzie, 7 vols. New York and Boston, 1907.

Madison—Life and Letters of Dolly Madison, Etc. By Allen C. Clarke. Washington, D. C., Press of the W. F. Roberts Company, 1914.

Madison Co., Ohio—History of Madison County, Ohio.

Magill Family Record—By Robert M. Magill. Richmond, Va., R. E. Magill, 1907.

Magna Charta Barons—The Magna Charta Barons and their American Descendants, etc. By C. H. Browning. Philadelphia, 1898.

MAJORS—The Majors and their Marriages, Etc. By James Branch Cabell. Richmond, Va., The W. C. Hill Printing Co., 1915.

MARSHALL—The Life of John Marshall. By Albert J. Beveridge. Boston and New York, Houghton-Mifflin Co., 1916.

MARSHALL—The Marshall Family. See "Paxton".

MARTIN—The Martin Family, Descendants of Thomas Martin, of Goochland Co., Va. By Irene D. Galloway. Fayetteville, Ark., 1906.

MARTIN—General Joseph Martin, Etc. By S. B. Weeks. Annual Report, Amer. Hist. Asso.

MASON—Life of George Mason. By Kate Mason Rowland. New York, G. P. Putnam's Sons, 1892.

MASON—The Public Life and Diplomatic Correspondence of James Mason, Etc. By his Daughter. The Stone Printing and Manufacturing Co., Roanoke, Va., 1903.

MASON—Life of Stevens Thomson Mason, the Boy Governor of Michigan. By Lawton T. Hemans. Lansing, Michigan, Historical Commission, 1920.

MASSIE—Nathaniel Massie a Pioneer of Ohio. By David Meade Massie. Robt. Clark Co., Cincinnati, 1896.

MATTHEWS (MATHES) FAMILY—By I. V. Van Deventer. Alexander Printing Company, Publishers, Kansas City, Missouri, 1925.

MAURY—Life of M. F. Maury. By Diana F. M. Corbin. London, 1888.

MAUZY—Genealogical Record of the Descendants of Henry Mauzy and Jacob Kisling. By Richard Mauzy. Harrisonburg, Va., 1911.

Maxwell—Maxwell History and Genealogy. By F. W. Houston, L. W. Blaine, E. D. Mallett. Indianapolis, 1916.

Md. Soc. Col. Wars—Society of Colonial Wars in the State of Maryland. Edited by Christopher Johnston. Baltimore, 1905.

MEADE—Andrew Meade of Ireland and Virginia, Etc. By P. Hamilton Baskervill. Richmond, Va., Old Dominion Press, 1921.

Meade I, II—Old Churches, Ministers and Families of Virginia. By Bishop Meade (2 vols.). Philadelphia, J. B. Lippincott Company, 1889.

MEMOIRS OF A HUGUENOT FAMILY—By Anne Maury. New York, 1872.

MEMOIR OF GOV. WM. SMITH.

MEMOIR OF M. R. T. HUNTER.

MEMORIES OF LIFE IN AND OUT OF THE ARMY IN VIRGINIA. Blackford. Compiled by Susan Leigh Blackford from original and contemporaneous correspondence and diaries. Privately printed. Lynchburg, Va., 1894.

MERCER—Life of Gen. Hugh Mercer. By J. F. Goolrick. New York and Washington, 1906.

MERCER-GARNETT FAMILY—Genealogy of the Mercer-Garnett Family of Essex Co., Va., Etc. By James Mercer Garnett. Richmond, Va., Whittet & Shepperson, 1910.

Meriwether [Minor's Meriwethers]—The Meriwethers and their connections. By Louisa H. A. Minor, Albany, N. Y., 1892. Joel Munsell's Sons, Publishers.

MHM—Maryland Historical Magazine, Baltimore, Md.

Miami Co., Ind.—History of Miami Co., Indiana. Chicago, Brant and Fuller, 1887.

Miami Co., Ohio—The History of Miami County, Ohio. Chicago, W. H. Beers and Co., 1880.

MIDDLESEX PARISH REGISTER—The parish register of Christ Church, Middlesex County, from 1653 to 1812. Richmond, W. E. Jones, 1897.

MILLER—Rev. Alexander Miller of Virginia and some of his descendants. By Milo Custer. Bloomington, Ill., 1910.

Millers of Millersburg—The Millers of Millersburg and their descendants, etc., compiled for Gustavus Hindman Miller of Chattanooga. By John Bailey Nicklin, Jr. Nashville, Brandon Printing Company, 1923.

Minor—The Minor Family of Virginia. By John B. Minor, 1923. J. P. Bell Co., Inc., Publishers, Lynchburg, Va.

MITTONG—Genealogy of the Mittong Family and Connections. By Benjamin Franklin Mittong, 1926.

MMV—Men of Mark in Virginia. Edited by Lyon G. Tyler, 5 volumes. Washington, D. C., 1906-1909.

Mo. HIS. COLLECTIONS—Missouri Historical Collections.

Monongahela I, II, III—Genealogy and personal history of the Upper Monongahela Valley, West Virginia, under the editorial supervision of Bernard L. Butcher. New York, Lewis Historical Publishing Co., 1912. 3 vols.

Monroe Co. (W. Va.)—A History of Monroe County, West Virginia. By Oren E. Morton. Staunton, Va., The McClure Publishing Co., 1916.

MONROE—Life of James Monroe. By George Morgan. Boston. Small, Maynard and Company, 1921.

Montague—History and Genealogy of Peter Montague of Nansemond and Lancaster Counties, Virginia, and his Descendants. Compiled and published by George Williams Montague. Amherst, Mass., Press of Carpenter & Morehouse, 1894.

Montgomery Co., Ohio—The History of Montgomery Co., Ohio. Chicago, W. H. Beers and Co., 1882.

MOORE—Six Centuries of the Moores of Fawley and their Descendants, Etc. By David Moore Hall. Printed for the Committee by C. E. Flanhart, Printers, Richmond, Va., 1904.

MOORE—Memoir of the Life of the Rev. Richard Channing Moore, D. D. By J. R. K. Henshaw. Philadelphia, 1842.

MOREHEAD—The Morehead Family of North Carolina and Virginia. By J. M. Morehead, III. New York, 1921. Privately printed.

MOREHEAD—John Motley Morehead and the Development of North Carolina. By B. A. Konkle, Etc. Philadelphia, 1922.

MORGAN MORGAN—Report of the Morgan Morgan Monument Commission. Charleston, W. Va., 1924.

Morgan [Francis Morgan, Etc.]—By Annie Noble Simms. From the Notes of William Owen Nixon Scott and from other Sources. Brand & Hutton, Inc., Printers, Savannah, Ga., 1920.

MORRISON—History of the Morrison Settlers of Londonderry, N. H., and Branches of the Morrison who settled * * * in Virginia. By L. A. Morrison. Boston, 1880.

Mortons and their Kin (The)—A genealogy and a source book. By Daniel Morton, M. D., F. A. C. S., St. Joseph, Mo., 1920. Volume One, "The Mortons"; Volume Two, "The Morton Kin".

A collection of genealogical material from original sources relating to the Morton family of Virginia and especially to John Morton and his descendants, together with a great amount of data concerning the following families kin to the Mortons: 1. Ashton, 2. Banks, 3. Batchellor, 4. Barner, 5. Beale, 6. Beckwith, 7. Bellfield, 8. Blanchan, 9. Bottomley, 10. Bos, 11. Caldwell, 12. Cocke, 13. Cooke, 14. Colhoun, 15. Colston, 16. Davis,

17. Dinwiddie, 18, DuBois, 19. Edwards, 20. Eltinge, 21. Gregory, 22. Haden, 23. Hawkins, 24. Hite, 25. Johnson, 26. Jorrissen, 27. Lane, 28. Means, 29. Meriwether, 30. Mothershead, 31. Mountjoy, 32. Pannill, 33. Payne, 34. Perrin, 35. Pryor, 36. Royall, 37, Slecht, 38. Smith, 39. Tarpley, 40. Terrell, 41. Thornton, 42. Van Meter, 43. Wood. There are hundreds of other surnames of interest to persons studying family history connected with Virginia, New York, Pennsylvania and Kentucky.
Only three copies of the work have been made. One set has been placed in the Library of Congress, Washington, D. C.; one set in the Newberry Library at Chicago, Ill., and another will eventually be placed in the Public Library at Kansas City.

MORTON—Morton Data. By Duval Morton, M. D. St. Joseph, Mo., 1901.

MOSELEY—Genealogy of the Moseley Family of Bedford County. By George Carrington Moseley. Richmond, Va., 1912.

Munsell's—Munsell's American Ancestry. Albany, N. Y. Vols. II-XII (1887-1899).

N

NANCE MEMORIAL—The Nance Memorial, Etc. By George W. Nance. Bloomington, Ill., G. E. Burke & Co., Printers, 1904.

NEFF GENEALOGY, 1896.

NEILL'S VIRGINIA CAROLORUM—See "Virginia Carolorum" infra.

New Eng. His. and Gen. Register—New England Historical and Genealogical Register.

New River—A History of the Middle New River Settlements and Contiguous Territory. By D. E. Johnston. Huntington, W. Va., 1906.

Norfolk—History of Norfolk County, Va. By William H. Stewart. Chicago, 1902.

Notable Families—Some Notable Families of America. By Annah Robinson Watson. New York, 1898.

NOURSE—James Nourse and his Descendants. By Maria C. Lyle. Lexington, Ky., 1897.

NOWLIN—Descendants of James Nowlin who came to Pittsylvania County, Va., from Ireland about 1700, etc., and of other Nowlins, as also a Record of the Descendants of George & J. H. Stone, from Pittsylvania Co., Va. By J. F. Nowlin. Salt Lake City, 1916.

O

OBITUARY RECORD OF YALE GRADUATES, 1921-22. New Haven, 1922. (Page Fam.)

OLD—The Olds (Old, Ould) Family in England and America. Compiled and published by Edson B. Olds. Washington, D. C., 1915.

Ogle Co., Ill.—History of Ogle County, Illinois. Chicago, H. F. Kelt and Co., 1878.

Old Alexandria—The History of Old Alexandria from July 13, 1749, to May 24, 1861. By Mary G. Powell, Richmond, Va. The William Byrd Press, Inc., 1928.

OLD CHAPEL—"Old Chapel", Clarke Co., Va. Berryville, Va., 1906.

Old King William—Old King William Homes and Families, etc. By Peyton Neale Clarke. J. P. Morton, Louisville, 1897.

Old Prince William—Landmarks of Old Prince William. 2 vols. The Old Dominion Press, Richmond, Va., 1924.

OVERWHARTON—Overwharton Parish, 1720 to 1760. Old Stafford County. Washington, D. C., The Sexton Printing Co., 1899.

P

Page—Genealogy of the Page Family in Virginia, etc. By Richard Channing Moore Page, 2nd ed. New York, Publishers' Printing Co., 1893.

PALMER, BRANCH, ETC., FAMILIES. By a Descendant. Houston, Texas, n. d.

Panhandle—History of the Panhandle. By J. Newton, etc. Wheeling, West Va., J. A. Caldwell, 1878.

PARKER IN AMERICA—Compiled and edited by Augustus G. Parker, Buffalo, N. Y. Niagara Publishing Co., Buffalo (n. d.). ("Macclesfield" Parkers, pp. 251-255).

PARKER—Descendants of George Parker and his wife of Accomac County. Compiled by Lawrence McRae. Greensboro, N. C., 1928.

Patrick Henry—Patrick Henry, Life, Correspondence and Speeches. By William Wirt Henry. New York, Charles Scribner's Sons, 1891. 3 vols.

PAULL-IRWINS—A Family Sketch. By Elizabeth Maxwell Paull. Privately printed, 1915.

PAXTON—The Paxtons. Their Origin in Scotland and their Migrations through England and Ireland to Pennsylvania whence they moved South and West. By W. M. Paxton. Platte City, Mo., 1903.

Paxton—The Marshall Family. By W. M. Paxton, Platte City, Mo. Cincinnati, Robert Clarke & Co., 1885.

PAYNE (Goochland)—Life and Letters of Dolly Madison. By Allen Clark, Washington, D. C., Press of W. F. Roberts Company, 1914.

PENCE—History of Judge John Pence and Descendants. Born in Shenandoah County, Virginia, 1775, Etc. Compiled and published by Kingsley Adolphus Pence. Denver, Colo., 1912.

PENDLETON—Memoirs of William Nelson Pendleton. By Susan P. Lee. Philadelphia, 1893.

Pendleton Co.—A History of Pendleton County, West Virginia. By O. F. Morton. Franklin, W. Va., 1910.

PENN FAMILY OF VIRGINIA. A Chronological Record from Christian Penn, 1621, Robert, 1621, William, 1635, Francis, 1635, etc. (n. p.), 1915.

PETERS—Reminiscences of Judge B. J. Peters. Mt. Sterling, Ky. (n. d.).

Peyton—History of Augusta County. By G. L. Peyton. Staunton, Va., 1882.

PEYTON—Memoir of John Howe Peyton. Staunton, 1894.

PILCHER—Historical Sketches of Campbell, Pilcher and Kindred Families. By Margaret C. Pilcher. Nashville, Tenn.

Pittsylvania—The History of Pittsylvania County, Virginia. By Maud Carter Clement, 1929. J. P. Bell Company, Inc., Lynchburg, Va.

Pocahontas Co., W. Va.—Historical Sketches of Pocahontas County, West Virginia. By William T. Price. Marlinton, W. Va., Price Brothers, Publishers, 1901.

POLLARD—Memoirs and Sketches. By Henry Robinson Pollard.

POTTER'S AMER. MONTHLY.

Potts—The Potts Family. By Dane Potts. Canonsburg, Pa. Published by the Compiler, 1901.

Powell—Biographical Sketch of Col. Levin Powell. By R. C. Powell. Alexandria, Va., 1877.

Preble—The Preble Family in America, 1636-1810. By G. H. Preble. Boston, 1868.

Preston—The Preston Family in Great Britain, New England and Virginia from 1040 to the Present Times. By L. A. Williams and William Bowker Preston. Salt Lake City, 1900.

Preston—Memoranda of the Preston Family. By Orlando Brown. Frankfort, Ky., 1842.

Preston Co., W. Va.—History of Preston Co. (W. Va.). By S. T. Wiley, assisted by A. W. Frederick. Kingwood, W. Va., The Journal Printing House, 1882.

Price—John Price the Emigrant to Jamestown Colony with some of his Descendants. By B. L. Price, 1910.

Price (*Culpeper*)—Thomas Price and his Descendants. A History and Genealogy. By Rev. John E. Cox. Printed in the Messenger Office, Owensville, Indiana, 1926.

Prichard—Descendants of William Prichard. By A. M. Prichard. Charleston, W. Va., March, 1912.

Proceedings of the Historical Society of East and West Baton Rouge, Vol. II, 1927-1928.

Proprietors of the Northern Neck—Chapters of Culpeper Genealogy. Privately printed. The Old Dominion Press, Richmond, Va., 1926.

Q

Quarrier—Genealogical Sketch of the Quarrier Family in America. A Genealogical Sketch and Table of the Quarrier Family of America. By A. T. Laidley. Charleston, W. Va., 1890.

Quisenberry—Genealogical Memoranda of the Quisenberry Family and other families. By A. C. Quisenberry. Washington, D. C., 1897.

R

Ragland—The Ragland Family. By Mrs. Philip H. Hale. St. Louis, Mo., 1928.

Randolph—The Poems and Amyntas of Thomas Randolph. Edited by J. J. Parry, Yale University Press, 1917.

Randolph—Randolph Genealogy. Descendants of Sir John Randolph. MS. (William Allan). (n. d.)

Randolph—Randolph Family of Virginia. Attributed in part to John Randolph of Roanoke, prob. pub. between 1914 and 1925.

Randolph Family of Virginia. Compiled by Anne Marie (Lyman) Randolph (n. p. n. d. pp. 15. Va. State Lib.)

Randolph—A Collection and Report on the old Randolph Epitaphs on Turkey Island, Curls, Mattoax and Tuckahoe (n. p. n. d.) [Wilson Miles Cary.]

Randolph Co., W. Va.—A History of Randolph Co., W. Va. By Dr. A. S. Bosworth. Elkins, W. Va., 1916.

RC—The Richmond Critic, published by W. Cabell Trueman. Edited by G. Watson James and R. A. Brock (genealogies).

Read—The Reads and Their Relatives. By Alice Read. Cincinnati, 1930.

Register of the Kentucky State Historical Association.

Renick—The Renick Family of Virginia. By E. I. Renick, 1889.

Researcher I, II—A Magazine of History and Genealogical Exchange. Owned and edited by Robert Armistead Stewart. Vols. I and II from October, 1926, to July, 1928. Dietz Printing Co., Richmond, Va.

Rhodes—Rhodes Family in America. Published by Nelson Osgood Rhodes. Los Angeles, Cal.

Ricks—Ricks Family of Virginia and North Carolina.

Ricks—History and Genealogy of the Ricks Family of America. Compiled by Guy S. Ricks, Concord, N. H. Press and Bindery of Skelton Publishing Co., Salt Lake City, 1908.

Ridley, etc.—Riddell, Riddle, Ridlon, Ridley. By R. T. Ridlon. Manhattan, N. H., 1884.

Ritchie Co., W. Va.—History of Ritchie Co., etc. By Minnie Kendall Lowther. Wheeling News Litho. Co., Wheeling, W. Va.

Ritchie [Thomas Ritchie]—By C. H. Ambler. Richmond, Va., 1913.

Rives—Reliques of the Rives (Ryves) Family. By James Rives Childs. J. P. Bell Co., Inc., Lynchburg, Va., 1929.

Roberdeau—Genealogy of the Roberdeau Family. By Roberdeau Buchanan. Washington, 1876, Joseph L. Pearson, Printers.

Robertson—Pocahontas and her Descendants, etc. By Wyndham Robertson. Richmond, 1887.

Robertson-Taylor—Donald Robertson * * * and Commodore Richard Taylor, of Orange County. Ancestry and Posterity. By William Kyle Anderson. Detroit, 1900.

Rockbridge Co.—A History of Rockbridge County, Virginia. By Oren F. Morton. Staunton, Va., The McClure Co., Inc., 1920.

Rockingham—A History of Rockingham County, Virginia. By John W. Wayland. Dayton, Va., Ruebush-Elkins Company, 1912.

Roger Jones—Capt. Roger Jones of London and Virginia, etc. By L. H. Jones (Albany, N. Y., 1891). New Edition with Supplements. (n. d.).

Rolfe—Rolfe Family Records (Vol. II). By R. T. and A. Gunther Heacham. Norfolk, Hazell, Watson & Viney. London and Aylesburg, 1914.

Rootes of Rosewell—By William Clayton Torrence (n. p., n. d.)

Rose—A Chart of the Descendants of Rev. Robert Rose. Prepared by W. G. Stanard. Richmond, William Ellis Jones, 1895.

Roush—History of the Roush Family in America. By Leslie Leroy Roush, A. B. Shenandoah Publishing House, Inc., Strasburg, Va., 1928.

RS—The Richmond Standard (weekly). Vols. I-III, 1878-1882. Genealogies by W. G. Stanard.

R. W. Johnson—The Ancestry of Rosalie Morris Johnson. By R. Winder Johnson. Privately printed, 1905.

Ruffin—The Papers of Thomas Ruffin. N. C. Historical Commission, 1918.

Ruffin and Other Genealogies (Beverley, Bland, Bolling, Byrd, de Jarnette, Meade, Randolph, Ruffin, Shippen, Skipwith, Taylor, Willing, Wormeley). Printed chart (Va. State Library). Compiled by R. B. Henry. (n. p. n. d.)

Russell—William Russell and his Descendants. By Anna R. des Cognets. Lexington, Ky., 1884.

Rust—The Rust Family (MS.). By E. Marshall Rust.

Ruvigny—The Plantagenet Roll of the Blood Royal, Etc. By the Marquis de Ruvigny and Rainevel. London, 1905.

S

St. Charles, etc., Mo.—History of St. Charles, Montgomery and Warren Counties, Missouri, etc. St. Louis. National Historical Company, 1885.

St. Louis—Encyclopedia of the History of St. Louis (4 vols.), edited by William Hyde and Howard L. Conrad. New York, Louisville, St. Louis. The Southern History Company. Haldeman, Conard & Co., Proprietors, 1899.

St. Mark's—A History of St. Mark's Parish, Culpeper Co., Va., etc. By Rev. Philip Slaughter, D. D., 1877.

St. Peter's Parish Register.

Sampson—The Sampson Family. By Lilla Briggs Sampson. Williams and Wilkins Co., Baltimore, Md. (Va. Sampsons, pp. 205-222).

Sangamon Co., Ill.—History of the Early Settlers of Sangamon County, Illinois. By John Carroll Power and Mrs. Sarah A. Power. Springfield, Ill., Edwin A. Wilson & Co., 1876.

Sanxay—The Sanxay Family. By F. F. Sanxay. New York, 1907. Privately printed.

SBN—The South in the Building of the Nation, etc. Vol. XI. Richmond, Va., 1909.

Scott—The Only Authentic Edition. Life and Services of Winfield Scott. By Edward S. Mansfield. New York, A. S. Barnes & Co., 1852.

Scruggs Genealogy, Etc. By Ethel Hastings Scruggs Dunklin. New York, Laplante & Dunklin Printing Company, 1912.

SHA—Southern Historical Association, Washington, D. C. Vol. IV, 1900; VII, 1902-1903; VIII, 1904.

Shearer—The Shearer-Akers Family of America. By Rev. James William Shearer, D. D. Somerville, N. J., 1918.

Shuey—History of the Shuey Family of America, Etc. By D. B. Shuey, A. M. Lancaster, Pa., 1876.

Southwest Virginia and the Valley. Historical and Biographical. Roanoke, Va., A. D. Smith & Co., 1892.

Southwest Virginia—Annals of Southwest Virginia, 1769-1800 (Botetourt, Fincastle, Montgomery, Washington, Wythe). By Lewis Preston Summers. Abingdon, Va., 1929.

Shenandoah Co.—A History of Shenandoah County, Virginia. By John W. Wayland, Ph. D. Shenandoah Publishing House, Strasburg, Va., 1927.

Shepherdstown—Historic Shepherdstown. By Danske Dandridge. Charlottesville, Va., 1910.

Shinn—The History of the Shinn Family in Europe and America. By J. M. Shinn. Chicago, 1903.

Simpson—Early Records of the Simpson Family, Etc. By Helen A. Simpson. Press of J. B. Lippincott Co., Philadelphia, 1927.

Six Centuries of the Moores of Fawley. See "Moore".

Skelton—The Skeltons of Paxton, Powhatan County, Virginia, and their Connections, including sketches of the families of Shelton, Gifford and Crane. By P. Hamilton Baskervill. Richmond, Va., Old Dominion Press, Inc., Printers, 1922.

Sketches and Recollections of Lynchburg, Virginia. By the oldest inhabitant. Richmond, C. H. Wynne, 1858.

Slaughter—Genealogy of the Slaughter Family since 1720. By Slaughter W. Ficklin. Charlottesville, Va., James Alexander, 1870.

SMITH—The Sydney Smith and Clagett-Price Genealogy. By Lucy Montgomery Smith Price. Printed by Shenandoah Publishing House, Strasburg, Va., 1927.

SMITH—Memoir of Gov. William Smith. By J. W. Bell. New York, 1891.

SMITH—Life of the Rev. William Smith (1880).

SMITH—Genealogy of the Smith Family of Essex County, Virginia.

SNEAD—The Sneads of Fluvanna. By Mrs. William E. Hatcher, 1910.

SOME COLONIAL MANSIONS, ETC. By T. A. Glenn. Philadelphia, H. T. Coates & Co., 1899.

SOUTHERN BIVOUAC.

Southside Va.—Notes on Southside Virginia. By Walter A. Watson. Edited by Mrs. Walter A. Watson. (Bulletin of the Virginia State Library, Vol. XV, September, 1925. Nos. 2-4.)

Speed—Records and Memorials of the Speed Family. By Thomas Speed. Louisville, Ky., 1892.

SPOTSWOOD—Genealogy of the Spotswood Family in Scotland and Virginia. By Charles Campbell. Albany, N. Y., J. Munsell, 1868.

Spotswood Letters—The Official Letters of Alexander Spotswood, etc. Virginia Historical Society, Richmond, Va., 1882.

Stark Co., Ohio—History of Stark Co., with an Outline sketch of Ohio. By William Henry Perrin. Chicago, Baskin and Battey, 1881.

STATEMENT OF FRANCIS CHARLES HUME. See "Hume".

STATHAM—The Descent of the Family of Statham. By Rev. S. P. H. Statham. London, 1924.

STEPHENSON—Genealogical and Biographical Record of William Stephenson. By Mrs. Elizabeth M. S. Fite. New York (n. d.).

STEWARTS OF BALLINTOY. By Rev. George Hall. Reprint.

STEWARTS OF BEECHWOOD. By Col. William H. Stewart. Privately printed.

STORRS—The Storrs Family, Etc. By Charles Storrs. Privately printed. New York, 1886.

STRATTON—A Book of Strattons, Etc. By Harriet R. Stratton. Grafton Press, 1908.

Strickler—Forerunners: a History or Genealogy of the Strickler Families, etc. Harrisonburg, Va., H. M. Strickler, 1925.

STROTHER—William Strother of Virginia and his Descendants.

STUART—Life of General J. E. B. Stuart.

Stubbs—Early Settlers of Alabama. By Col. J. E. Saunders, etc. With Notes and Genealogies by Elizabeth S. B. Stubbs. New Orleans, 1899.

STUBBS—The Descendants of John Stubbs of Cappahosic, Gloucester County, Virginia, 1652. By Dr. William Carter Stubbs. New Orleans, 1902.

SUBLETT—A Partial History of the French Huguenot by name Soblet. By S. S. Sublett. Richmond, 1896.

SULLIVANT—A Genealogical Family Memorial. By Joseph Sullivant. Columbus, Ohio, 1874.

Summers Co., W. Va.—History of Summers County from the earliest Settlement to the Present Time. By James H. Miller. Hinton, W. Va., 1908.

SWEARINGEN—Family Historical Register. Compiled by a member of the Family. Washington, 1884, and 2nd edition, Washington, 1894.

T

TABB—Father Tabb, His Life and Work, Etc. By Jennie Masters Tabb. Boston, 1921.

TALIAFERRO—Chart of the Descendants of Robert Taliaferro. By W. B. McGroarty. Falls Church, Va., 1927.

TAYLOR FAMILY OF VIRGINIA (1898).

TAZEWELL—Life and Character of Hon. Littleton Waller Tazewell. By H. B. Grigsby. Norfolk, 1860.

Tazewell II—Annals of Tazewell County, Va., from 1800 to 1922. By John Newton Harman, Sr., Vol. II. Richmond, Va., W. C. Hill.

TD—Times-Dispatch (newspaper), Richmond, Va. Genealogies by E. C. Mead, Mrs. Sally Nelson Robins, and others.

TERRELL—Genealogical Notes on the Tyrrall and Terrell Family of Virginia. By Edwin H. Terrell. San Antonio, Texas, 1907.

TERRELL—Further genealogical Notes on the Tyrrell-Terrell Family of Virginia, Etc. By Edwin H. Terrell, 2nd edition. San Antonio, Texas, 1909.

TERRELL—Tyrrell-Terrell Family of Virginia. By Edwin H. Terrell, 1907.

TERRELL—The Genealogy of Richmond and William Tyrrell or Terrell, Etc. Compiled and issued as a supplement to his "History of the Tyrrells". By Joseph Henry Tyrrell. Privately printed, 1910.

TERRILL—A Genealogy Line of the Terrills. By Alexander J. Quayle, 1921.

Thomas—The Thomas Book. By Lawrence Buckley Thomas, D. D., Henry T. Thomas Company, New York, 1896.

THOMAS (Southampton)—Life of Major-General George H. Thomas. By T. B. Van Horn, New York, 1882.

THOMAS HARDAWAY OF CHESTERFIELD Co. By Sarah D. Hubert. Richmond, Va., 1906.

THOMAS HORD, GENTLEMAN. See "Hord".

Thomas Ritchie—See "Ritchie".

Throckmorton Family—By C. Wickliffe Throckmorton. The Old Dominion Press, Richmond, Va., 1930.

Thomas Ritchie—A Study in Virginia Politics. By Charles Henry Ambler. Richmond, Va., Bell Book & Stationery Co., 1913.

THORNTON—A Sketch and Personal Reminiscences of Judge Anthony Thornton. Shelbyville, Ill., 1897.

TIERNAN—The Tiernan and other Families, Etc. By C. B. Tiernan, Baltimore, 1901.

TILLMAN—Tillman Genealogy. Nashville, Tenn., 1905.

TODD—The Virginia Todds. Compiled by J. R. Whitcraft. Philadelphia, Frankford Dispatch Publishing House, Philadelphia, 1913.

Trabue—A Corner in Celebrities. By Alice Elizabeth Trabue, 2nd ed. Geo. G. Fitter Company, Louisville, Ky., 1923.

TRACY—English Ancestry of Gov. Wm. Tracy of Va. (1620). By Dwight Tracy. New Haven, Conn., 1908.

Trezevant (from S. C.)—The Trezevant Family in the United States. By J. T. Trezevant. Columbia, S. C., 1914.

TRIMBLE—Autobiography and Correspondence of Allen Trimble, Gov. of Ohio, with a genealogy of the family. Cincinnati, 1909.

TUCKER—An account of the Tucker Family of Bermuda. By Thos. Addis Emmet, M. L., LL. D. New York, Bradstreet Press, 1898.

TUCKER—Tucker Family Tree. By Edward Tucker, Esq., of Bermuda.

Tucker Co., W. Va.—History of Tucker County, West Virginia, etc. By Hu Maxwell. Kingswood, W. Va., Preston Publishing Co., 1884.

Two Families—A History of Two Virginia Families Transplanted from County Kent, England. Thomas Baytop * * * John Catlett. By Dr. and Mrs. W. C. Stubbs. New Orleans, n. d.

Tyler's—Tyler's Quarterly Historical and Genealogical Magazine. Editor, Lyon G. Tyler. Richmond, 1920, plus.

TYLER—The Tylers of Mass., Conn., R. I., Va., and N. J. By W. Tyler Brigham.

V

VIRGINIA HERALDICA—Edited by William Armstrong Crozier. Virginia County Record Series, Vol. V. Published by The Genealogical Association. New York, MDCCCCVIII.

Va. His. Col.—Virginia Historical Collection.

Va. His. Mag.—Virginia Historical Magazine. Edited by Jefferson Wallace, Richmond, Va., July, 1891.

Valentine I, II, III, IV—The Edward Pleasant Valentine Papers. Four volumes. Published by the Valentine Museum, Richmond, Va. Whittet & Shepperson, Printers.

Van Meter—Genealogies and Sketches of Some Old Families. By B. F. Van Meter. Louisville, 1901.

VAN METRE—Origin and Descent of an American Van Metre Family. By Samuel Gordon Smyth. Privately printed, 1923.

VAWTER—The Vawter Family in America. By Grace W. Bicknell. Indianapolis, 1905.

VCR—Virginia County Records. By William Montgomery Crozier.

Venable—Venables of Virginia—An Account of the Ancestors and Descendants of Samuel Woodson Venable of "Springfield" and his brother William Lewis Venable of "Haymarket", both of Prince Edward County, Virginia. By Elizabeth Marshall Venable. n. p. 1925.

VESTRY BOOK OF CHRIST CHURCH PARISH.

VESTRY BOOK OF HENRICO PARISH. See "Henrico" above.

VHS COL.—VI and XI—Collections of the Virginia Historical Society, New Series, VI and XI. Richmond, Va., 1887 and 1892.

VIRGINIA CAROLORUM—By Edward D. Neill. Albany, N. Y., Joel Munsell's Sons, 1886.

VIRGINIA GAZETTE—Williamsburg, Va.

VIRGINIA HERALDICA—Edited by William Armstrong Crozier. Virginia County Record Series, Vol. V. Published by The Genealogical Association. New York, MDCCCCVIII.

VIRGINIA VALLEY RECORDS—By John W. Wayland, Dayton, Va. Ruebush, Elkins Co., Harrisonburg, Va., 1930.

Virkus I, II, III—The Abridged Compendium of American Genealogy. First Families of America. Edited by Frederick A. Virkus. A. N. Marquis & Company, Publishers, Chicago. Vol. I, 1925; Vol. II, 1926; Vol. III, 1928.

VM—Virginia Magazine of History and Biography. Published by the Virginia Historical Society, Richmond, Va. 37 Vols. (1895-1929, inclusive).

VSR—Magazine of the Sons of the Revolution in the State of Virginia, 1922-1925, edited by G. Watson James, Jr.; 1927-1929, edited by Clayton Torrence; 1929-, edited by Robert Armistead Stewart.

W

Waddell—Waddell's Annals of Augusta Co., Virginia, from 1726 to 1871. By Jos. A. Waddell, 2nd ed. Staunton, Va., C. R. Caldwell, 1902.

WADDELL—Memorials of an Academic Life, being an Historical Sketch of the Waddell Family, Richmond, 1891.

Walker-Wigton—Genealogy of the Descendants of John Walker, Wigton, Scotland, with Records of a few Allied Families. By Emma S. White, Kansas City, Mo., 1902.

WALLACE—Wallace Family in America. By J. H. Phelps. New York, 1914.

WALLACE—Genealogical Data pertaining to the Descendants of Peter Wallace and Elizabeth Woods his Wife. Compiled by George Selden Wallace. Cleveland, The Arthur H. Clarke Co., 1927.

WALLACE'S ILLUSTRATED WEEKLY—Richmond, Va., April 26, May 2, May 23, 1891.

WALLER—William S. Waller, with Family Genealogy.

WALTHALL—Walthall Family. By Ernest Taylor Walthall, 1906. Printed, Bound and Published by Walthall Printing Co., Richmond, Va.

WALTONS OF VIRGINIA—By Mrs. W. C. Stubbs.

WALTON—Notes on the Family of Edward Walton and some of his Connection. By Chas. Cortlandt Walton, Jr. Reprinted from the William and Mary Quarterly.

Warfield—The Founders of Anne Arundel and Howard Counties, Maryland. By J. D. Warfield. Baltimore, Md., 1905.

WASHINGTON—Washington Family. By W. C. Ford. New York, 1893.

WASHINGTON—The Pedigree and History of the Washington Family. By Albert Welles. New York, Society Library, 1879.

WASHINGTON—Mary and Martha * * * Washington. By B. J. Lossing. New York, 1886.

WASHINGTON—Wills of George Washington and his Immediate Ancestors. Edited by Worthington Chauncey Ford. Brooklyn, N. Y. Historical Publishing Club, 1891.

WASHINGTON—A Genealogical History of Thornton A. Washington. Washington, D. C., 1871.

WASHINGTON—Ancestry of Washington. By Henry F. Waters. Boston, 1889.

WASHINGTON—Maternal Ancestry and Nearest of Kin of Washington. A Monograph. By G. W. Ball. Washington, 1885.

WASHINGTON—Wills of the American Ancestors of George Washington. By J. N. Toner, M. D. Boston, 1891.

WATKINS—A Catalogue of the Descendants of Thomas Watkins of Chickahominy, Va. By F. N. Watkins (new ed.), Henderson, 1899.

Watson—"Of Sceptred Race". By Annah Robinson Watson. Early Printing & Publishing Co., Memphis, Tenn., 1910.

WATSON'S ROYAL LINEAGE—A Royal Lineage. Alfred the Great. By A. R. Watson. Richmond, Va., 1901.

WENGER—History of the Descendants of Christian Wenger, Etc. By Jonas G. Wenger, etc. 1903, Mennonite Publishing Co., Elkhart, Indiana.

West—West Family Register. By Latta Brock Stone. W. J. Roberts Co., Inc., Washington, D. C., 1928.

WEST—West Chart (Sir Thomas West, 2nd Lord De La Warr). Privately printed. By George Gregory. Richmond, Va., 1926.

WHALEY—The Whaley Family. By Rev. S. Whaley, 1901.

WHEELER—American Ancestors of the Children of Joseph and Daniella Wheeler. Wheeler, Ala. (n. d.).

Whitaker—Genealogy of the Campbell, Noble, Gordon, Shelton, Gilmour and Byrd Families, etc. By Mildred Campbell Whitaker (Mrs. Alexander Edward). St. Louis, Mo., 1927.

WHITE—Ancestry of the Children of J. W. White, M. D. By W. F. Creager. Philadelphia, 1898.

WIGGINTON GENEALOGY. Privately printed. (n. p., n. d.).

Willis—The Willis Family of Virginia, etc. By B. C. and R. H. Willis. Richmond, Va., n. d.

WINCHESTER AND ITS BEGINNINGS, 1743-1814—By Katherine Green. Printed by Shenandoah Publishing House, Strasburg, Va., 1926.

WINFREE—Winfree of Virginia. By Mrs. W. C. Stubbs. In Gulf State Historical Magazine.

WINSTON—Genealogy of Isaac Winston and Descendants. By Elizabeth W. C. Hendrick. New York, 1899.

Winston—Winston of Virginia and Allied Families. Compiled and edited by Clayton Torrence. Whittet & Shepperson, Richmond, Va., 1927.

Wise's Eastern Shore—Ye Kingdom of Accomacke on the Eastern Shore of Virginia in the Seventeenth Century. By Jennings C. Wise. Richmond, Va., 1911.

WISE—Col. John Wise of England and Virginia (1617-1695), His Ancestors and Descendants. By Jennings Cropper Wise (n. p., n. d.).

WISE—Life of Henry A. Wise of Virginia. By his grandson, the late Barton H. Wise. New York, The Macmillan Co., 1899.

WITHERS—Alexander Scott Withers. A Sketch. By Roy Byrd Cook, 1921.

WITHERS (*Stafford*)—Autobiography of an Octogenarian. By R. E. Withers. Roanoke, Va., 1907.

WM—William and Mary College Quarterly, owned and edited by Lyon G. Tyler, Williamsburg, Va., 27 vols. (1892-1920). After Dr. Tyler retired from the presidency of the College of William and Mary he continued his magazine as "Tyler's Historical and Genealogical Quarterly", Holdcroft, Va.

WM, 2d—William and Mary College Quarterly, Second Series (1921-). Editors, J. A. C. Chandler, E. G. Swem, Williamsburg, Va.

WOOD (*Valley of Virginia*)—History of the Wood Family. By James W. Wood, Luray, Va.

WOODFIN—Biography and Genealogy of the Woodfin Family. By Earnest S. Woodfin. New Orleans, La., 1928.

WOODLEY—The Woodleys of Isle of Wight County, Virginia. A Statement by James Francis Crocker. Portsmouth, Va., W. A. Fiske, Printer, 1914.

Woods-McAfee—The Woods-McAfee Memorial containing an Account of John Woods and James McAfee of Ireland and their Descendants in America, etc. By Rev. N. M. Woods, etc. Louisville, Ky., 1905.

Woodson—Historical Genealogy of the Woodsons and their Connections. Compiled by Henry Morton Woodson (Memphis). The Author, 1915.

WVM—West Virginia Historical Magazine, Charleston, W. Va.

Y

YATES—Memorials of a Family in England and Virginia. By A. E. Terrill. Privately printed, 1887.

YATES (*Caroline*)—Family Chart of Michael Yates. By Richard Yates.

Yeardley—Sir George Yeardley or Yardley, Governor and Captain General of Virginia, and Temperance Lady Yeardley * * * and some of their Descendants. By Thomas Teackle Upshur, Nassawadox, Northampton Co., Va.

YEARGAN—Genealogy of the Yeargan Family. By Leonidas H. and Hilary H. C. Yeargan. Nashville, Tenn., 1891.

YOUNG—Family Tree of Michael Cadet Young of Brunswick Co., Va. Compiled by C. D. Cowles, 1895.

Z

ZIMMERMAN—Zimmerman, Waters, and allied families. By Dorothy E. Z. Allen (n. p., n. d.).

INDEX

A

Aaron—Bruce IV, 91; Henry Co., 110.
Abbott (*Craig*)—Cyc. Va. Biog., V, 737.
    (*Page*)—Cyc. Va. Biog., IV, 334.
Abell—Albemarle, 137; Bruce IV, 324; Sangamon Co., Ill., 76.
Abernathy—Walker-Wigton, 80; 85-89.
Abney—Hayden, 381; Mackenzie II, 3-7; TD, Sept. 18, 1904; VM
    XXXIV, 357.
Abrahall—Keith, 27-28; TD, Sept. 15, 1907; WM, II, 266.
Abston—Pittsylvania, 144.
Acker—Bruce IV, 235.
Ackerly—Rockbridge, 470.
Ackiss—Antiquary III, 2; Norfolk, 908-911; 1016.
Acree—Bagby, 589.
Acrill—Tyler's VII, 212-213; VM, IV, 326.
Adair—BS, Oct. 25, 1908; Madison Co., O., 849; Rockbridge, 470.
    (*Giles*)—McIlhany, 232-235.
Adams—Rockbridge, 470; RS, I, 44; TD, Dec. 17, 24, 1905; Oct. 7,
    1906; Oct. 13, 1907; Virkus II, 171, 362; WM, VI, 29, 65,
    235; WM 2d, VI, 249-250.
    (*Alexandria*)—Avery I, 78; Munsell's IV, 157.
    (*Bedford*)—Hardy, 4-6.
    (*Campbell*)—Bruce V, 546; Campbell Co., 338-340; Clemens'
    Wills, 5; Virkus I, 409-410.
    (*Fairfax, from Md.*)—VM, VIII, 312-314, 420-421; IX, 200-201,
    313-314, 432-433; WM 2d, VI, 354, 356.
    (*Fauquier*)—Virkus I, 923; WM, XIX, 108-109.
    (*Frederick*)—Cartmell, 472-473.
    (*Halifax*)—Chappell, 342-369; Halifax, 102-105; VM, XI, 185.
    (*King William*)—Va. Gazette, April 7, 1781, p. 3.
    (*Lynchburg*)—Floyd, 57-62; Lewis, 346-347.
    (*New Kent*)—Cyc. Va. Biog., I, 169.
    (*Pittsylvania*)—Pittsylvania, 173.
    (*Richmond City*)—Crockett, 301; Hardy, 1-4; Lancaster, 118-122;
    Mackenzie VI, 8-12; RS, III, 15-16; Speed, 140-141; The
    Vestry Book of Henrico Parish, 183-187; VM, IV, 448-450;
    XIX, 444; XXII, 379, etc.; WM, V, 159-164.
    (*William, Fairfax Co.*)—WM 2d. VI, 354-356.
Adamson—Pendleton Co., 173.
Adcock (*Middlesex*)—Vestry Book of Christ Church Parish.
Addington—Bruce IV, 440; VI, 432.
Adkerson—Bruce IV, 373.
Affleck—Cartmell, 459.
Agath—WM, XXIV, 109-115.
Agee—TD, Dec. 18, 1910.
Aglionby—BS, Aug. 19, 1905.
Agnew—TD, May 31, 1908.
Agnor (*Agnew*)—Rockbridge, 470.
Agres—Rockbridge, 472.
Aiken—Cyc. Va. Biog., V, 746.

Ainslee—Winston, 261.
Akers—The Shearer-Akers Family (1915).
Akin—Virkus II, 35.
Albridgton—Tyler's IX, 209-210.
Albright—Rockbridge, 470.
Alden (*Middlesex*)—Vestry Book of Christ Church Parish.
Alderson—Barton I, R36-37; Hayden, 76; Shenandoah, 579.
Alexander—Alexander Family Records; Rockbridge, 244-245, 470-471; TD, Oct. 2, 1907; Oct. 11, 1908; Jan. 30, 1910; WM, V, 180; VI, 65; VII, 119.

    (*Augusta*)—Bruce VI, 83; Buford, 82-83; Cabell, etc., 492-596; Foote II, 99-105, 217-223; Life of Archibald Alexander, D. D., 3-14; Mackenzie III, 7-10; Marshall, 74-75, 159; RS, III, 2, 5; The Alexander Family, 13-17.

    (*Bedford*)—"Genealogy" (Weekes ed.), Vol. 14, p. 12.
    (*Campbell*)—Campbell Co., 341-345.
    (*Clarke*)—MMV, II, 3.
    (*Fairfax*)—Burgess, 133-136.
    (*Gloucester*)—Francis Morgan, 23-27; VM, XIV, 391.
    (*Highland*)—Highland Co., 257.
    (*King and Queen*)—Researcher II, 144.
    (*Mark*)—WM, XXV, 206-207.
    (*Northern Neck*)—"Genealogy", by W. M. Clemens, p. 25, 106; Kennedy I, 293-311.

    (*Rockbridge*)—Clemens' Wills, 5; Magna Charta Barons, 322; McClure, 125-126, 184-188; Rockbridge, 244-245, 470-471; SBN, XI, 5-6; VM, II, 331-332; Virkus I, 414.

    (*Stafford*)—Hardy, 7-14; Hayden, 180-182, 192-193; RS, II, 47, 49, 51; III, 35-37; VM, X, 315-316; WM, II, 87; VIII, 262-263; IX, 54-55, 252-254; X, 63-66, 132-134, 137-140, 178-185; XI, 60-66, 115-121, 247-251.

    (*Stafford, etc.*)—Hening VI, 399-402; RS, II, 47, 51.
    (*Timber Ridge*)—The Alexander Family (chart).
    (*Western Va.*)—Bruce V, 450.

Alford—Hayden, 507; VM, XXIII, 419-422.
Alfriend—Brock II, 765; SBN, XI, 7.
Allason—Hayden, 718-719.
Allegre—Huguenot Emigration, 80.
Allen—Hardin Co., O., 1034; Rockbridge, 471; TD, Nov. 13, Dec. 11, 1904; March 12, 1906; Nov. 10, 1907; Sept. 27, 1908; April 27, 1913; WM, VI, 69, 121, 130; VII, 254; WM, 2d, VI, 352-353.

    (*Albemarle*)—Watson, 206-209.
    (*Augusta*)—Boogher, 309, 314; Dunmore's War, 276, 339; Green's Ky. Families, 230-242; Mackenzie II, 85-86, 88; Tyler's IX, 259-265.

    (*Botetourt*)—Bruce IV, 54-55; Cyc. Va. Biog., IV, 332; MMV, IV, 5-6; Walker-Wigton, 300-301.
    (*Charlotte*)—DAR, 71, p. 130.
    (*Clarke*)—Lancaster, 459-460.
    (*Cumberland*)—Foote II, 223-235; Hampden-Sidney, 67-68; Life of Archibald Alexander, D. D., 178-179.
    (*Fauquier*)—Tyler's IX, 277-279.
    (*Frederick*)—Some Early Settlers (McCabe), 3-5.
    (*Goochland*)—WM, XXII, 194-196.
    (*Henrico*)—Valentine I, 1-37.
    (*Henry*)—Henry Co., 110-114.

(*James City*)—Researcher I, 175; TD, April 27, 1913; VM, XX, 95.

(*Lunenburg*)—Bruce V, 153; Old Free State II, 105-108; Virkus I, 899.

(*Middlesex*)—Vestry Book of Christ Church Parish.

(*Nansemond*)—Burgess, 485.

(*Pittsylvania*)—MMV, IV, 3-4.

(*Surry*)—Cyc. Va. Biog., I, 170; V, 637-639; Hening IV, 359-360; Kennedy II, 565-568; Lancaster, 50-53, 60-62; RC, II, 45; VM, VII, 211-212; WM, VIII, 110-113, 132-133.

Allerton—A History of the Allerton Family in the U. S., 1585-1885. By W. A. Allerton (New York, 1888); Allertons of New England and Virginia. By Isaac J. Greenwood, Boston, 1890 (Reprint from New Eng. His. and Gen. Reg., vol. 44, 1890); Lee, 329-330; Notable Families, 38-43; Researcher I, 228; VM, I, 199-200; WM, IV, 39, 171.

Alley (Ally)—TD, May 26, 1907.

Allibon—Hayden, 485.

Allison—Crockett, 266; Rockbridge, 471.

Allport—Bruce IV, 15.

Almond—Bruce V, 199; Hayden, 452.

Alphin—Albemarle, 137-138; Bruce VI, 227; Cyc. Va. Biog., IV, 322; Rockbridge, 471.

Alt—Pendleton Co., 173.

Altizer—Bruce IV, 477.

Amberger—WM, XXVI, 85.

Ambler—America Heraldica, 91; Bruce VI, 205; Burwell, 19-20; Culpeper, part 2, 143; Cyc. Va. Biog., IV, 353; Du Bellet I, 17-42, 53, 58-61, 63-79, 103-107, 113-116, 133-146, 223-225, 230-231, 234-236, 250-251; II, 1-40; Hardy, 14-21; Huguenot Emigration, XIV, XV; Kennedy I, 278-279, 604-605; Marshall, 42-45, 58, 142-143, 148-149, 251-252, 262-266, 361-362; RC, II, 19, 21, Jan. 20, 1889; RS, I, 39; TD, Jan. 28, 1906; Virkus I, 99, 649; VM, IX, 108; X, 51: XVIII, 378; XXXIII, 187-188; Willis, 128; WM, X, 151; XIV, 126-129.

Ames (*Eastern Shore*)—Bruce VI, 520; Cyc. Va. Biog., V, 611.

Amiss—Bruce V, 217-218.

Ammon—VM, XXXIV, 76-77.

Ammonet—SHA, III, 35-40—Jacob Ammonet of Va. and a part of his descendants.

Amory—Cyc. Va. Biog., V, 1059-1060; Two Families, 51, 84.

Amos—Bruce V, 355.

Anderson—Monograph of the Anderson, Clark, Marshall and McArthur Connection; Pendleton Co., 174-175; Rockbridge, 245, 471; TD, Sept. 17, 1905; Jan. 6, 1907; Oct. 11, 1908; March 5, 1911; June 29, Oct. 12, 1913; WM, IV, 127.

(*Albemarle*)—Albemarle, 138-139; Lewis, 33; McAllister, 48-54; RS, II, 49.

(*Amelia*)—TD, Nov. 16, 1913; VM, IV, 438-439; VSR, IV (No. 1), 69; WM, XIV, 32-33.

(*Augusta*)—Boogher, 305-306, 308-323; Crockett, 298; Maxwell, 241-249, 251-281, 558-569; Virkus I, 420; II, 331; VM, XXXV, 200.

(*Botetourt*)—Bruce V, 411; Cabell, etc., 336; Foote II, 584-586; McCormick, 72-73; MMV, III, 3-5; V, 16-18; RS, II, 49; Sangamon Co., Ill., 82; Thomas, 556a-556-.

(*Campbell*)—Campbell Co., 345-347; Cyc. Va. Biog., IV, 254.

(*Caroline*)—Caroline Co., 136-142.

(*Charles City*)—WM, IV, 127, 143, 148.
(*Chesterfield*)—Bruce V, 144; TD, Oct. 20, 1911.
(*David, Petersburg*)—WM, VI, 18-20.
(*Gloucester*)—TD, March 5, 1911; Virkus I, 110, 421; II, 388.
(*Hampshire*)—Munsell's XI, 15.
(*Hanover*)—Caroline Co., 116-121, 136-142; Crawfurdiana, 87-89; Crozier, VII, 67-69; English's Conquest of the Northwest, II, 1150; Green's Ky. Families, 171-172; Hampden-Sidney, 183; Mackenzie IV, 4-15; MMV, V, 21-22; Munsell's VII, 239; VIII, 230; XI, 197; RS, III, 24, 28, 31, 33, 35, 39, 48; SBN, XI, 15-16; TD, June 29, 1913; The Andersons of Gold Mine, Hanover Co.; Va. S. R., I, 41; Virkus I, 110, 421; VM, XII, 205; XX, 312-313; XXI, 87; XXV, 401-403; WM, XXI, 292.
(*Hanover and Albemarle*)—Cyc. Va. Biog., IV, 250.
(*Henry Co.*)—Henry Co., 114-116.
(*Henry, Henrico*)—VM, XXXII, 387-389.
(*Louisa*)—Crozier's Va. County Records, VI, 254, 258; Meriwethers, 51-52, 57, 60-62; MMV, V, 21-22.
(*Louisa and Albemarle*)—McAllister, 317.
(*Mecklenburg*)—Researcher I, 191.
(*Nelson*)—Crawfurdiana, 52.
(*New Kent*)—WM, 2d, VIII, 62-63.
(*Paulin*)—VM, XXXIII, 398.
(*Prince Edward*)—Bruce IV, 33.
(*Prince Edward, Cumberland, etc.*)—Venables of Va., 99-123.
(*Rappahannock*)—Bruce VI, 63.
(*Richmond*)—Price, 86-95.
(*Shenandoah and Pendleton*)—Shenandoah, 581-582.
(*Williamsburg*)—WM, XII, 116-118, 201-205.
Anderton (*Middlesex*)—Vestry Book of Christ Church Parish.
Andrews—Rockbridge, 471; WM, IV, 69, 284; V, 143.
(*Eastern Shore*)—Researcher I, 161; VM, II, 69-70.
(*Essex*)—Goode, 93-94, 175, 177, 306-311; Virkus II, 64.
(*Rev. Robert*)—Burgess, 55-56.
(*Williamsburg*)—VM, XXIV, 194; XXIX, 139-140; XXIII, 182 (for "Joseph Wilkerson" read "Biddle Wilkinson"); WM, III, 277-278; IX, 136; VI, 180.
(*York*)—WM, II, 165.
Angel—Crockett, 134.
Angell—Bruce V, 413.
Anglin—Bath Co., 188.
Ansell—Researcher, I, 226.
Anthony—Aris Sonis Focisque, 58-59; Bell, 24, 259; Cabell, etc., 320-322; Campbell Co., 347-350; Hampden-Sidney, 243; TD, Feb. 5, 26, 1905; March 3, 24, 1907.
(*Henry*)—VM, IX, 220, 328-331.
Apperson—Bruce VI, 282; MMV, III, 6-9; IV, 15-18; Researcher, I, 56; Speed, 164; TD, Aug. 10, 1913; Sept. 26, 1915; WM, VIII, 125.
Appleton—Vestry Book of Christ Church Parish; WM, IV, 41, 43.
Applewhite—Bruce IV, 553; WM, VII, 253, et seq.
Arbaugh—Pendleton Co., 175.
Arbogast—Hardin Co., O., 835; Highland Co., 257, 259.
Arbuckle—Dunmore's War, 103-104; Madison Co., O., 370; McCue, 184, 191-192, 207-208, 224-226, 232, 234-246.
Archer—TD, Oct. 7, 1907.
(*Appomattox and Chesterfield*)—DAR, 67, p. 266.

Ashton—ARP, II, 446-448; BS, July 12, Oct. 11, 1908; Cyc. Va. Biog.,
    I, 174; Hayden, 489, 630-633; Lee, 149-151; MMV, III, 10-
    11; Norfolk, 620; TD, Sept. 22, 1907; Dec. 13, 1908; WM,
    IV, 40; VII, 56, 94, 115-119, 174-178; VIII, 75; XIV, 66.
    (*Chatterton*)—VM, II, 27, 261-262; X, 292-293; XXV, 165;
    XXIX, 436-437; WM, XII, 247.
    (*Northumberland*)—VM, XI, 154; WM, IV, 40.
Aston—Magna Charta Barons, 159; Rockbridge, 472; TD, Sept. 22,
    1907; Virkus, II, 298; VM, III, 401-402; V, 91; XXIV, 67-
    68; WM, IV, 144, 148-149.
Astrop—Old Free State, II, 139.
Athey—Caroline Co., 367-369.
Atkins—Burgess, 936; Researcher II, 144.
Atkinson—Bristol Parish, 137-140; BS, May 14, 1905; Old King Wil-
    liam, 193-194; Rockbridge, 472; TD, Jan. 14, 1906.
    (*Alexandria*)—Avery I, 49.
    (*Dinwiddie*)—Burwell, 37-39; Foote II, 552-556; Hampden-Sid-
    ney, 260-261; Lancaster, 98; MMV, III, 12-13; Page (2d.
    ed.), 37-39, 191; VM, XV, 345-349; WM, IV, 270.
    (*Isle of Wight*)—Hardy, 135; Hayden, 281; Mackenzie I, 92.
    (*Northampton Co. and Ga.*)—History of Camden Co., Ga., p. 39.
Atkisson—Halifax, 105.
Atwell—Avery I, 128-129; Hayden, 15-16, 20, 166, 511.
Atwill—MMV, III, 14-15.
Atwood—MMV, III. 16-17; Southside Va., 86-87.
Aubrey—Clemens' Wills, 6.
Auld—Rockbridge, 472.
Auldridge—Pocahontas Co., 368-378.
Aulick—Cartmell, 498-499.
Austin—Burgess, 948; Hayden, 72, 120, 716; Montague, 140; Robertson,
    53; TD, June 16, 1912.
Avery—Avery I, 212; Burgess, 168-170.
Awbrey—Fothergill, 141; Old Prince William I, 153-154.
Ayers—Burgess, 864, 942; Pendleton Co., 176.
Aylesbury—Sangamon Co., Ill., 80.
Aylett—ARP, II, 443-446; Brock II, 761; Browning, C. D., 244-245;
    Burgess, 944-947; Cooke-Booth, 247-248; Cyc. Va. Biog., I,
    175; V, 824-825, 1089; Fothergill, 116; Hening VIII, 283-
    285; Kennedy I, 324-326; II, 17-18; Lee, 172; Magna Charta
    Barons, 322; MMV, I, 24; Old King William, 15-16, 26-28;
    Rockbridge, 472; RS, II, 35, 40, 49; TD, Oct. 11, 1908; April
    25, 1909; Virkus II, 115, 331; VM, IV, 468, 474; V, 355-356;
    XXV, 275; Watson, 219-220; WM, V, 34-35, 139; IX, 25, 172-
    174; XV, 70, 99-100; XIX, 183-184.
Aylmer—Hayden, 230; TD, Aug. 4, 1912; WM, I, 93.
Aylor—Bruce IV, 49; VI, 350; Madison Co., O., 759; Shenandoah, 582.
Ayres—Burgess, 62; Rockbridge, 472; WM, VII, 206.

B

Babb—Virkus III, 42.
Baber—Clemens' Wills, 7-8.
Bacheller (*Norfolk Co.*)—McIntosh II, 161-162.
Backus (*Amelia*)—Chappell, 247-250.
    (*Norfolk Co.*)—Norfolk, 1037.
Bacon—America Heraldica, 61; Bacons of Va. and their English An-
    cestry; Browning, C. D., 31-32, 347-348; Campbell's History

of Va., 311, 344; Goode, 472; Gosnald and Bacon, by J.
Henry Lea; Keith, 22-26, and chart; Meade I, 200; Neill's
Virginia Carolorum, 243; New Eng. His. and Gen. Reg.,
XXXVII; Peyton, 20; RS, I, 44; II, 19-20; III, 5, 26, 43;
TD, Sept. 17, 1905; Oct. 8, Nov. 26, 1905; Jan. 27, 1907; Sept.
19, 26, Oct. 3, 10, 1909; June 9, 30, 1912; April 9, 1916;
Valentine I, 38-101; VM, II, 125-129; Winston, 371-380, with
chart; WM, I, 230 (chart); II, 273-274; IV, 283.
(*Edmund, New Kent*)—WM, 2d, V, 182, 195.
(*Friston*)—RS, III, 26.
(*Nathaniel*)—RS, II, 30, 39; III, 26; VM, XII, 205; XXIX, 40-
41; WM, XXIII, 177-178.
(*Nathaniel, Jr.*)—RS, II, 19; VM, XIV, 411-419; XV, 65-70,
306-312; WM, II, 129-131; IX, 6.
(*Nathaniel, Sr.*)—RS, II, 39; WM, VIII, 223.
(*New Kent*)—Browning, R. D., III, 781-783; RS, II, 39; Thos.
Carter, 76-78; Valentine IV, 2235-2240; VSR, IV (No. 1),
40; WM, X, 267-271.

Bagby—Bagby,, 152-154, 300-301, 322-323; Bagby Family Tree; Bruce
V, 366; Cyc. Va. Biog., IV, 492, 554; MMV, V, 23; Rock-
bridge, 472; SBN, XI, 35; Virkus I, 436-437; III, 509; VM,
XXVII, 368.

Baggarly—Virkus II, 32; III, 510 (with arms).

Bagge—Meade I, 396; VM, XII, 299-300; XXI, 373-374.

Baggott—Montgomery Co., O., 356.

Baggs—Rockbridge, 472.

Bagley—Old Free State II, 112-116, 264-265.

Bagnall (*Isle of Wight*)—Kennedy I, 45-46; VM, VI, 41-42; WM,
VII, 219, 253.

Bagnell—Cyc. Va. Biog., I, 175.

Bagwell—Cyc. Va. Biog., I, 175; John Wise, 120-121; TD, Oct. 19,
1913; VM, V, 340; Yeardley, 20.

Bahen—Cyc. Va. Biog., V, 683-684.

Bailey—Auglaize Co., Ohio, 803-804; Henry Co., 126-130; New River,
377-378; Rockbridge, 472; St. Mark's; TD, March 17, 1907;
March 15, 1914. WM, 2d, II, 280.
(*Campbell*)—Campbell Co., 330-331.
(*Culpeper*)—Tyler's III, 54.
(*Frederick*)—Cartmell, 474.
(*Surry*)—Bruce IV, 355.

Bain—Norfolk, 555, 616.

Baird—WM, XII, 26.
(From N. Y.)—Cauthorn, 18, 47.

Baker—Caroline Co., 221-222; Habersham Chap. II, 393, 396; Pendle-
ton Co., 318; Rockbridge, 472; TD, Oct. 14, 1906; Virkus
II, 260.
(*Berkeley*)—Tyler's III, 51-53; WM, VI, 94-97.
(*Chesterfield*)—MMV, III, 24.
(*Frederick*)—Bruce IV, 411; Cartmell, 258, 277, 429-436; Cyc.
Va. Biog., V, 767-769; Jolliffe, 163-165; Kith and Kin,
171-185; MMV, V, 26-27.
(*Isle of Wight and Nansemond*)—Ancestors (Crocker); ARP,
I, 54-55; Cyc. Va. Biog., I, 175-176; V, 689; Virkus III,
83; VM, IV, 167-168; WM, IV, 26.

Barley (*Frederick*)—Cartmell, 496.
Barlow, Parlar, Berler (*Rockingham*)—WM, XXVI, 88.
Barlow (*Bath*)—Pocahontas Co., 184-188.
    (*Caroline*)—Munsell's IX, 88.
    (*Williamsburg and Portsmouth*)—Bruce V, 86; Burgess, 500;
      Cyc. Va. Biog., V, 913; Norfolk, 713.
    (*York*)—Burgess, 500.
Barnes—BS, Dec. 31, 1905; Burgess, 912; Hayden, 278, 599, 719; Marshall; New River, 381-382; TD, April 8, 1906.
    (*Frederick*)—Licking Co., O., 623.
    (*New Kent*)—Bruce IV, 22.
    (*Northern Neck*)—WM, XVII, 145.
Barnett—Bruce IV, 212; Mathews Family; Meriwethers, 68-69; Rockbridge, 473; Knox Co., Ill., 367; Johnson Co., Ind.; 588-589.
    (*Amherst and Nelson*)—WM, 2d, IV, 185-186.
    (*Augusta*)—Crockett, 428-429.
    (*Frederick*)—DAR, 76, p. 12.
    (*Hanover*)—Crawfurdiana, 25.
    (*Orange*)—DAR, 81, p. 72.
Barns (*Tazewell*)—Tazewell II, 333-336.
Barr—Brock II, 704; Bruce IV, 498; V, 28; Cartmell, 466-467.
Barradall—Bruton, 102-103; Meade I, 188-189; VHS Col. XI, 75; WM, II, 79.
Barraud—RS, II, 43; WM, VIII, 154, 190.
Barret—Buckners of Va., 36-37; Crawfurdiana, 67-68, 75-76; Culpeper, 105; Cyc. Va. Biog., I, 180-181; McAllister, 86-89; TD, Jan. 3, 1909; VM, VI; VSR, III (No. 3), 27; IV (No. 4), 42; The Rev. Robert Barret of Virginia and his descendants. Compiled by Edward A. Claypool, Chicago, Ill., 1907 (blue print); Watson, 205-206.
    (*Hanover*)—Mackenzie V, 570-572; VI, 273-277.
    (*Louisa*)—MMV, IV, 28-29; VM, XX, 208-209; XXIII, 142, 314.
Barrett—The Colonial Church, 249; VM, VI, 22; WM, VII, 201; IX, 241.
    (*Alexandria*)—Bruce VI, 130.
    (*Fredcrick*)—Cartmell, 474.
Barron—Beau Monde (weekly), Richmond, April 14, 1894; Bruce IV, 517; Burgess, 471-474, 896; 1329; MMV, II, 38; Norfolk, 489-490; SBN, XI, 49-52; VM, XII, 17.
Barrow—Cyc. Va. Biog., V, 721; Henry Co., 125-126; Virkus II, 210.
    (*Amelia*)—Old Free State II, 256-257.
    (*Brunswick*)—TD, Feb. 13, 1910; Nov. 16, 1913.
    (*Frederick*)—Sangamon Co., Ill., 98.
Barry (*Lunenburg*)—Old Free State II, 116-131; SBN, XI, 53-54.
Bartlett—Barbour Co., W. Va., 340-345; TD, April 2, 1905; VM, XIX, 68.
Bartley—DAR, 78, p. 210.
Barton—BS, Oct. 8, 1905; Cabell, etc., 349-350; Cyc. Va. Biog., IV, 529; V, 697; Du Bellet II, 746-750; Marshall, 353-356; McIlhany, 66-67; MMV, I, 139-142.
Bashaw—Sangamon Co., Ill., 99; WM, XIII, 292.
Baskervill—DAR, 80, p. 69; Hamiltons of Burnside, N. C., 109-111; VSR, V (No. 2), 46-47.
Baskerville—Cyc. Va. Biog., V, 867-868; Genealogy of the Baskerville Family; Additional Baskerville Genealogy; Goode, 120, 233-234, 380; Kith and Kin, 28, 37; RS, III, 44; TD, June 23, 1907; Virkus II. 107 (with arms); VM, XXI, 86, 222; XXVI, 278-279; XXVII, 76; WM, III, 182; XVII, 227-229.

Baskervyle—Cyc. Va. Biog., I, 181; WM, IV, 4.
Basket—Christ Church Register; Hayden, 525.
Bass—Burgess, 954; Jones, 203; RS, II, 46; TD, Aug. 27, 1911; Woodson, 232, 599.
Bassett—ARP II, 782-783; Browning, C. D., 32-33; BS, July 14, 21, 28; Aug. 4, 1907; Convention 1788, II, 370; Cyc. Va. Biog., I, 181; Henry Co., 120-125; Keith, 27-31; Kennedy II, 50-52; Lancaster, 264-266; McAllister, 122, 127; RS, III, 46; Spotswood Letters I, 63; TD, April 12, July 5, 1914; Tyler's II, 140-141; VM, I, 322-324, 453-456; II, 231-232; IV, 162; VIII, 399-400; XXII, 40; XXIII, 359; Willis, 125-127; Winston, 343-351; WM, II, 85, 217; V, 36-38; VI, 123, 125; VII, 146, 152.
　　(*New Kent*)—Hardy, 43-48.
Basye—Burgess, 953; Genealogy of the Cloyd, Basye, etc., Families of America, 207-223.
Batchelder—Christ Church Register; Morton Kin; Valentine I, 168-209; IV, 2245-2246; WM, III, 277; VSR, IV (No. 1), 38.
Batcheller—Researcher I, 250.
Bateman—Hayden, 480-481; WM, 2d, II, 181.
Bates—Bates et al., by Onward Bates; Bell, 3-4; Cyc. Va. Biog., I, 182; TD, Jan. 22, 1905; Sept. 2, 30, 1906; Aug. 25, 1907; VM, XI, 186; Walker-Wigton, 115-120; Woodson, 80, 227, 146; WM, VI, 122, 195; VIII, 44.
　　(*Goochland*)—DAR, 55, p. 301.
Batey—DAR, 46, p. 72.
Bathurst—Cyc. Va. Biog., I, 182; Griffith-Meriwether, 39-41; Roger Jones, 143-149, 277-281; RS, III, 5, 24; VM, XXIII, 294; VSR, III, 24; WM, II, 212; VIII, 98-100; XII, 67.
Batt—WM, I, 196-197.
Battaile—Fishback Family, 175, 265-266; Kennedy II, 79; McAllister, 75, 82; TD, Nov. 10, 1907; March 20, Sept. 11, Oct. 23, 1910; Aug. 27, 1911; VM, III, 1-2; IX, 213; XXVI, 408; WM, XX, 271; WM, 2d, I, 151; VII, 274-276.
Battaley—WM, V, 277.
Batte—Bristol Parish, 206; Cyc. Va. Biog., I, 182; Goode, 426; RS, II, 40; TD, Dec. 31, 1916; Jan. 7, 1917; VM, III, 328; VII, 438-440; X, 105-106; WM, I, 196-197; XXIV, 140, 207, 268-269.
Batteley—VM, XXXV, 41-42, 199-200.
Batten—WM, IV, 3.
Battey—Old King William, 187.
Battle—Bruce V, 53; DAR, 50, p. 168.
Baugh—Bruce V, 123; Cyc. Va. Biog., I, 182; Jones, 201; TD, Aug. 6, Sept. 24, 1911; Virginia Gazette, March 17, 1779; VM, VII, 423-424; XIII, 58; XIX, 193; WM, XV, 258; XXIV, 135.
Baughman—Cyc. Va. Biog., IV, 520; VSR, IV (No. 4), 27.
Baughn—Burgess, 8.
Bauserman—Bruce IV, 271.
Bauswell—Burgess, 957.
Baxter—Pocahontas Co., 419-421; Rockbridge, 246, 473; VM, XXXIV, 274.
　　(*Augusta*)—McClure, 188-190.
　　(*Rockingham*)—Foote II, 262-269.
Bayard—WM, VIII, 134, 207.
Bayless—DAR, 83, p. 192.
Bayley—Cyc. Va. Biog., I, 183.

Bayley, Bayly (*Richmond Co.*)—VM, X, 214.
Bayliss—Cartmell, 494; Hayden, 605-607, 623.
Baylor—Burgess, 1013; Cabell, etc., 337; Caroline Co., 371-379; Cartmell, 456; Cyc. Va. Biog., I, 183; Dinwiddie Papers II, 103-104; Hayden, 190; Mackenzie III, 367; Meade II, 464-465; "Mordecai Cooke", 23; Old King William, 28; RS, III, 2, 23; SBN, XI, 59-60; TD, Nov. 19, 1905; June 24, 1906; Sept. 4, 1910; July 16, 23, Aug. 13, 1916; Virkus III, 57; VM, VI, 197-199, 307-309, 432; XII, 95 (New Market); XIV, 438-439; XVI, 103; XXI, 89-96, 193-195; XXIV, 367-373; XXV, 315-323.
     (*King and Queen*)—VM, XXXIII, 404-405.
Bayly—Researcher I, 158, 222; VM, III, 182; WM, VII, 106.
     (*Eastern Shore*)—John Wise, 107-109.
     (*Middlesex*)—TD, March 15, 1917.
     (*Richmond Co.*)—VM, VIII, 422-423.
Baynard—Hayden, 463.
Bayne—Bruce V, 320; Cyc. Va. Biog., V, 1075; TD, Jan. 22, 1911; WM, XIII, 284-285.
Baynham—Caroline Co., 346-347; Halifax, 106-108; SBN, XI, 60-61.
Bayton—Hayden, 122.
Baytop—Cooke-Booth, 92, 121-122, 204-216; Cyc. Va. Biog., I, 183-184; Descendants of John Stubbs, 95-96; Francis Morgan, 27-33; RS, III, 31; TD, May 1, 8, 15, 22, 29, June 5, 1910; Two Families, 105-164; VM, XI, 69; XXIX, 42-43; WM, II, 234.
Bazile—Bruce IV, 134.
Beach—Avery I, 131; Burgess, 141, 932; Rockbridge, 473.
     (*Eastern Shore*)—WM, XVIII, 109-110.
Beale—Bruce V, 255; Cooke-Booth, 167-168; Hardy, 515; Hayden, 252, 737-739; Mackenzie IV, 195; MMV, IV, 97; Morton Kin; Pocahontas Co., 495-497; RC, III, 63; Shenandoah, 583; TD, Oct. 9, 1904; Nov. 26, 1905; Aug. 7, Oct. 16, 1910; Virkus I, 709; II, 191; III, 222; VM, IV, 463-464; XXIX, 360; XXXII, 51-54; VSR, 70; WM, I, 85; III, 68-69; XI, 124.
Beall—Burgess, 1014; Cooke-Booth, 249-250; Rockbridge, 473; SBN, XI, 61-62.
Bean—Bean Family of Hardy Co. (now W. Va.); Cartmell, 437-438; Halifax, 265; Millers of Millersburg, 161; Virkus III, 59.
Beamer—Bruce VI, 467.
Bear—Rockbridge, 473; Shenandoah, 583-584; Virkus III, 501.
Beard—ARP, I, 247; Rockbridge, 473; WM, XII, 64-65.
     (*Augusta*)—Mackenzie II, 83.
Beardsley—Hayden, 312.
Beasley—Burgess, 164; MMV, III, 29.
Beath—Pendleton Co., 333.
Beathe—Highland Co., 263.
Beatie—Bruce VI, 177.
Beattie (*Rockbridge*)—Draper Series, V, 196; King's Mountain, 495.
Beatty (*Frederick*)—Cartmell, 491-492.
Beaty—Rockbridge, 473.
Beauchamp—Hayden, 537, 735.
Beauford—See Buford.
Beaver—Rockbridge, 473; Strickler, 355.
Beazley—Bruce V. 255; Montague, 166.
     (*Greene*)—Cyc. Va. Biog., V, 1000.
Beck—Burgess, 728.

Beckham—Beckham Family in Virginia and the branches thereof in Ky., Tenn., Pa., and W. Va.; McCormick, 42-45. (*Orange and Culpeper*)—Virkus II, 263.
Beckley—See Bickley.
Beckwith—A New Baronetage, etc. (1769), I, 103-106; Bristol Parish, 131; Cyc. Va. Biog., I, 184; V, 606; Morton Kin; RS, IV, 23; The Beckwiths; WM, IV, 166; XIV, 140.
Bedford—Burgess, 316, 383; Halifax, 214; TD, Sept. 8, 1912; Virkus II, 209; III, 187; VM, XX, 197.
Bedell (Burwell)—Keith, 34.
Bedinger—Bittinger and Bedinger Families; Bruce V, 63; Burgess, 532-535; George Michael Bedinger, a Kentucky Pioneer, by Danske Dandridge (1909); Kennedy I, 564; Lee, 471-472; Shepherdstown, 54-59, 78, 80, 97, 131-134, 300-302; Welles' Washington Genealogy, 243.
Bee—Pendleton Co., 150-154.
Beecher—Cartmell, 492.
Beeks—Researcher II, 109-113.
Beers—Rockbridge, 473.
Beery—Bruce IV, 219.
Beets—Rockbridge, 473.
Beggs—Clemens' Wills, 9; The Book O' Beggs (1928).
Beheathland—Researcher I, 163; VM, VI, 363; XI, 363; XXXII, 353-354; WM, 2d, IX, 60-63.
Beirne—Boogher, 343-344; Bruce V, 393; Stubbs, 199; The Killing of Adam Caperton, 51-53.
Belcher—New River, 380; WM, XV, 259.
Bele—Rockbridge, 473.
Belfield—Barton II, 207-208; Griffith-Meriwether, 52-55, 60-61; Hening V, 285-287; Mortons and Their Kin, II, 477-479; Roger Jones, 56, 63-64, 182-184; RS, IV, 19; TD, Oct. 2, 1904; Aug. 13, 1916; Virkus II, 352; VM, XXXII, 63.
Bell—Rockbridge, 473; RS, III, 16; St. Mark's, 125; TD, May 26, 1912; WM, IX, 268.
    (*Accomac*)—Mackenzie VII, 66 et seq; Virkus I, 454; II, 266.
    (*Augusta*)—Bell Family in America; Boogher, 304-305, 311; Bruce V, 138; VI, 347; Burgess, 525-530; Mackenzie II, 82-105; McIlhany, 19-20; Peyton, 311; Virkus III, 345.
    (*Buckingham*)—Lancaster, 186-187; Marshall, 297-298.
    (*Fauquier*)—Burgess, 482.
    (*Frederick and Berkeley*)—Sangamon Co., Ill., 106.
    (*Hanover*)—Bell, 3.
    (*New Kent, Lunenburg, etc.*)—Old Free State II, 131-149; Virkus II, 267; III, 62.
    (*Northumberland*)—DAR, 74, p. 326.
Belote—Burgess, 57-59.
Belson—Valentine I, 210-211.
Belt—Bruce IV, 485; Goode, 275; Halifax, 110-113; Mackenzie II, 106.
Belvin—Burgess, 170-171, 237, 1226; Cyc. Va. Biog., IV, 124.
Benagh—Boddie, 80.
Bendall—Burgess, 735.
Bender—Braxton Co., W. Va., 350.
Benger—VM, II, 339-342.
Benn—Cyc. Va. Biog., I, 184; Norfolk, 712; WM, VII, 250.
Bennet—VM, VI, 38-39.
    (*Isle of Wight*)—VM, VI, 38-39.
Bennett—Burgess, 12, 59-60; Pendleton Co., 177-179; Rockbridge, 473; Sangamon Co., Ill., 110-112; TD, May 10, 1908; Feb. 25,

Best—Trabue, 50-52; Virkus II, 105; WM, VII, 251.
Bethel—Overwharton, 16.
Betts—Burgess, 531; Old Free State II, 149-154; TD, March 31, April 14, 1907; Virkus III, 488.
Beuhring—WVM, I, Oct., 1901, 33-34.
Beverage—Highland Co., 262-263.
Beveridge—Cyc. Va. Biog., IV, 244; Maxwell, 430-445.
Beverley—BS, Aug. 19, 21, 1906; Bruce V, 51; Buckners of Va., 119-120; Carter Family Tree; Cyc. Va. Biog., I, 185-186; Dinwiddie Papers II, 350-351; Du Bellet II, 234-235; Hening VIII, 166-168, 227-230, 280-283; Kennedy II, 337-354; Lancaster, 292, 295; Lee, 319-320; Meade II. 481; Neill's Virginia Carolorum; TD, Feb. 16, 1908; Nov. 7, 1909; Aug. 21, 1910; Thomas Carter, 282-283; Virkus III, 32, 133-134; VM, II, 405-413; III, 47-52, 169-176, 261-271, 383-392; XII, 317-318; XX, 116, 213-214, 332-333, 437-438; XXI, 97-102, 212-214, 305-306; XXII, 102-103, 297-301, 420 (Major Robert Beverley and His Descendants. By W. G. Stanard), XXXIII, 31, 85; XXXIV, 161-163; XXXVI, 333-334; VSR, I, 15; V (No. 2), 26, 59, 66; Wallace's Illustrated Weekly (Richmond), April, May, 1891; Winston, 142-147; WM, II, 272; VI, 173; XVII, 65.
   (*Fauquier*)—Bruce IV, 228.
Beverly (*Grayson*)—Researcher I, 125.
Bevill—The Beville Family of Virginia, etc. By Agnes B. V. Tedcastle. (Boston, privately printed, 1917); WM, XXXII, 389; XXXV, 279; WM, XV, 260.
Beville—Bruce V, 179.
Beyer (Beier)—The American Boyers, 3d ed., pp. 425-431.
Bibb—Albemarle, 143; Gilmer's Georgians, 107-111; Hampden-Sidney, 86; Hardy, 424-425, 549-551; SBN, XI, 78; Stubbs, 254-256, Thomas Carter, 128-129; Trabue, 28-30; VM, XVIII, 195-196.
Bibby (Bibbie)—Border Settlers, 221.
Bible—Coshocton Co., Ohio, 525; Highland Co., 353; Pendleton Co., 179-180.
Biby—Rockbridge, 474.
Bickers—Cyc. Va. Biog., V, 589.
Bickerton—VM, XXIX, 364, 366-367, 371; VSR, IV (No. 3), 29.
   (*Hanover*)—Winston, 87-90.
Bickley (Beckley)—A New Baronetage of England, etc., 1769, Vol. I, pp. 116-119; Convention 1788, I, 63-64; Cyc. Va. Biog., I, 186; Thos. Carter, 228; VM, XXX, 40-41; WM, IV, 250; V, 28-30, 124-127; IX, 241; X, 126-131; XI, 147.
Bidgood—Cyc. Va. Biog., V, 906; Norfolk, 871-872; Virkus I, 463.
Bigger—Armistead, 221; Brock II, 768; WM, XXV, 144.
Biggs—Crockett, 244.
Bilbro—Hardesty (*Bedford*), 417.
Bilisoly—Bruce VI, 18, 516; Cyc. Va. Biog., V, 1052-1053.
Billingsley—Bruce IV, 580.
Billington—ARP, II, 817; WM 2d, II, 124.
Billups—Brock II, 665; Burgess, 563; Cyc. Va. Biog., V, 885; TD, Sept. 12, 1909.
Binford—Kanawha, 857; Roger Jones, 86-87; TD, Sept. 27, Oct. 4, 1914; VSR, I (No. 3), 37; WM, V, 272.
Bingham (*Hanover*)—Virkus III, 78.
   (*King William*)—Tyler's X, 47-50.
Binkerd—Miami Co., Ind., 543.

Binns—Tyler's V, 140-141; WM 2d, II, 20-39.
    (*Surry*)—Rives, 495-498; WM, XX, 189-191.
Birchett—TD, March 30, 1913.
Birckhead—Virkus III, 59.
Bird (Byrd) (*King and Queen*)—Bagby, 323-324, 326-327, 355; VM, V, 356.
Bird—Bird Genealogy; Bruce IV, 511; Highland Co., 264-268; Pendleton Co., 333; TD, April 18, May 9, 1909.
    (*Valley of Va.*)—Cartmell, 259; Shenandoah, 584-585; Virkus II, 349.
Birdsong (*Sussex*)—Bruce VI, 557; VM, XIX, 46-47; WM,, XII, 16.
Biscoe—Arkansas, 265-269; Tyler's IX, 200-202.
Bish—Hardin Co., Ohio, 919.
Bishop—Albemarle, 144; Highland Co., 373; MMV, V, 32; Virkus III, 70; WM, III, 60.
Black—Albemarle, 144-145; Highland Co., 378; Pendleton Co., 180, 333; Rockbridge, 474; TD, Dec. 11, 1910.
    (*Montgomery*)—New River, 380-381.
    (*Prince George*)—WM, VIII, 148-150.
Blackburn—Bruce IV, 284; Buford, 132; Cyc. Va. Biog., I, 187; Marshall, 365; Meade II, 208; Virkus III, 514; VSR, I (No. 3), 47.
    (*Middlesex*)—Buford, 132-133, 171-173.
    (*Prince William*)—Hayden, 601-603, 633-638; Thomas, 556f-556g; WM, IV, 266-269.
    (*Washington Co.*)—Tyler's II, 263-268.
Blackburne (*Gloucester*)—WM, II, 219, 230.
Blackerby—Buckners of Va., 302.
Blackford—Brock II, 557-558; Bruce V, 8; Cyc. Va. Biog., V, 845-846; Du Bellet I, 189-194, 211-212, 225-227, 274, 279; II, 211-212; Kennedy II, 78; J. Marshall, 335-336, 385-386; Memories of Life In and Out of the Army in Virginia; MMV. III, 34-35; V, 37-38.
Blackman—WM, VI, 57; XXIV, 135-136.
Blackwell—Browning, R. D., III, 822; Bruce IV, 85, 276; Burgess, 535-537; Cyc. Va. Biog., I, 187; IV, 424; Fauquier Bulletin (No. 4), 486-499; Hardy, 49-70, 190; Hayden, 265-267, 271-277, 535; Hening VIII, 641-643; Millers of Millersburg, 125; MMV, III, 36-41; Old Free State II, 154-159; Roger Jones, 70; TD, Aug. 25, 1907; Jan. 5, 1908; Sept. 11, Oct. 16, 1910; Oct. 1, 1916; Thos. Carter, 351-352; Virkus III, 235; VM, XIX, 445; XX, 94-95; XXII, 438-441; XXIII, 101-103, 216-218, 326-331, 436-438; XXIV, 99-102, 204-206, 312-313; VSR, IV (No. 4), 37; WM, XX, 297.
    (*Hanover*)—Genealogy of Kilby, Tynes, etc., 35-36.
Bladen (*Fairfax*)—VM, X, 429.
Blagg—Highland Co., 267-268.
Blaikley (*York*)—WM, II, 212-213, 273.
Blain—Foote II, 294-301; Life of Gen. Hugh Mercer.
    (*Rev. Daniel*)—VSR, II (No. 2), 57.
Blair—Madison Co., Ohio, 989; Rockbridge, 474; RS, II, 9; Stubbs, 395-396; SBN, XI, 85-88; TD, Jan. 3, 1909; WM, VII, 63, 133; VIII, 36, 137.
    (*Archibald, Richmond City*)—WM, XVII, 225-226.
    (*Augusta*)—The Lyle Family, etc., 325-332.
    (*Richmond City*)—Foote II, 12-13; MMV, IV, 30-34; RS, II, 21; Virkus I, 473, 904; VM, I, 339.
    (*Western Va.*)—Grayson Co., 26-45, 50-52; Randolph Co., 311; SBN, XI, 84-86, 88-89.

(Williamsburg)—Blair, etc., 19-86; Brock II, 52; Bruce IV, 184; Bruton Church, 106-107; Hon. John Blair, Jr. An Address by H. T. Wickham, 1913; Kennedy I, 267-269; Lancaster, 15-16; Md. Soc. Col. Wars., II, 113; Va. His. Col., XI, 78-79; VM, IV, 161-162; VII, 154-155; IX, 110, 255; XXXI, 84-87; XXXII, 383-386; WM, I, 9-10; V, 279-281; XVII, 225-226.

Blake—Burgess, 696.

Blakemore—Davis, 105; VM, XVII, 91.

Blakey—Watkins, 37; WM, IX, 41.

Blanch—McIntosh I, 43, 77.

Blanchard *(Nansemond)*—N. C. His. Reg., I, 185.

Blancet—Kanawha, 686.

Bland—ARP, I, 279-281; Bagby, 324-325; Bland Papers (Petersburg, 1840), I, 13-15, 145, 160; Braxton Co., W. Va., 353; Bristol Parish, 147-163; Browning, R. D., III, 721-724; Campbell's History of Va., 670; Cyc. Va. Biog., I, 188; Goode, 54-55; Griffith-Meriwether, 52, 58-59; Hening VI, 303-308; Lee, 137-140; Mackenzie IV, 374; Meade I, 446-447; Pendleton Co., 180-181; RC (1888); Robertson, 32, 36, 45; RS, II, 14; III, 56; SBN, XI, 89-91; Southside Va., 133-136; TD, Feb. 12, 1905; Aug. 21, 1910; Feb. 25, 1912; VM, III, 206, 315-316; IV, 163; IX, 60, 66, 357; XIX, 445; XX, 238-239; VSR, I, 6; IV (No. 2), 26; V (No. 1), 71; (No. 2), 42; WM, III, 277; V, 150-157; VII, 231; VIII, 211 et seq; XVII, 267; XVIII, 69.
  (Charles City)—WM, XXVI, 139.
  (Highland)—Highland Co., 353.
  (John)—Familiae Minorum Gentium (Harleian Society), II, 421-427.
  (King and Queen)—Bagby, 324-325; Cyc. Va. Biog., V, 1059.
  (Norfolk Co.)—Cyc. Va. Biog., V, 1022.
  (Prince George)—Convention 1788, II, 380; Hampden-Sidney, 207; RC, I, 49; Stubbs, 381; Thomas Carter, 74-75; VM, X, 372-374; XXVIII, 353; WM, IV, 143-144, 148, 153, 269; V, 150-157; XV, 47.
  (Stafford)—VM, III, 206; WM, IV, 134.
  (Theodorick)—Md. Soc. Col. Wars, 107; Virkus I, 509-510; WM, XXVI, 39.

Blankenbaker—WM, XXVI, 85-88.

Blankenship—Crockett, 427-428.

Blankinship—TD, June 25, 1916; Feb. 4, 1917.

Blanks—Bruce V, 107; Cyc. Va. Biog., V, 653; MMV, IV, 37.

Blanton—Bruce IV, 149; V, 63; Caroline Co., 379-382; Cyc. Va. Biog., IV, 212; TD, Sept. 2, 1906; Virkus II, 271; III, 19.

Bledsoe—Cabell, etc., 229-230; Cisco, 55-190; Dunmore's War, 106; Hord (1898), 102-103, 137-138; Lewis, 138-139; McAllister, 371, 373; SBN, XI, 91-92; VM, VI, 345-346; VII, 2, 11-12; WM 2d, VII, 279.

Blennerhassett—TD, June 25, 1905.

Blewitt—Pendleton Co., 181.

Blizzard—Madison Co., Ohio, 728; Pendleton Co., 181-182.

Blood—WM, VI, 64.

Blosser—Shenandoah, 585-586; Strickler, 170-180; Virkus III, 501.

Blount *(Isle of Wight)*—ARP, II, 581; N. C. His. Reg., I, 34.
  (Surry)—VM, V, 202-204.

Blow—ARP, II, 785-788, 790-793, 801-802; Munsell's XI, 69; Norfolk, 494, 1029; TD, Nov. 29, 1908; Oct. 11, 1914; Virkus I, 93; II, 109; III, 177; WM, IV, 275-276.
Bloxom (*Accomac*)—Burgess, 845.
   (*Louisa*)—Bell, 3.
Blue—Burgess, 750; Hampshire, 701; Licking Co., Ohio, 622; Madison Co., Ohio, 852; TD, April 26, 1914.
Blunt—The Blunts of Isle of Wight County, Virginia. By James Francis Crocker (Portsmouth, Va., 1914).
Blythe—Cyc. Va. Biog., V, 839; TD, Jan. 7, 1906.
Board—Hardesty (*Bedford*)—413; Kanawha, 819, 948.
Boatwright—Bruce V, 501.
Boaz—Bruce IV, 46, 328.
Bocock—Bruce IV, 202; SBN, XI, 95; Virkus I, 478; VM, XXVII, 93; WM, XX, 296.
Boddie—Boddie and Allied Families.
Bodine—Hardin Co., Ohio, 991.
Bodkin—Highland Co., 268-270; Pendleton Co., 333; Rockbridge, 474.
Bogan—Rockbridge, 474; WM 2d, VII, 139.
Bogard—Pendleton Co., 318.
Boggess—Lindsay, 114-121.
Boggs—Hayden, 362-363; Miami Co., Ind., 507; Pendleton Co., 182-183; WVM, III, 202-203.
Bohannan—WM, VI, 198.
Bohannon—Cabell, etc., 316; WM, VI, 198.
Boils—Rockbridge, 474.
Boisseau—Bruce V, 443; Cyc. Va. Biog., V, 915; Habersham Chap II, 268-269, 276, 305, 342; Rives, 259-262; Tyler's X, 118-130; VM, XXII, 85-86; WM, V, 238; IX, 199; XIV, 139; WM 2d, II, 71-72.
Boivers—Highland Co., 353-354.
Boldero—WM, IV, 39.
Bolen—Bruce IV, 316; VI, 461; MMV, V, 39.
Bolithoe—VM, XXX, 39.
Bolling—ARP, I, 325-326; Baskerville, (89), 132-145; Bolling Genealogy (1868), 38 pages; Bolling Memoirs, edited by T. H. Wynne; Bristol Parish, 140-147; Browning, R. D., 3d, 20, 271, 276; BS, Nov. 5, 12, 19, 1905; Burgess, 539-541; Cabell, etc., 229-230; Campbell Co., 353-355; Cyc. Va. Biog., I, 189; IV, 522-523; V, 1032-1034; Du Bellet IV, 301-331; Goode, 64-65; Griffith-Meriwether, 52-57; Hayden, 478; Hening VIII, 291-293; Lancaster, 94-96, 183-185; LCJ, May 9, 1915 (II, 3); Lee, 506; Mackenzie II, 136-141; Md. Soc. Col. Wars, 113; Meade I, 78, etc.; N. E. His. and Gen. Reg., XXIV, 95; XXVI, 35; Old Free State II, 159-165; Old King William, 28; Robertson, 31-70; RS, II, 12-32; Ruvigny, 531; TD, Oct. 4, 1903; Aug. 28, 1904; May 20, 1906; May 19, 1907; July 18, Aug. 15, 1915; June 11, 1916; Virkus I, 296-297; II, 250; VM, I, 446-447; IV, 329-332; VII, 352-354; XII, 154-156; XXII, 103-107, 200, 215-217, 309-310, 331-333; VSR, I, 6; II (No. 3), 39; IV (No. 3), 21; (No. 4), 38-39; V (No. 2), 26, 43, 49; Willis, 74-76; WM, V, 275; VIII, 36; XVII, 68, 155.
   (*Center Hill, Petersburg*)—Munsell's V, 32-33; RS, III, 36.
   (*Prince George*)—Genealogy of the Bolling Family; Hardy, 71-80 Hord, 71-80; VM, XXI, 310-314, 422-427; XXIII, 322-324; XXIV, 196-197; XXV, 79, 411-412; XXVI, 405; WM, V, 275-276.

Boslow—Hardin Co., Ohio, 956.
Bosserman—Rockbridge, 474.
Bostick—Lewis, 155; McAllister, 387.
Boston—Burgess, 582-583; Mackenzie III, 54-55.
Boswell—Bruce VI, 311; Descendants of John Stubbs, 105-109; Old
    Free State, II, 171-176; TD, March 12, 1911; Virkus II,
    267; WM, VIII, 54.
Bosworth—Randolph Co., 306-308.
Boteler—Cartmell, 455.
Botkin—Madison Co., Ohio, 1147.
Bott—TD, Sept. 24, 1912; VM, XXXII, 387; WM, XIX, 63.
Bottom—WM, XV, 262.
Botts—Culpeper, 2, 46; Goode, 219, 367-368, 424-426; Kennedy II, 82-
    83; TD, July 22, 1906; Virkus III, 559; VM, XI, 449; Willis,
    74-76.
Bouce—Pendleton Co., 318.
Boucher—Cyc. Va. Biog., I, 191.
Boughton—Burgess, 1069.
Bouldin—Burgess, 584; Goode, 121, 195; Hardy, 81-83; Hayden, 312,
    319; Henry Co., 119; RS, III, 14, 16, 45; Southside Va.,
    156-157; TD, June 22, 1913; Tyler's IV, 438-439; Virkus
    II, 54; WM, V, 71; XII, 183-185.
Boulton—McAllister, 337-350.
Boulware—Bagby, 295, 325-326; Caroline Co., 384-388; Mackenzie
    IV, 384-386; MMV, V, 43-44; VM, V, 349.
Bourne—Grayson Co., 17-64.
    (*Culpeper*)—DAR, 80, p. 124.
Bourne (Bone)—Winston, 248-249.
Boush—Burgess, 589-590; Cyc. Va. Biog., I, 191; McIntosh II, 139-
    140; RC, II, 47; Researcher I, 118-124, 194, 252; Rockbridge,
    475; TD, March 29, 1908; VM, XXXI, 346; XXXV, 76-77;
    WM, II, 77; IV, 95.
Boutwell—Bruce IV, 447; Caroline Co., 382-384.
Bowcock—Albemarle, 145-147; Lewis, 297-298.
Bowden—Cyc. Va. Biog., IV, 417.
Bowdoin—ARP, II, 479-481, 486; Huguenot Emigration, XI, XII;
    Meade I, 254; Some Account of the Bowdoin Family; Vir-
    kus I, 86; WM, IV, 249; Yeardley, 30-31.
Bowe—Bruce IV, 25; Cyc. Va. Biog., IV, 425.
Bowen—Boogher, 333; Campbell, etc.; Cisco, 251-255; Crockett, 64-
    66; Cyc. Va. Biog., V, 785; Miami Co., Ind., 398; TD,
    Nov. 17, 1807; Virkus II, 169.
    (*Albemarle*)—Albemarle, 147-148.
    (*Tazewell*)—New River, 382, 386; Tazewell II, 341-356.
    (*Western Va.*)—Burgess, 557-578; Des Cognets, 56-66.
Bowers—Bruce IV, 289; Highland Co., 353-354; Strickler, 363.
    (*King and Queen*)—Burgess, 580-581.
Bowie—BS, Jan. 6, 13, 1907; Caroline Co., 388-392; St. Mark's, 149;
    TD, Feb. 23, March 15, 22, 1908; The Bowies and Their
    Kindred; Virkus I, 20; II, 320; VM, X, 306-307; WM, X,
    278; XXII, 299-300.
Bowker—Cyc. Va. Biog., I, 192; VM, VIII, 59-60; XI, 313.
Bowler (*Rappahannock*)—VSR, I (No. 2), 8; WM, VI, 30.
Bowles—Bruce V, 527; History of the Bowles Family, by T. A. Far-
    quhar (Philadelphia, 1907); MMV, I, 172-173; TD, Jan.
    26, April 19, 1908; Sept. 19, 1909; March 12, 1911; Feb.
    27, 1916; VM, XI, 68; WM, IX, 263.
    (*Bowlersville*)—Cyc. Va. Biog., IV, 538.

(*Lower Norfolk*)—McIntosh I, 77; II, 19; VM, XXVI, 280.
(*Norfolk*)—Mackenzie VII, 75, 352-353; VM, XXXII, 352-353.
Brayne—VM, II, 340; VSR, V (No. 2), 22; WM, X, 143-144.
Brazier—Meade II, 483.
Breathed (Breathitt)—TD, March 5, 1911.
Breckinridge (Breckenridge)—Browning, C. D., 3d, 556-557; Burgess,
    585-587; Cabell, etc., 232-236, 489-515; Cisco, 178, 180-181;
    des Cognets, 82-83; Dinwiddie Papers II, 531; Dunmore's
    War, 27; Joseph C. Breckinridge, Jr.; Kennedy I, 94-97,
    99-109, 451-459, 640-646; II, 588-591; Kith and Kin, 153-
    155; Mackenzie VII, 95; Marshall, 71-73; Meade II, 62;
    Munsell's XI, 22; Peyton, 304; Preston Family, 141-149;
    RS, II, 7; Sangamon Co., Ill., 136-138; SBN, XI, 115-119;
    Speed, 103-104; TD, Dec. 15, 1907; Virkus I, 398-399; II,
    274; VM, X, 432; XXVII, 157-159; Waddell, 38, 401-404.
Breeden—TD, June 2, 1907.
Bremond—Brock II, 690.
Brenaman—Bruce V, 48.
Brent—Bruce VI, 89; Burgess, 592-600; Cyc. Va. Biog., I, 193-194;
    Goode, 239; Md. Soc. Col. Wars, 7, 56; RC, March 17,
    1889; TD, July 29, 1906; VM, XIX, 445; WM, I, 17; IV,
    249, 251.
(*Charles*)—VM, XXXIV, 180-183, 280-285, 378-384.
(*Charlotte*)—VM, VIII, 105-106.
(*Dumfries*)—Hardy, 53-54, 88-91.
(*Giles and George*)—VM, XIX, 445; XXXV, 201-203.
(*Lancaster*)—ARP, II, 521-525, 527-530; Cartmell, 283, 490-491;
    Goode, 239-240, 384-385; Lee, 171; Marshall, 377-378; RC
    (1888); RS, II, 49; VM, XIV, 426-431; XV, 93-99, 450-
    453; XVI, 96-102, 211-213; XVII, 81-83, 194-197, 308-311,
    420-423; XVIII, 96-100, 224-226, 319-321; XIX, 94-96, 317-
    319, 433-435, 439-440; XX, 94-95.
(*Stafford*)—Hardy, 88-89; Hening V; Mackenzie I, 30-34; IV,
    522-523; VII, 101-112; Old Prince William I, 52; RC, II, 27,
    29, 31; SBN, XI, 119-120; VM, I, 123-124; II, 35-36; XI,
    70; XII, 292-294, 439-443; XIII, 105-112, 219-222, 318-321,
    435-441; XIV, 95-101, 209-215, 314-319, 426-431; XV, 93-99,
    194-199, 324-329, 450-453; XVI, 96-102, 211-213; XVII, 81-83,
    194-197, 308-311, 420-423; XVIII, 96-100, 224-226, 319-321.
    444-447; XIX, 94-96, 206-207, 317-319, 433-435; XX, 94-99,
    321-323, 433-434; XXI, 96-97; XXII, 201, 420; WM, IV, 40.
(*Stafford, etc.*)—Hening V, 292, 293.
Brenton—DAR, 76, p. 225.
Brereton—Cyc. Va. Biog., I, 194; WM, IV, 165; IX, 186.
Bressie—Burgess, 648; WM, VII, 212 et seq.
Brett—RS. III, 36, 43; WM, I, 108.
Brevard—Whitaker, 128.
Brewer—Bruce IV, 262; Cyc. Va. Biog., I, 102, 194; Kennedy II,
    509-512; RC, III, 16; TD, Aug. 11, Dec. 8, 1907; VM, III,
    182-184.
Brewster—Cyc. Va. Biog., I, 194; VM, XXVII, 295; WM, IV, 39.
(*Augusta*)—Maxwell, 204-206, 239-241.
Brice—Rockbridge, 475.
(*Lancaster*)—VM, V, 256.
Brickey—Hord (1898), 179-180.
Brickhouse—Burgess, 100.
Bridger—Convention 1788, II, 376; Cyc. Va. Biog., I, 195; Hening VI,

448-452; Meade I, 305; RS, II, 45; III, 28, 31, 37; TD, May 5, 1912; VM, II, 381-382; WM, VII, 212 et seq.
Bridges—Huguenot Emigration, 159-160; TD, Jan. 20, 1907.
Bridgforth—Old Free State II, 165-170.
Bridgland—Jones, 189-190.
Bridgman—Montgomery Co., Ohio, 447.
Bridwell—Overwharton, 12-15, 17-18, etc.
Briggs—Bruce VI, 493-494; Burgess, 817, 900; Convention 1788, II, 381; Cyc. Va. Biog., I, 195; Pendleton Co., 318; TD, April 5, 1908.
   (*Augusta*)—Green's Ky. Families, 205-208.
   (*Surry*)—VM, VII, 356; VSR, IV (No. 3), 20-21.
   (*Sussex*)—WM, 12 et seq.
Bright—Avery I, 82-83; Cyc. Va. Biog., V, 824; RS, III, 6.
   (*Elizabeth City Co.*)—WM, XII, 32-33.
Brightwell (*Prince Edward*)—Kanawha, 423.
Brillhart—Coshocton Co., O., 640.
Brinker—Cartmell, 488-489.
Brinkley—Cyc. Va. Biog., IV, 135-136.
Brisco—Culpeper, 87.
Briscoe—Hayden, 185; Highland Co., 271; Shepherdstown, 304; TD, June 5, 12, 1904; Nov. 14, 1909.
   (*From Md.*)—Mackenzie III, 84-88; IV, 191-192.
Bristow—Bruce V, 277, 373; Cyc. Va. Biog., I, 195; TD, Oct. 4, 1914; WM, II, 28, 233; XXI, 28-29.
   (*Robert*)—VM, XIII, 59-62; XXIV, 251.
Britt—Cyc. Va. Biog., IV, 179-180.
Brittain—Bruce VI, 362; TD, Jan. 30, 1906; Virkus III, 88.
Brittingham—Burgess, 150.
Britton—Sangamon Co., Ill., 140; TD, Jan. 30, 1906.
Broaddus—Caroline Co., 338-341, 392-393; Culpeper, part 2, 146-149; Cyc. Va. Biog., IV, 269; History of the Broaddus Family; Montague, 167, 291-292; TD, April 26, 1908; Virkus II, 20; VSR, I, 21.
Broadhurst (Brodhurst)—Cyc. Va. Biog., I, 196; VM, XVII, 226, 440-441; WM, I, 186; IV, 76, 88.
Broadnax (See Brodnax)—TD, July 26, 1914; Aug. 15, 1915; WM, VI, 60.
Broadribb—WM, XIV, 35-37.
Broadus—Life and Letters of John A. Broadus, by A. T. Robertson (Phila., Pa., 1901), 1-20; McAllister, 127-128; SBN, XI, 122-123, 135-139; St. Mark's, 194; TD, Jan. 28, 1906.
Broadwater—Burgess, 1059; Cyc. Va. Biog., I, 196; V, 782-784; Old Prince William, II, 413.
Brocas—Hayden, 229-230, 741; VM, I, 421-422; WM, I, 85.
Brock—Brock II, 549-550; Bruce V, 149; Cyc. Va. Biog.; III, 192; IV, 3; Virkus II, 125.
   (*Richmond*)—Munsell's VII, 153.
   (*Spotsylvania*)—Buckners of Va., 160-161; MMV, I, 181-182.
Brockenborough—Browning, C. D., 143.
Brockenbrough—Beau Monde, March 10, 1894; Browning, R. D., III, 769; BS, Oct. 23, 30, Nov. 6, 1904; Cyc. Va. Biog., I, 196; Goode, 402; Hayden, 110-111; Lancaster, 130-137; Meade II, 474-478; Moores of Fawley, 60, 67; Rockbridge, 246-247; RS, II, 34; III, 25; SBN, XI, 124; TD, July 17, 1910; Thomas Ritchie, 302-303; Virkus III, 301; VM, V, 447-449; VI, 82-85.
Brockett—Old Alexandria, 317-318; Avery I, 215.

Brockman—Albemarle, 149-150; History of the Hume, Kennedy and
    Brockman Families, 157-166.
Brodhead—VM, III, 212-213.
Brodhurst—WM, XVII, 226.
    (*Westmoreland*)—WM, IV, 76-77.
Brodnax (Broadnax)—Bruce IV, 108-110; Cyc. Va. Biog., I, 196;
    IV, 30; Hampden-Sidney, 129; Southside Va., 157; TD,
    Sept. 24, 1905; May 25, 1913; VM, XX, 91; XXIV, 417-
    420; WM, III, 111; XIV, 52-58, 135-138; XXI, 265-267.
    265-267.
Bromley—Bruce V, 27; Burgess, 1062.
Bronaugh—Burgess, 425, 427, 429-430; Cyc. Va. Biog., I, 196; Din-
    widdie Papers I, 111; Hayden, 534-536; Meade II, 229-
    230, 436, 483; TD, Aug. 15, 1908; Thomas Carter, 334-337,
    348-355; WM, XVII, 235-237; XIX, 127-128.
Broocke—Cauthorn, 41.
Brooke, Brook, Brooks—TD, April 1, 22, 1906; Feb. 27, April 10,
    June 19, Aug. 14, 1910; Sept. 14, 28, Oct. 12, 1913.
Brooke—ARP, I, 141; Bagby, 302-303, 326; Burgess, 587, 877, 1042; Cyc.
    Va. Biog., I, 196; IV, 10-12; Du Bellet I, 76-81, 147-149;
    II, 343-373, 367-368; Fauquier Bulletin, 381-382, 461-467;
    Goode, 314; Hening, VIII, 474-475; H. T. Harrison, 17;
    Kennedy I, 121, 555-556; II, 122-123; Mackenzie III, 313-
    314; Marshall, 53, 143-144; McAllister, 115; MMV, I, 43-45;
    Norfolk, 749-750, 832-835; RC, II, 50; III, 35; Thomas (1896),
    218-223; Tyler's IV, 437-438; Virkus III, 274; VM, II, 340;
    216-219, 321-325; XIII, 100-104, 223-224, 445-447; XIV, 106-
    108, 204, 325-327, 436-440; XV, 102-105, 200-204, 334-336,
    453-454; XVII, 88-92, 201-205, 423-425; XVIII, 103-104,
    233-234, 329-332, 454-456; XIX, 100-104, 208-211, 320-324,
    435-437; XX, 90-101, 215-218, 331, 434-437; XXIII, 193-195;
    XXIV, 309; VSR, II (No. 4), 45; WM, IV, 64; VI, 125;
    IX, 266; XI, 210-211; XXII, 67.
Brookes—WM, VII, 231.
Brooking—Southside Va., 157; VM, XXXV, 79, 201.
Brookman—Kanawha, 861.
Brooks—WM 2d, II, 184.
Broomhall—Quisenberry, 129-137.
Brough—Burgess, 641, 643; TD, Sept. 9, 1906 (Under "A Romance in
    a Virginia Family").
Broughton—Cyc. Va. Biog., V, 641-642; WM, XV, 212.
Broun—Chart of the descendants of William Broun the immigrant
    to Virginia, by Virginia M. Broun, 1911; Dr. Wm. Leroy
    Broun; Hardy, 435-438; Kanawha, 754-756, 767-771; SBN,
    XI, 125; TD, Jan. 17, 1904; Feb. 12, 1905; July 17, 1910;
    The Broun family and their kindred; WM, IX, 31; XIII,
    25-27; XX, 61-64.
Browder—Montague, 143, 248-255.
Brower—Montgomery Co., Ohio, 370.
Brown, Broun, Browne—TD, Jan. 17, 1904; Jan. 12, March 5, July 2,
    30, 1905; Oct. 13, 1907; May 17, 24, 1908; May 30, 1909;
    April 29, 1910; March 3, 1912.
Brown—Brown of Scotland and Maryland (also Virginia); Burgess,
    202, 738, 958; Green's Ky. Families, 54; Hayden, 147-201;
    Kennedy I, 673-674; RS, II, 7, 10; III, 6; TD, Feb. 12,
    1905; May 24, 1908.
    (*Albemarle and Hanover*)—Albemarle, 151-154; Randolph Co.,
    312-317.

(*Amherst*)—Bruce V, 13; Cabell, etc., 425-433.
(*Augusta*)—Peyton, 304; Trabue, 15-21; WM, IV, 248; IX, 19.
(*Augusta and Bath*)—Boogher, 380-382.
(*Bath*)—DAR, 50, p. 183.
(*Bedford*)—Hardesty, 413; Lancaster, 445; Rives, 528; Walker-Wigton, 127; WM, XII, 64-65.
(*Bedford and Petersburg*)—Bruce V, 356.
(*Campbell*)—Campbell Co., 351-353.
(*Chancellor John*)—Hayden, 504-506; Waddell, 387-388.
(*Charlotte*)—Virkus II, 277.
(*Culpeper*)—ARP II, 613; Cyc. Va. Biog., V, 1013; Culpeper, part 2, 46, 83-84; St. Mark's, 195.
(*Frederick*)—Cartmell, 484; Jolliffe, 113.
(*Frederick and Spotsylvania*)—Sangamon Co., Ill., 146.
(*Henry*)—Henry Co., 116-118.
(*Highland*)—Highland Co., 378-379.
(*Gloucester*)—Burgess, 202.
(*Greenbrier*)—VM, XXVII, 43.
(*Gustavus*)—Bruce IV, 222; Meade I, 400; II, 198, etc.; Old King William, 30; VSR, I (No. 3), 46; III (No. 4), 36; V (No. 2), 45.
(*Holladay's Cove*)—Munsell's VIII, 152.
(*John, Richmond*)—Cabell, etc., 347-349.
(*King George*)—VM, XXXIII, 89-91.
(*Mecklenburg*)—Duke, etc., 205-206.
(*Nelson*)—MMV, V, 45-47.
(*Norfolk*)—Hayden, 659.
(*Northampton*)—ARP, I, 344-345; R. W. Johnson, 3-8.
(*Petersburg*)—DAR, 76, p. 221.
(*Prince William*)—Genealogy of the Brown Family of Prince William; Hayden, 145-200; Kennedy II, 59-62; WVM, I No. 4), October, 1901, pp. 21-22.
(*Rev. John*)—Kennedy I, 650-652, 673-674.
(*Rev. John, Augusta*)—Dunmore's War, 27; Virkus II, 278.
(*Rockbridge*)—Cabell, etc., 524-525; Foote II, 61-71, 99; Hord (1898), 169; Rockbridge, 247-248, 475; SBN, XI, 130-131; Walker-Wigton, 151-156, 165-173; WVM, III, 79-93.
(*Tazewell*)—Bruce VI, 419.
(*Western Va.*)—Jolliffe, 185; WVM, I, Oct., 1901, 21-22.
(*Westmoreland*)—Mackenzie I, 235-236; MMV, V, 50-51.
(*William, Rappahannock*)—VM, XXXIII, 89-91.
(*Williamsburg*)—Cyc. Va. Biog., IV, 420.
(*Wythe*)—Johnson Co., Ind., 594.
Browne—John Wise, 108-109; RS, II, 17; III, 7; Welles' Washington Genealogy, 219.
(*Elsing Green*)—Bristol Parish, 168-170; Browning, C. D., 3d, 688-689; Lancaster, 268-269; VM, XXXII, 3; WM, V, 278.
(*Essex*)—Bruce V, 33; Cyc. Va. Biog., IV, 158.
(*From Salem, Mass.*)—America Heraldica, 54; Browning, C. D., 137-139; Cooke-Booth, 197-199.
(*James City*)—Rives, 510-512; WM, IV, 204, 279-280; VI, 119-120; VII, 110; VIII, 123; XXVI, 215.
(*Lower Norfolk*)—McIntosh I, 24-25.
(*Surry*)—Cyc. Va. Biog., I, 197; Griffith-Meriwether, 31-37; Lancaster, 57-59; Tyler's V, 134-135; VM, III, 148-153; V, 75; VII, 191-192; WM, XVI, 227-232.
(*William Burnet Browne*)—Cyc. Va. Biog., I, 197; WM, V, 278; VI, 68-69; WM 2d, II, 7-8. (See also above.)

Browning—Bruce V, 464; VI, 219; Buckners of Va., 227; Lewis, 131-135; McAllister, 367-370; MMV, III, 50-51; Munsell's V, 145; Roger Jones, 192-194; Virkus II, 357.
    (*Culpeper*)—Culpeper, part 2, 151-155; Munsell's XI, 169-170.
Brownlee—DAR, 50, p. 351; Rockbridge, 475.
Brownley—Cyc. Va. Biog., IV, 348.
Brownlow—Armstrong I, 40-44; SBN, XI, 132.
Broyles—Bruce V, 219.
Broyles (Bryol, Bryoll, Breil, Breile, etc.)—WM, XXVI, 89-95, 194.
Broyll (Broil)—Virkus II, 341; III, 632.
Bruce—BS, Sept. 24, Oct. 1, 1905; Cabell, etc., 325-327, 329-339; Hardesty (*Bedford*), 414; MMV, V, 54; RS, II, 47; SBN, XI, 133; Thomas, 556b-556c; Van Meter, 123; WM, VI, 112, 155.
    (*Frederick*)—Cartmell, 484; Du Bellet III, 42-43, 99-102, 159; Jolliffe, 99; Van Meter, 123.
    (*Halifax, etc.*)—Cyc. Va. Biog., I, 197-198; Halifax, 118-133; Lancaster, 427-431, 435-437; VM, XI, 197-200; 328-332, 441-443; XII, 93-96, 446-453; XXXIII, 327-330; XXXIV, 71.
    (*Norfolk Co.*)—McIntosh II, 92-93, 140-141, 156, 195.
Brugh—Bruce IV, 497.
Brumback—Cartmell, 493-494; Strickler, 181.
Brunk—Bruce IV, 110.
Brunskill—Meade II, 24, etc.
Brush—Rockbridge, 475.
Bryan—Armstrong II, 34; Hayden, 201-220; Lancaster, 250-251; Rockbridge, 475; TD, Oct. 27, 1912; Virkus III, 126.
    (*Alexandria*)—Hist. Encyc. of Ill., 164.
    (*Culpeper*)—Bristol Parish, 161; Culpeper, part 2, 150; Hist. Encyc. of Ill., 63; Memoirs of William Jennings Bryan, 19-21.
    (*From Georgia*)—Browning, R. D., III, 722-723; Cyc. Va. Biog., IV, 57-58, 68; Virkus I, 509; VSR, IV (No. 2), 24; V (No. 2), 39; Walker-Wigton, 122-126, 639.
    (*Isle of Wight*)—Virkus I, 85.
    (*Richmond*)—Lancaster, 113; Mackenzie VII, 119; VM, XVII (April No.)
    (*Stafford and King George*)—Cyc. Va. Biog., I, 198; WM, V,
    (*Valley of Va.*)—Dunmore's War, 220; Shenandoah, 648-649.
Bryant—Bruce IV, 353; Burgess, 647.
    (*Powhatan*)—Cyc. Va. Biog., V, 1099. 276-277.
    (*Southampton*)—MMV, IV, 39-41.
Bryarly—Cartmell. 484.
Brydon—Bruce IV, 76-77.
Bryoll—WM. XXVI, 89-95.
Buchan—Hayden, 2.
Buchanan—Dunmore's War, 174; Miami Co., Ohio, 729; MMV, III, 52-53; Rockbridge, 475.
    (*Augusta*)—Brock II. 705; Bruce IV. 154; Buchanan Family Records, 13-14; Dinwiddie Papers I, 268; Virkus I, 510; II, 141.
    (*Botetourt*)—Woods-McAfee, 201, 209, 234-249.
Bucher (Booker)—Cartmell. 492.
Buck (*James City*)—VM. XIX, 235-236; WM, VII, 230.
    (*Valley of Va.*)—Shenandoah, 631-634.
Buckey—Randolph Co., 311-312.
Buckingham—Johnson Co., Ky., 88; WM, I, 121.
Buckles—Miami Co., Ohio, 520.

(*Eastern Shore*)—ARP, I, 248; Mackenzie VI, 363; Warfield, 49-55.
(*Frederick*)—Cartmell, 496-498.
(*From New England*)—Brock II, 638-639.
(*Prince William*)—Barbour Co., W. Va., 349.
(*Surry*)—Burgess, 204-205.
Burgoyne—Pendleton Co., 185; TD, Nov. 22, 1903.
Burk—WM 2d, VIII, 58.
Burke—Bruce V, 263; MMV, IV, 44-45; New River, 386-387; Old King William, 117-118.
(*Caroline*)—Caroline Co., 394-395; Virkus III, 102.
Burket—Burgess, 194-195.
Burks—Buford, 182-183; Hardesty (*Amherst*), 436; Hardesty (*Bedford*), 414; MMV, II, 51-53; Rockbridge, 475.
Burnell—WM, VII, 242.
Burner—Barbour Co., W. Va., 350; Highland Co., 379; Strickler, 338.
Burnett (Burnet)—Virkus I, 526; WM, V, 278; VI, 69; VII, 242.
Burnham—Cyc. Va. Biog., I, 190; RC, II, 30; VM, I, 91; 256, 258; XVIII, 129-130; WM, II, 269.
Burnley—Burgess, 326, 570; Cyc. Va. Biog., I, 199; Du Bellet I, 100, 212-213; Marshall, 255.
(*Albemarle*)—Albemarle, 156-158.
(*Hanover*)—Winston, 451-458.
(*Orange*)—Burgess, 195-196, 326.
Burns—Highland Co., 354; Pendleton Co., 185.
Burris—DAR, 48, p. 64; Virkus III, 556.
Burroughs (*Lower Norfolk Co.*)—VM, V, 92; XV, 236.
Burrows—Cyc. Va. Biog., I, 190.
Burruss—Cyc. Va. Biog., V, 634, 1083; Kanawha, 902; Meriwethers, 90-91; Virkus III, 105.
Burton—Habersham Chap. II, 184-186, 213, 247-250, 313; LCJ, Nov. 8, 1914 (II, 3); Rockbridge, 475; TD, Feb. 26, April 16, 1911. WM, V, 72.
(*Amelia*)—WM, XV, 263-264.
(*Culpeper*)—Bruce VI, 413; WM, XI, 213-214.
(*Henrico*)—"Genealogy" (Weekes ed.), Vol. 5, pp. 89-90; Tyler's II, 113-114; 273-278.
(*Mecklenburg*)—VM, XXVIII, 55.
(*Orange*)—VM, IX, 206.
Burwell—America Heraldica, 121; ARP, II, 783; Browning, C. D., 32-34, 132-133; Browning, R. D., III, 735; Bruce VI, 234; BS, May 12, 19, 26, June 4, 1907; Burwell Genealogy, Compiled by Mrs. Owen Gleaves Rich, Huntington, W. Va.; Burwell's "Burwell Family": Cabell, etc., 546-547; Campbell's History of Va., 550; Carter Family Tree; Cartmell, 275-276; Cyc. Va. Biog., I, 64, 199-200; V, 598-600; Goode, 63-64, 289; Hampden-Sidney, 235; Hardy, 94-103; Hening VIII, 448-450, 481-483; Keith, 34-38, and chart; Addendum I; Kennedy I, 526, 545, 595-613; Lancaster, 53-57, 225- 230, 453-458; Mackenzie III, 367, 372; Marshall, 102-103, 144, 253, 348-349; Md. Soc. Col. Wars, 72; Meade I, 353-354; II, 290, etc.; Old Chapel, 25-27, 29, 31, 32, 34, 36-39, 44, 48, 50, 56-57, 63, 65, 74; Page (2d ed.), 69; Roger Jones, 45-46; RS, I, 40; II, 38; III, 42-45; IV, 1-2; TD, May 22, 1904; Oct. 8, 1905; June 28, Nov. 4, 1906; Sept. 15, 1907; June 21, 28, 1908; June 12, July 3, 1910; Nov. 12, 19, 1911; July 5, 1914; Virkus I, 524; II, 286; III, 31; VM, II, 232-233; IX, 358; X, 106-107, 177; XIX, 445; XX, 195-196;

XXIII, 156-157; XXIV, 262-268; XXVI, 284; XXXI, 357-359; VSR, II (No. 1), 70; V (No. 2), 23, 54; Willis, 123-124; Winston, 359-370; WM, I, 66-68; II, 218, 220-222, 231-233; III, 247; IV, 132; V, 176, 178, 244; VI, 99, 165, 245; VII, 44, 214, 311; XIV, 258-260; XV, 93, 162-163; XX, 167-168.

Bush—TD, Sept. 17, 1905.
   (*Frederick Co.*)—Du Bellet III, 17-24.
   (*Orange*)—Quisenberry, 77-95.
Bushong—Strickler, 290.
Bushring—Du Bellet IV, 342-343.
Bushrod—ARP, II, 450; Cyc. Va. Biog., I, 200; Hayden, 636; RC, II, 12; Tyler's III, 300-301; VM, XXIII, 49; WM, I, 90-91; VII, 96; XIV, 177-178; XVII, 63, 65.
Bussard—Highland Co., 271-272.
Buster—Albemarle, 158-159; TD, March 17, 1907; Virkus III, 235.
Bustin—McIntosh II, 289-290.
Butcher—Bruce IV, 205, 298; Hardin Co., Ohio, 617; Pendleton Co., 318; Price, 127-138; Randolph Co., 312; VM, XV, 60-62.
Butler—Bell, 26; BS, Nov. 27, 1904; Cyc. Va. Biog., I, 201; Green's Ky. Families, 272; Meade I, 166; TD, May 27, 1906; WM, VIII, 75.
   (*Amelia*)—WM, XV, 264.
   (*Hanover*)—Old King William, 30-32.
   (*Prince William*)—DAR, 83, p. 165.
   (*Richmond City*)—Brock II, 559.
   (*Dr. Samuel*)—Du Bellet I,, 254; Meade I, 310.
   (*Westmoreland*)—LCJ, Oct. 11, 1914 (III, 4); VM, III, 64-65, 203; V, 286-287; WM, IV, 166; XII, 268.
Buts—Keith Addenda, VI, VII.
Butt—Licking Co., Ohio, 625; Mackenzie VII, 76; Miami Co., Ind., 726-727; Rockbridge, 475.
   (*Berkeley Co.*)—Brock II, 706.
   (*Norfolk Co.*)—Burgess, 199-200; Cyc. Va. Biog., I, 201; V, 809; Mackenzie I, 62-65; McIntosh I, 48; II, 14-15, 94-95, 101, 115-117, 148-150, 188, 191, 198; Norfolk, 499-500, 536-537, 823-824, 877-878; Virkus I, 525; WM, XX, 187-188.
Butterworth—Bell, 25.
Button—Culpeper, 2. 47.
Butts—Kanawha, 518, 554; Keith Addenda VI, VII; VM, XXXII, 62.
Buxton—Cyc. Va. Biog., V, 956.
Buzzard—Pendleton Co., 318-319.
Byars—Brock II, 707; Lancaster, 466-468; Minor, 44.
Byers—Cartmell, 478; Hayden, 560; Rockbridge, 475.
Bynum—Habersham Chap. II, 18; TD, Sept. 8, 1912.
Byram—Overwharton, 10-11; Virkus I, 526.
Byrd—Adams Co., Ohio, 526-532; Balch's Provincial Papers, 125-131; Beau Monde ,April 7, 14, 1894; Bristol Parish, 195-196; Bruce V, 248; BS, Aug. 7, 1904; Campbell's History of Va., 429, 712; Cartmell, 449-450; Chaumiere Papers, 77, 79; Cyc. Va. Biog., I, 138, 151, 161; IV, 28-30; Glenn's Colonial Mansions, 57-58; Harper's New Monthly Mag., Vol. 42 (May, 1871); Hardy, 104-108; Kennedy II, 359-364; Lancaster, 68-69, etc.; Marshall, 96; McAllister, 114-115; Md. Soc. Col. Wars, 72; Meade I, 315; II, 290, etc.; New Eng. His. and Gen. Reg., XXXIV, 162; XXXVIII, 306; Old Chapel, 29, 32, 34, 36, 42-45, 49, 51, 53-54, 56; Old King William, 33; Pendleton Co., 185; Ragland, 37; RC, II, 14-15; SBN, XI, 149-

151; Sketches of Lynchburg, Va., 291-293; TD, Nov. 26, 1905; March 11, April 8, 1906; Jan. 10, 24, 31, 1909; May 31, Sept. 20, 1914; VM, VI, 346-358; IX, 80-88, 113-114; XII, 205-207, 317-318; XIX, 312-313, 443; XXVII, 97, 113-114; XXX, 295; VSR, II (No. 1), 75; IV (No. 2), 28-29; V (No. 2), 62; Whitaker, 86 et seq; Willis, 108-114; WM, VIII, 183; IX, 10.

(*Bath*)—Bruce IV, 75.

(*Henrico*)—Bruce V, 494; Dinwiddie Papers II, 110; MMV, I, 28-29; VM, XVI, 133-135; XIX, 312-313; XXX, 295.

(*Highland*)—Highland Co., 354-355.

(*King and Queen*)—Robertson-Taylor, 208-223.

(*Westover*)—America Heraldica, 142-143; Browning, C. D., 54-57; Browning, R. D., 3d, 183-187, 333; Du Bellet I, 247-248; Lancaster, 78-85; Tyler's II, 357; Virkus I, 525; VM, XXXII, 22-37; XXXV, 81-82, 221-245, 371-389; WM, IV, 144-146, 149, 154-156; WM, 2d, III, 246-249.

Byrne—Braxton Co., W. Va., 353-355.

(*Prince William*)—Buckners of Va., 190-191.

Bywaters—Cartmell, 478.

C

Cabaniss—Old King William, 166; TD, April 13, 1913; Virkus I, 40.

Cabell—Alstons and Allstons, 234-237; Bruce IV, 379; V, 158; BS, June 25, July 2, 1905; Cabells, etc., Campbell's History of Va., 626; Cyc. Va. Biog., I, 201-202; V, 751-754; Dupuy, 365-367; Fry Genealogy, 23; Hayden, 317-318; Kanawha, 725-726, 739; Lancaster, 198-203; Mackenzie VI, 113-118; VII, 142; Meade II, 60-63, etc.; MMV, I, 103-105; Munsell's IV, 65-66; V, 97-98; VIII, 204; Pittsylvania, 200; Robertson, 42-43; RS, I, 37, 39, 41, 43; II, 12, 17, 19, 40; III, 14, 34; Ruvigny, 531; SBN, XI, 150-153; Sketches of Lynchburg, 206-219; TD, Nov. 17, 24, 1912; Virkus I, 18-19; VM, XXVII, 79, 97, 364; XXIX, 261; VSR, I (No. 4), 53.

Cade—Researcher I, 258; Virkus II, 96; III, 415.

Cadwallader—Bell, 27; Bruce V, 192; Cartmell, 492.

Caffery—TD, July 9, 30, 1905; Aug. 2, 1914; Virkus I, 545.

Cahill—Henry Co., 134-136.

Caldwell—Bruce IV, 539; Burgess, 939-942, 1176; Cyc. Va. Biog., V, 735-736; McGavock Family, 83-84, 134; Mortons I, 63-65, 69-70, 200-203; II, 182-191, 598-656; Munsell's IX, 32; Old Free State II, 182-191; Rockbridge, 475; RS, II, 34; Sangamon Co., Ill., 165; TD, March 5, Dec. 3, 1905; Aug. 22, 1909; Virkus I, 44; III, 103, 415; VM, XIX, 92-94.

Cale—VM, XVIII, 416-417.

Calfree—New River, 387-388.

Calhoun—Hampden-Sidney, 62-63; Pendleton Co., 185-187.

(*Augusta*)—WM 2d, VI, 53-54; VII, 57-59.

(*Highland*)—Highland Co., 355.

(*Prince Edward*)—Foote II, 235-240.

Call—Browning, C. D., 180; Bruce IV, 126; Cyc. Va. Biog., V, 876; SBN, XI, 162-163.

Callahan—Cyc. Va. Biog., V, 682; Highland Co., 379.

(*Eastern Shore*)—TD, Nov. 2, 1913; Yeardley, 18, 20-24.

Calland—Pittsylvania, 101.

Callavan—Rockbridge, 476.

Callaway—Bruce V, 474; Cabell, etc., 295-296, 366-369; Campbell Co., 108-109, 358-363; Cyc. Va. Biog., I, 202; V, 835-838; Du Bellet II, 719-729; Hampden-Sidney, 69; Henry Co., 130-134; RS, III, 17, 21; TD, June 23, 1907; Virkus III, 109, 442; VM, VII, 9, 11, 16, 245; WM, III, 275.

Callender—DAR, 80, 225; TD, July 22, 1906.

Callis—Convention 1788, II, 378; Old Chapel, 25; Tyler's VIII, 275-277; VSR, III (No. 1), 39.

(*Louisa*)—Researcher II, 139-140.

Callison—Bruce V, 379.

Calloway—Buford, 264-267; Du Bellet II, 721-725.

Calmes—Cartmell, 470; Halifax, 134; Old Chapel, 25; Old Prince William I, 196; Shenandoah, 591; Two Families, 103-104; TD, Sept. 24, 1905.

Calthorpe—Armistead, 216-217; Cyc. Va. Biog., I, 202; VM, III, 185; V, 94; XXII, 422-423; VSR, I (No. 3), 52; IV (No. 4), 23; WM, II, 106-112, 160-168, 273-274; XIV, 286-287.

Calvert—LCJ, April 18, 1915 (II, 2); RS, III, 50; TD, Oct. 13, 1907.

(*Elizabeth City*)—Burgess, 903.

(*Maryland*)—Mackenzie VII, 105-106.

(*Norfolk*)—Antiquary I, 109, 113, 126; Cyc. Va. Biog., I, 202; McIntosh II, 205-208; VM, V, 436-439; with chart; VI, 73-75; WM, IV, 111.

(*Prince William, from Lord Baltimore*)—Mackenzie VI, 290-297; MHM, XVI, 50-59; 189-204, 313-318, 389-394; Shenandoah, 592.

Camden—Braxton Co., W. Va., 357-359; Bruce IV, 380; Hardesty (*Amherst*), 436; Rockbridge, 476.

Cameron—Quisenberry, 127-128; Virkus I, 534.

(*Augusta*)—Waddell, 354.

(*King and Queen*)—WM, XIV, 261.

(*Petersburg*)—Brock I, 251; Cyc Va. Biog., IV, 154; Hardesty, 388; MMV, IV, 49-56.

(*Rev. John*)—MMV, I, 106-111.

(*Western Va.*)—WVM, II, Oct., 1902, 57-65

Camm—WM, I, 71-72; III, 65; VIII, 246.

(*King & Queen*)—VM, XXXV, 33; WM, XIV, 130-131, 261-262; XXI, 140.

(*York*)—ARP, II, 798; VSR, IV (No. 4), 27; WM, IV, 61-62, 275-278; XIX, 28-30.

Camp—Habersham Chap. II, 292-295; Kanawha, 906-907; TD, July 23, 1911; VM, IX, 216-217; WM, IV, 206; V, 35.

(*Gloucester*)—Bruce IV, 195.

(*Norfolk*)—Cyc. Va. Biog., V, 916.

Campbell—Burgess, 1075, etc.; BS, Feb. 12, 1905; Clemens' "Genealogy", Jan., 1916; Cyc. Va. Biog., I, 203; Hardesty, 371-372; Hayden, 17-18, 165-167; Meade II, 160; Pendleton Co., 319; RS, I, 30, 32, 35, 38; II, 39, 45, 47; III, 1, 5, 7, 30, 44; IV, 3; TD, April 1, 8, 1906; May 12, 1907; May 14, 1911; June 14, 1914; Virkus II, 42; WM, VII, 60.

(*Albemarle*)—Kanawha, 540-543.

(*Amherst*)—Cyc. Va. Biog., V, 745; Hardesty, 436-437.

(*Augusta*)—Adams Co., Ohio, 301-303, 534-538; Culpeper, 77; Des Cognets, 62-64, 89-95; Dunmore's War, 39-40, 43, 47; Foote II, 114-121; Green's Ky. Families, 50-60; Goode; Historical Sketches of the Campbell, Pilcher and Kindred Families; King's Mountain, 378-402, 409-410; Lancaster, 476-481; Maxwell, 249-251; MMV, III, 60-62; Peyton, 307-308,

342-344; RS, II, 45, 47; SBN, XI, 169-174; Thos. Carter, 90;
VM, VII, 119-122, 126-127; VIII, 326; XXVII, 365; Walker-
Wigton, 3-5, 101, 104, 107, 240-242, 390-392; Woods-McAfee,
96.
(*Augusta, etc.*)—Cisco, 235-239; Kennedy II, 314.
(*Berkeley*)—Virkus I, 57.
(*Botetourt*)—Tyler's IX, 273-274.
(*Charles*)—Genealogy of the Spotswood Family.
(*Frederick*)—Cartmell, 425-429; Hardin Co., Ohio, 764.
(*Greenbrier*)—Adams Co., Ohio, 279-280.
(*Highland*)—Highland Co., 272-273.
(*King and Queen*)—Bagby, 370-371; Cooke-Booth, 213-215; Re-
searcher II, 140; Two Families, 130.
(*Norfolk*)—Tyler's I, 70-71.
(*Northumberland*)—Virkus I, 56.
(*Orange*)—DAR, 44, p. 77.
(*Prince Edward*)—Cabell, etc., 544-545.
(*Rev. Archibald*)—Meade II, 162.
(*Rockbridge*)—DAR, 59, p. 341; Rockbridge, 248, 476, 477.
(*Western Va.*)—Crockett, 191-194; WVM, II, Oct. 1902, 57-65.
(*Westmoreland*)—Kennedy II, 394; Lancaster, 323-324; Roger
Jones, 173; RS, I, 30, 32, 35, 38, 40, 48.
Candler—Campbell Co., 365-366; Hardin Co., Ohio, 992.
Cannon—Bruce IV, 167; VM, I, 469; II, 326.
(*Buckingham*)—VM, X, 100.
(*Richmond*)—VM, I, 342-343.
Cant—Cyc. Va. Biog., I, 203; VM, III, 14.
Canterbury—Kanawha, 966-967.
Cauthorne—Montague, 185.
Cantrall—Sangamon Co., Ill., 180-183.
Cantrell—BS, Jan. 1, 1905; Cantrill-Cantrell Genealogy.
Cantrill—TD, July 14, 1907.
Caperton—Killing of Adam Caperton, etc. (1918); New River, 388-
389; SBN, XI, 176; Virkus I, 299; II, 55; Woods-McAfee,
59-60, 309-313.
Capito—Kanawha, 427; Pendleton Co., 319.
Caplinger—Randolph Co., 322-325.
Capper—Bruce IV, 411; Cartmell, 442.
Capps—Bruce IV, 444; Burgess, 568; WM, VI, 194.
Carbaugh—Bruce V, 195.
Carden—Brock II, 707.
Carder—Barbour Co., W. Va., 351-358; Virkus III, 244.
Cardiff—Rockbridge, 477.
Cardoza—Cyc. Va. Biog., IV, 553.
Cardwell—Bruce IV, 191; Cyc. Va. Biog., IV, 103-104; Old King Wil-
liam, 185.
Cargill—Cyc. Va. Biog., I, 203; Virkus III, 365; WM, XXIII, 144-145.
Carleton—TD, June 28, 1914.
Carlile—Highland Co., 379-380.
Carlin—Avery I, 137; Braxton Co., W. Va., 365; Bruce VI, 125.
Carlock—Rockbridge, 477; TD, Feb. 13, 1916.
Carlton—Bagby, 364, 370; Halifax, 134-135; TD, April 12 ,1908; May
3, June 21, 1914.
Carlyle—Lancaster, 367-368.
(*Alexandria*)—Blair, etc., 193; Cyc. Va. Biog., I, 203; Descend-
ants of John and Sarah (Fairfax) Carlyle. By Richard
Henry Spencer (1910); WM, XVIII, 1-17, 201-212, 278-289.

Carmack—Brock II, 708-709.
Carmichael—Hayden, 216, 724; TD, Nov. 21, 1909; Walker-Wigton, 124.
Carne—Bruce VI, 146.
Carnefix—Hardesty (*Bedford*), 415.
Carner—Bruce V, 66.
Carnes—Knox Co., Ill., 427.
Carney—Burgess, 603; McIntosh I, 85; II, 8, 61, 85-86.
Carpenter—Braxton Co., W. Va., 360-364; Highland Co., 355-356; TD, Dec. 9, 16, 1906.
   (*Bath*)—Bath Co., 191.
   (*King & Queen*)—Cyc. Va. Biog., I, 203; MMV, I, 214-215; RS, I, 39; III, 21.
Carper—Burgess, 877; Rockbridge, 477.
Carr—Braxton Co., W. Va., 360; "Genealogy" (Clemens), VII, 139; Hardin Co., Ohio, 767; Pendleton Co., 187; Rockbridge, 477; RS, III, 19; SBN, XI, 179; VM, VII, 249.
   (*Albemarle*)—Albemarle, 159-163; Burgess, 600-603.
   (*King William*)—Cyc. Va. Biog., I, 204; WM, VIII, 106-108, 130-132.
   (*Loudoun*)—Munsell's VIII, 215; Virkus I, 552.
   (*Louisa*)—Hayden, 385; VM, II, 221-228; III, 208-217; V, 440-442; IX, 212; XIX, 205; WM, XXV$, 128.
   (*Nansemond*)—DAR, 75, p. 367.
   (*Spotsylvania*)—VM, XIX, 205.
   (*Thomas*)—Md. Soc. Col. Wars, 12.
Carrigan—TD, Nov. 2, 1913.
Carrington—Bruce IV, 27, 390; Burgess, 19; Cabell, etc., 156-168, 204-206, 272-273, 533-535, 537, 558-569, 605-610; Campbell's History of Va., 624; Cyc. Va. Biog., I, 204; V, 1029-1032; Du Bellet I, 47-48; Foote II, 575; Genealogy. Records, etc. Colonial Dames in State of New York, New York, MXCXXVII, 35-36; Goode, 128-130, 249-252, 389-390, 479; Halifax, 46-48, 135-139, 274-276; Hampden-Sidney, 22-23; Hardy, 303; SHA, V, 228-231; Kennedy II, 396; Lancaster, 437-438, 441; Marshall, 104-105; Meade II, 40; MMV, V, 61-62; RS, I, 45; II, 7, 35, 37; III, 14-15, 26 (Feb. 26, 1881); 27; R. W. Johnson, 49-54; St. Mark's, 164; TD, May 28, Aug. 20, 27; Sept. 3, Oct. 15, 1916; Virkus I, 76-77; II, 97; VSR, II (No. 2), 51; IV (No. 2), 37; V (No. 1), 80; Watkins, 28; WM, I, 225-226; WM 2d, X, 88.
Carroll—TD, July 14, 1912.
   (*Isle of Wight*)—Du Bellet I, 178.
   (*Louisa*)—Bruce IV, 363.
Carruthers—Kith and Kin, 146; SBN, XI, 183.
Carson—Burgess, 604-609; Cartmell, 492-493; Cyc. Va. Biog., IV, 71; MMV, IV, 50-60; Rockbridge, 477; VM, XXVII, 365.
   (*Campbell*)—DAR, 81, p. 330.
Carswell—DAR, 71, p. 77.
Carter—Bruce IV, 245; Cyc. Va. Biog., I, 204-205; Ellis, 29-30; Keith, 89; Meade II, 110-113; Rockbridge, 477; St. Mark's, 121-122; TD, Oct. 4, 1903; May 1, 15, Aug. 28, Sept. 25, 1904; Sept. 24, 1905; July 29, Aug. 26, Sept. 2, 1906; Sept. 15, 1907; April 19, Nov. 22, Dec. 27, 1908; Jan. 3, April 25, 1909; July 31, March 13, 1910; Dec. 29, 1912; Jan. 5, 12, 19, 26, Feb. 2, May 18, 1913; Feb. 8, 1914; VM, IV, 364-365; Whitaker, 112-113; WM, III, 205; V, 65, 256, 278; VI, 173; VIII, 9, 18, 189; X, 175.

(*Albemarle*)—Albemarle, 163-165.
(*Botctourt*)—DAR, 50, p. 118.
(*Corotoman*)—Armstrong II, 61-70; Browning, C. D., 55-56, 132-136, 143, 182-188; Browning, C. D., 3d, 184, 430, 571-572; Browning, R. D., III, 733-743; Bruce VI, 97; BS, Aug. 23, 1908; Cabell, etc., 266-267; Carter Family Tree; Culpeper, 53-54; Descendants of John Stubbs, ,101-102; Dinwiddie Papers II, 101-102; Dupuy, 256-257; Funsten-Meade, 23-24; Glenn's Some Colonial Mansions, 217-294; Hardy, 109-123; Hayden, 129-130, 140; Hening IV, 454-457; V, 300-305; VII, 478-480; VIII, 25-27, 214-222, 464-468, 486-488; Keith, 14-15, and chart, 87-88; Kennedy I, 589-590; II, 78; Lancaster, 98-104, 321-322, 333-338, 346-347, 375-376, 384-385; Lee. 356-362, 576; Mackenzie I, 77-79, 233; III, 373-374; McAllister, 119, 121-122, 125-127; Md. Soc. Col. Wars, 72; Meade II, 110-113; MMV, II, 64-67; IV, 61-63; Munsell's XI, 174; RC, June 18, July 2, 1888; Roger Jones, 159-167, 378-379; RS, II, 16, 42; III, 53; IV, 2; R. W. Johnson, Chart, 22-23, 36-37, 42-44; Virkus I, 85-86; VM, II, 430-435; IV, 436; V, 408-428; VI, 1-22, 88-90, 145-152, 260-265, 365-370; IX, 85, 358; XV, 426-427, 432-436; XVII, 217-218, 257; XXII, 380-382; XXIII, 162-172; XXV, 405; XXIX, 361-362 [will of Landon Carter]; XXX, 70-79; XXXI, 39-67, 254-255; XXXII, 18-22, 48-49; VSR, I (No. 4), 51-52; II (No. 1), 72; IV (No. 1), 36; V (No. 2), 18, 56, 61-62; Watson, 241-243; Welles' Washington Genealogy, 176-200; Willis, 103-107; WM, I, 138; IV, 16, with chart; V, 65.
(*Fauquier*)—Cyc. Va. Biog., V, 577.
(*Frederick*)—Cartmell, 493.
(*Halifax*)—Halifax, 274.
(*Hanover*)—Hardy, 124-126; TD, Feb. 8, 1914.
(*Henrico*)—Ellis, 13; Giles Carter of Virginia. By W. G. H. Carter (Baltimore, 1909).
(*Henry*)—Cyc. Va. Biog., V, 578.
(*Lancaster*)—Descendants of Capt. Thomas Carter of "Barford"; Du Bellet II, 192-248; Meade II, 110-117; RS, II, 16; Virkus II, 370; III, 32, 113.
(*Loudoun*)—Madison Co., Ohio, 1054.
(*Nelson*)—Bruce IV, 377.
(*Pittsylvania*)—Bruce IV, 421; Cyc. Va. Biog., IV, 499; Pittsylvania, 248-249.
(*Surry*)—VM, V, 213-214.
(*Thomas*)—Lee, 576; VM, V, 254-255; WM, IX, 34-37; XVII, 275-285; XVIII, 47-58, 89-103, 235-251; XIX, 116-137, 184-194; XX, 38-51.
(*York*)—Tyler's X, 205-206.
Carthers—Rockbridge, 477-478.
Cartmell—Cartmell, 284, 416-425; Sangamon Co., Ill, 193.
Cartmill—Madison Co., Ohio, 992.
Cartright—Rockbridge, 477.
Cartwright—DAR, 70, 242; Sangamon Co., Ill., 190-191.
Caruthers—Marshall, 158; Rockbridge, 248-249; RS, III, 2, 25.
Carver—VM, XXIII, 24; WM, III, 163-165; IV, 51-52.
(*Norfolk*)—Antiquary II, 48-49.
Cary—Armistead, 263-268; ARP, II, 784; Brock II, 774; Bruce VI, 415; BS, Nov. 25, Dec. 2, 9, 1906; Burgess, 903; Cary Family in America. By Henry Grosvenor, 1-2; Cyc. Va. Biog., I, 205-206; IV, 94-99; Goode, 281-285; Hening VII, 440-

444; VIII, 34-35; Keith, 39-41, and chart; Kennedy I, 247-287; Lancaster, 108, 258-259; Meade I, 455; N. C. His. Reg. II, 151; Page (2d ed.), 105-108, 258-259; RC, III, 32, 34, 36; Robertson, 33, 37-38; RC, III, 33, 34, 36; Rootes of Rosewell, 72-74; RS, II, 41; III, 31; TD, April 3, 17, May 29, 1904; Oct. 14, 28, Nov. 11, 1906; Jan. 6, 1907; Aug. 30, Sept. 6, Oct. 25, 1908; April 16, 1911; June 20, Oct. 31, 1915; Tyler's II, 284; Valentine I, 218-328; IV, 2247-2248; Virkus I, 541; III, 608; VM, VI, 320; VIII, 263-264; XIX, 445-446; VSR, II (No. 2), 59; (No. 3), 31; IV (No. 1), 32-33, 42; V (No. 2), 53; Winston, 353-357, with chart; WM, III, 276, 278; VI, 197, 230; IX, 45.

(*Devon, Bristol and James River*)—Sally Cary, 1916; The Virginia Carys, 1919; The Devon Carys (two vols.), 1920.
(*Gloucester*)—Tyler's I, 71.
(*Miles*)—Du Bellet II, 49-54, 61-98, 112-119, 122-126.
(*Warwick*)—Hardy, 128-132; Mackenzie I, 80-82; RC, III, 32, 34; Two Families, 146-147; VM, IX, 104-111, 213; X, 189-193; XXVII, 72; XXXII, 396; WM, II, 141; XV, 84,86.

Case—Crockett, 26.
Cash—Hayden, 84, 104; Rockbridge, 478.
　(*Amherst*)—Clemens' Wills, 16-17.
Caskey (*Rockbridge*)—Adams Co., Ohio, 539; Rockbridge, 478.
Caskie—Bruce IV, 394-395; V, 130; Cyc. Va. Biog., IV, 73-74, 141.
Cassady—DAR, 55, p. 101; Rockbridge, 478.
Cassel—MMV, IV, 64-65.
Cassell—Pendleton Co., 187.
Casteel—Rockbridge, 478.
Castle—Johnson Co., Ky., 101.
Castleman—Cabell, etc., 526-531; Virkus I, 91; VM, XXVII, 88.
Castor—Hardin Co., Ohio, 768.
Caswell (Casewell)—McIntosh I, 160, 185.
Catesby—RS, II, 51. See Jones.
Catchings—DAR, 25, p. 82.
Cather—Bruce IV, 393-394; V, 178-179; Cartmell, 475-476.
Catlett—Browning, R. D., III, 741; Buckners of Va., 119; Burgess, 610-614; Carter Family Tree; Cooke-Booth, 198, 201; Cyc. Va. Biog., I, 206; V, 988; Descendants of John Stubbs, 100-101; Hardy, 118-119; Hayden, 244, 280; Lancaster, 216-217; Life of Gen. Hugh Mercer, 123; MMV, V, 63-64; RC, III; St. Mark's, 156; TD, Sept. 22, Oct. 6, 13, 1907; Two Families, 1-104; VM, III, 62-64; IX, 207; XXIII, 381-382; XXVIII, 72; VRS, II (No. 1), 70; Zimmerman, 12-18.
Catlin—Cyc. Va. Biog., IV, 538.
Caton—Cyc. Va. Biog., V, 720; MMV, IV, 66-68; VM, XXIII, 171-174.
Caufield—Cyc. Va. Biog., I, 206-207.
Caulfield—Researcher I, 52.
Cauthorn—Burgess, 1120; Record of the Cauthorn Family.
Cave—Bruce IV, 451; Culpeper, 54-55; Cyc. Va. Biog., I, 206; Hayden, 12-13; St. Mark's, 122-125; TD, Nov. 25, 1906; Virkus III, 243.
Cavendish—Braxton Co., W. Va., 364.
Caw—Miami Co., Ohio, 677.
Cawfell—Rockbridge, 479.
Cawood—Avery I, 84-85.
Cawson—McIntosh II, 96, 113-114.
Cayce—WM, XXVI, 282.

Caylor—Mongtomery Co., Ohio, 398.
Cazenove—Avery I, 215-217, Huguenot Emigration XII, XIII.
Cecil—Brock II, 724; Bruce V, 566; Cyc. Va. Biog., IV, 133; MMV, IV, 69-70; New River, 395-396.
Cecil, Cissel—Warfield, 430.
Ceeley—Cyc. Va. Biog., I, 207; VM, XV, 177-178.
Chadwell—Coshocton Co., Ohio, 649.
Chaffin—Cyc. Va. Biog., V, 583.
Chalkley—Bruce VI, 179; Virkus I, 95; III, 116.
Chalmers—BS, Feb. 26, 1905; Halifax, 141-142; TD, Jan. 8, 1905.
Chamberlain—TD, Feb. 9, 1908.
    (*Essex, etc.*)—VM, VI, 191.
Chamberlayne—Hening V, 117-120; VI, 318-321; Jones, 315; WM, I, 18.
    (*Henrico*)—Beau Monde (weekly), March 31, 1894; Du Bellet III, 65-66; VM, XXIII, 157-159; VSR, IV (No. 2), 28; WM, XXIV, 270-271.
    (*King William*)—Burgess, 635-636.
    (*New Kent*)—Cyc. Va. Biog., I, 207; VM, XXVI, 145-150, 271-275; XXVII, 72; XXVIII, 235-238; WM, V, 78, 81; VIII, 182.
Chambers—Rockbridge, 478; Southside Va., 88.
    (*Mecklenburg*)—Goode, 124-125.
Chambliss—DAR, 82, p. 205; Rives; WM, XII, 17.
Champ—Pendleton Co., 187-188.
Champe—Burgess, 614-617; RS, III, 11; TD, Sept. 30, 1906; Jan. 20, 1907; Willis, 118-120; WM, XV, 124-125.
Champion—WM, VII, 249, 258, 262.
Chance (*Eastern Shore*)—Burgess, 617-619.
Chancellor—BS, Jan. 8, 1905; TD, Jan. 17, 1908.
Chandler—Bruce IV, 304; Cyc. Va. Biog., I, 207; Rockbridge, 478; TD, June 2, Aug. 11, 1907.
    (*Caroline*)—Caroline Co., 397-408.
Channell—Randolph Co., 321.
Chapin—Bruce IV, 558; VI, 28; Cyc. Va. Biog., I, 207; IV, 545-546.
Chapline—Chaplines from Va.; Draper Series, V, 87; TD, March 1, 8, Aug. 30, 1914.
Chapman—Browning, C. D., 39, 78; Hayden, 336-337; New River, 389-394; Notable Families, 52-53; RS, II, 47; III, 35-37; Tazewell Co., II, 352-356; TD, Dec. 28, 1913; April 16, 1916.
    (*Caroline*)—Caroline Co., 409-411.
    (*Culpeper*)—Buford, 187-196.
    (*Fairfax*)—RS, III, 35, 37; SBN, XI, 188-189; WM, X, 66, 134-135.
    (*Frederick*)—Madison Co., Ohio, 863.
    (*Giles*)—Kanawha, 674.
    (*Isle of Wight*)—VM, IX, 209.
    (*King William*)—WM, V, 67.
    (*New Kent*)—WM, IX, 137-142.
    (*Orange*)—McIlhany, 13-15; Shenandoah, 592; Virkus I, 546; Watson, 258.
    (*Richard*)—WM, VI, 60.
    (*Stafford*)—WM, IV, 164-165.
Chappell—Chappell, 14-265, 328, 370-382; Halifax, 142-243; Munsell's XII, 90; Rives, 684; VM, III, 416-420.
    (*Prince George*)—VM, XXIX, 101-102.
    (*Sussex*)—Bruce IV, 242.
Charleton—Cyc. Va. Biog., I, 207.
Charrington—Bruce VI, 361.

Charles—Virkus III, 424.
Chastain—Dupuy, 169, 249-252; Goode, 134-135; Halifax, 139-141; VM, XXXII, 395-396.
Chavis—Hardin Co., Ohio, 1038.
Cheadle (*Hanover*)—Burgess, 800.
Cheatham—LCJ, Oct. 4, 1914 (II, 11).
Cheatwood—Hardesty (Amherst), 437.
Cheatwood, Chitwood, Chetwood—WM, XXI, 202-203.
Cheesman (Chisman)—RC, II, 37; III, 45; VM, IV, 314; XXI, 63; WM, I, 81, 89-98; II, 9.
Cheesman—VM, I, 311-312; IV, 314-315.
Chenault—Munsell's X, 18-19; Quesenberry, 96-122; Stubbs, 429; TD, Oct. 22, 1916.
Chenoweth—Braxton Co., W. Va., 357-359; Cartmell, 467; History of the Chenoweth Family; Mackenzie II, 178-180; Randolph Co., 327; Tyler's III, 186-193; WM, XV; XX, 113-114.
Cherricholm—WM, VII, 247.
Cherry—DAR, 59, p. 13; Licking Co., O., 642.
    (*Norfolk Co.*)—Bruce IV, 545; McIntosh II, 117, 155, 215, 245.
Cheshire—Avery I, 138; Hampshire, 704.
Chesley—Cyc. Va. Biog., I, 207-208; VM, XIII, 63-64.
Chesterman (*Spotsylvania*)—Ragland, 21.
Chestnut—Highland Co., 273-274.
Chevalier, Chevalie—Montgomery Co., Ohio, 132; TD, June 17, July 1, 1906.
Chew—America Heraldica, 113; ARP, I, 219, 248-249; II, 499-500; Bowies, 380-381; Browning, R. D., 3d, 123; Burgess, 81-82; Cyc. Va. Biog., I, 208; Hayden, 672; Hening VI, 403; Kennedy I, 353-354; LCJ, Jan. 17, 1915 (II, 10); Life of Gen. Hugh Mercer, 108, 118-122; Mackenzie II, 181; RC, II, 22, 24, 26; St. Mark's, 145; TD, July 16, 1905; Oct. 24, 1909; Thomas, 253-255, 276-284; Thos. Carter, 281-282; Virkus II, 207; VM, I, 87-88, 197-198; III, 391-392; V, 341-342; VI, 345; VII, 195; VIII, 110; XXXII, 49-50; Wallace's Historical Mag., July, 1891, p. 14; Warfield, 109-112; WM 2d, VI, 199.
    (*Alexandria*)—Thomas, 251.
    (*Highland*)—Highland Co., 274-275.
    (*Orange*)—VM, II, 347.
    (*Spotsylvania*)—DAR, 56, p. 138.
Chewning (Chowning)—Virkus II, 104; III, 122.
Chicheley—VM, III, 39-40, 226-227; XVII, 144-146; WM, II, 150.
Chichester—ARP, II, 811-814; Bruce VI, 506; Cyc. Va. Biog., I, 208; IV, 226; Hayden, 91-95, 106-109; TD, Dec. 9, 1906; VM, XXI, 250-252; XXIII, 295-296.
Chichley—VM, III, 226-227; XXV, 56-58.
Chiddix—Brock II, 709.
Chilcott—Hayden, 92b.
Childress—Hardesty (*Amherst*), 437; Minor, 55; Rockbridge, 478.
Childrey—Brock II, 775.
Chiles—Campbell Co., 366-368; Cyc. Va. Biog., I, 208; Halifax, 282-283; TD, May 4, 1913; Virkus III, 65; VM, XIX, 104-106, 211-215, 324-325, 437-438; XX, 101-107; XXII, 425-426; Woodson, 646; WM, I, 75-78; VI, 147; VIII, 105-106; XVI, 285-286; XVIII, 106-108; WM 2d, III, 261-263.
Chilton—Cyc. Va. Biog., I, 208; Fauquier Bulletin, 321-329; Hardy, 133-141; Hayden, 536; Kanawha, 468, 797, 964-965; Mack-

enzie I, 89-96; Thos. Carter, 354-355, 361; Virkus III, 235;
   VM, XVII, 203; XXIII, 330-331; XXIV, 100; WM, X
   33; XV, 89-92, 191-192, 270-275.
   (*Lancaster*)—Burgess, 622-623.
Chinn—Bruce V, 288; VI, 275; BS, Feb. 5, 19, 1905; Hayden, 74-76,
   106-111, 120-121, 739; TD, Dec. 10, 1905; Aug. 19, 1906;
   Thomas Carter, 357-358; Virkus I, 483; III, 99; VM, XXIII,
   307; WM 2d, I, 294-295.
Chipley—Cartmell, 492.
Chisman (Cheesman)—Cyc. Va. Biog., I, 209; VSR, IV (No. 4), 22;
   WM, I, 81, 89-98; II, 7; XIII, 70; XIV, 116-117, 123-124,
   160-162.
Chiswell—Armistead, 56-61; Cyc. Va. Biog., I, 209; TD, Feb. 28,
   1909; VM, IV, 359; XXXII, 54; VSR, V (No. 2), 58; WM,
   II, 235; IX, 265.
Chittum—Rockbridge, 478.
Chitwood—Bruce IV, 466; VI, 197, 612; Virkus III, 121.
Chowning—WM, XI, 177; XII, 180.
Chrislip—Barbour Co., W. Va., 359-360.
Chrisman—Cartmell, 261-262; Green's Ky. Families, 26-27, 98-99;
   Mackenzie IV, 187.
Christian—LCJ, Aug. 30, 1914 (II, 1); New River, 395; RS, II, 43;
   St. Mark's, 188; TD, Aug. 21, 1904; July 2, 1912; VSR, I,
   21; Woodson, 59-60; WM, I, 176; VII, 110; XV, 198-201.
   (*Amherst*)—Major, 160; VM, IX, 424.
   (*Augusta*)—Culpeper, 77; Cyc. Va. Biog., I, 209-210; Dunmore's
   War, 206, 251-252, 429-430; Halifax, 143-144; History of the
   Battle of Pt. Pleasant, 25; Kennedy II, 401-403; Patrick
   Henry II, 641, 642; Peyton, 313-314; RS, II, 43; VHS,
   Col. VI, 143-144; VM, II, 348-349; XVI, 171; XIX, 313;
   XXVII, 164, 323; WM, VIII, 123, 124.
   (*Botetourt*)—Du Bellet II, 424-425.
   (*Buckingham*)—Bruce V, 59.
   (*Charles City*)—Burgess, 633-634; Cyc. Va. Biog., IV, 247-249,
   273; V, 780-782; Major, 53-55, 151-152; MMV, II, 70-71;
   V, 65-68; Tyler's X, 212; Virkus I, 549; II, 284; VSR, III
   (No. 4), 21; WM, V, 261-263; VIII, 70-74, 122-128, 265-271;
   IX, 47-52, 243-245; X, 279; XV, 198-201.
   (*Eastern Shore*)—VM, XXV, 419; Yeardley, 16-17.
   (*Hanover*)—VM, VIII, 104-105.
   (*New Kent*)—Bruce IV, 85; Tyler's X, 60-62.
Christmas—Cyc. Va. Biog., I, 210; TD, Dec. 24, 1905; March 22,
   1908; VM, IV, 202.
Chumbley—Bruce VI, 436.
Chunn—VM, VIII, 325.
Church—Highland Co., 380.
   (*Norfolk Co.*)—Cyc. Va. Biog., I, 210; Ellis, 58; McIntosh, I,
   191-192; II, 173-174.
Churchill—Fauquier Bulletin, 380; Hayden, 253, 294; Hening VII,
   157-159; Old Prince William I, 346; LEP, Feb. 8, March 1,
   1919; RC, II, 1; TD, Sept. 25, 1910; Virkus III, 116;
   VSR, II (No. 2), 61; WM, VII, 186-188; VIII, 47-50, 200-
   202; IX, 246, 249; X, 39-44; WM 2d, IV, 284-285.
   (*Middlesex*)—WM, IV, 201.
Churchman—Bruce IV, 206-207; Kanawha, 875; MMV, II, 74-75.
Clack—Burgess, 624-630; Cyc. Va. Biog., I, 210; Jones, 184; VM,
   VIII, 60-61; WM, III, 32, 42; XIX, 109-111.
Clagett—Avery I, 51; Crockett, 251.

(*Henrico*)—Brock II, 776; Bullington Chart. By Arthur B. Clarke; Virkus I, 561-562.
(*King William*)—Old King William, 139-140.
(*Louisa and Fluvanna*)—DAR, 47, p. 22.
(*New Kent*)—Bruce IV, 103.
(*Powhatan*)—Goode, 229-230, 373-375, 378, 427; Virkus I, 561.
Clarkson—Albemarle, 166-168; Kanawha, 715-719; Marshall, 99-100.
(*Fauquier*)—Hardy, 142-147.
Claud—Bruce VI, 527.
Clay—Cabell, etc., 286; Convention 1788, I, 255-260; II, 378-379; Kanawha, 433; Lewis, 103; Mackenzie V, 126-128; New River, 396, 398; RS, II, 1; Stubbs, 270-291, 359; TD, July 5, 1908; Feb. 25, 1912; April 6, 1913; Van Meter, 22-28, 168-171; Virkus II, 108; VM, III, 186; VII, 124-125; WM, VII, 239; XXIV, 142; WM 2d, II, 43, 129-130.
(*Henrico*)—RC, III, 19; Robertson-Taylor, 88-91, 156-161; Tillman Genealogy (Nashville, Tenn., 1905), 35-38; Virkus I, 187-188.
(*Pittsylvania*)—Pittsylvania, 202.
(*Powhatan*)—DAR, 56, p. 95.
Clayborne—Alstons and Allstons, 118-119.
Claypool—VM, II, 348.
Clayton—BS, Jan. 29, 1905; Cyc. Va. Biog., I, 212-213; Pendleton Co., 188; TD, March 5, 1905; Aug. 5, 1906; Aug. 19, Oct. 28, Nov. 25, 1906; Feb. 12, 1911.
(*Caroline, Samuel*)—VM, XXXIII, 93-94.
(*Charlotte*)—VM, XXXVII, 159-160.
(*Culpeper*)—Culpeper, 55-56, 107; Harris Genealogy. By G. D. Harris (Columbus, Miss., 1914), 90-91; Kennedy II, 453-462; Md. Soc. Col. Wars, 37; Rootes of Rosewell, 47-48, 64-72, 74-79; St. Mark's, 125-127.
(*Frederick*)—Cartmell, 483.
(*Gloucester*)—Convention 1788, II, 379; Cyc. Va. Biog., IV, 117-119; Tyler's VIII, 141-142, 207; Va. His. Mag. Edited by Jefferson Wallace (Richmond, Va., Oct., 1889), 25-29; Virkus III, 173; VM, IV, 163-164; XIV, 5; VSR, II (No. 1), 70; WM, II, 228-229, 236; III, 21; IV, 200; XVI, 141-142; WM 2d, VIII, 140, 317-318.
(*Loudoun*)—Walker-Wigton, 504-508.
(*New Kent*)—WM, XVI, 141-142.
(*Pittsylvania*)—Pittsylvania, 145, 267.
(*Samuel*)—VM, XXXIII, 93-96.
Claytor—Cyc. Va. Biog., V, 973-974 [confused in part with "Clayton"].
Cleavinger—Barbour Co., W. Va., 360-361.
Cleek—Bath Co., 191; Bruce VI, 67; Pocahontas Co., 379-381; Rockbridge, 478.
Clegg—TD, Sept. 25, 1910.
Cleghorn—Rockbridge, 478.
Clem—Bruce IV, 346; VI, 73.
Clement, Clements, Clemans—VM, XXXII, 292-298.
Clemens—Burgess, 634-635; Campbell Co., 377-378.
Clement—Campbell Co., 378-380; Cyc. Va. Biog., IV, 150; Thos. Carter, 142; VM, III, 274-275.
(*Campbell*)—Brock II, 561; Campbell Co., 378-380.
(*Surry*)—VM, XX, 195.
Clements—Cyc. Va. Biog., I, 213; Rockbridge, 478; TD, Nov. 9, 1913, March 15, 1914; Virkus II, 248; VM, II, 306.

(*Amherst*)—Hardesty, 438; Sangamon Co., Ill., 206.
(*Surry*)—Griffith-Meriwether, 29-31; VM, XX, 195.
Clendenen—Bruce IV, 481.
Clendennin—Pocahontas Co., 154-159.
Clendinen—WVM, IV, 189-213.
Cleveland—America Heraldica, 141; Draper Series, V, 210; King's Mountain, 425-454. 458; VM, VII, 4-5, 13, 123-124.
Clevenger—Cartmell, 474; TD, Aug. 22, 1909; WM, XX, 222.
Clevinger—Bruce VI, 503.
Clifton—Burgess, 45-49; Miami Co., Ind., 807; Pendleton Co., 319; VM, XXII, 273, 424-425; XXIII, 316-317; XXVI, 319-320.
Clinch—Cyc. Va. Biog., I, 213; Hening VI, 297-299.
Cline—Sangamon Co., Ill., 206.
Clinedinst—Bruce IV, 245, 360; Shenandoah, 594.
Clise—Virkus I, 337.
Clopton—Brock II, 695; Cyc. Va. Biog., I, 213; Douglas, 15; TD, Nov. 13, 27, 1904; July 23, Nov. 26, 1905; Sept. 19, 1909; Feb. 1, 1914; Virkus III, 126; VM, XXVIII, 239; XXX, 41-42; WM, V, 77, 80; X, 54-55; XI, 67-73; XVII, 294-296.
Clore—Virkus I, 445.
Clore, Clawre, Klor, Glore, etc.—WM, XXVI, 178-182.
Close—Hardin Co., Ohio, 771.
Clowder—TD, Nov. 7, 1909.
Clowes (*Loudoun*)——Avery I, 86.
Clowney—Rockbridge, 479.
Clowser—Cartmell, 440-441.
Cloyd—Cloyd, Basye and Tapp Families of America (Omaha), 1812, by A. D. Cloyd; Clemens' Wills, 19; Cloyd, etc.; Dunmore's War, 45; Genealogy of the Cloyd, Basye, etc. Families of America; McGavock Family, 16-18, 20, 41-42, 46, 153-156; New River, 398-401; Rockbridge, 478-479; Sangamon Co., Ill, 208; Woods-McAfee, 319.
Clyce—Rockbridge, 479.
Coakley—DAR, 83, p. 110.
Coalter—Bates, et al. of Va. and Md., 31-32, 36, 79-81, 83, 140-143; Bristol Parish, 160; Hayden, 215; Rockbridge, 479; TD, Feb. 6, 1910; VSR, IV (No. 2), 25; Walker-Wigton, 108-114, 120-122, 127-129, 639.
Coates—Bruce V, 305; Burgess, 912.
Coatney—Pendleton Co., 319.
Coats—Halifax, 284.
Cobb—BS, Jan. 26, Feb. 2, 1908; LCJ, Aug. 30, 1914 (II, 1); Rootes of Rosewell, 49-50; RS, II, 23; Something about the Dulaney (Dulany) Family and a Sketch of the Southern Cobb Family. By B. C. Dulany (Washington, D. C., n. d.), 73-86; TD, Aug. 27, 1911; Feb. 23, March 16, 1913.
(*Highland*)—Highland Co., 275.
Cobb-Cobbs—Bell, 6, etc.; Browning, C. D., 248; Halifax, 284; McAllister, 55-56, 104-108, 280, 311, 313; SBN, XI, 218-220; Virkus I, 557-558; III, 333; VM, IV, 209-210, 332-333; WM, XIX, 51-56.
(*Buckingham*)—VM, XXXIII, 201.
Cobbs—Bristol Parish, 45; BS, Nov. 10, 17, 24; Dec. 1, 8, 1907; July 26, 1908; Campbell Co., 380-385.
(*Amelia*)—Cyc. Va. Biog., I, 213.
(*Bedford*)—SBN, XI, 220.
(*Goochland and Ga.*)—VM, IV, 209.
Cochran—Albemarle, 168-169; Burgess, 491-492; Cartmell, 443; Cyc. Va. Biog., V, 1092-1093; Marshall, 68; Peyton, 296, 298-299,

312; Pocahontas Co., 422-426; Rockbridge, 479.
(*Augusta*)—Green's Ky. Families, 27.
(*Loudoun*)—Hardy, 435.
Cock—WM, IX, 47.
Cocke—Bristol Parish, 173, 184; Burgess, 246-248; Campbell Co.,
386-387; Cyc. Va. Biog., I, 213-215; Dunmore's War, 107;
Hampden-Sidney, 81; Morton's II, 664; Norfolk, 760-761;
RS, II, 31, 35, 37, 40, 44, 52; III, 8, 20, 40; TD, Nov. 1
1908; Nov. 19, 1916; VHS. Col. (1886), 164-204; VM, IV,
86-96, 212-217, 322-332, 430-451, 457; V, 71-89, 181-198, 449;
VII, 253; X, 100-101, 202, 306-307; (1902-3), 102-104, 209-210;
(1903-1904); XXVIII, 365-366; Watkins, 21; WM, I, 18;
III, 204; VI, 29, 166; VIII, 151; X, 174; WM 2d, IX, 49-59.
(*Amelia*)—DAR, 69, p. 23.
(*Halifax*)—Halifax, 284-285.
(*Henrico*)—Browning, C. D., 66; Browning, C. D., 3d, 621;
Cabell, etc., 603-604; Dupuy, 249-258; Huguenot Emigration,
194-204, 405-414; Lancaster, 104-105, 168, 173-178, 187-191;
MMV, III, 76-77; RS, II, 31-33, 35, 45; Two Families, 156;
Tyler's VIII, 212-213; Virkus II, 147, 283; VM, III, 282-
292, 396, 405-414; IV, 86-96, 212-217, 322-332, 431-448; V,
71-89; XXVI, 407; WM, III, 204; IV, 247; XV, 87-88;
XVI, 233-234; XXVII, 140-143.
(*Henrico and Augusta*)—Albemarle, 169-171.
(*James*)—RS, II, 32, 34.
(*Lancaster*)—VM, V, 195-197 (also Cox).
(*Lower Norfolk Co.*)—McIntosh I, 98, 172-173.
(*Middlesex*)—Browning, C. D., 3d, 621; Two Families, 156.
(*Princess Anne*)—WM, IV, 15, 94; XVI, 232-233.
(*Richard*)—ARP, I, 327-328; Browning, C. D., 66; Bruce V,
507; Cox Family, 46-52; Du Bellet II, 158-159; MMV, III,
74-77; Mortons II, 658; Randolph Family (Va. State Li-
brary), 11-12; RS, II, 33, 35, 37, 40, 45; Tyler's VII, 212;
Virkus I, 557, 908; II, 283; III, 130; VM, XXXV, 27-29;
VSR, I (No. 3), 41; IV (No. 2), 39; V (No. 1), 73.
(*Stafford*)—(*Catesby*)—VM, XXVI, 71-72.
(*Surry*)—WM, V, 114-117; XV, 87-88; XVI, 232-233.
(*Surry and Lower Norfolk*)—VM, V, 181-189.
(*Thomas*)—Mortons II, 661.
(*Walter*)—WM, XVI, 233.
(*William*)—WM, XVI, 232.
(*Dr. William*)—Old Prince William, I, 155-156.
(*Williamsburg*)—Bruton Church, 89; RC, III, 53; RS, II, 52;
Spotswood Letters II, 8-9; Two Families, 153; VM, IV,
322-332; V, 189-194; X, 100; XXVI, 71-72; WM, IV, 67;
X, 174-175.
Cocke (Cox)—Bruce VI, 307; Wise.
Cockerell—Burgess, 571.
Cockerill—TD, May 5, 1912; WM, III, 69.
(*Loudoun*)—Adams Co., Ohio, 311, 313, 712-715, 914-915.
Cockersham—WM, VIII, 161.
Cockrell—Virkus I, 559; RS, IV, 3.
Cockrill—Armstrong III, 21; Munsell's XI, 185.
(*Richmond Co.*)—DAR, 81, p. 66.
Cockroft—McIntosh I, 103-104.
Codd—Cyc. Va. Biog., I, 215; VM, X, 374-375; XXIII, 382-384; XXV,
53-55; XXIX, 43-44.
Codrington—RS, II, 35, 37.

Coe—Cartmell, 463-464; Sangamon Co., Ill., 209.
Cofer—Bruce IV, 75-76; Hardesty (*Bedford*), 415.
Coff—Randolph Co., 325.
Coffee—Bell, 27.
Coffey—Kanawha, 985.
Coffield—TD, Oct. 15, 1905.
Coffman (Kauffman)—Cyc. Va. Biog., IV, 73; Licking Co., O., 643, 647; Shenandoah, 594-596; Strickler, 240-244.
Cofield—WM 2d, VIII, 62.
Cogbill—Bruce IV, 78.
Coggin—Bruce VI, 509.
Coghill—America Heraldica, 114, 161; Caroline Co., 415-416; TD, Sept. 25, 1906; The Family of Coghill—1377 to 1879. By James Henry Coghill, 1879.
Cohen—Burgess, 1031.
Cohenour—Rockbridge, 479.
Coke—Beau Monde (weekly), Richmond, Va., March 3, 1894; Brock II, 776; Coke of Trusley (London, 1880). By B. J. T. Coke; Cyc. Va. Biog., I, 215; Du Bellet I, 156-157; VM, XXIX, 344-345; WM, III, 120; VII, 127-129; XVIII, 103-104.
  (*Williamsburg*)—VM, XXIX, 344-345.
Coker—Virkus I, 559.
Colaw—Bruce VI, 190; Highland Co., 275-277.
Colbert—Bruce V, 70; Burgess, 636-637.
Cole—BS, Nov. 6, 1904; Cyc. Va. Biog., I, 215; V, 654; Old King William, 36-37; RS, II, 4, 31-32; TD, Feb. 17, March 10, April 14, 1907; Nov. 5, 1911; July 5, 1914; VM, XVIII, 416-417; XXXII, 60; WM, XXIV, 199-200.
  (*Charles City*)—Albemarle, 171.
  (*Nutmeg Quarter*)—VM, XIX, 189-190.
  (*Pittsylvania*)—MMV, III, 78.
  (*Warwick*)—Browning, C. D., 78; Hampden-Sidney, 101; Norfolk, 747-748; VM, II, 382-383; IX, 429-430; Winston, 315-322; WM, I, 142-143; V, 177-181; XIV, 165-166; XXI, 292-293; XXII, 62-64.
  (*Westmorland*)—VM, XXII, 26-28.
Coleman—Bristol Parish, 202; Bruce VI, 576; Marshall, 130-131; MMV, III, 85-89; Old King William, 38; TD, Feb. 2, March 29, April 26, 1908; Sept. 4, 1910; April 23, 1911; Virkus II, 114; VSR, I (No. 2), 25-26; V (No. 2), 37; Six Centuries of the Moores of Fawley, 50-51, 60.
  (*Caroline*)—Bruce VI, 511-512; Caroline Co., 121-127, 416-420; Coghill, 109; Cyc. Va. Biog., I, 215; Marshall, 211-212, 234, 236-240; Stubbs, 514-515; Tyler's IV, 440-441; Virkus II, 340; III, 439; VM, V, 77.
  (*Culpeper*)—Culpeper, 56; St. Mark's, 128.
  (*Cumberland*)—Pittsylvania, 159, 199.
  (*Essex*)—Francis Morgan, 109-120.
  (*Gloucester*)—Descendants of John Stubbs, 110-112; Francis Morgan, 104-108; Old Free State II, 191-194.
  (*Goochland*)—WM 2d, VII, 178.
  (*Halifax*)—Baskerville Family, 116, 121-122; Additional Baskerville Genealogy, 141-146; Du Bellet II, 413-416; Halifax, 149-152, 288-289; Hampden-Sidney, 53.
  (*Hanover*)—Boddie, 76-77, 80-81; Du Bellet II, 409-411; SBN, XI, 221; TD, March 29, 1908.
  (*King and Queen*)—Tyler's VI, 52-59, 147-148; VSR, I (No. 2), 3.

(*Lunenburg*)—Old Free State II, 191-194.
(*Miscellaneous*)—Stubbs, 519.
(*Richmond City*)—VSR, V (No. 1), 84.
(*Williamsburg*)—VM, XV, 102-103.
Coles—Browning, C. D., 3d, 621; Browning, R. D., 3d, 21; BS, Sept.
4, Dec. 4, 18, 1904; Culpeper, 76; Cyc. Va. Biog., I, 216;
V, 647-652, 995-997; Halifax, 286; Kennedy I, 641; II, 379-
381; Lancaster, 413-417, 442-443; Meade II, 15; RS, III,
26; St. Mark's, 186; Vestry Book of Henrico Parish, 177-
178; Virkus I, 563; III, 240-241; VM, VII, 101-102, 326-
329, 429-432; XV, 114-115; XXI, 203; WM, IV, 105; VIII,
158; WM 2d, VII, 32-33.
(*Albemarle and Hanover*)—Albemarle, 172-173; Governor Ed-
ward Coles. Ed. by C. W. Alvord (Ill. State His. Library,
Springfield, Ill., 1920), 18-21; His Encyc. of Ill., 110; Knox
Co., Ill., 115; Sketch of Edward Coles (Washburn).
(*Pittsylvania*)—Pittsylvania, 201.
(*Richmond City*)—VM, XV, 111-115.
Collclough—Cyc. Va. Biog., I, 215.
Collett—Pendleton Co., 319; Randolph Co., 319-320.
Colley—Brock II, 711.
Collier (Collyer)—Boddie, 76-77, 80-81; Coshocton Co., Ohio, 655;
Cyc. Va. Biog., I, 216; V, 1087; Goode, 50-50b, 78b, 276-
278, 404-406; Habersham Chap. II, 187-188; Hardy, 148-
163; Old Free State II, 374-375; Rockbridge, 479; SBN,
XI, 221; Thos. Carter, 274-275; Trezevant, 78-79, 120; Ty-
ler's IV, 445; Virkus I, 648; VM, XVIII, 303-304; WM,
III, 278.
(*Vines*)—Burgess, 82-86.
(*York*)—Tyler's IV, 445; VI, 52-59, 147-148; X, 52-53; WM,
VIII, 202-203, 255-257; IX, 183-185.
Collingsworth—Avery I, 139; Fothergill, 166, 190.
Collins—Cartmell, 481-482; Halifax, 285; Pocahontas Co., 412-415;
Rockbridge, 479.
(*Culpeper*)—Brock II, 561.
(*King and Queen*)—Bagby, 327.
(*Norfolk Co.*)—McIntosh I, 43, 195.
Collup—Crockett, 225, et seq.
Colonna—Bruce V, 510-511; MMV, II, 76.
Colony (*Eastern Shore*)—Burgess, 252-255.
Colquitt—Goode, 98; SBN, XI, 223; Virkus II, 88.
Colston—ARP, II, 728-730, 819; BS, April 8, 1906; Cartmell, 454-455;
Cyc. Va. Biog., I, 216; Du Bellet I, 93-94, 188, 292; II,
236-238; Griffith-Meriwether, 60-61; Hening VII, 633-638;
VIII, 168-170; Marshall, 45-47, 105-106, 112-115, 218-219,
222, 334-335; Md. Soc. Col. Wars, 109; Mortons II, 688-
689; RC, II, 10; VM, XV, 204; XXV, 279-282; WM, III,
132; IV, 27-28, 203.
Colt—WM, V, 41.
Colter—Green's Ky. Families, 52-53.
Colvill—Old Prince William I, 276.
Colville—Cyc. Va. Biog., I, 215; Licking Co., O., 639; Shenandoah,
657; WM, VI, 62.
Colvin (*Culpeper*)—Bruce IV, 241; Burgess, 470-471.
Combs—Madison Co., Ohio, 1047; Shenandoah, 632.
Comer—Miami Co., Ind., 407; Southside Va., 89; Virkus I, 563.
Virkus I, 563.

Cooksey—Burgess, 311-312; Old Free State II, 384.
Cooley—Grayson Co., 186-188.
Coombs—DAR, 48, p. 295; Mackenzie III, 47; WM 2d, I, 297.
Coons (Countz)—Virkus II, 363.
Coontz—Barbour Co., W. Va., 366-367.
Cooper—BS, Jan. 8, 1905; Pocahontas Co., 476-481; Rockbridge, 479; RS, III, 36.
    (*Botetourt*)—Sangamon Co., Ill., 224-225.
    (*Hampshire*)—Hampshire, 702-703.
    (*Henry*)—VM, IX, 220, 329-331.
    (*Isle of Wight*)—VM, XXI, 63; XXIX, 297.
    (*Norfolk*)—Cooper and Allied Families.
    (*Norfolk Co.*)—McIntosh I, 127, 147; II, 64, 128, 293.
    (*Northumberland*)—Cyc. Va. Biog., I, 217.
Cootes—Cyc. Va. Biog., V, 1117.
Cope—Hardin Co., Ohio, 895.
Copeland—WM, VII, 307.
Copenhaver—Bruce IV, 579; VI, 277; Tazewell II, 339-341; [Copenhover] Virkus II, 141.
Copes—Cyc. Va. Biog., V, 950.
Copland (*Richmond*)—WM, XIV, 44-45, 217-230; XV, 57-63.
Coplinger—Pendleton Co., 319-320.
Copp—Bruce IV, 312; Hardin Co., Ohio, 933.
Coppage—Burgess, 592; WM, XI, 138-139.
Coppridge—Bruce IV, 420.
Corbett—Highland Co., 356.
Corbin—ARP, II, 453-455; Bagby, 78-79, 327-328; BS, Oct. 2, 16, 23, Nov. 6, 20, 1904; Caroline Co., 420-421; Carter Family Tree; Chart Pedigree of the Corbin Family; Cyc. Va. Biog., I, 217-218; Hardy, 171-181; Hening VII, 458-461; Kennedy II, 67-74; LCJ, Oct. 18, 1914 (III, 4); Lee, 83-89; Meade II, 145-146; II, 145; RC, II, 11-13; Roger Jones, 55; RS, III, 20, 38; Spotswood Letters I, 78; TD, July 2, 23, Sept. 17, 1905; Feb. 13, March 6, June 12, Sept. 11, Oct. 23, 1910; Virkus III, 257-258; VM, XVI, 92-93; XVII, 401-403; XIX, 310-311; XXI, 204-205; XXII, 98; XXIII, 160-161; XXVIII, 281-283, 370-373; XXIX, 124-125, 243-251, 374-382, 520-526; XXX, 80-85, 309-318, 403-407; XXXI, 80-83, 170; XXXIV, 358-359; VSR, II (No. 2), 53; V (No. 2), 19; WM, III, 166.
    (*Culpeper*)—Knox Co., Ill., 427; VM, XXXVII, 57-59.
    (*Eastern Shore*)—John Wise, 107.
    (*Richmond Co.*)—Virkus III, 32; VM, XXXIV, 358-359.
Corbitt—Bruce IV, 537, 545-546.
Cordell—Hayden, 637-639; RS, III, 6.
Corder—Bruce VI, 343.
Corderoy (Cordray)—VM, XXIV, 385.
Cordery—WM, III, 41.
Corey—TD, July 3, 1904.
Corington—Burgess, 277.
Cork—Kanawha, 967-970.
Corker—Cyc. Va. Biog., I, 218; WM, VII, 232.
Corley—Braxton Co., W. Va., 365-368; Cyc. Va. Biog., IV, 437-438.
Corling—WM, V, 233; XII, 197.
Corn—Burgess, 861; DAR, 82, p. 12.
Cornelison—DAR, 74, p. 233.
Cornelius—Hardesty (*Bedford*), 416.

(*Berkeley*)—Cox Family, 60-62.
(*Chesterfield*)—Chappell, 197; Cyc. Va. Biog., V, 875.
(*Grayson*)—Cox Family, 53-60; Grayson Co., 167-171.
(*Hampshire*)—Cox Family, 63-64.
(*King and Queen*)—Bagby, 365.
(*Loudoun*)—Bruce IV, 114.
(*Scott*)—Bruce IV, 442-443; MMV, III, 96-97.
(*Westmoreland*)—Hardy, 189-190.
Cox (Cocke)—Bruce VI, 307.
Coxe—Cyc. Va. Biog., I, 218; DAR, 40, p. 313.
Coyle—Kanawha, 455.
Coyner—Bruce VI, 356.
Crabb—Cyc. Va. Biog., I, 218.
Crabbe—VM, XX, 293-294.
Crabtree—Burgess, 131; Tazewell II, 172.
Cracraft—DAR, 83, p. 1-2.
Craddock—Bruce V, 401; Cyc. Va. Biog., I, 218; Halifax, 152-156,
    289-291; MMV, II, 83-86; Southside Va., 89-90, 158; TD,
    July 30, 1905.
Crafton—Sangamon Co., Ill., 233.
Craghead—Henry Co., 136-137.
Craig, Craik—TD, May 22, 29; June 5, 1904; March 12, 1905.
Craig—Cyc. Va. Biog., IV, 46; Rockbridge, 480.
    (*Adam*)—WM, I, 19.
    (*Augusta*)—Boogher, 292-307; Bruce VI, 121; Foote II, 28-33;
        Munsell's XI, 136; Waddell's Annals of Augusta Co., 39-40.
        40, 388-392.
    (*Lunenburg*)—Jones, 289-291; Old Free State II, 348-349.
    (*Orange*)—DAR, 75, p. 37.
    (*Rockingham*)—Munsell's XI, 136.
    (*Washington Co.*)—Brock II, 714-715.
    (*Williamsburg*)—WM, X, 124-125.
Craighead—DAR, 42, p. 11, 235.
Craighill—Blair, etc., 199-292; Brock II, 562-563.
Craik—Browning, C. D., 97-98; Browning, C. D., 3d, 487-489; Din-
    widdie Papers I, 115; Fry Memoir, 76; Hayden, 341-343;
    Mackenzie V, 203; Magna Charta Barons, 136.
Cralle (Crawley)—Burgess, 460-462; Hayden, 117-120.
Cralle—Bruce V, 429; Cabell, etc., 544; Hampden-Sidney, 208; Old
    Free State II, 342-344, 352-354; VM, XII, 81-82.
    (*Nottoway*)—Jones, 287-288.
Crane—Cyc. Va. Biog., IV, 543; Hayden, 308, 315, 720; TD, March
    26, Aug. 27, 1905.
Cranford—TD, March 27, 1910.
Crashaw, Croshaw—Cyc. Va. Biog., I, 218; VM, I, 84; XXX, 278-279.
Craven—Albemarle, 173-174; Avery I, 87; Rockbridge, 480.
Cravens—Boogher, 379-380.
Crawford—Burgess, 463-466; Montague, 149-150; Rockbridge, 480;
    RS, II, 6; III, 28; TD, Oct. 22, 1905; July 5, 1908; Feb.
    28, March 14, 21, 28, April 11, 18, 25, May 2, 9, 1915; Virkus
    II, 306.
    (*Amherst*)—Gilmer's Georgians, 123-127.
    (*Augusta*)—Boogher, 311; Crawford Family Records. By W.
        M. Clemens (New York, 1914), 9-18; McIlhany, 59-63;
        Peyton, 314-315; Randolph Co., 327-329; Waddell's Annals
        of Augusta, 205-209.
    (*Berkeley*)—Crawfurdiana, 77-78; RS, III, 32; VHS. Col. VI,
        184.

Crouch—Cyc. Va. Biog., V, 1106; Douglas, 181; Du Bellet II, 709; Pocahontas Co., 564, 567; Randolph Co., 317-319; RS, IV, 2; SBN, XI, 235.
Croushorn—Cyc. Va. Biog., V, 907.
Crow—DAR, 46, p. 174; Sangamon Co., Ill., 235.
Crowder—Bruce IV, 388; Sangamon Co., Ill., 237-238; TD, Nov. 5, 1905.
Croxton—DAR, 55, p. 285; Old King William, 125-126.
Crudup—Boddie, 91-97.
Crummett—Highland Co., 356-357; Pendleton Co., 77-80, 191-192.
Crump—Bruce IV, 39; Cyc. Va. Biog., I, 219; IV, 151; V, 978; TD, Oct. 14, Dec. 9, 1906; March 24, 1907; May 23, 1909; VM, V, 348; WM, XXVI, 139.
   (*Alexandria*)—Avery I, 141.
   (*Isle of Wight*)—Burgess, 87-90.
   (*James City*)—Virkus III, 415; VM, IV, 75.
   (*New Kent*)—MMV, I, 281-282; WM, XXVI, 139-140.
Crutcher—LCJ, Nov. 8, 1914 (II, 3); LEP, March 15, 1919; Munsell's IX, 20.
Crutchfield—Life of Gen. Hugh Mercer, 120-121; VM, XXXII, 397-398.
Crute—Bruce V, 143.
Cryder—Madison Co., Ohio, 868.
Culbertson—Genealogy of the Culbertson Family.
Cullen—Du Bellet II, 711; RS, IV, 3.
Cullingsworth—Brock II, 779.
Culpeper—Cyc. Va. Biog., I, 219; VM, XX, 16, 93-94; XXX, 391-393.
   (*English*)—Proprietors of the Northern Neck (Privately printed); VM, XXXIII, 113-153, 223-267, 333-358; Chart, VM, April, 1925; XXXIV, 19-64.
   (*Norfolk Co.*)—McIntosh I, 169.
Culpepper (*Norfolk Co.*)—Cyc. Va. Biog., IV, 381.
Culton—Clemens' Wills, 23; Rockbridge, 480.
Cummings—Kanawha, 692; RS, III, 2.
   (*Augusta*)—Green's Ky. Families, 158-160.
   (*Fauquier*)—DAR, 70, p. 152.
   (*Washington Co.*)—Brock II, 715; Foote II, 121-125; Thomas Carter, 87-90, 92-96.
   (*Western Va.*)—Dunmore's War, 81, 152.
Cummins—Licking Co., O., 640; Rockbridge, 480.
Cundiff—Hardesty (Bedford), 416.
Cunningham—Braxton Co., W. Va., 368-369; Kanawha, 659; Pendleton Co., 192-193; Rockbridge, 480-481; TD, July 1, Dec. 30, 1906; May 26, 1907; Feb. 28, 1909; WM, III, 266.
   (*Amherst*)—Hardesty, 438.
   (*Augusta*)—DAR, 83, p. 125; Waddell, 261.
   (*Frederick*)—Munsell's XII, 204.
   (*Hardy*)—Van Meter, 105-107, 166-168.
   (*Highland*)—Highland Co., 357.
   (*Washington Co.*)—Foote II, 121-125.
   (*West Va.*)—Randolph Co., 330-331.
   (*William*)—Burgess, 636-637.
Curd—Coghill, 106; Douglas, 103, 182-183; TD, May 31, 1908; WM, XXV, 67.
Curle—Barton I, R97-98, 109; Burgess, 486-487; Cyc. Va. Biog., I, 219; Kennedy I, 269-271; Spotswood Letters I, XXXI, XXXIII; TD, Dec. 16, 1906; Tyler's II, 140; VM, XXXV,

26-27; WM, IX, 125; XXVI, 286.
(*Campbell*)—Bell, 77, 79.
Curling (Norfolk Co.)—McIntosh I, 174, 185; II, 80, 311.
Currell—WM, V, 255; XII, 183.
Currence—Randolph Co., 334-339.
Currie—Marshall, 180; RS, V, 20; Virkus II, 86.
  (*Halifax*)—Halifax, 45; Hayden, 239; Tyler's VII, 139.
  (*Lancaster*)—Cyc. Va. Biog., I, 219-220; Hayden, 239; Montague, 69; Roger Jones, 110; Tyler's VII, 139; WM, XXI, 141.
Currin—Grayson Co., 100-103.
Curry—Highland Co., 277-278; Pocahontas Co., 311-315, 492-495; Rockbridge, 481; Sangamon Co., Ill., 384.
  (*Augusta*)—MMV, II, 89-91; Virkus III, 530.
Curtis—TD, Dec. 31, 1911; July 28, 1912; May 18, 1913; Feb. 15, 1914; WM, IX, 47.
  (*Gloucester*)—Cooke-Booth, 223-224; Cyc. Va. Biog., V, 635; VM, V, 344; XIV, 92.
  (*Middlesex*)—Cyc. Va. Biog., I, 220; Thos. Carter, 285-286.
  (*West Va.*)—Randolph Co., 325-326.
  (*York*)—Cyc. Va. Biog., V, 941.
Custard—Pendleton Co., 320.
Custer—The Custer Family.
Custis—ARP, I, 90, 345-347; II, 483; Boogher, 328-329; Browning, C. D., 3d, 538-539; BS, Dec. 15, 22, 29, 1907; Jan. 5, 12, 19, 1908; County Court Note Book V, Nos. 3, 4, 5; Supplement for Aug., Oct. and Dec., 1925; Custis Reminiscences, 113; Harrison, Waples, etc., 88-108; John Wise, 85, 99-103; Kennedy II, 47-49; Lancaster, 371-372, 482-484; Lee, 456-461; Mary and Martha Washington. By B. J. Lossing (New York, 1886), 83-97; Marshall, 264; Meade I, 262; Neill's Virginia Carolorum, 208; Potter's Amer. Monthly, VI, 85; RS, III, 15; R. W. Johnson, Chart, 28-29, 32, 33; TD, Jan. 14, 1906; March 3, 1907; March 21, 1909; VM, III, 319-321; IV, 64-66, 421; XVII, 404-412; XVIII, 84-85; XXV, 77; XXXII, 238-239; XXXIV, 371; Wise's Eastern Shore, 279-280, 331-334, 348-350; WM, III, 258-261; IV, 66; V, 35-36.
Cutchins—Bruce IV, 84.
Cutherell—McIntosh II, 16-17.
Cutler—Burgess, 18, 246.
  (*Dinwiddie*)—Tyler's VIII, 64-65.
Cutlip—Braxton Co., W. Va., 359.
Cutts—RS, III, 6; St. Mark's, 186.

D

Dabbs—Cyc. Va. Biog., V, 653.
Dabney (d'Aubigny)—Albemarle, 174-175; Brock II, 601; Cabell, etc., 561; Campbell Co., 388; Cooke-Booth, 83-84; Culpeper; Dabney's Sketch of the Dabney Family with Some of Their Family Records; Dabneys of Va.; Du Bellet III, 28-30, 59-65, 123-126, 178-180; IV, 87-93; Gilmer's Georgians, 166; Hampden-Sidney, 272; Kennedy I, 674; II, 379; Life and Letters of Robert Lewis Dabney. By F. C. Johnson (Richmond, Va., 1903), 120; Mreiwethers, 71-72; Minor, 72-100; Munsell's VI, 91 (for Fewell, read Ferrell), 166; RS, II, 34;

III, 24; SBN, XI, 284-251; Sketches of Lynchburg, 245, 246;
St. Mark's, 186; TD, Jan. 3, 10, 1904; Valentine I, 396-429;
IV, 2254-2255; VM, II, 332-333; VI, 306; Walker-Wigton,
157-158; Willis, 55; WM, IV, 103.
(*Albemarle and Hanover*)—Albemarle, 175.
Dade—BS, Oct. 11, 1908; Burgess, 73; Culpeper, 87; Cyc. Va. Biog.,
I, 220; Hayden, 731-733; Lewis, 45; McAllister, 123; St.
Mark's, 58; TD, March 6, 1910; VM, II, 121; XX, 210-
212, 323-329; WM, VIII, 205; XII, 245-250.
Dagg—Clemens' Wills, 24; Cyc. Va. Biog., II, 281-282.
Daggy—Pendleton Co., 320.
Dahmer—Pendleton Co., 193-194.
Dailey—Burgess, 780-782; Winchester and Its Beginnings. By Kath-
erine Green, 363.
Daingerfield—Avery I, 53; Bruce V, 250; Cyc. Va. Biog., I, 220;
Hardy, 46; Mackenzie I, 69; TD, Feb. 20, 1910; Virkus
I, 45; III, 217; Woods-McAfee, 270-271; WM, VI, 207;
VIII, 96-100; IX, 188-189, 202; XII, 69-70; XVII, 65-66.
See also "Dangerfield."
Dalbey—Madison Co., Ohio, 869.
Dale—Cyc. Va. Biog., I, 220; McIntosh II, 44, 123, 292-293; Meade
I, 278; Norfolk, 489; Rockbridge, 481; SBN, XI, 252-254;
Thos. Carter, 12-22.
(*Lancaster*)—VM, XXIX, 435; WM, XVII, 196-202.
Dalton—ARP, II, 655-657; Burgess, 1364; Hughes, 77-109; RC, 162
(P-VSL); Rockbridge, 481.
(*Rockingham*)—Hughes, etc., 80-90, 93-105.
Dame—Kennedy I, 536;Page (2d. ed.), 198; Munsell's VII, 189.
Dameron—Hardesty (*Amherst*), 438; Munsell's IV, 58-59; Tyler's IV,
54-58, 117-122; VIII, 42-52; WM, XII, 100.
Dance—WM, XXVI, 50-55; WM 2d, VII, 190.
D'Ances, Dancey, Dancie, Dansie—TD, July 21, 1907.
Dancey—Culpeper, part 2, 81-83.
Dancy—Virkus I, 55.
Dancy, Dansey—VM, V, 338.
Dandridge—Armistead, 272; Browning, C. D., 243-245, 291-292; Brown-
ing, C. D., 3, 446-447; Burgess, 261; Culpeper, 72-73; Cyc.
Va. Biog., I, 220-221; Dunmore's War, 24; Hening VI, 322,
428-432; VII, 296-297, 486-487; VIII, 224-227, 638-639; Henry
Co., 143-152; Huguenot Emigration, 145; Kennedy II, 13-
62, 411; Lindsay, 22; Mackenzie I, 117-120; Old King
William, 39-40; Patrick Henry II, 634; Robertson, 33, 36,
45-46; RS, II, 10, 12, 21; Shepherdstown, 312-314; Spots-
wood Genealogy, 23; TD, Dec. 25, 1904; Aug. 13, 1905;
Oct. 11, 1908; March 30, 1913; The Dandridges of Virginia.
By Wilson Miles Cary; VSR, I (No. 2), 12-13; IV (No. 3),
26-27; VM, XI, 216-217, 423; XIV, 116-117; XV, 430-431;
XXII, 96-97; XXXII, 237-238; WM, I, 224; III, 168; V, 30-
39, 81-82, 139-140; VI, 250-251; VIII, 271; X, 102; XII, 126-
127; XIV, 267-268; XX, 249; WVM, V, 153.
Dandy—Virkus I, 55.
Dangerfield, Daingerfeild—VM, XXXII, 134-135.
Dangerfield—Amer. His. Review, Oct. 1900, 77-107; Griffith-Meri-
wether, 42-44; Kennedy I, 195; Meade I, 405-406; RS, III,
6; TD, Feb. 4, 1912; VM, XXV, 239-241; Willis, 121-122;
WM, XVII, 65-66.
Daniel—Campbell Co., 388-392; Du Bellet II, 221-222; Goode, 49, 77,
78b, 273-274, 403-404; Hampden-Sidney, 32, 263-264; Hayden,

291-330; Kennedy I, 558, 742; McAllister, 95, 97; Montague, 88-89, 127-132, 211-214, 354-355; MMV, I, 226-233; RS, I, 32; III, 51; SBN, XI, 254-257; TD, May 14, Oct. 1, 22, 1905; June 17, Oct. 28, Nov. 18, Dec. 9, 1906; Jan. 21, 1917; Tyler's VIII, 181-184, 285; Watkins, 18; Woodson, 69, 134; WM, XII, 205.
    (*Goochland and Albemarle*)—VSR, II (No. 3), 46.
Daniels—Randolph Co., W. Va., 339-341.
Danner—Cartmell, 490.
Darby—Burkeley, 204.
Darden—Burgess, 86; DAR, 82, p. 280; TD, May 6, 1906.
Dark—Burgess, 79; TD, Oct. 22, 1905.
Darke—Berkeley, 198-199; Convention 1788, II, 368; Cyc. Va. Biog., II, 277; Shepherdstown, 255-261.
Darlington—Adams Co., Ohio, 546-547; Burgess, 781-782.
    (*Frederick*)—Adams Co., Ohio, 251-256; Cartmell, 482.
Darnall—Fauquier Bulletin, 317.
Darnell (*Fauquier*)—DAR, 83, p. 180.
Darrell—VM, XVII, 115.
Darst—Cyc. Va. Biog., IV, 47; Kanawha, 519; Shenandoah, 597.
Dashiell—Minor, 59.
    (*Richmond*)—Dashiell Family Records.
Daugherty—Pocahontas Co., 400-404.
Daughtrey—MMV, V, 87.
Davenport—Old King William, 190-191;RS, II, 26.
    (*Berkeley*)—DAR, 74, p. 64.
    (*Mathews*)—DAR, 81, p. 82; WM, VII, 17, 152.
    (*Miscellaneous*)—Researcher I, 253-257.
    (*Richmond*)—VM, IV, 319.
    (*Richmond City*)—MMV, IV, 82-86.
    (*Williamsburg*)—Cyc. Va. Biog., I, 221; WM, V, 271-272.
Daves—Md. Soc. Col. Wars, 20; Virkus III, 415.
Davidson—BS, March 4, 11, 1906; Green's Ky. Families, 188-189; New River, 401.
    (*Rockbridge*)—McCormick, 34-37; Rockbridge, 249, 481-482.
    (*West Va.*)—Ritchie Co., 49.
Davies—Bristol Parish, 203; Bruce V, 422; VI, 444; BS, Oct. 21, 28; Nov. 4, 1906; Campbell Co., 393-397; TD, June 10, 24, Aug. 5, Dec. 2, 1906; Tyler's VIII, 140-141, 207-209; WM, VIII, 267.
    (*Amherst*)—Cabell, etc., 245-247, 285-288; TD, June 18, 25, Aug. 5, Dec. 2, 1906.
    (*Nicholas*)—Tyler's VIII, 140-141.
    (*Rockbridge*)—Clemens' Wills, 25-26.
    (*Samuel*)—Cyc. Va. Biog., I, 221; Foote I, 157-158; VHS, Col. VI, 93-94.
Daviess—Marshall, 78.
Davis—Braxton Co., W. Va., 371; BS, Jan. 22, 1905; Burgess, 639-647; Campbell Co., 392-393; Harrison Co., 369; Monongahela II, 723-726; Pendleton Co., 194-197; Rockbridge, 482; Shenandoah, 597-598; TD, Dec. 30, 1906; May 2, 1909; March 25, April 8, May 6, 1917; WM, I, 79.
    (*Albemarle*)—DAR, 74, p. 294; MMV, III, 109.
    (*Albemarle and Middlesex*)—Albemarle, 176.
    (*Amherst*)—Burgess, 639-640; Ellis, 15; Floyd, 11-12.
    (*Augusta*)—Barbour Co., W. Va., 378.
    (*Bedford*)—Bell, 28, 252-257.
    (*Campbell and Louisa*)—Bruce IV, 359.

(*Charles City*)—Bruce IV, 364.
(*Charlotte, Prince Edward and Lunenburg*)—Old Free State II, 194-203.
(*Cumberland*)—Bruce IV, 143.
(*Elizabeth City*)—Burgess, 641-645.
(*Essex*)—Burgess, 646-647.
(*Gloucester*)—Bruce V, 379.
(*Greensville*)—Burgess, 645.
(*Hanover*)—DAR, 70, p. 149.
(*Henrico*)—N. C. His. Reg. I, 637.
(*Highland*)—Highland Co., 278.
(*Isle of Wight*)—Cyc. Va. Biog., I, 221; IV, 365; MMV, IV, 97-99; WM, VII, 225 et seq.
(*King and Queen*)—Bagby, 332.
(*Logan*)—Burgess, 645-646.
(*Middlesex*)—MMV, III, 109; Virkus I, 88-89; Watson, 318-322.
(*Pittsylvania*)—VM, XIX, 424.
(*Prince William*)—Burgess, 640; Monongahela II, 825-827.
(*Richmond City*)—Cyc. Va. Biog., IV, 228.
(*Spotsylvania*)—Boogher, 324-328; Thos. Carter, 154-184, 382-388; VM, XII, 434-437; WM, XVIII, 239-241; XX, 38-46.
(*Stafford*)—VM, XII, 325-328, 434-437; XXXVI, 372.
(*Surry*)—MMV, IV, 90.
(*Woodstock*)—John G. Davis (by Huntley), 10-12.
Davison—Cartmell, 258-259; Cyc. Va. Biog., II, 366-367; Du Bellet III, 67-72, 130-136.
Davisson—Harrison Co., W. Va., 371; McIlhany, 139-140.
Dawkes—Cyc. Va. Biog., I, 221.
Dawley (*Norfolk*)—Antiquary III, 135-136; ARP, II, 781.
Dawson—A Collection of Family Records of Various Families Bearing the Name of Dawson. By Charles C. Dawson. (Dawson Family Record); Albemarle, 176-179; Hist. Encyc. of Ill., 129; Rockbridge, 482; WM, I, 53, et seq.; VI, 123, 216; VII, 148; IX, 222.
(*Amherst*)—Hardesty, 439.
(*Bedford*)—Kanawha, 287.
(*Fairfax*)—Sangamon Co., Ill., 244.
(*Lynchburg*)—Goode, 60.
(*Spotsylvania*)—Convention 1788, I, 314.
(*Williamsburg*)—Cyc. Va. Biog., I, 221-222; WM, II, 51-52, 153; V, 208, 211; XI, 92-93.
Day—Cyc. Va. Biog., I, 222; V, 1100; TD, Feb. 11, 1906; VM, XXXII, 291.
(*Charlotte*)—DAR, 78, p. 18.
(*Isle of Wight*)—WM, III, 167-168; VII, 211, et seq.
Dayton—Barbour Co., W. Va., 369.
Deaderick (Dietrick)—Armstrong I, 59-60, 72-75.
Deadrick (*Frederick*)—Knoxville, Tenn., Sentinel, about 1909.
Deal (*James City*)—MMV, V, 90.
Deal (Dale)—Rockbridge, 482.
Deale—McIntosh II, 156-157.
Deall (*Norfolk Co.*)—McIntosh II, 50-51.
Dean—Berkeley Co., 242-243; Pendleton Co., 197; Rockbridge, 482; RS, III, 17.
Deane—Burgess, 884-885; Hampden-Sidney, 171.
Deans—Bruce IV, 123.
Dearing—Bruce V, 351; VI, 69-70; Cyc. Va. Biog., V, 961-962.
Dearmont—Bruce V, 430; Cartmell, 455.

Death—Cyc. Va. Biog., I, 222.
Deaton—Bruce IV, 437; Cyc. Va. Biog., IV, 500.
Deaver—Highland Co., 380.
Debnam—TD, March 19, 1911.
Debusk—Brock II, 717.
De Butts—Bruce VI, 394; Carlyle, 30; Cyc. Va. Biog., I, 222.
De Cordy—Brock II, 667.
Dedman—Albemarle, 179; Burgess, 424; Woods-McAfee, 371-385.
Deem—Ritchie Co., 220-223.
Deering—Campbell Co., 397-399.
Deeton—Avery I, 143.
De Farge—Old King William, 66.
De Friece—Bruce VI, 254.
Degge—WM, XXI, 86-87, 193-198.
De Graffenried (Graffenreidt)—History of the de Graffenried Family
    from 1191 A. D. to 1925. By Thomas P. de Graffenried
    (1925); Old Free State II, 203-210; Stubbs, 291-293, 309-
    316; TD, Nov. 3, 1912; Virkus III, 38, 150; VM, XIV, 243;
    XXIX, 13; WM, X, 191; XI, 74.
    (*Christopher*)—Baron Christoph von Graffenried's Acount of the
        Founding of New Bern, etc., N. C. Hist. Com. (Raleigh,
        1920), 27-30, 96-97; TD, Nov. 3, 1912; WM, XV, 201-204.
    (*Switzerland*)—TD, July 22, 1906.
De Hart—Monroe Co., 333.
De Haven—Cartmell, 481; Clemens' Wills, 27.
Deihl—Highland Co., 278-279.
Deitrick—Old King William, 186.
De Jarnette—Bruce VI, 472; Caroline Co., 423-424; Francis Morgan,
    81-85; Halifax, 291-292; MMV, IV, 100-103; TD, June 16,
    1907; WM, XXV, 268-274.
Delaney—Bruce IV, 91.
Delany—Cyc. Va. Biog., I, 222.
Delk—WM, XVIII, 65-66.
Delke—Cyc. Va. Biog., I, 222.
Dellinger—Bruce VI, 440; Cartmell, 490.
Demint—DAR, 80, p. 319.
Demoville—Burgess, 445; WM, XXIV, 143.
Denby—Virkus I, 242; II, 101.
    (*Norfolk*)—McIntosh II, 300.
De Neuville—WM, VI, 59.
Denit—Bruce IV, 461.
Dennett—WM, XVII, 227; WM 2d, V, 200-203.
Denning—MMV, II, 98-99.
Dennison—Rockbridge, 482.
Denny—DAR, 78, p. 153; RS, III, 7; SBN, XI, 275-276; Virkus I,
    544; MMV, I, 23.
Dent—Boogher, 346-347; DAR, 55, p. 438; Monongahela III, 1309-
    1312; Preston Co., 346.
    (*From Md.*)—Mackenzie III, 153-154.
Denton—Halifax, 293; Shenandoah, 598.
Denver—Cartmell, 425-426, 477-478.
Denwood—ARP, I, 149.
Depew, Dupuy—TD, Oct. 27, 1907.
De Priest—Douglas, 186; TD, Sept. 3, 1905; WM, XII, 103.
De Quasie—Fayette Co., 540.
De Rieux—Albemarle, 360; VSR, I, 32; WM, XVII, 20.
Derrick—Kanawha, 586.
Derry—TD, Oct. 1, 1905.

Deshazo—Henry Co., 156-160.
De Shields—Bruce V, 300.
Deskin—TD, Dec. 2, 1906.
Deskins—Tazewell II, 371-374.
Devany—Bruce IV, 455.
Dever—Highland Co., 279.
Devericks—Highland Co., 279-280.
Devier—Bruce IV, 239.
Devine—Burgess, 216.
Devoe—RS, III, 17.
Dew—Bagby, 291-293, 304-305, 365; Bruce VI, 643; Cyc. Va. Biog.,
    IV, 279; MMV, II, 94-95; WM, XXVII, 135.
    (*King and Queen*)—VSR, II (No. 2), 68.
Deweese—Miami Co., Ohio, 523, 545-546.
Dewey—Cyc. Va. Biog., I, 222-223.
De Witt—Bruce V, 131; Hardesty (*Bedford*), 416; Preston Co., 341;
    Strickler, 75.
Deyerle—Bruce IV, 211; Strickler, 60.
Dibrell—Crockett, 114-118; Huguenot Emigration, 23; McAllister,
    189-197, 211-271; MMV, V, 96-97.
Dice—Burgess, 213; Pendleton Co., 197-199.
Dick (*Fredericksburg*)—Burgess, 1101; Cyc. Va. Biog., I, 223; WM,
    XVIII, 112.
Dickenson—Barbour Co., W. Va., 379; Grayson Co., 54-59; Pendle-
    ton Co., 199; TD, June 2, 1907.
Dickerson—Albemarle, 179; Baskerville Family, Table I; Rives, 395.
    (*Caroline and Pittsylvania*)—DAR, 47, p. 23.
Dickey—Bagby, 332; Old King William, 40-41; Rockbridge, 482.
Dickie—Bruce IV, 355; Chappell, 266-382.
Dickins—Virkus III, 153.
Dickinson, Dickerson—Caroline Vo., 424, 426.
Dickinson—TD, June 30, Aug. 18, 1907; March 16, 1913.
    (*Bath*)—Dunmore's War, 272; WVM, II, 54-56 (April, 1902).
    (*Caroline*)—Buckners of Va., 87-89; Burgess, 878; Kanawha, 527.
    (*Prince Edward*)—Cabell, etc., 372-374; Dupuy, 228-231; Hugue-
    not Emigration, 165-166.
    (*Spotsylvania*)—DAR, 72, p. 159.
Dickson—Armistead, 131; Monroe Co., 334; Rockbridge, 482.
    (*Lunenburg*)—DAR, 72, p. 159.
Didlake—Bruce VI, 343; Burgess, 207, 468; RS, II, 46.
Dietrick—Miami Co., Ohio, 817.
Digges—America Heraldica, 125-163; Browning, C. D., 10, 75-78;
    Browning, C. D., 3d, 700-701; Browning, R. D., III, XXIX;
    Burgess, 209-215; Convention 1788, II, 382; Cyc. Va. Biog.,
    I, 223; II, 9; IV, 179; Lee, 311-312; Magna Charta Barons,
    152-153; Mackenzie I, 68; Md. Soc. Col. Wars, 57; Meade
    I, 238-240, 244-245; RS, II, 24; Southern Bivouac (1888);
    [Digges, Diggs]—TD, March 12, 1905; Feb. 25, April 1,
    1906; May 28, June 4, Aug. 20, 27, Sept. 3, 10, 17, 24, Nov.
    5, 1911; VM, IV, 168-169; IX, 358; X, 377-378; XIV, 305;
    XVII, 381; XIX, 350, 357-358; XXIII, 47-48, 160; XXX,
    362-364; XXXII, 47-48; WM, I, 80-88, 140-154, 208-213;
    II, 81-82; III, 143; V, 127-128; X, 67; XV, 36-39.
    (*Fauquier*)—Burgess, 1362.
    (*Richmond Co.*)—WM, XVII, 67.
Diggs—Bagby, IV, 365; TD, March 12, 1925.
Digman—Barbour Co., W. Va., 379.
Dilke—VM, I, 443; III, 277; XX, 41.

Dillard—Brock II, 563, 603; Bruce IV, 467; V, 129, 311; Henry Co., 67, 152-156; Hughes, etc., 54-61; King's Mountain, 468; McCue, 186, 194, 211-212; Montague, 148-149, 258; Pittsylvania, 96; TD, June 2, 1912; Thos. Carter, 61-62; VM, XIX, 425; XXIII, 375.
  (*Amherst*)—DAR, 72, p. 157.
Dillon (*Prince Edward, etc.*)—Bruce V, 456-457; Cantrill-Cantrell Genealogy, 46-47; Hampden-Sidney, 226-227; Henry Co., 166; Madison Co., Ohio, 1019; MMV, V, 100-102; Sangamon Co., Ill., 251.
  (*West Va.*)—Monroe Co., 335.
Dimitry—Du Bellet IV, 145-190.
Dimmock—Kennedy I, 53-54.
Dinges—Cartmell, 489.
Dingledine—Bruce IV, 197; Rockbridge, 482.
Dinwiddie—Dinwiddie Papers I, VII-XXVIII; Du Bellet II, 600-605; TD, April 12, 1908; Jan. 24, 1909; VM, XIX, 283.
  (*Bath*)—WM, XVIII, 67.
  (*Highland Co.*)—Highland Co., 380.
Dipnall (Dipdall)—Cyc. Va. Biog., I, 223.
Disart—King's Mountain, 404.
Dishman—Virkus III, 163.
Dismukes—DAR, 43, p. 298; Habersham Chap. II, 532.
Dispanet—Cartmell, 439.
Diuguid—Bruce V, 135; Campbell Co., 403-404.
Dix—Pittsylvania, 95.
Dixon—Cooke-Booth, 237; Hayden, 477-478; Rootes of Rosewell, 38-40, 45-47; RS, III, 16; TD, Nov. 5, 1911; WM, I, 20; III, 256; X, 272-273; XIX, 106-107.
  (*Gloucester*)—Cyc. Va. Biog., I, 223-224; VM, XIX, 283-287; XX, 292; WM, III, 29-31.
  (*Isle of Wight*)—Boddie, 105-106.
  (*Spotsylvania*)—Cyc. Va. Biog., I, 224.
Doak—Cyc. Va. Biog., I, 224; "Genealogy" (Clemens'), VII, 167; Hampden-Sidney, 25-26; Irvins, Doaks, etc.; Rockbridge, 482.
  (*Loudoun*)—Adams Co., Ohio, 730.
Dobbs—TD, Feb. 15, 1914; Virkus III, 164.
Dobie—Cooke-Booth, 53-54; Norfolk, 690.
Dobyns—Hardesty (*Bedford*), 417.
Dodd—Cyc. Va. Biog., V, 633; Berkeley, 175-176.
  (*Pittsylvania*)—Bruce V, 114-115.
Doddridge—Hayden, 659, 662-663; WVM, II, Jan., 1902, 54-68.
Dodman—WM, IV, 41; VII, 232.
Dods—Rockbridge, 482.
Dodson—Bruce IV, 218; Burgess, 619; Cyc. Va. Biog., IV, 155.
Doggett—Avery I, 130; Burgess, 217-220; Cyc. Va. Biog., I, 224; IV, 362; TD, Feb. 23, March 22, 1908; VM, XXVI, 410; WM, XII, 181.
Doherty—Sangamon Co., Ill., 257.
Dold—Cyc. Va. Biog., IV, 480; Rockbridge, 483.
Dollins—Albemarle, 180.
Dolly—Pendleton Co., 199-201.
Donaho—Rockbridge, 483.
Donald—Bruce VI, 314; TD, July 1, 1906; VM, XXIX, 401.
Donaldson—Miami Co., Ind., 685.
Doneghy—Mackenzie VII, 188-189.
Donelson—Armstrong II, 88, et seq.; Cisco, 245-247; County Court

Note Book, VI, Nos. 2, 3, 4; Pittsylvania, 153; SBN, XI, 547-548; Virkus I, 185-186; VM, VII, 15; XXIII, 80.
Doniphan—Marshall, 301; Memoir of Gov. Wm. Smith; Price, 96-105; Virkus III, 383; WM, XVI, 290-291.
Donnald—Rockbridge, 483.
Donnally—Kanawha, 816; WVM, I, July, 1901, 52-64.
Donnan—Brock II, 555; Bruce IV, 17.
Donne—VM, IX, 176; X, 427.
Donnell—DAR, 48, p. 280.
Dooley—Brock II, 779; Bruce V, 272.
Doosing—Bruce V, 567.
Doran—Funk, 294.
Dorman—McCue, 32, 47, 67-68, 70, 93-94, 123, 145-146; Rockbridge, 249, 483.
Dormer—Cyc. Va. Biog., I, 224-225.
Dornin—Cyc. Va. Biog., IV, 428.
Dorrington—WM, XII, 127.
Dorsey—Burgess, 221, 827-828.
Dorson (*Isle of Wight*)—Boddie, 98-102.
  (*Williamsburg*)—WM, XI, 92-93.
Dortch—Virkus III, 165.
Doster—Cartmell, 484.
Doswell—VM, XXII, 90-91; VSR, IV (No. 4), 39; WM, VIII, 126-127; XXIV, 55.
Dotson—Bruce IV, 471; Ritchie Co., 142-145.
Dougherty—Burgess, 201; Rockbridge, 483.
Doughty—VM, V, 288-290.
Douglas, Douglass—TD, Aug. 14, 1904; March 26, 1905.
Douglas—Bell; Burgess, 223, 912; Campbell Co., 403; Cyc. Va. Biog., V, 990-992; Goode, 354; RS, III, 6; WM, VIII, 127.
  (*Eastern Shore*)—Cyc Va. Biog., I, 224; John Wise, 76-81.
  (*Frederick*)—Cartmell, 457.
  (*Garallan*)—John Wise, 289-304; Virkus III, 490; VM, III, 336-337.
  (*Goochland*)—Douglas Register.
  (*Highland*)—Highland Co., 280.
  (*Loudoun*)—Browning, C. D., 58; Cyc. Va. Biog., I, 225; Genealogical Chart (by John S. Wise); Sangamon Co., Ill., 261.
  (*Petersburg*)—VM, XXXVII, 66.
  (*Rev. William*)—Meriwethers, 123-129.
Douglass—Albemarle, 180; Campbell Co., 403-404; Cyc. Va. Biog., II, 255; Harrison Co., 382-383; Ritchie Co., 175-181; Rockbridge, 483; Shenandoah, 598-599.
Douthat—Du Bellet I, 164-167, 174-175; Lancaster, 73; Lewis, 42, 49; Marshall, 96, 204-205, 321-322; McAllister, 113, 116; Monongahela II, 625-626; Rockbridge, 483; RS, III, 2; VM, VI, 79.
Dove—Pendleton Co., 201.
Dovell—Bruce VI, 525.
Dowd—DAR, 82, p. 205.
Dowdall—DAR, 53, p. 258.
Dowdell, Dowdal—TD, April 22, 1906.
Dowdell—DAR, 47, p. 36.
Dowdle—Virkus II, 98.
Dowdy—Monroe Co., 335.
Dowell—Albemarle, 181.
Downe, Downes (*Elizabeth City*)—VM, XXII, 26; XXV, 243-244.

Downing—Bruce V, 169; Hardy, 185-193; MMV, II, 98-99; VM, XXII, 440; WM, XXIV, 189-193; XXV, 41-51, 96-106.
Downman—Cyc. Va. Biog., I, 225; Hardy, 40-42; Hayden, 72-74, 101-102, 122-123, 125-126, 137-138, 738-739; Mackenzie II, 43; VM, XXV, 241-243; WM, III, 17; IV, 16, chart; XVIII, 138-141; WM 2d, VIII, chart op. p. 33.
Downs—Cyc. Va. Biog., I, 225.
Downton—Burgess, 228; Tyler's IX, 134.
Dowse—Cyc. Va. Biog., I, 225.
Doyle—Bruce IV, 431; Highland Co., 280-281.
Doyley—Cyc. Va. Biog., I, 225-226; VM, XII, 300-301.
Dragoo—Jolliffe, 102, 195-197.
Drake—TD, June 19, July 3, 1904.
    (*Isle of Wight*)—Boddie, 108-109.
    (*Loudoun*)—Price, 128.
    (*Mecklenburg*)—Hamiltons of Burnside, N. C., 102-103.
    (*Western Va.*)—Dunmore's War, 78; Ritchie Co., 38-39.
Draper—Bruce VI, 479; Crockett, 22, 269; Dunmore's War, 64; McClure, 203; SBN, XI, 292-294; Virkus III, 168.
Drew—Convention 1788, II, 370; Cyc. Va. Biog., I, 226; Virkus III, 439.
Drewry—Burgess, 41, 84, 229.
    (*Henry Co.*)—Henry Co., 164.
    (*King William*)—MMV, I, 277-278.
    (*Southampton*)—Bruce IV, 20; MMV, V, 108-111; Virkus I, 585.
Drinkard—Halifax, 159-160.
Drinkwater—Clemens' Wills, 29.
Drinnon—Pocahontas Co., 459-464.
Driscoll—Avery I, 146; Bruce IV, 214.
Driver—Bruce IV, 295-296; WM, VII, 237, 240, et seq.
Dromgoole—Southside Va., 17-19; TD, July 22, 1906.
Drone—Fishback Family, 107.
Drummond—Rockbridge, 483; TD, Feb. 22, 1914; WM, VI, 259; VII, 108.
    (*Accomac*)—Burgess, 65-67, 930; XXXIII, 29.
    (*James City Co.*)—Cyc. Va. Biog., I, 226; VM, XXII, 234.
    (*William*)—Cyc. Va. Biog., I, 226; VM, XVIII, 2-3.
Drumwright—TD, Dec. 25, 1904.
Dryden—Rockbridge, 483.
Du Bois—TD, July 31, 1904.
Duckwall—Miami Co., Ind., 581, 754.
Dudley—Bagby, 365, 373-375; Barton I, R11; Buckners of Virginia, 171; Burgess, 230-232, 236; Des Cognets, 54-55, 79; Garrard, 82-84, 87; Joseph C. Breckinridge (By E. D. Warfield, 1898), 10-13; Mackenzie V, 198-201; MMV, IV, 109-110; V, 112-114; Stubbs, 386-391; TD, Nov. 20, 1904; Dec. 4, 1910; July 16, 1911; VM, V, 209-210, 430; XXIII, 148-149; WM, XI, 141.
    (*Hanover*)—Whitaker, 229.
    (*King William*)—Bruce IV, 140.
    (*Richmond City*)—SBN, XI, 299.
Duerson—TD, June 16, 1907.
Duff—Burgess, 506; Monongahela II, 713-714; Rockbridge, 483.
Duffey—Avery I, 147.
Duffield—Highland Co., 380; Pocahontas Co., 451-454.
Dugger—Virkus III, 379.

Duke—Armstrong III, 34; Bruce IV, 50; Cyc. Va. Biog., IV, 136; Duke, etc., 257-395; Kennedy I, 471-472; Marshall, 178-183, 282-290; MMV, II, 100-102; Page (2d ed.), 229-230; RS, III, 2; TD, March 6, 1904; Tyler's VII, 213-214; Virkus II, 127; VM, VI, 319-320; VII, 400; X, 96; WM, II, 275; IX, 6.
 (*Albemarle*)—Albemarle, 181-182; Bruce V, 6-7.
 (*Berkeley*)—WVM, IV, 70-71.
Dulaney, Dulany—Shenandoah, 599-601; Something About the Dulaney (Dulany) Family; TD, July 12, 1908.
Dulany, Delaney (*Madison Co.*)—Virkus III, 536; VM, XXXV, 88.
Dulany (*From Maryland*)—Browning, R. D., 3d, 60-63; Ellis, 22; Mackenzie II, 46-47; Md. His. Mag., XIII, 157; MMV, I, 74-76.
Dulin—Braxton Co., W. Va., 372.
Dumas—Cartmell, 484.
Dumire, Domire—Tucker Co., W. Va., 392-397.
Dunbar—Kanawha, 957; Old King William, 40-41; TD, Jan. 28, Feb. 18, 1906.
 (*Frederick*)—Adams Co., Ohio, 730-733.
Duncan—DAR, 83, p. 50; Pittsylvania, 167.
 (*Western Va.*)—WVM, II, April, 1902, 74-76.
Duncanson—TD, Dec. 19, 1909; Feb. 6, 1910; VSR, V (No. 1), 22-28.
Dundas (*Alexandria*)—Browning, C. D., 3d, 201.
 (*Norfolk Co.*)—McIntosh I, 148.
Dunford—Burgess, 236-238.
Dunkum—Albemarle, 183.
Dunkle—Pendleton Co., 201, 320.
Dunlap—Alleghany, 198-199; Burgess, 241-243; Cartmell, 442; Monroe Co., 336-337; Rockbridge, 249-251, 483-484; WVM, III, 255-259.
 (*Augusta and Rockbridge*)—Virkus I, 281; II, 335-338; III, 499.
 (*King and Queen*)—Cyc. Va. Biog., I, 226.
Dunleavy—WM 2d, VI, 48.
Dunlop—Cyc. Va. Biog., I, 226; WM, VI, 6; VII, 69, 215; VIII, 61.
 (*Petersburg*)—Bruce IV, 379; Mackenzie I, 499; Magna Charta Barons, 442-444; MMV, V, 119; Virkus II, 220.
Dunn—Burgess, 240-241; Monroe Co., 337; Rockbridge, 484; TD, March 17, 1907.
 (*Augusta*)—Maxwell, 185-190, 206-224, 228-239.
 (*Miscellaneous*)—Stubbs, 377-386.
 (*Petersburg*)—Jones, 34.
 (*Washington Co.*)—Brock II, 717; MMV, III, 117-118.
Dunnavant—WM 2d, VI, 47.
Dunnington—Bruce V, 270; Monongahela II, 787-789.
Dunscombe—Cabell, etc., 277-278; Cyc. Va. Biog., I, 227; WM, VIII, 268.
Dunsmore—Cyc. Va. Biog., V, 814; MMV, II, 109-110; Monroe Co., 337-338.
Dunster—WM, VII, 222.
Dunton—Burgess, 451.
Dupree—DAR, 47, p. 119.
Du Puy—BS, Dec. 11, 1904.
Dupuy—Bruce V, 166; Douglas, 381; Goode, 173; Henry Co., 162-164; Huguenot Emigration, 151-182; Kith and Kin, 27-28, 37; Meade I, 467-468; Norfolk, 530-531; Southside Va., 150; TD, April 7, 1907; The Huguenot Bartholomew Dupuy, etc.;

Thomas Carter, 70-71; Va. His. Col. V (1886), 151-182; Virkus III, 134; Watkins, 25-26; Woodson, 48, 177, 276. 177, 276.
Durand—Cyc. Va. Biog., I, 226-227.
Durrett—Albemarle, 183-185.
Dustheimer—Licking Co., Ohio, 654.
Dutton—Brock II, 718.
Du Val—LCJ, Aug. 2, 1914, p. 15.
   (Md. and Henrico)—DAR, 70, p. 250.
Duval—Arkansas, 140-143; Cyc. Va. Biog., II, 249; Des Cognets, 96-99; Huguenot Emigration, 31; Kennedy II, 272; Knox Co., Ill., 272; Robertson, 43; SBN, XI, 306-308; TD, July 8, 1906; Jan. 22, 1911; VM, XIII, 224; WM, VIII, 269.
Duvall—Bruce V, 133; Cyc. Va. Biog., I, 227; WM, XX, 110.
Dwire—Burgess, 215.
Dye—Monongahela II, 860-861; Ritchie Co., 60-61.
Dyer—Albemarle, 185-186; Alleghany, 200; Barbour Co., W. Va., 378; Henry Co., 160-162; Highland Co., 357; Pendleton Co., 201-203.
   (Albemarle)—Albemarle, 185-186; Lancaster, 417-419; Virkus III, 383.
Dykes—Cyc. Va. Biog., I, 227; WM, V, 186.
Dymoke—Thomas Carter, 26-35.
Dyson *(Nottoway)*—Southside Va., 92,158.

E

Eaches—Old Alexandria, 321.
Eades—Albemarle, 186.
Eagle—Highland Co., 281-282.
Eakin—Rockbridge, 484.
Earle—Cartmell, 445; Habersham Chap. II, 406-408; History and Genealogy of the Earles of Secaucus, etc., by Rev. Isaac Earle (Marquette, Mich.), 69, 72-82, 99-111, 253-254; Mackenzie II, 238-240; VI, 209-210; Montague, 192-193, 323-325, 385-386; Munsell's VII, 65; XI, 100; TD, Aug. 11, 1907; Virkus II, 28, 208, 291; III, 244.
   (Clarke)—Randolph Co., 341-342.
   (Frederick and S. C.)—Earle, 110-114, 116-121, 181.
Early—Albemarle, 187-188; Bruce IV, 373; VI, 175; Buford, 263-269; Cabell, etc., 548-549; Campbell Co., 197-202, 404-408; Convention 1788, II, 371; Cyc. Va. Biog., IV, 114-115; "Early in America"; "Family of Early Which Settled on the Eastern Shore"; Hampden-Sidney, 71; Rives, 523; TD, June 11, July 2, Aug. 27, 1905; Dec. 10, 1916; Virkus III, 442; VM, XIX, 198.
   (Bedford)—DAR, 81, p. 80.
Earnest—Bruce IV, 157.
Easley—Bell, 29; Bruce IV, 512; Cyc. Va. Biog., V, 663; Halifax, 160-169, 293-294; MMV, I, 82-83; TD, Jan. 22, 1905; Virkus I, 586.
East—Bruce V, 563; Burgess, 179; Cyc. Va. Biog., IV, 479; TD, May 12, 1907.
Easter—SBN, XI, 311.
Easton—DAR, 74, p. 109.
Eastwood—Burgess, 179-180.
   (Norfolk Co.)—McIntosh I, 137.

Eaton—Baskerville Family, 99, 101-115, 994; Cyc. Va. Biog., I, 227; Rockbridge, 484; TD, June 23, 1907; Virkus I, 729, 803; VSR, V (No. 2), 47.
Eberly—MMV, II, 113.
Eberman—Pendleton Co., 320; Randolph Co., 342.
Ebert—Cartmell, 484-485.
Eccles—Johnson Co., Ind., 606.
Echols—MMV, I, 114-116; V, 124-133; Rockbridge, 251-252, 484.
    (*Halifax*)—Monroe Co., 338-340.
Eckard—Highland Co., 357; Pendleton Co., 203-204.
Eddins—Lewis, 299; Virkus III, 502.
Edgar—Montgomery Co., Ohio, 165; Monroe Co., W. Va., 340-341.
Edington—Rockbridge, 484.
Edins—Hardin Co., Ohio, 922.
Edley—Rockbridge, 484.
Edloe (Edlow)—Armistead, 277; Cyc. Va. Biog., I, 228; Hening VI, 297-299; TD, Jan. 4, Feb. 22, 1914; VM, V, 96-97; VI, 404-405; VSR, II (No. 2), 52; IV (No. 2), 39; WM, VI, 29-30; VII, 54; VIII, 113-114; XV, 282-283; XVI, 141.
Edmiston—DAR, 46, p. 73; Pocahontas Co., 168-175, 439-442.
Edmond—Highland Co., 380.
Edmonds (*Fauquier*)—Burgess, 181; VM, XXIII, 103, 216-217.
    (*Lancaster*)—Bruce V, 365.
Edmondson, Edmiston—King's Mountain, 402-408.
Edmondson, Edmondston, Edmiston—Dunmore's War, 84.
Edmondson—Rockbridge, 252, 484; TD, Dec. 14, 1913.
    (*Augusta*)—DAR, 48, p. 237.
    (*Frederick*)—Cartmell, 490.
    (*Halifax*)—Brock II, 621; Halifax, 169-170; Monongahela II, 636-638.
Edmunds—Convention 1788, II, 381; Dupuy, 215-218; Halifax, 171-172 (for "Littlejohn" read "Littleton"); Huguenot Emigration, 156-157; St. Mark's, 140; Watkins, 32.
    (*Lancaster*)—Hardy, 52.
    (*Surry*)—Mackenzie V, 447; VM, XXXII, 59; VSR, V (No. 1), 78.
    (*Surry, etc.*)—Cyc. Va. Biog., I, 228; Virkus III, 241; VSR, V (No. 1), 28-58.
Edmundson (*Essex*)—Cyc. Va. Biog., I, 228; Tyler's VII, 185-191, 263-264.
    (*Halifax*)—Halifax, 294.
    (*Lunenburg*)—Old Free State II, 210-213.
Edrington—Hayden, 252; Munsell's VII, 238.
Edwards—BS, Oct. 30, Nov. 6, 1904; Culpeper, 67-68; Cyc. Va. Biog., V, 925; Marshall, 122; TD, Dec. 23, 1906.
    (*Ambrose*)—DAR, 70, p. 212.
    (*Brunswick*)—Cyc. Va. Biog., I, 228.
    (*James City*)—VSR. IV (No. 1), 34-35.
    (*Jefferson Co.*)—DAR, 81, p. 81.
    (*King William*)—Old King William, 115-194.
    (*Lancaster*)—Hayden, 98-99; Norfolk, 622-625; VM, V, 259-260.
    (*Louisa*)—Old King William, 112-114.
    (*Norfolk*)—Cyc. Va. Biog., IV, 361.
    (*Northern Neck*)—"Historic Sketches of the Edwards and Todd Families."
    (*Northumberland*)—Brock II, 668; Browning, R. D., III, 767.
    (*Stafford*)—Garrard, 44-54; Hardy, 241; SBN, XI, 312-314.

Estill, Estell, Estelle, Estil—TD, April 21, 1907; Dec. 20, 27, 1914; Jan. 3, 1915.

Estill—Alleghany, 200-201; Highland Co., 381; Monroe Co., 342; Peyton, 292; Rockbridge, 252-253; Waddell's Annals of Augusta Co., 321.

Etheridge—McIntosh II, 88, 162, 164-165, 194, 231, 285-286, 302; Norfolk, 649, 672, 783; VM, XXVI, 409.

Eubank—Albemarle, 188-189; Bagby, 305-306, 365; Bruce V, 432; VI, 12; Ellis, 20-21.

Eustace—Hayden, 261, 271-272, 277-278; Kennedy II, 410; VM, XXXIV, 346-347; WM, XI, 209-210.

Evans—Bruce V, 331; Knox Co., Ill., 563; Licking Co., Ohio, 663; Monroe Co., W. Va., 343; Rockbridge, 484; WM, VII, 245.

   (*Berkeley*)—Berkeley, 194-195, 427; DAR, 41, p. 67.

   (*Campbell*)—Campbell Co., 408-410.

   (*Monongalia*)—DAR, 81, p. 86; Monongahela II, 484-486; III, 1316-1321; Virkus III, 560.

   (Peter)—Virkus II, 380.

   (*Loudoun*)—Clemens' Wills, 32-33; DAR, 76, p. 203.

Evelyn—Browning, R. D., III, XXIII; TD, Dec. 22, 1907; VM, VII, 296-297; IX, 172-173; WM, X, 172.

Everard—Cyc. Va. Biog., I, 231; Funsten-Meade, 28-29; N. E. His. and Gen. Reg., XXXVIII, 166; Sir Richard Everard, etc., by Marshall Delancey Heyward, Pub. So. His. Asso., Vol. 2; VSR, V (No. 2), 51; WM, IX, 123.

Everett—Albemarle, 189-190; Bruce V, 222; Crawfurdiana, 79-80; RS, IV, 5.

Everhart—Coshocton Co., Ohio, 579.

Everette (*Southampton*)—Cyc. Va. Biog., IV, 366.

Everly—Cartmell, 490; Preston Co., 428.

Evick—Hardin Co., Ohio, 1000; Highland Co., 357; Pendleton Co., 204-205.

Ewell—Cyc. Va. Biog., I, 231; Hayden, 331-334; Hord (1898), 107-108; LCJ, Aug. 23, 1914 (p. 9); Mackenzie V, 202-206; MMV, III, 127-128; WM, IV, 41; XII, 177.

   (*Eastern Shore*)—VM, XI, 313.

   (*Princess Anne*)—Bruce IV, 425.

Ewell (Yowell)—WM, IV, 41.

Ewers (*Loudoun and Hampshire*)—Hampshire, 705.

Ewing—Clan Ewing; Dunmore's War, 423; Monroe Co., 343; Ewing Family and Cognate Branches; Ewing Family Chart; Hardesty (*Bedford*), 1417; McGavock Family, 24-26, 40, 58-59, 90, 112-113, 157-158; Pocahontas Co., 616-617; Rockbridge, 484; VM, IX, 215-216; WVM, IV, 203-213.

Exline—Coshocton Co., Ohio, 676; Virkus III, 182.

Exum—Valentine I, 430-449; WM, VII, 253-254, 264; XXVII, 57-58.

Eye—Highland Co., 357; Pendleton Co., 205-207.

Eyre—ARP, II, 485; Cyc. Va. Biog., I, 231; Md. Soc. Col. Wars, 22; Meade I, 259; VM, VI, 418; XIX, 421-422.

Eyres (Eyre)—Cyc. Va. Biog., I, 231.

Eyster—Bruce V, 555.

Ezekiel—SBN, XI, 331.

F

Face—Burgess, 560-561.

Fadeley—Avery I, 149.

Fagg—Albemarle, 190-191.

Fairburn—Funk, 234.
Fairchild (Westmoreland)—Johnson Co., Ky., 222.
Fairfax (*England and Virginia*)—Herald and Genealogist, London, 1863, Vol. IV, 44; VI, 385-507, 604-630; Proprietors of the Northern Neck, Chapters of Culpeper Genealogy (1926); Sally Cary, by W. M. Cary (New York, 1916); Slaughter's Life of Randolph Fairfax (1878), 62-66; The Fairfaxes of England and America in the Seventeenth and Eighteenth Centuries, by E. D. Neil, Albany, N. Y., 1868; VM, IV, 102-104; VIII, 11-15; IX, 108-109; XI, 212-214; XXXIII, 113-153, 223-267, 333-358; XXXIV, 19-64, 181; America Heraldica, 165; ARP, II, 641, 649; Browning, C. D., 166-167; Browning, C. D., 3d, 222-225; Carlyle, 17-18, 29; Cyc. Va. Biog., I, 231-232; Dinwiddie Papers, I, 19-20; Du Bellet II, 165-186; Funsten-Meade, IV, 30-32, 44, with chart; Goode, 114, 378, 456; Kennedy I, 285; Lee, 147-148; Lineage Book, Order of Washington, 115-116; Mackenzie II, 264-283; Magna Charta Barons, 153-154; Meade II, 106-110; New York Gen. and Biog. Record, XXIV, 3; Preston Co., W. Va., 344, 420; RS, IV, 20; TD, Nov. 29, 1903; Dec. 15, 1907; Thomas, 303-312; Virkus II, 380; III, 608; WM, II, 151; III, 266; VII, 60; XVIII, 210-211; WVM, Vol. II (Jan. 1902), 9-19.
(*Barons*)—Burke's Peerage and Baronetage (1904), 587-588.
(*From Maryland*)—Browning, C. D., 3d, 304; Cartmell, 118, 248-249; Lindsay, 110-113; MMV, I, 48-50; IV, 115-118; Munsell's V, 114.
(*John*)—An Historic Sketch of the Two Fairfax Families in Virginia (New York, 1913), 25-26; Cartmell, 134-136, 244-247, 275.
(*Prince William*)—Du Bellet II, 188-190; McIlhany, 245-247.
Faison—Bruce V, 449; Virkus III, 596.
Farant—Cyc. Va. Biog., IV, 502.
Farinholt—Bruce IV, 127.
Faris (*West Va.*)—Virkus III, 199.
Faris (Farris)—Rockbridge, 484.
Farish—Bruce IV, 42; Kith and Kin, 47-48, 56.
(*Albemarle and Caroline*)—Albemarle, 191-192; Burgess, 1111.
Farley—Monroe Co., 454; Old Free State II, 147; RS, II, 14, 44; Stubbs, 481; VM, IX, 213; XX, 178-179; WM, III, 166.
(*Archer's Hope*)—Cyc. Va. Biog., I, 232; VM, XXX, 265.
Farlow—Cyc. Va. Biog., I, 232.
Farmbrough—Monroe Co., 343.
Farmer—Cyc. Va. Biog., I, 232; DAR, 46, p. 327; Halifax, 295-296.
Farnefold—Cyc. Va. Biog., 232; VM, XXII, 399-400; XXVIII, 131.
Farrar—Albemarle, 192; Cyc. Va. Biog., I, 232-233; Douglas, 63 (Ferrer); RS; TD, Feb. 22, 1914; Virkus II, 42; III, 481; VM, I, 419; III, 359-361; VII, 69, 319-322, 432-434; VIII, 97-98, 206-209, 424-427; IX, 203-205, 322-324; X, 86-87, 206-207, 308-310; XIX, 429-430; XXVIII, 219.
Farrell—Cyc. Va. Biog., I, 233; VM, IV, 146; WM, IV, 5; V, 77, 80-81.
Farrier—Bruce VI, 596.
Farris—BS, Jan. 22, 1905.
Farrow—Burgess, 374; Cyc. Va. Biog., II, 284; DAR, 55, p. 114; SBN, XI, 337-338; VM, XXXIV, 346.
Fassaker, Fossaker—VM, XV, 178.
Fatherly—Bruce VI, 512.

Faucett—Burgess, 783.
Faulcon—Cyc. Va. Biog., I, 233; VM; XXXIV, 227-228.
Faulconer—Bruce V, 298.
Faulkner—Bruce V, 160.
   (*Berkeley*)—Berkeley Co., 169-174, 196-198, 202; Cartmell, 467-468.
   (*Essex*)—MMV, V, 144-145.
   (*Frederick, from Md.*)—VSR, IV (No. 4), 26.
   (*Halifax*)—Halifax, 173-176; MMV, III, 131-132; V, 144-145.
   (*Mecklenburg*)—Bruce IV, 85-86.
   (*Valley of Va.*)—SBN, XI, 338-339.
   (*Winchester*)—Cartmell, 496.
Fauntleroy—Bagby, 332-334, 365; Browning, C. D., 142-144; Browning, R. D., III, 766-772; BS, Jan. 8, 1905; Campbell Co., 399-401; Cartmell, 450-451; Cyc. Va. Biog., I, 233; De Bow's Review, XXXVI; Du Bellet III, 147-148, 184-185; IV, 294-300; Hayden, 96, 110-111; Magna Charta Barons, 135-136; Meade II, 478-481; "Mordecai Cooke", 31; Roger Jones, 167-181; SBN, XI, 339-340; TD, April 29, May 13, 27 (correction), 1906; Jan. 31, Feb. 21, 1909; Va. His. Mag., edited by Jefferson Wallace (July, 1891), 1-18; Virkus I, 106; III, 87; VM, XV, 215, 436; XXXII, 128-129; XXXV, 204-205; VSR, V (No. 2), 27; WM, II, 272.
Fauquier—WM, VIII, 171.
Faure, Fore—Crozier VII, 161-165; WM, XX, 67.
Fawdoin (Fawdown)—Cyc. Va. Biog., I, 233.
Fawdon—VM, XXIX, 297; WM, VII, 215, et seq.
Fawcett (Fossett)—Cyc. Va. Biog., I, 233.
Fawcett—Cartmell, 494; Prseton Co., 345, 428.
Fayson—Tyler's VI, 270-271.
Fearn—Cisco, 113, 124-126; Habersham Chap. II, 569-570; McAllister, 272-279.
Featherston (*Lynchburg*)—Floyd, 68-69; Hardesty (*Bedford*), 417; Jones, 187.
Feild—Armistead, 246-247; Bristol Parish, 173-174; Brock II, 641-642; Cyc. Va. Biog., I, 233-234; Goode, 244; Keith, Addendum I.
   (*Henrico*)—VM, IV, 10-11; W M 2d, IX, 144-147.
   (*Peter*)—Researcher I, 33; Tyler's VII, 53-54; VSR, IV (No. 1), 31.
Felgate—Cyc. Va. Biog., I, 234; RC, II, 45; TD, Nov. 10, 1907; VM, II, 181-182; XIX, 400; XXIX, 297; WM, I, 83.
Felton—Barbour Co., W. Va., 382.
Fenn—Winston, 307.
Fenter—Rockbridge, 485.
Fentress—Bruce VI, 463; MMV, V, 148-149; Norfolk, 638-639, 696-699.
Fenwick (*Lower Norfolk*)—Fenwick Allied Ancestry, 26-27; McIntosh I, 69-70.
Ferebee—McIntosh II, 318-319; Researcher I, 193-194, 252.
Fergus—Miami Co., Ohio, 633.
Ferguson—Bruce VI, 117, 415; Randolph Co., 343-344; Sangamon Co., Ill., 295.
Fern (*Isle of Wight*)—VM, VI, 39-41.
Fernyhough—Cauthorn, 14.
Ferrer—Neill's Virginia Carolorum, 42.
Ferrel—Bruce IV, 490.
Ferrell—Brock II, 640; Bruce V, 174; VI, 385.
   (*Bedford*)—Bell, 96.
Ferris—Valentine I, 450-459; VSR, IV (No. 1), 39.

Fetherngill—Johnson Co., Ind., 607.

Fetterlock—TD, April 19, 1908; March 19, 1911; June 22, 1913.

Ficklen—Bruce VI, 389; Du Bellet III, 167; TD, Jan. 24, 1907; Virkus I, 598.

Ficklin—Albemarle, 192; Bruce V, 241; Ficklin Family, etc.; Virkus III, 167.

Field, Feild—Record of all the Field Family in America whose ancestors were in the country prior to 1700.

Field—Dunmore's War, 113-114; Records of all the Field Family, etc.; Tazewell II, 380-381; TD, Nov. 11, 1906; June 29, 1913; Woods-McAfee, 298-299.

 (*Albemarle*)—Albemarle, 194.

 (*Augusta*)—Preston Co., 346-347, 429.

 (*Culpeper*)—Culpeper, 57-58; part 2, 143; St. Mark's, 130-132; Virkus III, 126.

 (*Gloucester*)—Burgess, 1114; Roger Jones, 100-101; Two Families, 121.

 (*Kin gand Queen*)—C ooke-Booth, 200-204; WM, VII, 92.

 (*Petersburg*)—WM, XIV, 113.

Fielding, Feilding—WM, XVIII, 243-251.

Fielding (*King and Queen*)—WM, IX, 264.

 (*Northumberland*)—Cyc. Va. Biog., I, 234; Thomas Carter, 155-158; VM, XI, 453-456; XII, 99-102, 214-215; XIV, 205-207; WM, IX, 264-265; XVIII, 243-246, 248-251.

Fields—Tazewell II, 380-381.

Fife—VM, XI, 204-205; XXVII, 174.

Figgatt—Jones, 190-191.

Filbrun—Miami Co., Ohio, 633.

Filmer—Cyc. Va. Biog., I, 234; Mackenzie IV, 173-174; VM, XV, 181-182; XXI, 153-154; XXIV, 158-162; XXV, 327-328; XXIX, 347.

Finch—Cyc. Va. Biog., IV, 157; V, 1094; Goode, 331-332; TD, Sept. 17, 1905.

 (*Charles City*)—WM, XVI, 140.

Fink—Kanawha, 790; Rockbridge, 485; Tucker Co., 406.

Finkle—Quisenberry, 138-154.|

Finley—Burgess, 1123; Marshall, 160; Rockbridge, 485; TD, Jan. 12, 1908.

Finnell—Monongahela, 558-560.

Finney—Henry Co., 176-178; VM, IV, 216; VSR, V (No. 1), 70.

 (*Amelia*)—Watkins, 39.

 (*Henrico*)—Huguenot Emigration, 78; VM, XII, 26.

 (*West Va.*)—Kanawha, 696.

Finnie—DAR, 70, p. 22.

Firebaugh—Bruce V, 419.

Firestone—Rockbridge, 485; Virkus III, 189.

Firth—TD, June 23, 1907.

Fishback—Adams Co., Ohio, 178-179; Bruce IV, 500; Cyc. Va. Biog., I, 234; Genealogy of the Fishback Family in America, by W. M. Kemper (New York, 1914); Hardy, 212-216; VM, XXXIV, 153-157.

Fishburne—Bruce IV, 55; VI, 178; MMV, II, 116-117.

Fisher—Braxton Co., W. Va., 378-379; Burgess, 99-104; Pendleton Co., 320-321; RS, II, 2; TD, June 2, 1907; May 10, 1914.

 (*Augusta*)—Tucker Co., 407.

 (*Campbell*)—Bell, 77.

 (*Eastern Shore*)—Bruce VI, 512; Burgess, 99-104; Hening VIII, 440-442.

(*Fauquier*)—VM, XXIII, 308-309.
(*Franklin Co.*)—Miami Co., Ind., 688-690.
(*Highland*)—Highland Co., 284.
(*Richmond City*)—Du Bellet, I, 51-52, 94-97, 99, 202-205; II, 752-812; McIlhany, 28-29; WM, XVII, 100-139, 148-176.
(*Shenandoah*)—Bruce IV, 195.
Fitch—Albemarle, 194; TD, Feb. 25, 1906.
Fitchett—Burgess, 16.
Fitzgerald—Bruce IV, 188; BS, Jan. 8, 1905; Hardy, 217-218; Montgomery Co., Ohio, 312; Pittsylvania, 172; TD, May 19, 1907; Whitaker, 124.
(*Amelia*)—Habersham Chap. II, 450.
(*Buckingham*)—Bruce IV, 253.
(*Nottoway*)—Southside Va., 97, 160-162.
(*Pittsylvania*)—The Nowlin-Stone Genealogy, 491-507.
(*Prince Edward*)—Cabell, etc., 358.
Fitzhugh—America Heraldica, 143; ARP, II, 755-758; Bruce IV, 29; V, 465; BS, Dec. 17, 24, 1905; Burgess, 210, 246, 947; Carter Family Tree; Cooke-Booth, 210-211, 246; Crozier, VII, 108-111; Crozier's Va. County Records VI, 298-299; Culpeper, 109; Cyc. Va. Biog., I, 324-326; II, 9; De Bow's Review, XXVI, 133; Du Bellet I, 201; II, 551-580; Funsten-Meade, 33-34; Habersham Chap. II, 110-111; Hardy, 219-237; Hayden, 87, 263; Lancaster, 349-354; Lee, 89-90; Life of George Mason (Rowland), I, 377; Mackenzie I, 70-71, 365-366; II, 297; Md. Soc. Col. Wars, 110; Meade II, 192; MMV, IV, 119-120; RS, II, 30, 51; TD, Aug. 30, 1903; Oct. 24, 1909; Thomas, 315-316; Thomas Carter, 349; Two Families, 34-35, 140-141, 145-146; Virkus I, 603-604; II, 115, 213; III, 190-191; VM, I, 411-415; II, 276-280; IV, 467-468; VII, 196-199, 317-319, 425-427; VIII, 91-95, 209-211, 314-317, 430-432; IX, 99-104, 208, 431; XV, 7; XIX, 96, 446; XXIX, 105-107; XXX, 20; Welles' Washington Genealogy, 252; WM, I, 20; II, 22; III, 68, 141-142, 199; V, 142.
Fitzpatrick—Burgess, 121; Cabell, etc., 605-606; DAR, 81, p. 164; Monroe Co., 343.
FitzRandolph—Monongahela III, 926-928.
Flanagan—Bruce IV, 318; Burgess, 892.
Flanary—Bruce IV, 508.
Flannagan—Bruce IV, 128; VI, 351.
Fleece—Burgess, 105-107.
Fleenor—Brock II, 719-720.
Fleet—Bagby, 307, 334-335, 357, 361; Browning, R. D., III, 821; Cyc. Va. Biog., I, 236-237; II, 365; Hayden, 234-235; Magna Charta Barons, 328-335; Montague, 315-317, 384; Munsell's IX, 233; RC, II, 44; III, 13; TD, Feb. 11, 1912; VM, II, 71-76; V, 253-254; XXIII (royal descent), 429-430; XXVI, 309; XXVII, 77; XXVIII, 342-343; XXX, 365.
Fleete—Convention 1788, II, 377.
Fleischmann (Fleshman, Fleishman)—WM, XXVI, 183-185.
Fleisher—Highland Co., 284-285.
Fleming—Bolling Gen., 25; Bruce V, 73; Cyc. Va. Biog., I, 236; Du Bellet II, 403-416; Goode, 211; Marshall, 337; Lancaster, 181-182; Rockbridge, 485; TD, March 27, 1904; April 9, 1911.

(*Botetourt*)—Convention 1788, II, 40-54; Dinwiddie Papers II, 335-336; Dunmore's War, 428-429; History of the Battle of Pt. Pleasant, 25; Peyton, 344-345; VM, V, 260-268.

(*Charles*)—RS, II, 20, 23; IV, 1; VM, X, 11-12.
(*Cumberland, etc.*)—Robertson, 32-34, 38, 50.
(*Hanover*)—Du Bellet I, 147.
(*Highland*)—Highland Co., 286.
(*Monongalia*)—Virkus III, 85.
(*New Kent*)—Mackenzie II, 137; VM, XXIII, 214-216, 325-326, 441-443; XXIV, 94-97, 206-210, 327-333, 440-443; XXV, 211; WM, XII, 45-47.
(*West Va.*)—Monongahela II, 401-426.
Flemmens—Pocahontas Co., 274-278.
Fleshman—Monroe Co., 343-344.
Fletcher—Bruce VI, 103; Cyc. Va. Biog., V, 732; Southside Va., 97, 162-163; TD, March 8, 1908.
(*Charlotte*)—Hord (1898), 70, 71, 321.
(*Fauquier*)—Bruce IV, 149, 420-421; VI, 103.
(*Rockbridge*)—Rockbridge, 485; Sangamon Co., Ill., 299-302.
Flinn—Hardin Co., Ohio, 1056; Pendleton Co., 321.
Flint—Cyc. Va. Biog., I, 237; Monroe Co., 344; Rockbridge, 485.
Flinton—Cyc. Va. Biog., I, 237.
Flippin—Bruce VI, 445.
Flippo—Bruce V, 405.
Flood—Bruce VI, 313; Cyc. Va. Biog., I, 237; MMV, II, 118-120; TD, Oct. 12, 1913; Virkus III, 167; VSR, V (No. 1), 41; WM, VII, 232.
(*Surry*)—WM, XVI, 224-226.
Flory—Bruce IV, 270, 331; Cyc. Va. Biog., V, 691.
Flournoy—Brock II, 782; Buckners of Va., 23; Cabell, etc., 354-364; Cyc. Va. Biog., II, 237; Dupuy, 217; Halifax, 176-178; Hampshire, 706; Kanawha, 792-795; LCJ, July 11, 1915 (II, 5); RS, I, 37; III, 14; TD, May 16, 1909; VM, I, 469; II, 81-90, 190-213, 318-327, 437-447; III, 67-79, 414-416; IV, 97-101; Walker-Wigton, 159-160; Watkins, 20; WM, XVI, 283-284.
(*Prince Edward*)—Venables of Va., 195-197.
Flowers—DAR, 56, p. 243.
Floyd—Adams Co., Ohio, 338; Brock I, 156-164, 217-219; Campbell Co., 410-412; Carter Family Tree; Cyc. Va. Biog., I, 237; Dunmore's War, 9; Floyd's Biographical Genealogies of the Va.-Kentucky Families; Floyd's Hart Family; Hardesty, 367-368; Highland Co., 381; History of Camden County, Ga., by T. Vocelle (1914), 71-74; LEP, April 12, 19, 1919, pp. 6, 15; Life and Diary of John Floyd, by C. H. Ambler (Richmond, Va., 1918), 9-32; Louisville's First Families, 153-176; MMV, II, 209-211; Preston Family, by W. B. Preston, 189-190; RS, II, 7; SBN, XI, 351-353; TD, May 7, July 16, 30, Sept. 10, Oct. 15, 1905; Nov. 24, Dec. 29, 1907; May 2, 1909; VM, VII, 16; Waddell's Annals of Augusta Co., 219.
Foley—Bruce IV, 334; Sangamon Co., Ill., 304.
Foliott, Folliott—WM, I, 213.
Folkes—Brock II, 566; TD, Sept. 10, 24, 1911.
Folks—Highland Co., 286.
Folliott—ARP, II, 801; Cyc. Va. Biog., I, 237; VM, XVI, 93.
Fontaine—Cooke-Booth, 265-268; Culpeper, 39-41, 75-76; Cyc. Va. Biog., I, 237-238; IV, 78; Dinwiddie Papers II, 589 (Fontain); Du Bellet II, 215; IV, 384-388; Halifax, 296-297; Henry Co., 174-176; Huguenot Emigration, 119-150; Kanawha, 592-593; Kennedy I, 633-684; LEP, Feb. 15, 1919;

Meade I, 465; Memoirs of a Huguenot Family; MMV, V, 150-151; Old King William, 51-54; Patrick Henry II, 634-635; Stubbs, 293-297; TD, Aug. 9, 1903; July 18, 1909; April 3, 1910; Valentine I, 460-485; Virkus III, 140, 407; VM, III, 432; VI, 208, 305-307; XXII, 195-197; VSR, IV (No. 1), 42; WM, XIX, 180-181.

Foote—Cyc. Va. Biog., I, 238; Foote Family, Vol. I, 552-555; Hardy, 9-10; Hayden, 303; Hord (1898), 82-83; Lewis, 45-46; McAllister, 123-124; Old Prince William I, 193; SBN, XI, 354-356; VM, II, 269-270; VII, 73-75, 201-203; XXX, 393-394.

Forbes—Culpeper, 80; WM, XII, 216-217.

    (*Dumries*)—Willis, 79.

    (*Fredericksburg*)—Life of Gen. Hugh Mercer, 118-119.

Ford—Bruce IV, 343; Cyc. Va. Biog., I, 238; V, 935; Henry Co., 173-174; Monongahela, III, 1071-1072; Rockbridge, 485.

    (*Fauquier*)—Sangamon Co., Ill., 304.

    (*Prince Edward*)—Bruce IV, 139.

Ford (Foard) (*Nottoway*)—WM 2d, VI, 248-249.

Forehand—Rockbridge, 485.

Foreman—Barbour Co., W. Va., 385; Cartmell, 495.

    (*Norfolk Co.*)—Bruce VI, 157; Cyc. Va. Biog., IV, 236; McIntosh I, 123; II, 33-34, 125-126.

Forest—TD, Sept. 25, 1906.

Forman—Marshall, 229-233.

    (*Nansemond*)—N. C. His. Reg., I, 544.

Forrest—LCJ, Feb. 21, 1915 (II, 5); RS, III, 37; TD, July 14, 1912.

Forsyth—RS, III, 23.

    (*Spotsylvania*)—Forsyth of Nydie, etc. By Forsyth de Fronsac, New Market, Va., 1888, 19-21.

Forsythe—Rockbridge, 485; TD, Sept. 30, 1903.

Fortune—Bruce IV, 363; Sangamon Co., Ill., 306.

Fortune (Forchan)—Rockbridge, 485.

Foscue—TD, July 12, Sept. 13, 1914.

Fossaker—Cyc. Va. Biog., I, 238.

Foster—Coshocton Co., Ohio, 502; Rockbridge, 485.

    (*Culpeper*)—Monroe Co., 344.

    (*Fairfax*)—Stubbs, 366-367.

    (*Louisa*)—Sangamon Co., Ill., 309.

    (*Lower Norfolk*)—Virkus III, 496.

    (*Mathews*)—Cyc. Va. Biog., I, 238; MMV, I, 56-57; WM, II, 217-218.

    (*Westmoreland*)—DAR, 83, p. 25.

Foulke—Hayden, 658.

Foulks—Draper Series V, 151-152.

Fourqurean—Halifax, 178-179; Huguenot Emigration, 33.

Foushee—VM, VII, 239.

Foutch, Fouche (*Loudoun*)—Sangamon Co., Ill., 310.

Foutz—Rockbridge, 485.

Fowke (Fouke)—America Heraldica, 117; ARP, II, 805; BS, Sept. 17, 1905; Cyc. Va. Biog., I, 238-239; Dinwiddie Papers I, XXIV, XXV; Hayden, 154-161, 743-745; Mackenzie V, 314-315; Meade II, 482; MHM, XVI, 1-19; Munsell's VI, 137; Old King William, 55; RC, III, 18; Southern Bivouac (1886), 727; TD, Dec. 20, 1903; VM, III, 322-323; XXIV, 386; XXIX, 347-349; VSR, V (No. 2), 45-46.

Fowkes—Sangamon Co., Ill., 311.

Fowle—Avery I, 55-57; Old Alexandria, 322.

Fowler—Annals of the Fowler Family; Brock II, 721; Cyc. Va. Biog., I, 230; Rockbridge, 485; Sangamon Co., Ill., 312.
Fowlkes—Southside Va., 98, 163-164.
Fox—Hayden, 21; Rives, 514; RS, III, 23; TD, Nov. 5, 19, 1905; July 16, 1911; Virkus II, 340.
  (*Brunswick*)—DAR, 56, p. 7.
  (*Gloucester*)—Cooke-Booth, 231-237; Cyc. Va. Biog., I, 239; Lewis, 48-49; McAllister, 113; Winston, 310; WM, III, 33-34, 168, 183, 184.
  (*Highland*)—Highland Co., 286-287.
  (*King William*)—Cyc. Va. Biog., I, 239; VM, VIII, 382-385; Winston, 310-314; WM, XVII, 303-304; XX, 262-266; XXVI, 129-138.
  (*Lancaster*)—Barton I, R23; II, 195-196; Cyc. Va. Biog., I, 239; Hayden, 60-61; Mackenzie II, 39; RS, II, 17; WM, VIII, 108-109; XVII, 59-63.
  (*Nelson*)—Braxton Co., W. Va., 376-377.
Foxall (Foxhall)—VM, XIV, 301-302.
Foxhall—VM, XXX, 40.
Frail—Highland Co., 381.
Frame—ARP, I, 287; Braxton Co., W. Va., 377.
France—Bruce IV, 28.
Francis—Bruce IV, 495; Cyc. Va. Biog., I, 240.
Francisco—Stubbs, 198-199; The Romantic Record of Peter Francisco (Porter and Albertson), 1929, pp. 91-103; Tyler's VII, 288; WM, XIII, 217-219; XIV, 6-8, 107-111.
  (*Peter*)—Cyc. Va. Biog., II, 278.
  (*Valley of Va.*)—VM, XIV, 123.
Franklin—Hayden, 658; TD, Oct. 30, Nov. 13, 1904.
  (*Campbell*)—Campbell Co., 412-414.
  (*Orange*)—King's Mountain, 458-459.
Fravel—Bruce IV, 112; Hampshire, 706.
Fray—Bruce VI, 199.
Frayser—Virkus I, 562.
Frazer (Fraser)—Burgess, 1104.
Frazer—Kanawha, 485.
Frazier—Bruce IV, 412; Rockbridge, 485.
  (*Augusta*)—Virkus I, 215-216; III, 197.
  (*Giles*)—Bruce VI, 321.
Freeman—TD, July 10, 1910; Aug. 28, 1912; Virkus III, 182-183.
  (*Bridges*)—Old King William, 57.
  (*Culpeper*)—Culpeper, 13.
  (*James City*)—VM, IV, 422.
  (*York*)—WM, II, 164-165; Virkus I, 916; III, 428.
Freis—Cartmell, 472.
French—Crockett, 230-233; Halifax, 180-184; New River, 402-405; SBN, XI, 367; TD, Sept. 4, 18, Oct. 30, 1904; Jan. 22, 1905; Virkus II, 142; VM, II, 340; VSR, V (No. 2), 28.
  (*Fredericksburg*)—VM, XI, 334.
  (*Giles*)—Bruce V, 488.
  (*King George*)—WM, XII, 269-270.
  (*Richmond Co.*)—Cyc. Va. Biog., I. 240; WM, XII, 271.
  (*Spotsylvania*)—Life of Gen. Hugh Mercer, 126-127; VM, II, 340.
  (*Westmoreland*)—DAR, 81, p. 93.
Fretwell—Albemarle, 195.
Friel—Pocahontas Co., 175-186.
Friend—Braxton Co., W. Va., 378; Bruce VI, 460; Pendleton Co., 321; Randolph Co., 343; Thos. Carter, 82-83.
  (*Chesterfield*)—TD, Aug. 27, Sept. 24, 1911.

Fritts—Bruce V, 327.
Frogg—DAR, 44, p. 139; Dunmore's War, 280-281.
Froman—Cartmell, 262-263.
Frush—Rockbridge, 485.
Fry (Frye)—Brock II, 782; Culpeper, 58-59; Dinwiddie Papers I, 7-8; Goode, 119; Green's Ky. Families, 152-154; Lewis, 296; Licking Co., Ohio, 667; Marshall, 124; Meade I, 405; MMV, IV, 132-133; Rootes of Rosewell, 55-56; RS, III, 28; Speed, 80-88; St. Mark's, 132-134; TD, March 13, 1904; June 26, Oct. 2, Nov. 2, 13, 1904; April 18, 1909; April 23, 1916; VM, XIII, 144-145; WM, II, 150; V, 161; X, 258-259; XVII, 169.
  (*Augusta*)—Bruce IV, 251.
  (*Joshua*)—Albemarle, 197-198; Cyc. Va. Biog., I, 240; V, 600-601; Memoir of Col. Joshua Fry; Mackenzie VI, 15-17; WM, V, 161.
Frye, Fry—Frye Genealogy, by Ellen F. Barker, New York, 1920; TD, Oct. 2, 1904.
  (*Frederick*)—WM, X, 209-210.
Fudge—Bath Co., 194; Bruce VI, 537.
Fugate—Bruce IV, 470; VI, 345.
Fugitt—Avery I, 151.
Fugua—Clemens' Wills (*Bedford*), 35.
Fulcher—McIntosh II, 26.
Fulgham (*Isle of Wight*)—VM, II, 392; WM, VII, 227, et seq.
Fuller—Rockbridge, 485 (*Montgomery*); Miami Co., Ohio, 647.
Fullerton—The Stewarts of Ballintoy, by the Rev. George Hall (reprint), p. 14.
Fulkerson—Hughes, etc., 69-72; Shenandoah, 601.
Full—Pendleton Co., 321-322.
Fuller—Rockbridge, 485.
Fuls—Hardin Co., Ohio, 979.
Fulton—Rockbridge, 485-486; RS, III, 2.
Fultz—Pendleton Co., 207.
Funk—Bruce, V, 75; Funk Family History, 213, et seq; Shenandoah, 601-602.
Funkhouser—Bruce IV, 293; V, 326, 443; Cartmell, 494; Shenandoah, 602-603.
Funsten—Cartmell, 458; Minor, 59; The Ancestors and Descendants of Colonel David Funsten and his Wife, Susanna Everard Meade (Funsten-Meade), 1-21.
Fuqua—Brock II, 722; Knox Co., Ill., 269; TD, April 22, 1906; June 16, Aug. 4, 1907; Woodson, 652.

G

Gaar—Virkus III, 360.
Gabbert—Kanawha, 544-545; Rockbridge, 486.
Gaddis—DAR, 81, p. 256.
Gainer—Barbour Co., W. Va., 389; DAR, 82, p. 209.
Gaines—Bagby, 335-336; Buckners of Va., 230-232; Cisco, 248-249; Cooke-Booth, 112-113; Culpeper, 98; Cyc. Va. Biog., I, 240; Goode, 124, 290, 470; SHA, II, 160-161, 168-172; Hughes, etc., 195-197; Mackenzie VI, 245; Nourse Family of Va., 45-47; SBN, XI, 576-578; TD, Sept. 11, Dec. 18, 1904; July 9, 1905; March 3, Oct. 13, 1907; Jan. 10, 1915; July 9, Sept. 3, 1916; Thos. Carter, 47-48.
  (*Amherst*)—Cyc. Va. Biog., IV, 505.

(*Charlotte*)—DAR, 81, p. 243; Brock II, 784; Sangamon Co., Ill., 321.
(*Culpeper*)—Armstrong I, 76-99; Kanawha, 550-554; St. Mark's, 164.
(*Culpeper*) (Not descended from Daniel Gaines)—The Gaines Genealogy. Our Line from 1620 to 1918, by J. P. Gaines, Calhoun, Ga., 1918.
(*Hanover*)—RS, III, 14.
Galt—Burgess, 142, 274; RS, III, 32, Sangamon Co., Ill., 19; WM, (*King and Queen*)—Cyc. Va. Biog., V, 932-933.
(*Orange*)—DAR, 82, p. 296.
(*Prince William*)—Cyc. Va. Biog., V, 730.
Galbraith—Rockbridge, 486; WM, XII, 98.
Gale—Cyc. Va. Biog., I, 241.
Galford—Pocahontas Co., 269-274.
Gall—Barbour Co., W. Va., 386-387; Highland Co., 381.
Gallaher—BS, Jan. 29, Feb. 12, 1905; Kanawha, 745; Mackenzie III, 103-104; WVM, I, October, 1901, 29-30.
Gallahue—Virkus III, 487.
Galt—Burgess, 142, 274; RS, III, 32; WM, VIII, 259-262; WM 2d, VIII, 40.
(*Fluvanna*)—Lancaster, 195-196.
(*Norfolk*)—Convention 1788, I, XII, XIII; SBN, XI, 380-381.
(*Williamsburg*)—Cyc. Va. Biog., I, 241; III, 176.
Gamble—Bates, et al. of Va. and Mo., 62-63, 123-130; Cabell, etc., 255-257; Cyc. Va. Biog., II, 241-242; Gilmer's Georgians; Goode, 401; Kennedy I, 96-99, 463-465; Lancaster, 156-157; RS, II, 2, 51; IV, 20, 24; TD, Sept. 9, 25, 1906; VSR, I, 10; VM, XIX, 280; Waddell's Annals of Augusta Co., 307, 309; Walker-Wigton, 71-72, 114-115.
Gamewell—Rockbridge, 486.
Gandy—Monongahela III, 1087-1089; Randolph Co., 345-346.
Gannaway—Hardesty (*Amherst*), 439; Researcher, Vol. II; WM 2d, VII, 177-180.
Gannt—Albemarle, 198.
Gant—Biog. Encyc. of Ky. (1877), 404.
Gany—Cyc. Va. Biog., I, 241.
Garber—Armistead, 164-166; Bruce IV, 189, 272, 292-295; Goode, 407.
Garden (*Prince Edward*)—VM, XXIV, 201.
Gardiner—Rockbridge, 486.
Gardner, Gardiner—TD, Nov. 19, 1905; April 4, 1915.
Gardner—Highland Co., 287; Sangamon Co., Ill., 322; Virkus III, 266.
(*Albemarle*)—Kanawha, 549.
(*Albemarle and Russell*)—Bruce VI, 145.
(*Rockbridge*)—Kanawha, 946.
Garland—Arkansas, 307-311; Burwell, 17; Cabell, etc., 275-276, 379-380; Campbell Co., 414-416; Du Bellet II, 424; Floyd, 102-105; Grayson Co., 141-147; Hampden-Sidney, 264-265, 282-283; Hening VI, 311-314; VIII, 442-444; Kennedy II, 399-401; Munsell's X, 21; RS, X, 21; SBN, XI, 383-384; TD, April 23, June 18, 1905, July 26, Aug. 3, 10, 1908; Dec. 28, 1913; June 25, 1916; WM, IV, 280.
(*Albemarle*)—Albemarle, 198-201; Sangamon Co., Ill., 324.
Garlick—Cyc. Va. Biog., V, 933; WM, IV, 167, 270; XVI, 100-103.
Garlington—Buford, 225; Chappell, 330-341; Hayden, 243, 259-260; WM, XII, 266.
Garner—Bruce VI, 218; Burgess, 141, 461, 556; Rockbridge, 486; TD, June 10, 1906.

(Stafford)—Cyc. Va. Biog., V, 592.
(West Va.)—Ritchie Co., 132-133.
Garnes—Kanawha, 622.
Garnett—Bagby, 293-295, 337-338; Bruce V, 535; Burgess, 136-139; Culpeper, 59-60; Cyc. Va. Biog., I, 241; II, 232-233; IV, 175; Genealogy of the Mercer-Garnett Family of Essex Co., Va., by J. M. Garnett, Richmond, 1910; Green's Ky. Families, 197-198; John Wise, 191-196; Kennedy I, 501; Mackenzie I, 190-192; MMV, IV, 134, 136; Norfolk, 607-608; RS, III, 11 (Oct 13, 1880), 14, 23, 26, 93; SBN, XI, 384-386; St. Mark's, 134-136; TD, Sept. 2, 1906; Aug. 28, Sept. 11, 1910; Aug. 18, 1912, March 9, 1913; VM, XV, 103-104; XXXIII, 29-30; Walker-Wigton, 604-605; WM, XVIII, 17-37, 71-89.
Garr—Garr Genealogy; Munsell's XII, 33; Virkus III, 94.
Garrard—Gov. Garrard of Ky., etc., His Descendants and Relatives, by Anna R. des Cognets, Lexington, Ky., 1898; SBN, XI, 387-388; Woodson, 286, 455-456.
(Jacob, Stafford)—Garrard, 110-128.
(Stafford)—Virkus I, 118; II, 268.
(William, Stafford)—Van Meter, 22.
Garrett—Hardesty *(Bedford)*, 418; Madison Co., Ohio, 1021; TD, Oct. 28, 1906; Yeardley, 12-14.
(Albemarle)—Albemarle, 201-203.
(Caroline)—Caroline Co., 427.
(King and Queen)—Bruce V, 346.
(Larkin)—Old King William, 134.
(Loudoun)—MMV, IV, 137-138.
(Norfolk Co., from Eastern Shore)—Stewarts of Beechwood (privately printed).
(Williamsburg)—MMV, IV, 137-138.
Garrison—Brock II, 784; Bruce IV, 290; Cyc. Va. Biog., V, 727; Rockbridge, 486; TD, July 27, 1913.
Garst—Bruce VI, 548.
Garten—Summers Co., 686-688.
Garth—Albemarle, 203-205; Bruce IV, 52; Cisco, 90-91, 142, 161; Des Cognets, 85-86.
Garthwright—Bullington Chart, by Arthur B. Clarke (Va. State Library).
Garvey—Rockbridge. 486; Sangamon Co., Ill, 325.
Garvin—Bruce V, 188-190; Rockbridge, 486.
Gary—Bruce IV, 387; DAR, 82, p. 34; TD, Oct. 14, 1906.
Gasaway—Miami Co., Ind., 565.
Gascoigne (Gascoine)—DAR, 49, p. 106; TD, April 26, 1914.
Gaskin—Monongahela III, 1115-1116.
Gaskins—Adams Co., Ohio, 753; Cyc. Va. Biog., I, 241; Hayden, 272, 438, 440-441; TD, May 10, 1914; VM, V, 345-346; VSR, III (No. 3), 36, 43; WM, I, 146; XI, 276-280.
Gates—Kanawha, 610; TD, July 14, 1907.
Gatewood—Bruce V, 440; Burgess, 489; Caroline Co., 428; Kanawha, 959; Montague, 192; RS, III, 31; Shenandoah, 603; TD, Feb. 14, June 2, 1911; Aug. 18, Dec. 11, 1912; Welles' Washington Genealogy, 237; WVM, IV, 304-306.
Gathright—Biog. Cyc. of Ky. (1896), 94; Virkus I, 619-620.
Gay—Alleghany, 201-202; Bath Co., 194; Clemens' Wills, 36; Monongahela I, 384; Pocahontas Co., 128-131, 511-513; Rockbridge, 253, 486-487; Virkus II, 223; III, 500-501.
(Augusta)—Virkus II, 340.

Gilkeson—Bruce VI, 462; Cartmell, 444; Hampshire, 708; Pendleton
    Co., 207; Rockbridge, 487.
    (*Frederick*)—McClure, 204-210.
Gill—Hardesty (*Amherst*), 439; Rockbridge, 487; Virkus II, 284.
    (*Bedford*)—Virkus I, 145.
    (*Botetourt*)—DAR, 72, p. 229.
    (*York*)—Cyc. Va. Biog., I, 242; VM, VI, 93.
Gillespie—Houston Family, 358-364; Rockbridge, 487.
    Rockbridge, 487.
    (*Bath*)—Braxton Co., W. Va., 381-382.
    (*Frederick*)—DAR, 45, p. 244.
    (*Tazewell*)—New River, 405-406; Tazewell II, 381-412.
Gillett (*Eastern Shore*)—John Wise, 83-84.
Gilliam—Bristol Parish, 174-177; Bruce IV, 375: V, 243; Burgess,
    938-939; Campbell Co., 417-419; Cyc. Va. Biog., IV, 88;
    Keith, Addendum III; Montgomery Co., Ohio, 320; Roger
    Jones, 157-158; RS, II, 32; III, 33, 35, 40; Sanxay Family,
    by F. F. Sanxay, 116-122; TD, Dec. 18, 25, 1904; April
    5, 1908; July 6, 13, 1913.
    (*Charles City*)—VSR, Jan., 1928, 50-70.
    (*Petersburg*)—Cyc. Va. Biog., IV, 369-371; VM, XXX, 66.
    (*Prince George*)—Bruce IV, 16; VSR, III (No. 3), 32; WM,
    XII, 62-64.
    (*Rockingham*)—Montgomery Co., Ohio, 297.
Gillispie—Kanawha, 742-743.
Gilman (*Hanover*)—Cyc. Va. Biog., IV, 480.
Gilmer—Albemarle, 206-208; Brock I, 180-194; Bruce VI, 447; Cyc.
    Va. Biog., II, 249; Cabell, etc., 564; Dinwiddie Papers II,
    336; Gilmer's Georgians, 9-31; Hardesty, 373; Kennedy I,
    102-103, 455-456, 473-475; Life of Gen. Hugh Mercer, 100,
    115-116; Lancaster, 411-412; McAllister, 316-317, 324; Meri-
    wethers, 58-59, 62-68, 146-147; MMV, IV, 139-141; Munsell's
    V, 99-100; Page (2d ed.), 221-222; Peyton, 288-289, 293;
    RS, I, 46; TD, June 18, 25, 1905; May 30, 1915; Tyler's
    II, 133-134; VHS, Col. VI, 71-74; Virkus I, 906; II, 263-
    264; VM, XXIV, 222; XXIX, 282; VSR, I, 65-66; II (No.
    1), 66; WM, XV, 225-227; XVI, 142; XX, 214-215.
    (*Highland*)—Highland Co., 287-288.
    (*Russell*)—Brock II, 724; Bruce VI, 229.
Gilmore—Clemens' Wills, 38; Rockbridge, 487-488.
Gilmour—Whitaker, 82-83.
Gilvin—Old King William, 176.
Ginger—Rockbridge, 488.
Girty—Shenandoah, 624.
Gish—Bruce VI, 469.
Gissage—WM, X, 126.
Gist—Burgess, 51-55; RS, III, 3.
Given—Alleghany, 202-203; Braxton Co., W. Va., 382-383; Monroe
    Co., 345.
    (*Augusta*)—Virkus II, 339.
    (*Highland*)—Highland Co., 381.
Givens—Bruce IV, 428, 474.
Givin—Highland Co., 292-294.
Glaize—Bruce V, 185; Cartmell, 471-472; Lower Shenandoah, 673-
    675, 699.
Glascock, Glasscock—Bruce VI, 327; Hayden, 61; Sangamon Co., Ill.,
    331; VM, XV, 84; WM, XII, 100, 102.

Glasgow—Bruce IV, 425; VI, 54; Cabell, etc., 292-293; McCormick, 119-124; Rockbridge, 253-254, 304-306, 488; TD, Aug. 11, 1912; Virkus I, 922; II, 110; III, 617.
    (*Rockbridge*)—Thomas, 556j-556k.
Glass—Bruce IV, 5; Campbell Co., 224-227; Cartmell, 413-416; Cyc. Va. Biog., V, 618-619; Foote II, 24; MMV, IV, 142-144; 488; VM, XXVII, 85, 356-357.
    (*Amherst*)—Bruce IV, 410; Cyc. Va. Biog., V, 618-619.
    (*Frederick*)—Cartmell, 274-275, 290-291.
    (*Valley of Va.*)—MMV, I, 311-315; Lower Shenandoah, 738-739.
Glasscock—Cyc. Va. Biog., I, 241; Kanawha, 489; Monongahela III, 1044-1045; TD, Aug. 18, 1912.
Glassell—Culpeper, 60; Cyc. Va. Biog., I, 242; Hayden, 1-44; St. Mark's, 136-138; TD, Nov. 26, Dec. 3, 10, 1916; VSR, V (No. 2), 39.
Glazebrook—Genealogy of Kilby, Tynes, etc., Families, 33-36; TD, Oct. 16, 1910; Virkus II, 115.
Gleaves—DAR, 72, p. 144; Crockett, 68-71.
Glenn—Burgess, 116-118; Tyler's X, 137; Virkus III, 87.
    (*Halifax*)—Glenn Family (MS), by Robert S. Phifer.
Glover—Glover Memorials and Genealogies, by Annie Glover (Boston, 1887); Licking Co., Ohio, 677; Ritchie Co., 87.
Goad—Braxton Co., W. Va., 383; Bruce VI, 573.
Gobble—Brock II, 725.
Gochnauer—Bruce VI, 250.
Goddin—Barton I, R80-81; Brock II, 785; Genealogy of the Goddin Family; Randolph Co., 345; TD, Nov. 29, 1908; Tyler's II, 172-173.
Godfrey (*Norfolk Co.*)—Cyc. Va. Biog., I, 241; McIntosh I, 200-201; II, 19-20, 47, 57-61, 83-84, 96-97, 190.
Godsey—Bruce V, 176; Chappell, 175-176.
Godwin—Barton II, 68; TD, April 29, 1906; VM, V, 198-201; VI, 85-86
    (*Isle of Wight*)—Cyc. Va. Biog., I, 242; RS, III, 34.
    (*Nansemond*)—Cyc. Va. Biog., I, 242-243; VM, XXXV, 442.
Godwyn (*Isle of Wight*)—RS, III, 34.
Goff—Bruce V, 510; Harrison Co., W. Va., 379; Preston Co., I, 353, 434; Randolph Co., 346; Ritchie Co., 280-294.
Goffigan (*Eastern Shore*)—Burgess, 120-121.
Goggin—Buford, 133; Burgess, 118-119; Campbell Co., 419-420; Cyc. Va. Biog., IV, 502; TD, June 2, 1907; Virkus I, 203.
Gold—Cartmell, 461-462; Lower Shenandoah, 713-714; Rockbridge, 488.
Golladay—Bruce IV, 352; Shenandoah, 603.
Gooch—America Heraldica, 166; ARP, II, 730; Cyc. Va. Biog., I, 243; Genealogical Narrative of the Hart Family, Memphis, 1882, pp. 78-82; Hart Family; McCue, 47; McIlhany, 136-137, 232-233; MMV, II, 136-137; TD, Dec. 6, 1903; Jan. 17, 1909; VM, XI, 74; WM, II, 15-16, 141, 235; IV, 197; V, 110-112; VI, 194; XVI, 17; Woods-McAfee, 375-376.
Gooch, Gouge (*Hanover and Albemarle*)—Albemarle, 208-210.
Gleason—Bruce IV, 301.
Good—Bruce IV, 305, 326, 403; Kanawha, 367; Miami Co., Ind., 587; Montgomery Co., Ohio (TH), 402; Pendleton Co., 207-208, 322; Rockbridge, 488.
Goodall—Burgess, 211-212; Convention 1788, II, 375; Cyc. Va. Biog., II, 362-363; TD, July 30, 1905.
Goodbar—Rockbridge, 488.

Goode—Biog. Cyc. of Ohio, III, 680; Burwell, 11-22, 32-33; Cyc. Va. Biog., I, 243-244; IV, 101-102; V, 1063; Goode's Virginia Cousins; MMV, III, 143-145; Munsell's III, 21; IV, 101-102; TD, Feb. 23, 1908; Virkus I, 625; VM, IV, 454-456; XXX, 396-397.

Goodhart—Biog. Cyc. of Ohio, II, 332.

Goodin—Goodwin (1899), 48.

Goodloe—Bruce V, 14, 434; Munsell's XII, 17; Virkus III, 103; Woods-McAfee, 315-316.

Goodman (*Albemarle*)—Albemarle, 210; Kith and Kin, 66.

(*Bedford*)—Hardesty, 418.

Goodpasture—TD, Feb. 13, 1916.

Goodrich—Cyc. Va. Biog., I, 243.

(*Amherst*)—St. Charles, etc., Mo., 733, 787.

(*Isle of Wight*)—Convention 1788, II, 46; Tyler's II, 130-131; 207; VM, XI, 83; XIV, 443-444; XV, 160-165.

(*Old Rappahannock*)—VM, XI, 74; XX, 93-94.

(*Old Prince George*)—VM, XXIX, 102.

(*Old Rappahannock, Thomas*)—VM, XXXII, 61.

Goodwin—Cyc. Va. Biog., I, 244; Goodwin Families of America (Supplement to William & Mary College Quarterly, 1899); Hardesty (*Amherst*), 440; Kanawha, 406; MMV, III, 225-226; Rockbridge, 488; TD, March 25, April 15, 1906.

(*Botetourt and Tazewell*)—Goodwin ('99), 17-18.

(*Dinwiddie*)—Goodwin ('99), 135-138, 140-142.

(*Elizabeth City*)—Goodwin ('99), 52.

(*Harrison*)—Goodwin ('99), 16-17, 146.

(*York*)—Goodwin ('99), 1-5, 23-24; WM, II, 84, 266.

Goodwyn (*Dinwiddie*)—Goodwin ('99), 19-22, 26-37, 140-142; Thos. Carter, 79-80.

(*Surry*)—WM, XXVI, 126-127.

(*Sussex*)—VM, XXI, 443-444.

Goodykoontz—Grayson Co., 190-198.

Gookin—America Heraldica, 64; Cyc. Va. Biog., I, 244; Mackenzie VII, 77; N. E. His. and Gen. Reg., I, 345-352; RS, IV, 14; VM, V, 435-436, 458; Chart in Col. V; VI, 91; XIX, 141.

Goolrick—Bruce V, 237.

Goolsby—Albemarle, 211.

Goosley—WM, I, 152; VII, 39.

Gordan—RC (1888).

Gordon—Bristol Parish, 203; Bruce IV, 3; BS, May 7, 1905; Cyc. Va. Biog., V, 796-799; Rockbridge, 488; RS, III, 31, 37; TD, Dec. 27, 1903; Jan. 3, 1904; Jan. 2, 1910; March 20, April 10, 1910.

(*Albemarle*)—Albemarle, 211-212; Cyc. Va. Biog., II, 110-111.

(*Alexandria*)—Gordons in Virginia, by A. C. Gordon (Hackensack, N. J., 1918), 108-111.

(*Blandford and Essex*)—Gordons in Virginia, 86-90.

(*Clarke*)—Bruce V, 85.

(*Fairfax*)—Munsell's X, 56-57.

(*Falmouth and Fredericksburg*)—Gordons in Virginia, 98-107.

(*Fauquier*)—Hayden, 615-623.

(*Frederick*)—Auglaize Co., Ohio, 381-382.

(*Fredericksburg*)—Kennedy I, 654; Virkus I, 625.

(*James*)—Col. James Gordon of Lancaster.

(*Jefferson*)—Lower Shenandoah, 755.

(*Kenmore*)—Hayden, 724.

(*Lancaster*)—Bruce IV, 159; Cyc. Va. Biog., I, 244-245; Gordons in Virginia, 7-85; Hayden, 249-253; Mackenzie VII,

Grandstaff—Bruce IV, 336-337.
Grandy—Kennedy I, 49; McIntosh I, 115-116.
Grant—Rockbridge, 488; TD, Dec. 2, 1906.
    (*Chesterfield and Richmond City*)—VSR, IV (No. 4), 24.
    (*Fauquier*)—Hord Family of Va., Supplement, 103-108; VSR,
      II (No. 1), 62.
    (*Frederick*)—Cartmell, 460.
    (*New Kent*)—Munsell's VII, 72.
    (*Washington Co.*)—Brock II, 725.
Grattan—Cabell, etc., 256-257; Gilmer's Georgians, 31; Meriwethers,
    59; MMV, IV, 147-148.
Gravatt—Bruce V, 387; Caroline Co., 437-439; MMV, IV, 149-150;
    Virkus I, 628.
Gravley—Brock II, 605-606; Henry Co., 169-173.
Graves—Bruce IV, 274, 276; VI, 403-404; Cyc. Va. Biog., I, 246; V,
    624-625; LCJ, March 14, 1915 (II, 5); Rockbridge, 439;
    TD, March 14, 1911; June 22, 1913; Virkus I, 185; WM,
    XII, 121-123.
    (*Culpeper*)—Biog. Cyc. of Ky. (1898), 266-267.
    (*Pittsylvania*)—Bruce VI, 581.
    (*York*)—Burgess, 500; WM, II, 271; III, 202-203, 280.
    (*York, etc.*)—Kennedy II, 545-546.
Gravely—MMV, V, 170-172.
Gray—Burgess, 500-504; Miami Co., Ohio, 690; RS, III, 36; St.
    Mark's, 121; TD, July 22, 1906; Jan. 2, 1910; Oct. 26, 1913;
    Valentine I, 486-591.
    (*Augusta*)—Brock II, 726.
    (*Culpeper*)—Culpeper, 81; part 2, 140; Cyc. Va. Biog., I, 246-
    247; Rootes of Rosewell, 44-45, 59-64.
    (*Fluvanna*)—Bruce IV, 196.
    (*Goochland*)—Cyc. Va. Biog., IV, 207.
    (*Prince Edward*)—Bruce IV, 101-102.
    (*Rockbridge*)—Rockbridge, 488-489; Woods-McAfee, 97.
    (*Southampton*)—Cyc. Va. Biog., II, 111.
    (*Stafford*)—SHA, II, 162-164; Virkus I, 628; VM, X, 101, 202;
    XI, 210.
    (*Surry*)—Cyc. Va. Biog., I, 246-247; Stubbs, 380; VSR, III
    (No. 3), 30, 36; IV (No. 1), 40; VM, III, 402-404; V,
    77, 201-202; XXX, 64-66, 294.
    (*Surry and Prince Edward*)—Valentine IV, 2256-2267.
    (*Washington Co.*)—Brock II, 727; Bruce VI, 294.
    (*Westmoreland*)—Virkus II, 143; VM, XII, 267-271.
Graybeal—Tazewell II, 428-431.
Grayson—Burgess, 279-288; Cabell, etc., 452-454; Convention 1788,
    I, 194-210; Cyc. Va. Biog., V, 883; Hayden, 303, 534; TD,
    Sept. 8, 1907; Tyler's V, 195-208, 261-268; VI, 201-202;
    VII, 54-56; VIII, 119-126, 141-143; Warfield, 240.
    (*Spotsylvania*)—Albemarle, 214; Two Families, 99-100.
Greathouse—Braxton Co., 384; Panhandle, 358; Preston Co., 354, 435.
Greear—Bruce VI, 327, 552.
Green, Greene—TD, March 26, April 30, 1905; May 27, 1906; May 23,
    June 6, 1909; July 7, 1912.
Green—Burgess, 504-506; Meade; Rockbridge, 489; RS, II, 46; III,
    16, 18, 52; Slaughter's Fry Genealogy.
    (*Amelia*)—Bruce VI, 120; Dupuy, 252; Hayden, 548-550; Hugue-
    not Emigration, 196-197; Mackenzie IV, 174-175; The Ewing
    Family and Cognate Branches, by P. K. and M. E. Ewing

(n. p.), 1911, 132-152; Tyler's V, 135-138; VI, 37-43; WM 2d, IV, 94-98.
(*Berryman*)—VM, XV, 84.
(*Culpeper*)—BS, Dec. 31, 1905; Burgess, 506; Culpeper, 61-69; Cyc. Va. Biog., I, 247; II, 223; V, 832-833; Du Bellet II, 398-402; Glengarry McDonalds, 112-119, 153-161; Hardy, 238-247; Hayden, 548-550; Lancaster, 141-142; Lower Shenandoah, 614-616; Marshall, 118-124, 261; McAllister, 175-177; Munsell's IV, 16; RS, III, 18-19; Shenandoah, 604-605; St. Mark's, 138-142; Thomas Ritchie, by C. H. Ambler (Richmond, Va., 1913), 320; Virkus III, 121; VM, VIII, 77-80, 213-216, 317-318, 421-424; IX, 207-208, 427-428; XIX, 446; XXIII, 101, 103.
(*Fauquier*)—DAR, 59, p. 294.
(*Gloucester*)—Barton II, 13-15.
(*Grief*)—Mackenzie II, 507.
(*Halifax*)—Brock II, 622.
(*Halifax, Berryman*)—Halifax, 184-198.
(*James City*)—WM 2d, VI, 203-204.
(*King George*)—Virkus, III, 274.
(*Loudoun*)—Sangamon Co., Ill., 340-341.
(*Orange*)—Marshall, 86-88, 226-227; Robertson-Taylor, 50, 80-84, 150-154; Speed, 83-84, 87; VSR, III (No. 3), 37.
(*Prince William*)—Lower Shenandoah, 741-742.
(*Scott Co.*)—Johnson Co., Ky., 235.
(*Thomas*)—Tyler's V, 135-138.
(*Warwick*)—Cabell, etc., 306-307, 312-313.
(*Westmoreland*)—Tyler's VII, 199-203; VIII, 287-288.
(*West Va.*)—Monroe Co., 347.
Greenawalt—Pendleton Co., 208-209.
Greene (*Clarke*)—Bruce V, 486.
    (*Warwick*)—RS, II, 34; Tyler's V, 135-138.
Greenhill—Cyc. Va. Biog., I, 248.
Greenhow—VHS Col. XI, 72, 77; VM, XXIX, 144; WM, VII, 17; XVII, 273-275.
Greening—Sangamon Co., Ill., 338.
Greenlee—Green's Ky. Families, 9-12; Marshall, 64-65; McCormick, 31; Peyton, 67-74; Rockbridge, 254-256, 489; WM, X, 208.
Greenway (*Dinwiddie*)—Meade; Tyler's VIII, 65-66.
Greenwood—Ancestry and Descendants of Thomas Greenwood of Newton, Mass., and John Greenwood of Virginia; Sangamon Co., Ill., 335.
Greer—Rockbridge, 489.
Greever—Tazewell II, 431-440; Virkus III, 500-501.
Gregg—Bruce VI, 98; Hening VIII, 163-166.
Gregory—BS, Jan. 15, 1905; Dupuy, 283-284; Hardesty, 377-378; Montague, 122-123; RS, II. 4: Slaughter's Fry Genealogy; St. Charles, etc., Mo., 791; TD, Nov. 20, Dec. 4, 18, 1904; March 12, 26, May 26, June 15, 1905; Jan. 24, 1915; VM, XXVII, 180-181, 363; West Chart (Lord Delaware), privately printed, Richmond, Va.
    (*Alexandria*)—Old Alexandria, 319-321.
    (*Charles City*)—Brock I, 202-203; Burgess, 50-51, 507-509; WM, XI, 266-268; XVI, 141.
    (*Essex*)—Cyc. Va. Biog., I, 248.
    (*Fredericksburg*)—St. Louis, II, 945.
    (*King William*)—Cooke-Booth, 92-93; MMV, V, 171-172; Old King William, 37, 58-61; RS, II, 4; Tyler's VIII, 264-266;

VM, V, 162-163; XXVI, 84-86; Winston, 253-265, with chart;
supplement, 9-10.
(*Lunenburg*)—Bruce IV, 563; Cyc. Va. Biog., V, 704.
(*Nansemond*)—Crocker "Ancestors"; VM, XV, 442-444; XVI,
(*Pittsylvania*)—Pittsylvania, 172.
XVI, 90-92, 103-104, 201-203; XVII, 99, 316-318.
(*Rappahannock and Essex*)—Winston, 237-250.
Gregson—Cyc. Va. Biog., I, 248.
Grendon—VM, XIV, 207-208.
Grendon, Grindon, Grindall—VM, I, 441-442; Cyc. Va. Biog., I, 248.
Gresham—Bagby, 338-340; Goode, 338; Gresham Family, by W. Mac-
farlane Jones (Richmond, Va., 1924); TD, Sept. 24, 1905;
April 5, 1914; Jan. 3, Nov. 28, 1915; June 4, Nov. 12, 1916;
Virkus II, 341.
(*Chesterfield*)—Bruce IV, 57.
(*King and Queen*)—WM 2d, VIII, 312.
(*Princess Anne*)—Bruce IV, 423.
Gribble (*Loudoun*)—Preston Co., 355.
Grice—Bruce VI, 16; Cyc. Va. Biog., V, 758.
Griffen—Highland Co., 289.
Griffin—Cyc. Va. Biog., II, 111; Hayden, 110; Huguenot Emigration,
XI; LCJ, April 4, 1915 (II, 10); Ritchie Co., 234; RS, I,
10; III, 21; TD, Dec. 2, 1906; July 11, 1909; Virkus II,
300; VM, I, 254-256; VSR, IV (No. 2), 39-40.
(*Alexandria*)—Avery I, 155-156.
(*Augusta*)—RS, III, 11.
(*Nansemond*)—Cyc. Va. Biog., IV, 506.
(*Northumberland*)—Cyc. Va. Biog., I, 249; VM, I, 471-472.
(*Richmond Co.*)—Browning, C. D., 113-114; 3d, 616-618; Cyc.
Va. Biog., I, 249; McAllister, 114, 116-117; VM, V, 433;
XVII, 435; XXIII, 430-434.
(*Roanoke*)—MMV, III, 148-150.
(*York*)—Cyc. Va. Biog., I, 248-249.
Griffith, Griffon—TD, Aug. 28, 1904.
Griffith—Bruce IV, 505; V, 382; VI, 176; Miami Co., Ind., 774.
(*Frederick*)—Cartmell, 468-469; Lower Shenandoah, 710-711.
Grigg—DAR, 47, p. 238.
Griggs—Brock II, 607; Griggs Family; Henry Co., 178-181.
Griggs—Timberlake; Lower Shenandoah, 658-661.
Grigsby—BS, May 21, 1905; Convention 1788, I, V, IX, XXI; Cyc.
Va. Biog., II, 224; Lineage Book, Order of Washington,
125; McIlhany, 226; Norfolk, 491-492; Rockbridge, 256, 489;
Virkus III, 371; WM, IX, 268-269.
Grigsley—Clemens' Wills, 40-41.
Grimes—BHNC, VI, 243; Burgess, 548-549; McIntosh I, 153; Meade
II ,373; Montgomery Co., Ohio, 167; Norfolk, 520-523;
Pocahontas Co., 188-195; Virkus I, 55.
(*Alexandria*)—Avery I, 156.
(*Fairfax*)—Preston Co., 355.
Grimshaw—BS, March 5, 1905.
Grimsley—Bruce VI, 414.
Grinnan—Bruce IV, 188; Culpeper, part 2, 79; Hayden, 10-12, 29-44;
VSR, V (No. 2), 38; Walker-Wigton, 124-125, 129; WM 2d,
I, 159-160.
Grizzard—Bruce IV, 72, 363.
Grogg—Highland Co., 289-290.
Gromarrian—Hening VIII, 643-646.
Groner—Brock II, 553.

Gwatkin—Cyc. Va. Biog., V, 877; "Genealogy" (Weekes ed.), Vol.
  p. 45; WM, V, 210-211.
Gwin—Bath Co., 194; Highland Co., 292-294; TD, March 1, May 5,
  1907.
Gwinn—Monroe Co., 348-349; Rockbridge, 489; Summers Co., 656-663.
Gwyn, Gwynn, Gwinn, Gwin—TD, Sept. 25, 1906; Dec. 4, 1910.
Gwyn, Gwynne (*Gloucester*)—Cooke-Booth, 28-29.
Gwyn (Rev. John)—VM, IV, 204, 206-207.
  (*York*)—Cyc. Va. Biog., I, 249.
Gwynn (*Gloucester*)—Hayden, 469; H e n i n g VIII, 483-484; WM,
  XVIII, 60-62.

H

Haas—McCormick, 203, 204.
Hack—Cyc. Va. Biog., I, 250; Hayden, 243-244; Tyler's VII, 253-262;
  IX, 64-65.
Hacke—VM, V, 256-258; WM, VIII, 237.
Hacker—Cyc. Va. Biog., I, 250; Harrison Co., 372.
Hackett—Cyc. Va. Biog., I, 250.
Hackley—Burgess, 558; Hampden-Sidney, 20-21.
Hackney—DAR, 53, p. 455.
Haddan—Randolph Co., 354.
Haddox—Ritchie Co., 136-137, 604-607.
Haden—Bruce IV, 52-53.
Haeger—Cyc. Va. Biog., I, 250.
Hagan—Brock II, 786; Cyc. Va. Biog., IV, 48.
Hager—Clemens' Wills, 41; Johnson Co., Ky., 237.
Hagerman—St. Louis, II, 971.
Hague—Clemens' Wills, 41.
Haigler—Pendleton Co., 322; Randolph Co., 353.
Hailey—Biog. Cyc. of Ky. (1896), 183.
Haines—Cyc. Va. Biog., I, 252.
Hairston—Cabell, etc., 471-472; Campbell Co., 420-422; Clemens' Wills,
  42; Crawfurdiana, 106; Cyc. Va. Biog., I, 250; IV, 117;
  Henry Co., 80; Hughes, etc., 146-149; MMV, IV, 157-159;
  Pittsylvania, 94, etc.; Tyler's VI, 66-67; Virkus II, 124.
Hakes—The Hakes Family, by Harvey Hakes.
Halbert—Sangamon Co., Ill., 347; Virkus II, 341.
Hale (Heale)—TD, Aug. 16, 1908.
Hale—Biog. Cyc. of Ky. (1896), 267; Grayson Co., 104-140; Hale Fam-
  ily Chart, by Ann Gleaves Rich (Wytheville, Va., n. d.);
  Hardy, 53; Kanawha, 926-930; New River, 406-410; Woods-
  McAfee, 231.
Halfaker—Johnson Co., Ind., 611.
Hall—Burwell Chart; Carter Family Tree; Coshocton Co., Ohio, 649;
  Johnson Co., Ky., 253; Rockbridge, 489-490; Sangamon
  Co., Ill., 350-351; Shenandoah, 633; TD, Aug. 25, 1907;
  WM, IV, 247; VII, 109; IX, 123.
  (*Albemarle*)—Bruce IV, 185.
  (*Augusta*)—Bruce IV, 258.
  (*Culpeper*)—Md. Soc. Col. Wars, 31; Virkus III, 222.
  (*Elisha*)—His. of Cecil Co., Md., 481.
  (*Fredericksburg*)—WM, XXII, 134-139, 265-270.
  (*Jacob*)—Six Centuries of the Moores of Fawley, 53-55, 60-62.
  (*Lancaster*)—Bruce V, 343.
  (*Leesburg*)—Kanawha, 617.
  (*Prince William*)—DAR, 42, p. 46.

(*Richmond*)—Goode, 355; MMV, I, 77-79.
(*Ritchie Co., W. Va.*)—Kanawha, 703; Ritchie Co., 43-113, 181-182, 199-201, 241-247.
(*Stafford*)—Bruce V, 347.
(*William*)—VM, XXXI, 339.
(*Winchester, etc.*)—WM, XXII, 134-139.
Hallam—Ritchie Co., 609-610; VM, V, 212.
Halleburton—Halifax, 299-300.
Halley—Mackenzie II, 302-307.
Halliburton—Munsell's V, 85-86.
Halliday (*Norfolk Co.*)—McIntosh II, 79.
Halliman—WM, VII, 247.
Hallows—Barton II, 26-27.
Halsey—Bruce IV, 367-368; Hayden, 35-36; Munsell's IV, 226.
Halstead—Crocker's "Ancestors", 26-28.
Halterman—Highland Co., 294-295; Monongahela II, 769-770.
Ham—Cyc. Va. Biog., I, 250.
Hamaker—Cyc. Va. Biog., V, 619.
Hamersley—Hampden-Sidney, 237.
Hames—DAR, 78, p. 143.
Hamil—Rockbridge, 491.
Hamilton—Alleghany, 203-204; Rockbridge, 490-491; RS, III, 24; St. Mark's, 158, 185; TD, March 12, 1905; April 24, 1910; VSR, I, 12; V (No. 2), 48.
(*Amelia*)—DAR, 72, p. 285.
(*Augusta*)—Ancestry and Descendants of Lieut. John Henderson, 36-37; Boogher, 296-297; Historical Sketches of Campbell, Pilcher, etc.; John Wise, 322-336, 343; Waddell's Annals of Augusta Co., 91,494.
(*Cumberland*)—Kanawha, 880.
(*Frederick*)—Virkus I, 181.
(*Henry Co.*)—Henry Co., 181-182.
(*Highland*)—Highland Co., 357-358.
(*Petersburg*)—Hamiltons of Burnside, N. C., 104-105.
(*Rockbridge*)—Monroe Co., 349.
(*Spotsylvania*)—Culpeper, 87.
(*Valley of Va.*)—McCormick, 141-191.
(*West Va.*)—Ritchie Co., 218-219.
Hamlett—Henry Co., 75; TD, Sept. 8, Oct. 20, 1912.
Hamlin—Bruce VI, 466-467; Cyc. Va. Biog., I, 250; WM, XI, 59-60; XXIV, 288-289.
Hamm—Bruce IV, 40.!
Hammack—Cartmell, 489.
Hammaker—Kanawha, 467.
Hammer—Cyc. Va. Biog., V, 700; Highland Co., 358; Pendleton Co., 209-210.
Hammitt—Crockett, 51.
Hammond—Bruce VI, 358; Cyc. Va. Biog., I, 251; Rockbridge, 491; Sangamon Co., Ill., 354; TD, Oct. 23, 1910.
(*Richmond Co.*)—King's Mountain, 467; Mo. His. Soc. Cols., Vol. IV (No. 4), 1920; SBN, XI, 436-438; VM, XI, 186.
Hammontree—Coshocton Co., Ohio, 695.
Hamner—Albemarle, 214-216; Hampden-Sidney, 208-209, 212-213, 273.
Hamor—Cyc. Va. Biog., I, 251; Neill's Virginia Carolorum, 19; VM, I, 86; XIX, 140, 219; XXVI, 122; XXIX, 297; WM, X, 168.
Hampton—Biog. Cyc. of Ky. (1896), 341; History and Genealogy of the Earles, etc., 114-116; King's Mountain, 83; Rockbridge, 491; RS, II, 17; Sangamon Co., Ill., 396; Stubbs, 123-124;

TD, April 12, 1908; Nov. 26, 1911; Dec. 3, 10, 17, 1911; Thos. Carter, 194-199; Two Families, 36, 100-103; VM, II, 309-310; Virkus III, 316.

Hamrick—Barbour Co., W. Va., 389-391.

Hanby—Hughes, etc., 120-122; Pittsylvania, 95.

Hancher—Cartmell, 484.

Hancock—Bruce VI, 439; TD, May 6, June 10, 17, 24, Aug. 19, 1906; Jan. 24, 1915; Virkus II, 39-40; III, 93; VM, XXXII, 413-416; XXXIII, 107-112, 212-215, 316-321, 416-420; Woodson, 651.

(*Albemarle*)—Albemarle, 214-216.
(*Botetourt*)—Johnstons of Salisbury, 178-184, 205-214; RS, IV, 11 (Oct. 30, 1880).
(*Charlotte*)—Bruce V, 103-104.
(*Franklin*)—Bruce VI, 395.
(*Goochland*)—Bruce VI, 279-281.
(*Henrico*)—VM, XXXIII, 107-112, 212-215, 316-321, 416-419.
(*Lower Norfolk*)—Armistead, 164; McIntosh I, 113-114.
(*Surry and Sussex*)—VM, XXXIII, 419-420.

Hand—VSR, I (No. 3), 45; Monroe Co., 349-350.

Handford—VM, XIII, 199-200; XVI, 71.

Handley—DAR, 71, p. 1; Monroe Co., 350.

Haney—DAR, 82, p. 41.

Hangar—McCue, 54, 98, 148; Rockbridge, 148.

Hanger—Peyton, 316; Rockbridge, 491; TD, Aug. 6, 1911.

Hankins—Coshocton Co., Ohio, 690; Tazewell II, 440-445; WM, XII, 28.

Hankla—Bruce IV, 528.

Hanks—Campbell Co., 422-423.

Hanmer—TD, June 5, 1904.

Hanna—Bell, 30; Biog. Cyc. of Ky. (1896), 100-101; VM, XVI, 205-206.

Hannah—Adams Co., Ohio, 565-566; Bruce V, 558; Pocahontas Co., 218-229; Rockbridge, 491.

(*Charlotte*)—Cabell, etc., 283.

Hannon (*Botetourt*)—WVM, I, October, 1901, p. 15.

Hansard—Speed, 150-151.

Hansborough—Culpeper, part 2, 139; MMV, I, 242-244.

Hansel—Highland Co., 295.

Hansford—ARP, II, 800-801; Kanawha, 462; TD, Feb. 5, June 11, 1911; July 21, 1912; Tucker Co., 416; Tyler's II, 270.

(*King George*)—Hayden, 726.
(*Norfolk*)—Burgess, 564-565.
(*Orange*)—WVM, IV, 49-56.
(*York*)—WM, III, 246.

Haralson—Virkus I, 625; III, 405.

Harbaugh—Miami Co., Ohio, 524.

Harbert—Crockett, 104-105, 109, 114; Harrison Co., 373.

Harber—Miami Co., Ind., 697.

Harbeson—Green's Ky. Families; Marshall, 363; RS, III, 149.

Harcum—Burgess, 570-572.

Hardaway—Bruce V, 551; Genealogical Statement—Allen; Goodwin, 99, 136-137; Habersham Chap. II, 201-202, 226-228, 296-297; Jones, 297; Southside Va., 100, 162-163; Thos. Hardaway of Chesterfield Co., etc., by Sarah D. Hubert (Richmond, Va., 1906); VSR, V (No. 2), 52; WM, II, 141; XX, 216-217.

(*Brunswick*)—DAR, 78, p. 16.

Hardbarger—Rockbridge, 491.
Hardesty—Cartmell, 454; Lower Shenandoah, 677-678.
Hardidge (Hardick)—ARP, II, 449-450; VM, XV, 429-430.
Hardiman—Cyc. Va. Biog., I, 251. See also Hardyman.
Hardin, Harding—RS, II, 17.
Hardin—Albemarle, 217; Draper Series, V, 163; Fauquier Bulletin,
    469-470; Green's Ky. Families, 177-183; Van Meter, 76-77;
    Virkus I, 626; III, 408; VM, IV, 121; VII, 192.
    (*Middlesex*)—VM, XXXV, 416.
Harding (Harden)—Bruce IV, 384; Randolph Co., W. Va., 350; RS,
    III, 7; WM, VIII, 75.
    (*Henrico*)—Crawfurdiana, 112-113; Ellis, 7; RS, IV, 9.
    (*Northumberland*)—Tyler's II, 104-110.
Hardman—Ritchie Co., 50-54, 92-94.
Hardway—Highland Co., 381.
Hardwich—WM, IV, 40.
Hardwick, Hardidge—WM 2d, III, 97-112, 157.
Hardwick—Armstrong II, 129-149; Cyc. Va. Biog., I, 251; Fothergill,
    103, 126; WM, XXII, 182-191; XXIII, 59.
Hardy, Hardin, Harding—Valentine II, 591-617.
Hardy—Bruce IV, 55, 407; V, 162; Hardy, 261-268; Monongahela
    III, 1050-1052; Rockbridge, 491; Virkus II, 287; VM, XIX,
    446; WM, IV, 247; VII, 234, et seq.
    (*Isle of Wight*)—Convention 1788, II, 137-138; Cyc. Va. Biog.,
    I, 251; VM, VIII, 387.
    (*Lunenburg*)—Buford, 295-299; Old Free State II, 216-280.
    (*Winchester*)—Bruce V, 35.
Hardyman—ARP, I, 278-279; VM, V, 82; VII, 354-355; WM, V, 272-
    273; VIII, 126; XI, 47-49.
Hare—Cabell, etc., 597; New River, 410-412; WM, VIII, 227.
    (*King and Queen*)—Cabell, etc., 260-263.
Hargis—Sangamon Co., Ill., 361.
Hargrave (*Caroline*)—Bell, 9-10, 54-56.
    (*Charles City*)—WM 2d, VIII, 136.
Hargrove—McIntosh I, 100; II, 5.
Harland—LCJ, Nov. 22, 1914 (II, 5).
Harlan—Munsell's VII, 18; Sangamon Co., Ill., 362.
Harless—Kanawha, 393.
Harlowe—Cyc. Va. Biog., I, 252.
Harman—Bruce VI, 159, 166; Cyc. Va. Biog., V, 818; Harman Gene-
    alogy; MMV, II, 161-162, 165-166, 169-171; IV, 167-169;
    News Leader (Richmond, Va.), Feb. 8, 1929, p. 8; Pendleton
    Co., 211-212; Tazewell II, 445-459.
Harmanson—Barton II, 147-148; Cyc. Va. Biog., I, 252; Mackenzie
    VII, 69, et seq; WM, VII, 108; Yeardley, 8-15.
Harmer (*Ambrose*)—VM, IX, 178.
    (*Eastern Shore*)—Cyc. Va. Biog., I, 252; VM, III, 273-274;
    XIX, 230; XXIX, 36-37.
    (*Frederick*)—Cartmell, 459.
    (*West Va.*)—Monongahela II, 698-700.
Harmon—Harman-Harmon Genealogy. J. N. Harmon, Sr. Rich-
    mond, Va., 1923; McGavock Family, 91; Shenandoah, 605.
Harned—WM, XX, 108.
Harness—Rockbridge, 491.
    (*Western Va.*)—Alleghany, 304; Van Meter, 171-173.
Harnsbarger—Rockbridge, 491: Monroe Co., 350.
Harnsberger—Bruce IV, 417; Rockingham Co., 360-361.

Harold—Highland Co., 358; Pendleton Co., 213-214.
Harper—Albemarle, 218; Cyc. Va. Biog., II, 261; Du Bellet I, 157;
(*Alexandria*)—Burgess, 1417.
Hampshire, 710; McAllister, 49-51; Old Alexandria, 313-
314; Pendleton Co., 393-397; Randolph Co., 351-352; Rock-
bridge, 491; TD, July 22, 1906; Virkus III, 219.
(*Essex*)—WM, III, 204, 273.
(*Sussex*)—Stubbs, 343.
Harpine—Bruce IV, 273.
Harpole—Pendleton Co., 322.
Harrell—Bruce V, 446; Cyc. Va. Biog., V, 609.
Harr—Monongahela II, 473-475.
Harrell—Cyc. Va. Biog., V, 609.
Harris—Burgess, 566-570; Harris Family in Va. from 1611 to 1914,
by T. H. Harris, n. p., n. d.; Harris Chart; Rockbridge,
491; TD, April 10, May 8, 1904; June 4, 1905; July 8, Oct.
21, 29, 1906; April 10, May 8, 1904; March 31, June 2, 1912;
Nov. 23, Dec. 14, 1913; Oct. 4, 1915; Jan. 10, 1915.
(*Albemarle*)—Albemarle, 219-222; Harris Genealogy, by G. D.
Harris (Columbus, Miss., 1914), 51-53; MMV, V, 195-196;
Woods-McAfee, 306-307.
(*Brunswick*)—DAR, 70, p. 93; Habersham, Chap. II, 147; Stubbs,
311-312.
(*Elizabeth City*)—VM, XXII, 160-172 (Capt. John).
(*Fauquier*)—Woodson, 605-606.
(*Goochland*)—Douglas, 24-25.
(*Greenville*)—DAR, 82, p. 321.
(*Hanover*)—Cyc. Va. Biog., I, 252; Goodwyn Fam. of America;
History of Rockingham Co., 356-357; Mackenzie VII, 265;
Munsell's X, 103.
(*Hayne, Devon, Eng., and Northumberland*)—VM, XX, 294.
(*Henrico*)—Browning, R. D., III, 804-806; Chart of the Descend-
ants of Capt. Thos. Harris; Cyc. Va. Biog., I, 252; RC, III,
33; VM, IV, 79, 248-249; VSR, III (No. 4), 21-22; WM,
VII, 237, et seq.; WM 2d, VIII, 134.
(*Isle of Wight*)—Green's Ky. Families, 198-199; Habersham
Chap. II, 147-148; Harris Genealogy, by G. D. Harris (Co-
lumbus, Miss., 1914); Stubbs, 243-245.
(*Loudoun*)—Licking Co., Ohio, 693.
(*Nelson*)—Bruce IV, 380.
(*Northumberland*)—Cyc. Va. Biog., I, 252; VM, XXIII, 308,
418-419; XXV, 417-419.
(*Powhatan*)—Bruce V, 55.
(*Spotsylvania*)—Bruce V, 67; Cyc. Va. Biog., V, 749.
(*West Va.*)—Randolph Co., 350; Ritchie Co., 33-35.
Harrison—BS, April 30, 1905; Dec. 16, 23, 30, 1906; Bruce V, 183-
184; Burgess, 572-577; Hening VII, 455-457; Keith Addenda
I-VII; SBN, XI, 452-457; Sketches of Lynchburg, 94-96;
TD. Sept. 27, 1903; June 24, July 29, Aug. 19, Sept. 2, Oct.
7, Nov. 11, 25, 1906; Feb. 24, March 10, April 28, Oct. 20,
27, 1907; Sept. 13, 27, Nov. 29, 1908; June 13, 20, 27, July
4, 18, Aug. 1, Oct. 17, 1909; Jan. 9, Aug. 7, 1910; May 11,
1913; Aug. 15, 1915.
(*Albemarle*)—Albemarle, 222-223.
(*Amelia*)—Brock II, 607-608.
(*Andrew, Essex*)—VSR, VII (No. 2), 33-50.
(*Augusta and Rockingham*)—Boogher, 373-379; Waddell's Annals
of Augusta, 152.

(*Botetourt*)—Crockett, 238-244.
(*Brunswick*)—Trezevant, 62-64; WM, XVIII, 62-63.
(*Brunswick, Gabriel*)—VM, XXIV, 193.
(*Burr*)—DAR, 70, p. 67; Monongahela III, 1024-1025.
(*Campbell*)—Campbell Co., 357-358.
(*Fluvanna*)—RS, III, 20.
(*Franklin Co.*)—Brock II, 727.
(*Gessner*)—Cyc. Va. Biog., II, 225-226; V, 1004.
(*Goochland*)—Pittsylvania, 183.
(*Isle of Wight*)—Ancestors, by James F. Crocker, 35-37.
(*Orange and Augusta*)—VSR, IV (No. 4), 28.
(*Dumfries*)—Harrison Co., W. Va., 389-390.
(*James River*)—Bristol Parish, 28, 177, 188, 230; Brock II, 643-
  645; Browning, C. D., 3d, 34-36, 66, 78, 186-187, 254-257,
  446-447; Browning, R. D., III, 155, 737-738, 751; Burwell,
  27; Cabell, etc., 236-240, 515-526, 531; Campbell's History of
  Va., 654; Carter Family Tree; Carter Henry Harrison. A
  Memoir, by W. J. Abbot (New York, 1895), 51-52; Con-
  vention 1788, I, 183-186; Cyc. Va. Biog., I, 253; IV, 473,
  478; Des Cognets, 51-52; Dinwiddie Papers II, 241-242;
  Du Bellet I, 51, 94-201, 275-279; II, 485-549; Hardy, 282-
  296, 426; Hayden, 183-186, 248; Hening III, 538-540; VIII,
  66-68, 510-515, 538-540; His. Encyc. of Ill., 222-223; Keith,
  41-52, and chart; Addenda II-VII; Kennedy I, 536, 540-541;
  II, 149-150; Lancaster, 63-70, 86-90, 186, 197-198; Lee;
  Lower Shenandoah, 645-646; Mackenzie III, 108-109, 371, 375;
  McGavock Family, 131; Meade I, 311; MMV, II, 172-
  173; Munsell's VI, 28; Old Chapel, 59, 66-67, 69; Old Free
  State II, 311-312; Page (2d ed.), 263-264, 266-269; RC, II,
  18, 41, 43, 45; III, 3; RS, II, 24-27, 38, 41; Robertson;
  SBN, XI, 452-453; Some Colonial Mansions (Glenn), 411-
  429; Spotswood Letters II, 41; Thomas Ritchie, by C. H.
  Ambler (Richmond, Va., 1913), 302; Tyler's VII, 286-287;
  Virkus I, 25-27, 62, 167, 605, 794; II, 346; III, 173, 228, 439;
  VM, II, 233, 235; III, 124-131; VI, 190, 233-236; VII, 283,
  357-358; VIII, 265-266, 329; X, 103-104; XIV, 441-442;
  XVII, 378; XIX, 446; XXIV, 421-422; XXX, 408-412;
  XXXI, 83-87, 180-182, 277-283, 361-380; XXXII, 97-104,
  199-202, 298-304, 404-410; XXXIII, 97-103, 205-208, 312, 316,
  410-416; XXXIV, 84-92, 183-187, 285-287, 384-388; XXXV,
  89-93, 207-211, 302-309, 451-455; XXXVI, 389-399; XXXVII,
  176-179; XXXVIII, 86-91; VSR, V (No. 2), 66; WM, I,
  152; IV, 146-147, 150; VII, 39; VIII, 36; X, 109-112, 140;
  XIV, 164-165; WM 2d, II, 12-15.
(*Northern Virginia*)—Cyc. Va. Biog., I, 253; Fauquier Bulletin,
  484; H. T. Harrison, 211-213; Hayden, 510-513; MMV, II,
  174-176; Roger Jones, 113-115; Shenandoah, 606-607; Virkus
  II, 386; VM, XXIII, 214-216, 331-333, 443-445; XXIV,
  97-99, 211-213, 314-315.
(*Prince George*)—DAR, 48, p. 327.
(*Richmond Co.*)—Tyler's VII, 286-287.
(*Rockbridge*)—Sangamon Co., Ill., 358-359.
(*Rockingham*)—Dunmore's War, 272; McAllister, 125, 127-128.
(*Rockingham and Augusta*)—Boogher, 373-379.
(*Skimino*)—Aris Sonis Focisque [Harrisons of Skimino]; Bruce
  IV, 12; Du Bellet II, 93-98; Memoir by Fairfax and Francis
  B. Harrison (privately printed, 1910); RS, II, 41.
(*Tazewell*)—Tazewell II, 394-395.

(*Westmorland*)—Draper Series V, 335; Tyler's VI, 205-206.
(*West Va.*)—Berkeley, 184, 231.
(*York*)—Baskerville Family, 96-97.
Harrod—VM, VII, 15.
Hart—Bruce VI, 323; Randolph Co., W. Va., 352-353; Rockbridge, 491; TD, Feb. 9, 16, 1913.
    (*Albemarle*)—Albemarle, 223-224; Bruce IV, 510; Hampden-Sidney, 273-274.
    (*Halifax*)—Halifax, 198-199.
    (*Hanover*)—Habersham Chap. II, 380-385; Virkus III, 417.
    (*King and Queen*)—DAR, 44, p. 31.
Harter—Miami Co., Ind., 679.
Hartless—Rockbridge, 491.
Hartley—Brock II, 645; Monongahela II, 736-737; III, 1154-1158.
Hartman—Pendleton Co., 219-220.
Hartsook—Cabell, etc., 609-610.
Hartwell—Cyc. Va. Biog., I, 253-254; Major, 130-132; VM, IV, 146-147; XXI, 359; WM, VI, 34; VII, 62.
Harvey, Harvie—TD, July 8, 1906; April 21, May 12, 1907.
Harvey—Monroe Co., 350-351; Rockbridge, 491.
    (*Botetourt*)—Thos. Carter, 356.
Harvie—Du Bellet I, 87-88, 171-173; Gilmer's Georgians, 62, 139; Green's Ky. Families, 89-90; Marshall, 100-101, 207-208; McGavock Family, 124; Old King William, 159; The Harvie Family (Richmond, Va., 1928), VHS Col. VI, 83; WVM, II, Oct., 1902, 44-46.
    (*Albemarle*)—Albemarle, 224-225; Virkus III, 25.
    (*Amelia*)—Crockett, 298.
Harwood—Bagby, 307-308, 340; Bruce IV, 490; V, 342; Cyc. Va. Biog., I, 234; IV, 447; V, 723; Hardy, 470-471; RC, II, 48; RS, II, 32; III, 36; TD, July 27, 1913; Virkus II, 60.
    (*Charles City*)—Lancaster, 70-73; VM, II, 184-185; IV, 90-91; V, 187.
    (*Elizabeth City*)—WM, I, 96.
    (*King and Queen*)—Bagby, 307-308, 333, 340-341; VM, II, 183-185; WM, X, 198-200.
    (*Warwick*)—TD, July 27, 1913; VM, II, 183-184; WM, XI, 264-265.
Haskins—Brock II, 787; Southside Va., 164; WM, XXV, 199-200.
Hatch—Bruce V, 88.
Hatcher—Bates, et al. of Va. and Mo., 36-37, 85-86, 96-102, 139-140; Bruce IV, 73; Cyc. Va. Biog., I, 254; Dupuy, 260-261; Hardin Co., Ohio, 937; McAllister, 255-266; MMV, V, 197-199; TD, Aug. 9, 1908; VM, V, 98-100; VI, 404; WM, XXIV, 267; XXV, 91; XXVII, 192; Woodson, 68.
Hatchet, Hatchett—TD, Dec. 25, 1904; Feb. 18, 1906; April 21, 1912.
Hatchett—Old Free State II, 280-289.
Hathaway—Bruce V, 563; Genealogy of the Kemper Family, Appendix, p. 1.
Hatton—Rockbridge, 491; TD, Dec. 14, 1913.
    (*Norfolk Co.*)—Brock II, 671; McIntosh II, 197.
Hauck—Lower Shenandoah, 785-786.
Haviland—Cyc. Va. Biog., I, 254-255.
Haw—Virkus II, 346.
Hawes—Buckners of Va., 132; Caroline Co., 440-441; Cyc. Va. Biog., IV, 252; SBN, XII, 446; Virkus II, 148; Pendleton Co., 322.
Hawkins—Garrard, 77-81; Hardesty (*Bedford*), 419; TD, June 7, 1914; Virkus III, 216; VM, III, 36-37, 92; IV, 151-152.

(*Botetourt*)—Green's Ky. Families, 78.
(*Culpeper*)—DAR, 70, p. 13.
(*Essex*)—Cyc. Va. Biog., I, 255; Hord Family Supplement, 89-90.
(*Frederick*)—VM, X, 105.
(*Gloucester*)—DAR, 81, p. 321.
(*King William*)—Memoranda of the Hawkins Family, by Gen. J. S. Hawkins.
(*Old Rappahannock*)—VM, IV, 151-152.
(*Shenandoah*)—Montgomery Co., Ohio, 297.
Hawley—Crockett, 289; Cyc. Va. Biog., I, 107-108; Thos. Carter, 112-113; VM, XXVI, 383.
Hawse—Bruce IV, 280.
Hawthorne—Major, 128-130; Old Free State II, 156-157, 263-265.
Haxall—ARP, I, 321-322; Bristol Parish, 178-181; Brock II, 788; Hayden, 582-583; Virkus I, 168; VSR, V (No. 2), 44; WM, XII, 47-52.
Hay—RS, II, 45.
(*Anthony*)—Cyc. Va. Biog., I, 253; Tyler's VIII, 277-278.
(*Clarke*)—Cyc. Va. Biog., V, 608; Old Chapel, 30, 36, 39, 45.
(*Southampton*)—WM, XV, 84-87.
(*Williamsburg*)—Cyc. Va. Biog., I, 253; WM, III, 127, 166; V, 272.
(*York*)—Cyc. Va. Biog., I, 253; VM, III, 337.
Hayden—Hayden, 26.
Hayes, Hays—TD, April 29, 1906; May 12, 1907; March 3, 1912.
Hayes—Burgess, 563-564; Goode, 84-85; RS, III, 45.
(*Gloucester*)—DAR, 47, p. 24.
(*Isle of Wight*)—Cyc. Va. Biog., IV, 446.
Hayhurst—Ritchie Co., 342-343.
Haymaker—Cartmell, 465-466; Johnson Co., Ind., 614.
Haymond—Braxton Co., 386-387; Harrison Co., W. Va., 369-371, 379-380, 393; Haymond Family (1903); Monongahela I, 527-531; II, 803-805; Randolph Co., 354; Ritchie Co., 125-132; WVM, IV, 232-241.
Haynes—Alleghany, 204; Bagby, 366; Cyc. Va. Biog., I, 255; Tyler's I, 68; VM, XXXII, 60.
(*Gloucester*)—VM, XV, 427-428.
(*West Va.*)—Monroe Co., 351-352; Summers Co., 558-561.
Haynie, Hayney—Cyc. Va. Biog., I, 255-256; VM, XXII, 88-90; WM, VIII, 42.
Hayrick—Cyc. Va. Biog., I, 256.
Hays—Biog. Encyc. of Ky. (1877), 281; WM, IX, 247.
(*Albemarle*)—Albemarle, 225-226.
(*Augusta*)—Waddell's Annals of Augusta Co., 38.
(*Rockbridge*)—Rockbridge, 491-492; Walker-Wigton, 495-511.
Hayslet—Rockbridge, 492.
Hayter—Brock II, 729.
Haythe—Campbell Co., 423-424.
Hayward—Cyc. Va. Biog., I, 256; VM, I, 274.
(*Westmoreland*)—VM, IX, 332-333.
Head (*Albemarle*)—Cisco, 264-266; Virkus I, 331-332.
Headley—Bruce V, 431.
Heady—DAR, 48, p. 191.
Heale—Cyc. Va. Biog., I, 256; Hayden, 55; Hening VIII, 63-65; Tyler's VII, 287; VM, XVIII, 82.
Heale, Hale—TD, Aug. 16, 1908; Thos. Carter, 343-344, 355-356; WM, XVII, 202-203, 296-300.
Heale, Hele—Woodson, 135, 214, 353.

Heard—Habersham Chap. II, 451-460; Pittsylvania, 143; Virkus III, 181; VM, XIX, 425.
Heater—Braxton Co., 388-389; Bruce V, 195; Cartmell, 489-490.
(*Loudoun*)—Lower Shenandoah, 725-726.
Heath—BS, Nov. 27, Dec. 4, 1904; Burgess, 892; Cyc. Va. Biog., II, 113; Hayden, 514; Lineage Book (Order of Washington), 135-136; TD, Jan. 29, 1905; Aug. 5, Sept. 9, 1906; WM, XI, 207; XXIV, 109-115.
Heaton—Ritchie Co., 30-32.
Heatwole—Bruce V, 22; Heatwole Family of America, by Cornelius Heatwole (n. p., 1907); History of the Heatwole Family, by C. J. Heatwole, 1908.
Hebb—Tucker Co., 415, 419.
Hedges—Biog. Cyc. of Ohio, II, 404; Duke, etc., 43-46, 403-404.
Hedgman—Burgess, 280; Cyc. Va. Biog., I, 256; Hayden, 303, 309, 742.
Hedgpeth (*Nansemond*)—N. C. His. Reg., I, 109.
Hedrick—Highland Co., 359; Monroe Co., 353; Pendleton Co., 220-223; Summers Co., 544.
Heflebower—Hampshire, 711.
Hefner—Virkus II, 136.
Heironomous—Cartmell, 481.
Heiskell—Shenandoah, 607-608; TD, March 12, 1905.
Heizer—Rockbridge, 492.
Hele, Heale—John Wise, 343-347.
Helm—Auglaize Co., Ohio, 672-673; Burgess, 889; Cartmell, 470-471; Green's Ky. Families, 216-220; Hughes, etc., 209-212; Jolliffe, 103; Mackenzie VII, 275; TD, April 21, 1907; Virkus I, 334; VM, XVII, 90-91.
Helmick—Highland Co., 459; Pendleton Co., 223-224; Tucker Co., 417.
Helms—Highland Co., 295; TD, April 21, 1907.
Helphrey—Licking Co., Ohio, 682, 695.
Hempenstall—Highland Co., 381.
Henderson—Johnson Co., Ind., 615; Meade II, 233; Rockbridge, 492; RS, II, 23; TD, Sept. 10, Nov. 26, Dec. 3, 1905; July 9, 1911; Aug. 29, 1915; June 11, July 16, 1916; Tyler's X, 60; WM, VIII, 135.
(*Accomac*)—Burgess, 890-892.
(*Albemarle*)—Albemarle, 226-228; Habersham Chap. II, 199; Hughes, etc., 209-212; McCue, 182-183, 195-198, 212-214, 239.
(*Alexander*)—Henderson Chronicles, etc., by J. W. McCue [n. p.], 1913.
(*Augusta*)—Virkus III, 47; WM 2d, III, 259.
(*Alexandria*)—Avery I, 158-159.
(*Cumberland*)—Bruce IV, 311.
(*Dumfries*)—Hayden, 723.
(*Fairfax*)—RC, II, 18, 39.
(*Greenbrier*)—Ancestry and Descendants of Lieut. John Henderson, by J. L. Miller (Richmond, Va., 1902); Thos. Carter, 191-194; WVM, V, 108-114.
(*Hanover*)—Cyc. Va. Biog., V, 944; Hughes, etc., 218-263, 277-289; Mackenzie IV, 177-178; VM, XXXIII, 379-380.
(*Highland*)—Highland Co., 381.
(*Pittsylvania*)—St. Louis II, 1016.
(*Rev. James*)—Brock II, 752; Cabell, etc., 426, 435-436.
(*Western Va.*)—McClure, 212; Monroe Co., 353.
Hendree—Virkus III, 44.
Hendren—DAR, 48. p. 393; McCue, 16.
Hendricks—DAR, 80, p. 4.

Herndon—Burgess, 899-900; King's Mountain, 456, 461-462; Life of Gen. Hugh Mercer, 108, 125-126; Montague, 173, 300-302, 379-381; Sangamon Co., Ill., 372; TD, May 14, 1905; July 8, 22, 1906; Aug. 22, 1909; Virkus III, 238; VM, IX, 318-322, 439-441; X, 90-92, 200-201, 304-306, 441-443; XI, 98-101, 203-205, 332-335, 448-451; XII, 109-111, 212-214.

Herold—Highland Co., 358-359.

Herrell—Cartmell, 442.

Herrick—Cyc. Va. Biog., I, 257.

Herring—Boogher, 339; Bruce IV, 287; Highland Co., 382.

Herron—Rockbridge, 492.

Hervey—Panhandle, 349.

Hesser—Sangamon Co., Ill, 373.

Heterick—Lower Shenandoah, 698-699.

Heth—Bruce VI, 192; Hardy, 426; Lancaster, 160-161; MMV, II, 183-184; RS, II, 26; VSR, IV (No. 3), 20.

Hethrick—Cartmell, 484.

Hevener—Bruce VI, 85, 192; Highland Co., 295-297; Pendleton Co., 224-226.

Hewell—TD, April 30, 1905.

Hewes—TD, Oct. 9, 1904.

Heyman—Cyc. Va. Biog., I, 257; VM, XI, 158-159; XXV, 379.

Heymond—The Heymond Family, by Henry Heymond (Morgantown, W. Va., 1903).

Heyward (*York*)—Cyc. Va. Biog., I, 257 [Howard]; WM, II, 98-99.

Hiatt—Mackenzie V, 280-283; TD, June 2, 1912.

Hickey—Licking Co., Ohio, 687; RS, II, 49.

Hicklin—Alleghany, 205; Bath Co., 195; Highland Co., 297-298.

Hickman—Buford, 208-209; Cyc. Va. Biog., I, 257; Dupuy, 369-370; Goode, 101-103, 200-201; Harrison Co., 383-384; Lewis, 131-186; McAllister, 366-367, 370-400; McCormick, 87-89; Rockbridge, 492; Roger Jones, 189-192; Virkus I, 334; III, 35; VM, XXXIV, 216-219, 372-373; WM, III, 248; X, 204-205.
(*Culpeper*)—DAR, 81, p. 129.
(*Highland*)—Highland Co., 382.

Hicks—Burgess, 907-908; Cyc. Va. Biog., V, 730; Genealogical Statement, by Capt. C. T. Allen, 45-46; Highland Co., 298; Rockbridge, 492; TD, Aug. 20, 1905; May 13, July 1, 1906; July 28, 1912; VSR, I (No. 2), 28; WM, XI, 130-131.
(*Washington Co.*)—Brock II, 730.

Hickson—Bruce V, 86; TD, Dec. 9, 1906.

Hiden—Culpeper, part 2, 139; Willis, 54.

Hidy—Highland Co., 298-299.

Hiers—Rockbridge, 492.

Hiestand—Biog. Cyc. of Ohio, II, 547; Shenandoah, 609.

Hiett—Bruce V, 87; Cartmell, 484; Hampshire, 709.

Higdon (*Alexandria Co.*)—Burgess, 900-901.

Higginbotham—Bruce IV, 435; Burgess, 902; Cabell, etc., 317-318; Kanawha, 806-807, 834; Monongahela II, 773; Monroe Co., 354; Tazewell II, 459-471; Virkus II, 241; III, 459; WM, XXVI, 205-213, 265-274; XXVII, 45-56, 123-129, 294-298.

Higgins—Bruce IV, 14; Jolliffe, 95; Virkus II, 380.

Higginson—ARP, II, 464-465; Cyc. Va. Biog., I, 112, 257; Higginsons of England and America, part I (Boston, 1903); VM, IV, 207; VSR, V (No. 1), 76; Winston, 120-122; WM, II, 220, 231; III, 136; V, 186-187; VI, 69; XIX, 292-293.

High—Kanawha, 810.

Higinbotham—Monongahela II, 593-594.

Hill—BS, Feb. 16, 23, March 1, 8, 15, 1908; Burgess, 902-905; Hayden, 388; Old King William; Rockbridge, 492; RS, III, 38; St. Mark's, 193; TD, June 9, July 21, Aug. 4, 25, 1907; Jan. 28, 1912; Feb. 1, 1914; Jan. 31, 1915.
  (*Amelia*)—WM 2d, I, 215.
  (*Brunswick*)—Stubbs, 384-386; BHNC, VIII, 224.
  (*Buckingham*)—Cyc. Va. Biog., II, 113.
  (*Charles City*)—Brock I, 253; II, 789; VM, III, 319-321; WM, III, 66; IV, 147.
  (*Chesterfield*)—DAR, 76, p. 218.
  (*Culpeper*)—Culpeper, 111; part 2, 85-86, 94-96; St. Mark's, 193 (Ambrose Powell Hill).
  (*Cumberland*)—Hampden-Sidney, 78-79.
  (*Eastern Shore*)—John Wise, 81-82.
  (*Elizabeth City*)—Cyc. Va. Biog., I, 257; VM, XXVII, 36.
  (*Henry Co.*)—Henry Co., 182-187.
  (*Isle of Wight*)—Crocker, 29-35; Cys. Va. Biog., I, 258; WM, VII, 232 et seq.
  (*King and Queen*)—Bagby, 72-73, 76, 343-344; Burgess, 1466; Cyc. Va. Biog., I, 257; Old King William, 64-67, 148; VSR, I, 4; VM, XXXIV, 369-370; XXXVII, 24; WM, XVI, 97-99.
  (*King William*)—VM, XV, 102; XXVII, 94.
  (*Lower Norfolk*)—Cyc. Va. Biog., I, 257-258.
  (*Petersburg*)—Cyc. Va. Biog., V, 843.
  (*Rockingham*)—DAR, 82, p. 372.
  (*Shirley*)—BS, Feb. 16, 23, March 1, 8, 15, 1908; RS, III, 38; VM, III, 156-159; X, 107; XIV, 171; WM, IV, 147, 150.
  (*Thomas*)—VM, XI, 60-61.
  (*Warwick*)—Burgess, 903-905.
  (*West Va.*)—Pocahontas Co., 117-122.
  (*Wood Co.*)—DAR, 78, p. 299.
  (*York*)—Cyc. Va. Biog., I, 258; WM, I, 91; VII, 108; VIII, 256
Hille—Pendleton Co., 224, 322.
Hilliard—Rockbridge, 492; Virkus III, 635 (with arms).
Hillis—Rockbridge, 492.
Hillman—Bruce V, 38.
Hillyard—Bruce V, 182.
Hillyer—RS, I, 38, 40, 48.
Hilton—Goode, 110; RS, I, 48.
Hinchman—Bruce IV, 358; Monroe Co., 354.
Hinclker—Cartmell, 482.
Hinds—Rockbridge, 492.
  (*Berkeley*)—Ewing Family, etc., 136-137.
Hinegarner—Highland Co., 299.
Hiner—Highland Co., 299-302; Miami Co., Ind., 698; Pendleton Co., 226-227.
Hines (*Campbell*)—Descendants of Henry Hines, Sr. (1732-1810), Louisville, 1925; Monroe Co., W. Va., 354-355.
Hinkle—Highland Co., 359; Pendleton Co., 228-230.
Hinkston—DAR, 83, p. 197.
Hinton—Bruce V, 155; MMV, IV, 179-182; WM, II, 150.
  (*Western Va.*)—WM, XX, 110-111.
Hipkins—Fothergill, 184; Tiernan, etc., 416.
Hiser—Pendleton Co., 230.
Hisey—Licking Co., Ohio, 683.
Hissom—Kanawha, 507.

Holbrook—Rockbridge, 493.
Holcomb—Highland Co., 382; Kennedy I, 100-101.
Holcombe—America Heraldica, 141-142; Campbell Co., 427-428; Hampden-Sidney, 43, 115-116; Holcombe Genealogy; SBN, XI, 503; WM 2d, VIII, 318.
Hold—Alleghany, 206-207.
Holden—Descendants of John Stubbs, 32; WM, V, 176.
Holder—DAR, 80, p. 180.
Holderby—Cyc. Va. Biog., I, 259; WVM, I, Oct., 1901, 28-29 (No. 4).
Holeman—"Grafton Johnson", 78.
Holford—VM, III, 328.
Holiday—Cyc. Va. Biog., I, 259.
Holladay—Armstrong II, 161-172 [Holloday]; Campbell Co., 427-428; Hayden, 356-376; TD, March 24, Sept. 15, 1907; Tyler's IV, 447-448; VSR, III (No. 3), 26.
    (*Nansemond*)—Cyc. Va. Biog., V, 1019.
    (*Spotsylvania*)—Burgess, 913-915; Lewis, 147; McAllister, 367, 377-378, 386; Tyler's II, 257-262; Virkus I, 363-364.
Holland—Cyc. Va. Biog., I, 259; IV, 25, 374; TD, March 27, April 17, 1904; Jan. 14, 1912; WM, IV, 206.
    (*Eastern Shore*)—TD, Nov. 9, 1913; Yeardley, 27-28.
    (*Halifax*)—Chappell, 231-233.
Hollawell—McIntosh II, 288-289.
Hollenback—WVM, I, Oct., 1901, 27-28.
Hollenshade—Miami Co., Ind., 775.
Holliday—Armstrong II, 161, et seq.; Brock I, 248-251; Hardesty, 387; Lower Shenandoah, 575-578; TD, April 28, 1907.
Hollier—Cyc. Va. Biog., I, 259.
Hollingsworth—Adams Co., Ohio, 574-577; Armstrong II, 175; Biog. Cyc. of Ohio, II, 417; Bruce IV, 346; Cartmell, 292-295; Hollingsworth Genealogical Memoranda; Descendants of Valentine Hollingsworth, Sr. (Louisville, Ky., 1925), 3-5, 37, 54-57, 101, 161-164; Jolliffe, 143-153; Lancaster, 449-450; WM 2d, I, 298.
Holloway—Bell, 30-31; Burgess, 917-918; Cyc. Va. Biog., I, 259; Pendleton Co., 231; Van Meter, 94-95; Virkus II, 95, 304.
    (*Caroline*)—McIlhany, 27-28.
Hollows—Cyc. Va. Biog., I, 259.
Holman—Cyc. Va. Biog., I, 259; Rockbridge, 493.
Holmes—Hardin Co., Ohio, 1005; Rockbridge, 493; Southside Va., 157.
    (*Frederick*)—Berkeley, 222-223.
Holmwood—Cyc. Va. Biog., I, 259.
Holston—DAR, 83, p. 73.
Holt—Braxton Co., W. Va., 384-385; Bruce IV, 548; Halifax, 304; Hardesty (*Bedford*), 419; Highland Co., 382; SBN, XI, 507; TD, March 13, April 17, 1904; Oct. 21, 1906; Tyler's VII, 277-285; VM, V, 452-453; XIX, 236-237 (Randall); WM, XVII, 154; XIX, 144.
    (*Alexandria*)—Avery I, 160.
    (*German*)—WM, XXVI, 185.
    (*Orange*)—BHNC, VII, 160.
    (*Surry*)—Cyc. Va. Biog., I, 260; VM, XXV, 231.
    (*Surry and Norfolk*)—Cyc. Va. Biog., I, 259-260; VM, XIV, 438.
    (*West Va.*)—Monongahela III, 923-926.
Holtsapfel—WM 2d, VIII, 59.
Holtzclaw—Cyc. Va. Biog., I, 260; Fauquier Bulletin, 204; VM, XI, 233-234; XXIX, 98-100.
Honaker—Monroe Co., 356.

Hone—Cyc. Va. Biog., I, 260; Family Record of the Moreheads, 21-22; VM, IV, 4; Winston, 151-157; WM, VI, 98.
Honeyman—Miami Co., Ohio, 650.
Honeywood—Cyc. Va. Biog., I, 266; WM, III, 64.
Honyman—DAR, 72, p. 85.
Hood—Highland Co., 303.
Hooe—Avery I, 59; BS, March 22, 1908; Cyc. Va. Biog., I, 260; V, 807-808; De Bow's Review, XIX, 265; Family Records of "The Moreheads", Los Angeles, n. d., 21-22; Fauquier Bulletin, 97-98; Hayden, 716-719; Hooe Genealogy (1891), 4 pages; Lancaster, 347-349; Meade; RS, III, 5; TD, Jan. 18, March 8, 1914; Throckmorton, 346; Tyler's IX, 204-206; Virkus II, 319; VM, III, 301; IV, 427-429; XII, 319-320; XXI, 287; VSR, V (No. 2), 29; WM, II, 88; VII, 119.
Hooes—TD, March 27, 1910.
Hooff—Old Alexandria, 323.
Hook—Bruce V, 189-190, 225; Highland Co., 303; VM, XXXIV, 149-150.
Hooke—Highland Co., 416; VM, III, 22-23.
Hooker (Henrico)—Valentine II, 618.
Hoomes—Caroline Co., 356-358; VM, XXXVIII, 74.
Hooper (Buckingham)—Rives, 607.
Hoover—Alleghany, 205; Braxton Co., W. Va., 385, 389; Bruce IV, 287, 371, 491; V, 100; Cartmell, 140-141, 464-465; Highland Co., 359-360; Pendleton Co., 232-233.
Hope—Armistead, 132-133; Bruce VI, 522; Cyc. Va. Biog., I, 260; IV, 165; V, 821-822; LCJ, Nov. 22, 1914 (II, 5); Norfolk, 496-499, 753-754; TD, Feb. 18, 1906; WM, VIII, 257-258.
Hopkins—Alleghany, 205; Biog. Cyc. of Ky. (1896), 361; Crozier, VI, 286, 288; Hardesty (Bedford), 419; Hopkins Genealogy; Meade I, 460; Pendleton Co., 231; Rockbridge, 493; RS, II, 31; SBN, XI, 512-513; Stubbs, 87-93, 437-438; Tazewell II, 471-476; TD, May 15, 29, June 19, 1904; WM, XII, 131.
    (Albemarle)—Albemarle, 229-230; DAR, 75, p. 210.
    (Arthur)—Thos. Carter, 124-133; VM, XXXIV, 381.
    (New Kent)—Bruce VI, 187-188; Cabell, etc., 140-141.
    (Northampton)—VM, V, 429.
    (Pittsylvania)—Pittsylvania, 46.
    (Winchester)—Mackenzie III, 373.
Hopson—Habersham Chap. II, 288-292, 307-309, 641-642.
    (Halifax)—Ragland, 29, 38, 69, 75, 109.
Hopwood—MMV, V, 208-210; Shenandoah, 610-611.
Hord—Buckners of Va., 96-97, 105; Cyc. Va. Biog., IV, 309; Family Record of the Moreheads, 63; Genealogy of the Hord Family, Phila., 1898; Hord Family in Virginia, Supplement, by A. H. Hord, n. p. 1915; Mackenzie I, 249-252; Munsell's III, 27; IV, 45-46; XI, 211; Photostat Copy of the History of the Hord Family, by Robert Hord; Thomas Hord, Gentleman, A Supplement to the Genealogy of the Hord Family, 1903; Va. S. R., I, 61; VSR, II (No. 1), 61.
Horn—Douglas, 69; Rockbridge, 493.
Hornbeck—Randolph Co., 355.
Hornby—Cyc. Va. Biog., I, 260; VM, XXXII, 51; WM, XVII, 246.
Horner—Arkansas, 120-131; Blair, etc., 209-257; Bruce IV, 526; V, 27; Hayden, 170-172, 186-190, 196-200; TD, June 6, 20, 1909.
Hornsberger—Sangamon Co., Ill., 358.
Hornsby—BS, Oct. 16, 1904; Burgess, 830; Notable Families, 99; VHS, Col. XI, 72; Watson, 102-104; WM, XVII, 169, 246.

(*Rockingham*)—Biog. Cyc. of Ohio, II, 380.
(*West Va.*)—Braxton Co., 393-394; Ritchie Co., 18-22.
Hughart (*Bath*)—Alleghany, 206; Fayette Co., W. Va., 627-628.
Hughlette (Hulett)—DAR, 72, p. 61.
Hughson—Bruce V, 448.
Huguley—Habersham Chap. II, 163.
Huie—Hayden, 599.
Hulett—DAR, 67, p. 82.
Hull—Bruce VI, 191; Hayden, 444, 446; Rockbridge, 494; TD, April
  15, 1906; Feb. 3, 1907; VM, XI, 332-333; WM, XXIII, 188,
  190.
  (*Augusta*)—Virkus I, 565.
  (*Highland*)—Highland Co., 303-305.
  (*Northumberland*)—Cyc. Va. Biog., I, 261.
  (*Pendleton*)—Van Meter, 81-82.
Hume—History of the Hume, etc., Families, 9-74, 265-269; LCJ, Jan.
  17, 1915 (II, 10); Madison Co., Ohio, 372, 889; MMV,
  IV, 203-207; Munsell's XII, 9; Norfolk, 532, 568; Register
  of the Ken. His. Soc., XII, 85-112; Statement of Francis
  Charles Hume (bound with Pamphlets of Va. Geneal., Va.
  His. Soc.); Virkus I, 399-400; II, 123; III, 69, 261-262;
  VM, XX, 381-421; WM, VI, 251; VIII, 84-91.
  (*Portsmouth*)—Cyc. Va. Biog., V, 677; BHNC, IV, 213-217.
  (*Spotsylvania*)—Cyc. Va. Biog., I, 261-262.
Humphrey—Buford, 82; Virkus I, 399-400; Rockbridge, 494.
Humphreys—MMV, III, 173-175; Rockbridge, 494.
  (*Augusta*)—Virkus II, 337; III, 499.
  (*Greenbrier*)—Braxton Co., W. Va., 385; Virkus II, 136.
  (*Smyth*)—MMV, I, 89-91.
  (*West Va.*)—Monroe Co., 359-360.
Hundley—Bruce V, 105; Cyc. Va. Biog., IV, 484; Mackenzie VI, 168-
  173; MMV, III, 176-178; Old King William, 67, 119.
Hungerford—DAR, 78, p. 289; Lineage Book, Order of Washington,
  145-146.
Hunnicutt—Bell, 137; WM, XXVII, 34-44, 113-122.
Hunt—TD, April 15, 1906; WM, XXII, 193.
  (*Charles City*)—Cyc. Va. Biog., I, 202; WM, IV, 124-125.
  (*Hanover*)—Pittsylvania, 195.
Hunter—Biog. Encyc. of Ky. (1877), 414; BS, Nov. 11, 18, 1906; Ellis,
  27; Hunter Family of Va. (1895), 50 pages; St. Mark's,
  153; TD, Aug. 22, 1909; Virkus III, 263; WM, II, 76; VII,
  12, 14, 145, 154.
  (*Alexandria*)—Virkus I, 628.
  (*Augusta*)—Hunter Family Register. Descendants of Samuel
    Hunter of Augusta Co., Va., Dubuque, Iowa, 1895.
  (*Bedford*)—Virkus I, 131-132.
  (*Berkeley*)—Berkeley, 222; Hampden-Sidney, 229-230.
  (*Campbell*)—Campbell Co., 430-432.
  (*Elizabeth City*)—Cyc. Va. Biog., I, 202; VM, XXXII, 246;
    WM, XIV, 149-150.
  (*Essex*)—Genealogy of the Mercer-Garnett Family of Essex
    Co., Va., by J. M. Garnett (Richmond, 1910), 20; Kennedy
    II, 153-157; Memoir of R. M. T. Hunter, 13-28; RS, III, 11.
  (*Fairfax*)—Records of Hunter, etc.; RS, III, 35, 36.
  (*Fredericksburg*)—WM 2d, I, 148-149.
  (*Norfolk*)—Brock II, 672-673; Lineage Book, Order of Wash-
    ington, 146-148.
  (*Princess Anne*)—Antiquary I, 127; WM, II, 76-77.

(*Rockbridge*)—McCue, 175, 180-181, 184, 188-191, 201-207, 217, 220-224; Rockbridge, 494.

(*Valley of Va.*)—Culpeper, 100; Kennedy II, 131-137, 144; Lower Shenandoah, 580-582, 634-635; Mackenzie I, 235; VM, XI, 217-218; WVM, V, 151-155.

Hunton—Bruce V, 3; Burgess, 212; Cyc. Va. Biog., IV, 535-537; Hardy, 91-93; Hayden, 274; MMV, I, 302-308; TD, April 12, 1908; Virkus I, 403; WM, XII, 96, 179, 182-183.

Huntsberry—Cartmell, 454, 463.

Hupman—Highland Co., 305-306.

Hurst—Border Settlers, 324; Bruce VI, 16; Cyc. Va. Biog., IV, 378; Tyler's I, 170-171.

Hurt—Brock II, 646; Caroline Co., 441-444; Cyc. Va. Biog., V, 866; Halifax, 207-210, 305-306; MMV, III, 181-183; Old Free State II, 251.

Husher—Ritchie Co., 189-190.

Huston—Biog. Cyc. of Ohio, II, 358; Green's Ky. Families, 278-281.

Hutcherson (*Pittsylvania*)—St. Charles, etc., Mo., 1098.

Hutcheson—Burgess, 155; Cyc. Va. Biog., V, 586-589; TD, March 13, April 17, 1904.

(*Augusta*)—McClure, 212.

(*Mecklenburg*)—Bruce V, 109; Virkus II, 97.

(*Rockbridge*)—Bruce IV, 169.

(*Shenandoah*)—Bruce IV, 253.

Hutchings (*Norfolk*)—Cyc. Va. Biog., I, 262; VM, XV, 379-380.

(*Pittsylvania*)—Brock II, 608; Thos. Carter, 138-139; VM, XX, 195.

Hutchinson—Braxton Co., 394-395; Burgess, 860, 937; Monroe Co., 360; Rockbridge, 495; TD, Nov. 20, 1904.

(*James City*)—Cyc. Va. Biog., I, 262.

(*King and Queen*)—Bagby, 344-345.

Hutchison (*Loudoun*)—MMV, II, 191-193.

Hutt—Bruce V, 291; Cyc. Va. Biog., I, 262; Kanawha, 957; TD, Oct. 7, 1906; WM, XV, 191.

Hutter—Bruce V, 136-137; Mackenzie II, 413.

Hutton—Bruce V, 466; MMV, IV, 208-209; Randolph Co., W. Va., 346-350; Rockbridge, 495.

Hyatt—Bruce V, 435; VI, 147.

Hyde—Miami Co., Ohio, 597; RS, II, 27; TD, Aug. 13, 1905; July 21, 1912.

(*Augusta*)—McCue, 16-17, 28-29, 56-57, 104-106, 152.

(*York*)—Cyc. Va. Biog., I, 262; WM, I, 86-87; VI, 126; XIV, 148-149.

Hyden (*Stafford*)—DAR, 56, p. 93.

Hyer—Braxton Co., W. Va., 389-392.

Hylton—Bruce VI, 615.

Hyman—Ritchie Co., 87-88.

Hymes—Rockbridge, 495.

Hypes (*Botetourt*)—St. Louis II, 1089.

Hyslop—Bruce VI, 518.

I

Ice—Barbour Co., W. Va., 405; Monongahela III, 1020-1024.

I'Anson—Armistead, 278; Jones, 189.

Imborden—McCue, 52-53, 97-98, 148.

Ingles—Bruce IV, 454-455; Cyc. Va. Biog., I, 263; WM, VI, 88; VII, 151 et seq.

J

386-388; Ritchie Co., 83-86; Rockbridge, 495; TD, Dec. 25, 1904.
(*Bath*)—Braxton Co., W. Va., 396-397.
(*Cumberland*)—DAR, 48, p. 179.
(*Frederick*)—Bruce IV, 409; Cartmell, 473; Lower Shenandoah, 760-761.
(*Harrison*)—Convention 1788, II, 66-70.
(*Norfolk*)—WM, XII, 200-201.
(*Prince William*)—Clemens' Wills, 49.
("*Stonewall*")—Brock I, 262; Early Life and Letters of Stonewall Jackson (Arnold, 1916).
Jacob (*Hampshire*)—DAR, 81, p. 87; LEP, Feb. 15, 1919.
Jacobs (*Amherst*)—Crawfurdiana, 20a, 29, 45-46.
Jagoe—VM, XXXVI, 140, 300.
James—RS, III, 11; Pocahontas Co., 347-351; Rockbridge, 495; Stubbs, 225; WM, V, 276; VI, 127.
(*Bedford*)—Adams Co., Ohio, 188-189.
(*Highland*)—Highland Co., 382.
(*Lancaster*)—Bruce V, 295.
(*Loudoun*)—Coshocton Co., Ohio, 712; Cyc. Va. Biog., IV, 187; Munsell's IX, 95.
(*Northampton*)—Burgess, 298-301; Virkus I, 655.
(*Northern Neck*)—VM, XXXIII, 308-309; XXXIV, 82-83, 273.
(*Pittsylvania*)—Bruce V, 505; Pittsylvania, 259.
(*Princess Anne*)—Antiquary III, 5; VM, XV, 229-230.
(*Spotsylvania*)—Genealogy of the Cloyd, Basye, etc., Families of America, 245-246.
(*Westmoreland*)—Munsell's IX, 95; XI, 216; "Rev. Colin Dew James", Journal of Ill. State His. Society, Jan., 1917.
(*West Virginia*)—Munsell's XI, 216.
Jameson—Albemarle, 234; Alleghany, 207; Knox Co., Ill., 876; Mackenzie IV, 386-387; Millers of Millersburg, 73; Rockbridge, 495; TD, June 29, 1913; Virkus III, 642; WM, II, 12; III, 199-201; V, 90; VIII, 251-255.
(*Charlotte*)—Hampden-Sidney, 94-95.
(*Norfolk*)—WM, XIII, 67-69.
(*York*)—VM, XXV, 285; WM, V, 90-94.
Jameson—Virkus III, 271.
Jamison—Bruce VI, 161; Clemens' Wills, 49; Virkus II, 87; III, 272.
Jamisson—WM 2d, VIII, 131.
Janney—Bruce V, 517; Cyc. Va. Biog., IV, 411; Jolliffe, 164, 170; Munsell's XI, 117; SHA, VIII, 119-128, 196-208, 275-286; Virkus III, 271, 443.
(*Loudoun*)—Lower Shenandoah, 734.
Jaquelin (Jacquelin)—America Heraldica, 91; BS, Feb. 25, 1906; Cyc. Va. Biog., I, 264; Du Bellet, I, 1-22; Huguenot Emigration, XIV; VM, XXXVII, 156; VSR, V (No. 2), 22; WM, IV, 49-51; V, 51-52.
Jaqueline (Jacqueline)—Kennedy I, 286-287.
Jarman—Bruce IV, 203.
Jarratt—Brock II, 646; Bruce IV, 70; TD, March 17, 1907.
Jarrett—Kanawha, 461, 575; Sangamon Co., Ill., 408-409; Tyler's IX, 122-124.
Javins—Avery I, 162.
Jarvis—Bruce V, 469.
(*Petersburg*)—Brock II, 647.
Jayne—Johnson Co., Ky., 304.
Jefferies (Jeffreys)—TD, Feb. 3, April 21, 1907.

Jefferies—Sangamon Co., Ill., 416.
    (*Cumberland*)—Cyc. Va. Biog., V, 688.
Jeffers—WM, VI, 25-26.
Jefferson—Albemarle, 235-238; Browning, R. D., III, 719-720; Cabell,
    etc., 387-388; Campbell's His. of Va., 604; Cyc. Va. Biog.,
    I, 264; Dinwiddie Papers II, 95; Goode, 44; Lancaster, 402-
    405; Md. Soc. Col. Wars, 12; Old Free State II, 289-297;
    Pittsylvania, 95; Randall's Life of Jefferson, I, 17; RC, II,
    4; Slaughter's Fry Genealogy, 22; TD, Oct. 29, 1916; The
    True Thomas Jefferson, by W. E. Curtis (Phila., 1901), 17-
    54; Tyler's VI, 199-201, 264-270; VII, 49-53, 119-124; VIII,
    39-41; Virkus III, 610; VM, I, 208-212; XXIII, 79, 173-175;
    XXV, 407-411; XXVI, 321-324; XXIX, 499-500; XXXVII,
    163-164; WM, XXIII, 181-182.
    (*Peter*)—Cyc. Va. Biog., V, 868; Researcher I, 33, with chart;
    VSR, IV (No. 1), 31.
    (*Western Va.*)—Lower Shenandoah, 776.
Jeffress—Halifax, 212-215; Southside Va., 165.
Jelf (Chelf)—Thos. Carter, 184-186; WM, XX, 46-49.
Jellis—Bruce V, 364; Cyc. Va. Biog., IV, 164; V, 920.
Jenings (Edmund)—Cyc. Va. Biog., I, 131, 264-265; Lee, 300-301;
    Meade; RS, III, 38; The Curio I, 160-161; WM, X, 33.
    (*Elizabeth City*)—WM, IX, 124.
    (*Isle of Wight*)—WM, IV, 112-113.
    (*York*)—Dinwiddie Papers II, 419; Hardy, 301; RC, II, 11;
    III, 5; Thomas, 344; VM, IV, 366; VI, 399; XII, 306-310;
    XIX, 188-189, 359; XX, 93; XXV, 379; XXIX, 349-350;
    WM, III, 154; IX, 124.
Jenkins—Barbour Co., W. Va., 408-409; Bruce V, 122; WM, IX, 129-
    130.
    (*Nansemond*)—Cyc. Va. Biog., IV, 383.
    (*Orange*)—Munsell's IV, 174.
    (*Rockbridge*)—McCormick, 92-94.
    (*Southampton*)—Cyc. Va. Biog., IV, 406.
Jenney (*Loudoun*)—Clemens' Wills, 49.
Jennings—Campbell Co., 436-437; Cyc. Va. Biog., I, 265; Hardesty
    (*Amherst*), 441; LCJ, Aug. 22, 1905 (II, 5); Southside Va.,
    165; TD, April 10, May 8, July 17, Oct. 30, 1904; Jan. 14,
    1906; Sept. 22, 1907; Tyler's IX, 277; VM; XII, 306-310.
    (*Cumberland*)—Montague, 142-143, 243-248.
    (*Elizabeth City*)—Kennedy I, 57-59; Tyler's IV, 425-437.
    (*Fauquier*)—Virkus III, 274.
    (*Isle of Wight*)—VM, XXII, 48.
Jerdone—Cyc. Va. Biog., I, 265; TD, March 3, 1907; Sept. 5, 1909;
    WM, V, 21-22, 70; VI, 37-38; VII, 42; XI, 153-160, 236-242;
    XII, 32; XIV, 141-145.
Jesse—Bruce VI, 114.
Jeter—Bruce IV, 135; Cyc. Va. Biog., V, 731; Hardesty (*Bedford*),
    420; TD, Nov. 25, 1906.
Jett—Fothergill, 182, 187; Mackenzie VI, 292; Ritchie Co., 257-258;
    WM, XVII, 20-26.
Jiggetts—Ragland, 119.
Jobe—Shenandoah, 612.
John—Montgomery Co., Ohio, 403.
    (*Loudoun*)—Clemens' Wills, 50.
Johns—Bruce IV, 224; Dupuy, 189; VM, XXXV, 78-79.
    (*Highland*)—Highland Co., 306-307.

Jolliff (Jolloff)—McIntosh II, 55-56.
Jolliffe—Cartmell, 484; Jolliffe Family of Virginia (1893), 245 pages; Lower Shenandoah, 644-645; Monongahela I, 390-395.
Jones—Bristol Parish, 138; BS, Jan. 7, 1906; Grayson Co., 148-161; Johnson Co., Ill., 622; Rockbridge, 495; St. Mark's, 191; TD, April 23, May 28, June 11, July 2, 1905; April 22, May 6, 20, 1906; May 12, 1907; Sept. 14, 28, Oct. 12, 1913; Aug. 23, 1914; WM, I, 22; II, 150, 210; IV, 188, 245; V, 192; VII, 60; VIII, 191; IX, 40.
(*Abingdon, Warwick, Southampton*)—Ridley, 482.
(*Albemarle*)—Albemarle, 238-240; Cabell, etc., 307-312.
(*Amelia*)—Chappell, 199-200; Cyc. Va. Biog., V, 1073; Hening VIII, 276-277; Huguenot Emigration, 141-142; John Burgwyn, Benjamin Cardiman and John Jones Virginian, by Walter B. Jones, Montgomery, Ala. (privately printed, 1913); Jones, 320-321; MMV, III, 187; Southside Va., 105-108, 165-171; VM, IV, 274-275, 284-288, 464-467; V, 103; XV, 317-318.
(*Bartholomew*)—VSR, II (No. 2), 56.
(*Bedford*)—Brock II, 733; Hardesty, 420-421.
(*Brunswick*)—Brock II, 673; Bruce V, 80-81; Burgess, 517-519; Cyc. Va. Biog., V, 828-830; Goode, 121-122, 235-237, 380-382, 384; John Jones Virginian, 77-116.
(*Brunswick, Charles City and Prince George*)—Jones, 243, et seq.
(*Cadwallader*)—Burgess, 519-520.
(*Cadwallader, Stafford*)—VM, XXI, 323-340.
(*Campbell*)—Campbell Co., 443-446.
(*Caroline*)—Sangamon Co., Ill., 418.
(*Clarke*)—Lower Shenandoah, 650-653.
(*Culpeper*)—Buckners of Va., 239; Culpeper, part 2, 89-94; Hayden, 159; Sangamon Co., Ill., 417.
(*Cumberland*)—Stubbs, 217-221.
(*Dinwiddie*)—Convention 1788, II, 369.
(*Edmundson*)—Family of Hoge, 51.
(*Elizabeth City*)—Du Bellet II, 307-308.
(*Emanuel*)—Cooke-Booth, 220-224, 261-265; Cyc. Va. Biog., I, 267; VM, IV, 162; VIII, 61-62; WM, II, 150, 210; III, 31-32, 42, 116; IV, 188; XI, 132-136.
(*Essex*)—Hening VIII, 159-162.
(*Frederick*)—Cartmell, 499-504; Lower Shenandoah, 771.
(*Gabriel*)—Buckners of Va., 222-224; Convention 1788, II, 16-19; Du Bellet I, 87, 157-158, 251-254.
(*Gabriel, Augusta*)—Marshall, 255-257, 319-320, 356-357; Waddell's Annals of Augusta, 81-84; WVM, II, April, 1902, 19-30; Oct., 1902, 46-47.
(*Gabriel,Culpeper*)—Burgess, 521; Culpeper, part 2, 89-94; Hayden, 150; VM, XXI, 87-88, 428.
(*Gabriel, Frederick*)—Marshall, 145-146, 201-202, 255-257, 319-320, 356-357. See "Gabriel, Augusta", above.
(*Gabriel, Rockingham*)—Cyc. Va. Biog., I, 267; Green's Ky. Families, 86-87; Rockingham, 350-351.
(*Gloucester*)—Tyler XI, 141-142.
(*Goochland*)—Douglas, 109.
(*Hampshire*)—DAR, 49, p. 184.
(*Harrison, Cumberland*)—American Ancestry of Joseph and Daniella Wheeler, 12, 18, 166.
(*Henry Co.*)—Brock II, 790; Henry Co., 83-86, 194-200.
(*Highland*)—Highland Co., 307-309.

(*Isle of Wight*)—DAR, 72, p. 85.
(*James City, Rev. Bartholomew*)—VSR, I, 12-13.
(*King George*)—DAR, 51, p. 306.
(*Lancaster*)—Burgess, 1016.
(*Middlesex*)—Bruce V, 546; VM, V, 164-165; WM, IX, 40-41.
(*Nansemond*)—N. C. His. Reg., I, 96.
(*Northumberland*)—WM, XXVII, 134-135.
(*Nottoway*)—Brock II, 648; Hampden-Sidney, 87-88.
(*Orange*)—Johnson Co., Ind., 621; WM 2d, I, 287-289; II, 133.
(*Orlando*)—Cyc. Va. Biog., I, 268; VM, VIII, 261.
(*Page*)—Brock II, 570-571.
(*Peter*)—Cyc. Va. Biog., I, 268; Old Free State II, 306, 342-344;
   Virkus I, 933; VSR, V (No. 1), 68; WM, XIX, 287-292.
(*Pittsylvania*)—DAR, 81, p. 80; Pittsylvania, 218.
(*Prince George*)—DAR, 59, p. 241; VM, XXIX, 100-101; Virkus
   I, 933; VSR, I, 29.
(*Rappahannock*)—Sangamon Co., Ill., 419.
(*Rice*)—Essex, 46.
(*Richmond Co.*)—Bruce VI, 33-34.
(*Robert, Northumberland*)—WM, XXIII, 191-202, 261-271;
   XXVII, 134.
(*Rockingham*)—SHA, II, 157-158.
(*Roger*)—Browning, R. D., III, 770; Bruce IV, 540; Capt. Roger
   Jones of London and Virginia; Cooke-Booth, 209-210; Cyc.
   Va. Biog., I, 268-269; Hardy, 330-331; Kennedy I, 675-676;
   Lee, 365-369; Major Thomas ap Thomas Jones of Bathurst;
   Mackenzie IV, 273-297; MMV, 237-240; Two Families, 140;
   Virkus II, 353-358; VM, V, 192-194; VI, 306; XXI, 317-
   320; VSR, III (No. 3), 39.
(*Rowland*)—VSR, II (No. 2), 54; WM, II, 150; V, 192-197;
   VIII, 191-192; XXV, 211.
(*Spotsylvania*)—DAR, 51, p. 283.
(*Warwick*)—Alstons and Allstons, 285-291; MMV, III, 184-185;
   Tyler's VI, 44-48, 146; VII, 134-136; VIII, 282-283; IX,
   280-283, 436-437; X, 211-212; WM, XII, 179.
(*West Va.*)—Monroe Co., 364.
(*York*)—Brock II, 691; Bruce IV, 558.
Jopling—Brock II, 609; Hardesty (Bedford), 421; Virkus II, 307.
Jordan—Bell, 257-258; Cabell, etc., 127-129, 144; Chappell, 173-174;
   Cyc. Va. Biog., I, 269-270; Halifax, 215-219, 221; Tarrisons
   of Skimino, 23-24; Pendleton Co., 236; Rockbridge, 259-260,
   496; Summers Co., 377-384; TD, Oct. 2, 1904; March 25,
   Dec. 10, 1905; Nov. 29, 1908; May 10, 1914; Valentine II.
   626-771; IV, 2268-2274; VSR, IV (No. 1), 43; (No. 4),
   25; WM, V, 282; VII, 231, et seq; X, 32; XIV, 32-33;
   XXVII, 121-122; WM 2d, VIII, 36.
(*Highland*)—Highland Co., 309-310.
(*Isle of Wight and Nansemond*)—VM, III, 186.
(*Nansemond*)—Virkus III, 598; WM, XXVII, 121-122.
(*Prince George*)—VSR, III (No. 1), 39-40.
(*Southampton*)—Bell, 102.
(*Surry*)—VM, IV, 2-4; XIV, 205; WM, IV, 196; XVI, 288-
   290.
(*West Va.*)—Pocahontas Co., 500-505.
Jordon—TD, March 12, 1905; Sept. 25, 1906.
Jouett—Albemarle, 240-242; Draper Series V, 304; His. Encyc. of
   Ill., 309-310; Mackenzie II, 86-88; SBN, XII, 27; VHS Col.

VI, 89; VM, VIII, 419; XI, 97; XXXVII, 27; VSR, April, 1923, 22-27.
Joyes—LEP, March 22, 1916, p. 6; Louisville's First Families, 91-100.
Joyner—Bruce IV, 579.
Joynes—Burgess, 522-525; Meade; MMV, IV, 222-223; RS, II, 34; WM, X, 145-147.
Judd (*Brunswick*)—Cisco, 266-269.
Jude—Burgess, 547.
Judkins—Cyc. Va. Biog., V, 982.
Judy—Highland Co., 360; Pendleton Co., 236-238.
Julian—Buford, 226; Munsell's VII, 173; VM, V, 455-456.
Jump—Burgess, 1375.
Junk—Knox Co., Ill., 289.
Junkin—Rockbridge, 260; TD, Sept. 12, 1909.
Jury—Licking Co., Ohio, 699.
Juxon—Baskerville Family (90); VM, XV, 318-320; XX, 91; WM, XVII, 229.

K

Kabler—Campbell Co., 446-447.
Kagey—Bruce IV, 191; Strickler, 158.
Kagy—Shenandoah, 613.
Kaifer—WM, XXVI, 186.
Karicofe—Highland Co., 382.
Karns—Hardesty (*Bedford*), 421.
Kaufman, Kauffman—Arkansas, 300-307; Strickler, 231.
Kay—WM, VII, 118, 245, et seq.
Kaylor—Hampshire, 714.
Kean—Brock II, 571; Caroline Co., 157; Cyc. Va. Biog., I, 30, 34; Dupuy, 228;; Griffith-Meriwether, 169-171; Page (2d ed.), 262; Virkus I, 352-353; II, 33.
Keaton—Monroe Co., 366.
Kech—Price, 46.
Kee—Pendleton Co., 238; Pocahontas Co., 292-298.
Keeling—Cyc. Va. Biog., I, 270; Ellis, 40; Mackenzie VII, 78; McIntosh I, 33, 67, 86-87; Norfolk, 652, 865; RC, III, 41; VM, IV, 200-201.
Keen—Bruce IV, 239; Cyc. Va. Biog., IV, 423; Pittyslvania, 260; Virkus III, 312.
(*James City*)—"Grafton Johnson", 121.
Keenan—Monroe Co., 365.
Keene—ARP, II, 451; WM, VIII, 45-46.
(*Fayette*)—Green's Ky. Families, 61.
(*Northumberland*)—VM, I, 472-473.
Keeran—Licking Co., Ohio, 705.
Keesee—Bullington Chart, by Arthur B. Clarke (Va. State Library); Virkus I, 562.
Keeton—Cyc. Va. Biog., I, 270.
Keezel—Bruce V, 227; MMV, III, 194-195; Rockingham, 361-362.
Keger—Rockingham, 496.
Kegley—Bruce VI, 573.
Keim—Keim and Allied Families.
Keist—Coshocton Co., Ohio, 717.
Keister—Bruce IV, 234, 297; Highland Co., 360; Monroe Co., 366; Pendleton Co., 239-240.
Keith—Bruce VI, 162-163; Cyc. Va. Biog., I, 270; V, 604, 870-872; Fauquier Bulletin, 287; Habersham Chap. II, 45-46; Mar-

shall, 24-31; Meade II, 216; MMV, II, 227-228; Rockbridge,
496; VSR, IV (No. 2), 38; V (No. 2), 53; VM, XXIV, 313.
(*Fauquier*)—Hayden, 267-268; Mackenzie I, 96.
(*Frederick*)—WM, XX, 104-108.
(*Rev. George*)—VM, III, 279-280; XXIII, 20, 144.
(*Rev. James*)—Hardy, 311-314.
(*Loudoun*)—Stark Co., Ohio, 618.
(*Rev. William*)—Browning, C. D., 3d, 630-631.
Keitz—Highland Co., 382.
Kell—Avery I, 165.
Kellam—Bruce IV, 429.
Kellar—Monongahela II, 649-650.
Keller—Rockbridge, 496; RS, IV, 3; Shenandoah, 613-614.,
Kelley (*Loudoun*)—Preston Co., 366, 445-446.
Kello (*Southampton*)—VM, XXXVII, 66.
Kelly—Albemarle, 242-244; Barbour Co., W. Va., 411; Brock II, 734-
735; Bruce, IV, 429; Rockbridge, 496; TD, March 5, 1911.
(*Highland*)—Highland Co., 310.
(*Loudoun*)—Preston Co., 366, 445-446.
(*Smyth*)—Bruce IV, 12.
(*Westmoreland*)—WM, XV, 129-131; XVII, 27-33.
Kelso—Rockbridge, 496; Walker-Wigton, 74-79, 641.
(*Bedford*)—Hardesty, 421.
Kemp—Cooke-Booth, 32, 33; Cyc. Va. Biog., I, 270-271; History of
Kemp and Kempe Families; TD, Dec. 6, 1908; Two Fam-
ilies, 122, 123; VHS Col. XI, 76, 77; VM, I, 420-421; II,
174-176; III, 40-42; VIII, 128; XX, 71-75; WM, II, 226,
235; III, 69, 70; Zimmerman, 36-44.
(*Caroline*)—Munsell's V, 143.
Kempe—WM, III, 69.
Kemper—Boogher, 302-303; Brock I, 242; Bruce III, 166; IV, 229;
Cyc. Va. Biog., I, 271; Genealogy of the Kemper Family;
Munsell's IV, 63; V, 108; Virkus I, 171; III, 100, 451; VM,
XI, 231-232.
Kencaster—Johnson Co., Ind., 580.
Kendall—Cyc. Va. Biog., I, 271; Kanawha, 555; TD, Sept. 10, 1905;
Aug. 5, 1906 [Kendal]; Ritchie Co., 322-328.
(*Eastern Shore*)—Hening VI, 443; VIII, 278-279; VM, XIX,
10-12; WM, XVIII, 108; VSR, IV (No. 4), 31.
Kender—Rockbridge, 296.
Kendig—Bruce V, 94-95.
Kendrick—Brock II, 736.
Kennedy—History of the Hume, Kennedy and Brockman Families,
by W. E. Brockman, Washington, 1916, 113-132; Mackenzie
I, 296-298; Rockbridge, 496.
(*Augusta*)—Mackenzie VII, 279.
(*Bedford*)—DAR, 82, p. 105.
(*Jefferson Co., from Md.*)—Kennedy I, 369-433.
(*Valley of Va.*)—Kith and Kin, 191-196.
Kenner—Cyc. Va. Biog., I, 271; Hayden, 82, 83; RS, II, 17; TD, April
23, 1905; VM, IX, 201-202; XX, 213, 214; WM, VIII, 109,
110; IX, 185-187; XIV, 173-181; XVII, 63.
Kennerly—Bruce IV, 186; Lower Shenandoah, 661-662; Mo. His. Soc.
Collection, pp. 88-123; VM, XX, 430-431.
Kenney—Grayson Co., 205-206.
(*Nelson*)—Waddell's Annals of Augusta Co., 338.
Kennon—Additional Baskerville Genealogy, 155-156; Baskerville Fam-
ily, 147-149; Bolling Genealogy, 23; Bristol Parish, 182-

187; Browning, C. D., 3d, 620-621; BS, June 18, 1906; Cyc.
Va. Biog., I, 271-272; Du Bellet I, 203; Hampden-Sidney,
159; Lancaster, 165; McAllister, 27, 102; Robertson; RC,
II, 89; RS, II, 45; TD, April 7, 28, 1907; Nov. 10, 1912;
Aug. 15, 1915; VM, V, 90-91; XIII, 91; XXIX, 497-498;
XXXI, 297; XXXII, 389-391; VSR, V (No. 1), 80; (No. 2),
49; Watson, 235; Woodson, 138, 217; WM, III, 203, 275;
V, 172; XIV, 132-135, 268-275; XV, 45-46; XIX, 165-167.
Kent—Burgess, 747-748; Crockett, 286-307; McGavock Family, 15-16,
35-39, 77-78, 81-84, 86-88, 101, 132-133, 137, 156-157; MMV,
V, 241-242; TD, May 7, 1905; April 28, 1907; Virkus II,
166; III, 290; Bruce VI, 290.
   (*Louisa*)—MMV, I, 117-119.
   (*Wythe*)—Cyc. Va. Biog., V, 969.
Kenton—SBN, XII, 35-36; Fauquier Bulletin, 189-195.
Kenurd—Browning, C. D., 3d, 620, 621.
Kenyon—TD, Jan. 22, 1911.
Keplinger—Pendleton Co., 238.
Ker (*Augusta*)—MMV, IV, 232-233.
Kerby—Armistead, 212-213; VSR, IV (No. 4), 22; WM, XVII, 301-
302.
   (*York*)—WM, XIV, 154-158.
Kercheval—Cartmell, 439.
Kerker—WM, XXVI, 186.
Kern—Bruce VI, 49; Cartmell, 460-461.
Kernes—Burgess, 750.
Kerns—Lower Shenandoah, 707.
Kerr—Albemarle, 244-245; Bruce IV, 577; N. C. His. Reg. I, 517;
Rockbridge, 496; RS, III, 28.
   (*Augusta*)—McClure, 124-125.
   (*Williamsburg*)—Tyler's IV, 39-41.
Kersey—Avery I, 166; Burgess, 69-70.
Kesling—Miami Co., Ind., 730.
Kessler—Miami Co., Ohio, 836.
Kessner—Pendleton Co., 238-239.
Ketterman—Pendleton Co., 238.
Key—Albemarle, 245-246; Hayden, 167-169, 182-185; Key and Allied
Families, by Mrs. Susan G. Lane (Statesboro, Ga.); Mar-
shall, 27-29; RS, III, 20; TD, Jan. 1, 15, Feb. 5, March
5, 1905.
Keyes—Sangamon Co., Ill., 427.
Keys—Rockbridge, 496.
Keyser—Bruce IV, 426; Cyc. Va. Biog., IV, 392.
Kidd—Rockbridge, 496; Sketches of Lynchburg, Va., 200-202.
   (*King and Queen*)—Cyc. Va. Biog., V, 794.
   (*Middlesex*)—DAR, 42, p. 103.
   (*Nelson*)—Braxton Co., W. Va., 399.
Kidder—Funsten-Meade, 40-41.
Kiddy—Rockbridge, 496.
Kiger—Rockbridge, 496.
Kilby—Brock II, 660; Cyc. Va. Biog., IV, 385; Genealogy of Kilby,
Tynes, etc., by C. M. Kilby (Lynchburg, Va., 1924), 5-14;
Norfolk, 633-634; TD, May 14, 1905.
Kilgore—Burgess, 653, 838.
Killingsworth—Highland Co., 310.
Kilpatrick—Rockbridge, 496.
Kimble—Pendleton Co., 243.
Kimbrough—Crawfurdiana, 47, 59-61.

Lake (*Fauquier*)—Sangamon Co., Ill., 438-439.
Lakes—Hardesty (*Bedford*), 422.
Lamb—Cyc. Va. Biog., I, 273; V, 571; Pendleton Co., 245-246.
    (*Charles City Co.*)—Bruce IV, 237.
    (*Highland*)—Highland Co., 311.
    (*Norfolk*)—MMV, I, 190-194.
    (*Sussex*)—MMV, III, 201.
    (*York*)—WM, III, 126-128, 203-204; VII, 51-54, 109-112.
Lambert—Pendleton Co., 246-249; Rockbridge, 498.
    (*Fauquier*)—MMV, IV, 236-237.
    (*Richmond City*)—Hardy, 426.
    (*Westmoreland*)—Fothergill, 122.
    (*Winchester*)—McIlhany, 132.
Lamkin—Fothergill, 152, etc.
Lamme—DAR, 69, p. 285.
Lampkin—Thos. Carter, 250.
Lampton—Ardery (Ky. Court and Other Records), 156.
Lancaster—Lancaster, 420-421; TD, Oct. 20, 1912; Virkus I, 186-187;
    VSR, I, 31.
Lance—Rockbridge, 498.
Land—Mackenzie VII, 73; Norfolk, 789-790, 914; Virkus I, 454.
Landcraft (*Nelson*)—Summers Co., 586-588.
Lander—DAR, 78, pp. 194-195.
Landes—Bruce VI, 90.
Landis—Pendleton Co., 249.
Landon—Cyc. Va. Biog., I, 273; Descendants of John Stubbs, 103;
    Keith, 88; VM, II, 430-433; IV, 364-365; XXXII, 262-263;
    WM, XII, 264 (note).
Landrum—DAR, 70, p. 209.
    (*Amherst*)—Hardesty, 441.
    (*Westmoreland*)—Burgess, 923-930.
Lane—Culpeper, 63, 65, 67; Habersham Chap. II, 92.
    (*Fairfax*)—Kennedy II, 228-231.
    (*Fluvanna*)—Bruce V, 330.
    (*Mathews*)—Cyc. Va. Biog., V, 776-777; Kennedy II, 231-236;
    MMV, I, 145-146.
    (*Miscellaneous*)—Kennedy II, 207-208, 237-259.
    (*Prince William*)—Glengarry McDonalds, 332-333.
    (*Spotsylvania*)—Kennedy II, 236.
    (*Westmoreland*)—Kennedy II, 237-259.
    (*Western Va.*)—WVM, I, Oct., 1901, 26-27.
Lang—Barbour Co., W. Va., 416-420.
Langborn—WM, XV, 257; XIX, 104-107.
Langborne—Armistead, 271; Cooke-Booth, 221; Old King William,
    17-18; WN, IV, 166.
Langbourn—Cyc. Va. Biog., I, 274; WM, V, 39.
Langfitt—DAR, 50, p. 105; Panhandle, 440.
Langford—Bruce IV, 323.
Langham—Madison Co., Ohio, 368.
Langhorne—Brock II, 573-574; Bruce III, 409; IV, 317; V, 215-216;
    BS, Dec. 25, 1904; Buford, 175-176; Campbell Co., 447-
    449; Cyc. Va. Biog., I, 274; IV, 395-399; Hardy, 315-319;
    Mackenzie II, 404-421; Marshall, 296-208; McGavock Fam-
    ily, 76, 78, 122-123, 151; Norfolk, 885-886; Sketches of
    Lynchburg, Va., 164-171; TD, Dec. 23, 1906; Feb. 10, 1907;
    Virkus I, 139; II, 24; VM, VIII, 319; XXIX, 437-438;
    XXXIII, 92-93, 311.

Langley—Cyc. Va. Biog., I, 274; Ellis, 55; Mackenzie VII, 73; McIntosh I, 123; II, 66-68, 169-170, 172, 211-212, 220, 259, 311; TD, July 5, 1908; Dec. 21, 1913; WM, XIX, 194-199.

Langston—RS, I, 44; Valentine II, 772-778; IV, 2242-2243; VM, XXVIII, 139-140.

Langtry—McCue, 226-227, 239-240, 242, 244, 246.

Lanham—Bruce VI, 123.

Lanier—Crozier VII, 67-72; Cyc. Va. Biog., I, 274; Harris Genealogy, by G. D. Harris, 104-106; Lanier Biography (1877), 87 pp.; Pittsylvania, 48, 213; Stubbs, 243, 311; Thos. Carter, 139; TD, March 19, June 25, 1916; Tyler's III, 126-141, 143-147, 210-211; Virkus I, 17, 193; III, 298; VM, XXVIII, 341; XXIX, 102; Welles' Washington Genealogy, 112, etc.; WM, III, 71-74, 137; IV, 35-36; XII, 18; XV, 77-79; XVII, 69-70.

Lankford—Cyc. Va. Biog., I, 274; Pittsylvania, 96, 194; VM, XXIII, 376.

Lanphier—Sangamon Co., Ill., 442.

Lansdowne—Hord (1898), 138-139.

Lantz—Highland Co., 311-312; Pendleton Co., 249; Ritchie Co., 149.

Lapsley—Clemens' Wills, 52 (Lapesly); Kith and Kin, 127; Rockbridge, 498; Woods-McAfee, 126-132, 278-288.

Larew—Monroe Co., 367-368; Rockbridge, 498.

Larkin—Rockbridge, 498.

Larrick—Bruce V, 198-199; Cartmell, 438, 486-487; Cyc. Va. Biog., V, 872-873; Lower Shenandoah, 694, 751-752.

Larue—Six Generations of Larues and Allied Families, by O. M. Mather, 1921; WM, XX, 101-102; WM 2d, I, 215.

La Rue—Bath Co., 196; Bruce IV, 220; Lower Shenandoah, 656-657.

Lassiter—Brock II, 648; MMV, IV, 238-239; V, 252-253; VM, XXVI, 410; XXVII, 93-94; XXX, 395-396.

Laswell—Sangamon Co., Ill., 444.

Latane—Bagby, 68, 366; Bruce VI, 106, 126; Cyc. Va. Biog., I, 274; Huguenot Emigration, 29; Montague, 68-69; MMV, IV, 240-241; Roger Jones, 136-140; Thomas Ritchie, 301; VM, VIII, 58-59; XI, 103-104.

Latham—Brock II, 575, 738; Fishback Family, 186-188, 274, 279-280, 283-285; Habersham Chap. II, 70, 92; Sangamon Co., Ill., 445.

Latimer—Burgess, 896.

Lauck—DAR, 46, p. 269.

Laughlin—Rockbridge, 498.

Laurens— (*Amelia*)—DAR, 51, p. 262.

Lavender—Summers Co., 384-385.

Laverty—Bath Co., 196.

Lavinder—Henry Co., 212-216.

Law—Ritchie Co., 264-265; Rockbridge, 498.

La Warre—TD, Nov. 22, 1908.

Lawless—Cyc. Va. Biog., IV, 171; MMV, II, 242.

Lawrence—Licking Co., Ohio, 706; Pendleton Co., 250; Rockbridge, 498; TD, May 12, 1907.

(*Isle of Wight*)—N. C. His. Reg., I, 90.

Lawson—Bruce V, 159; BS, May 12, 1907; Cyc. Va. Biog., I, 275; Rockbridge, 498 TD, March 3, 1907.

(*Halifax*)—Halifax, 225-227, 313.

(*Lancaster*)—Kemper Family Appendix I, II; Thos. Carter, 136; VM, IV, 202-203, 313-314; V, 284; XXVI, 384; WM, XVIII, 237.

(*Lower Norfolk*)—Antiquary I, 48-55; Habersham Chap II, 580; McIntosh II, 144-145: VM, V, 152-153.
(*Northern Neck*)—WM, XVIII, 237.
(*Norfolk and Princess Anne*)—Burton I, R68-69.
(*Prince Edward*)—Hampden-Sidney, 72-73; MMV, IV, 244-250.
(*Princess Anne*)—WM, IV, 16.
(*Richmond Co.*)—VM, XXIX, 360.
Laydon—Cyc. Va. Biog., I, 275; VM, II, 69.
Layfield—Ritchie Co., 183.
Layman—Bruce IV, 433, 463; VI, 404.
Layne—Highland Co., 312-313, 382.
Layton—Licking Co., Ohio, 709.
Lea—Bruce IV, 171; TD, May 26, 1907; March 29, 1914.
Leach—Highland Co., 312-313; Pendleton Co., 250.
(*Prince Edward*)—Monroe Co., 368-369.
Leachman—Bruce V, 458.
Leadbeater (*Alexandria*)—Bruce VI, 567; MMV, V, 254-255.
League (*Jefferson Co.*)—Braxton Co., W. Va., 400.
Leake—Albemarle, 248-250; Bruce IV, 193, 488; Cyc. Va. Biog., IV, 105-106; Foote II, 87-88; Hampden-Sidney, 125; McGavock Family, 54; MMV, V, 256-257; Munsell's X, 25-26; Scruggs Genealogy, by Ethel S. Dunklin, 218-219; TD, Feb. 14, 28, 1904; Virkus II, 33; III, 301; VM, XI, 417-419; Woodson, 120; WM, VI, 198; WM 2d, VI, 349-350.
(*Rockingham*)—DAR, 56, p. 19.
Lear—Cyc. Va. Biog., I, 139, 275; DAR, 82, p. 151; RC, III, 30, 46; VM, XVII, 228-231; Winston, 323-325; WM, VII, 309-310, 316; IX, 124.
(*Fauquier*)—Burgess, 418-419.
Leatherbury—Yeardley, 26-27.
Leatherman—Hampshire, 715.
Lecky—Cyc. Va. Biog., V, 665.
Ledbetter—DAR, 80, p. 353; Virkus III, 449.
Lee—Bruce II, 511; VI, 393; Campbell's History of Va., 659, 745; Cartmell, 458; Convention 1788, II, 368; Cyc. Va. Biog., I, 134, 276; V, 712-714; Lower Shenandoah, 588-589; Rockbridge, 261; TD, Nov. 8, Dec. 27, 1903; Dec. 17, 1905; Jan. 21, May 6, 1906; Jan. 27, Aug. 4, 1907; Sept. 26, Oct. 3, 10, Nov. 14, 1909; March 10, 1912; March 2, 1913; May 16, 1915; WM, VI, 191, 212; VII, 97, 203; VIII, 46; X, 134, 140.
(*Amelia*)—Virkus II, 69.
(*Amherst*)—TD, March 2, 1912.
(*Bedford*)—Hardesty, 422; Thos. Carter, 84.
(*Campbell*)—Campbell Co., 449-452.
(*Elizabeth City*)—Cyc. Va. Biog., IV, 367.
(*Essex*)—DAR, 72, p. 134.
(*Hancock*)—Hening VI, 443; VIII, 278-279.
(*Hanover*)—Bruce IV, 117.
(*Lunenburg*)—Bruce V, 39; Old Free State II, 297-299.
(*Middlesex*)—Montague, 109-110, 321-322.
(*Norfolk*)—Bruce IV, 29.
(*Ohio*)—Miami Co., Ohio, 641.
(*Richards*)—VM, XXXIV, 373.
(*Richard Henry*)—DAR, 55, p. 293.
(*Warwick*)—Tyler's VII, 136-138.
(*Westmoreland*)—America Heraldica, 66, 170; ARP, II, 455-458; Bruce V, 43, 46: Carter Family Tree; Cyc. Va. Biog., V, 772-774; Du Bellet I, 228-229; II, 208, 216, 218-232, 249-

266; IV, 83-85; Fothergill, 158, etc.; Funsten-Meade, 42-43; Hardy, 320-335; Hayden, 96-98, 341-343, 739; Hening VI, 443; Kennedy I, 317-337; Lancaster, 309-310; Lee Family of Virginia and Maryland, from 1300 to 1866, by E. C. Mead (New York, 1871); Lee Family of Va. (1868), 114 pp.; (1872), 11 pp.; (1890), 11 pp.; (1892), 23 pp.; (1895), 586 pp.; Lee's Lee of Virginia; Mackenzie I, 311-319; McAllister, 198-210; McIlhany, 254-255; Meade II, 136-143, 170-171; MMV, I, 235-236; V, 260-265; Notable Families, 54-59; Old Chapel, 60-61, 70; RC, I, 47, 49-51; RS, II, 44, 48; III, 38, 40; IV, 2, 8, 18, 21; R. W. Johnson, 39; SBN, XII, 66-88; Stratford Hall and the Lees, by F. W. Alexander (Oakgrove, Va., 1912); Virkus I, 327; III, 329; VM, II, 219; V, 222, 350-351; VI, 255-260; XX, 243; XXVII, 97; XXXIV, 104-107, 373; VSR, III (No. 3), 40; V (No. 1), 69-70; Warfield, 226-227; WM, II, 247-249; III, 265; IV, 37-38; IX, 197-198; XI, 206-207; see also Bibliography.

(*York*)—Tyler's VII, 136-138; WM, IV, 38; XXIV, 46-54, 215-216.

Leece—Tazewell II, 418-419.
Leech—Rockbridge, 498.
Leedy—Bruce V, 228; Cyc. Va. Biog., V, 699, 1038-1041.
Leeper—Stark Co., Ohio, 709.
Leftwich—Bruce VI, 185-186; BS, Aug. 13, 20, 1905; Campbell Co., 452-455; Cyc. Va. Biog., IV, 207; Summers Co., W. Va., 331-332; TD, Sept. 29, 1912; Virkus II, 300.
Legg—Fothergill, 37.
Leggett—Ritchie Co., 334-337.
Le Grand—Cabell, etc., 212; Cyc. Va. Biog., I, 277; Hampden-Sidney, 55-56, 184; Huguenot Emigration, 75; TD, Oct. 20, 1912; VSR, I, 31; WM, IX, 273; XXIV, 284-285.
Le Hew—Bruce V, 159.
Leigh—Bruce VI, 562, 641; Cyc. Va. Biog., IV, 327; Halifax, 227-228; Marshall, 111, 221-222; Meade I, 451; MMV, III, 209-210; RC, II, 10; RS, II, 41; III, 14; IV, 2; SBN, XII, 89; TD, Feb. 26, 1911; March 29, 1914; Virkus II, 140; VM, XXIX, 156-157; XXXII, 62-63; VSR, III (No. 1), 36; Watkins, 40-41.
(*Norfolk*)—ARP, II, 781.
Leiper (*Richmond City*)—Thomas, 435.
Leister—Rockbridge, 498.
Leitch—Meriwethers, 51-52.
Leith—Mathews Family, 34.
Le Master—Armistead, 180-182.
Lemen—Bruce IV, 310.
Lemley—Cartmell, 492.
Lemon—Kanawha, 510-511.
(*Botetourt*)—Ritchie Co., 384-385.
Le Neve—VM, XXIV, 307-308.
Lenoir—DAR, 59, p. 203.
Leonard—Cyc. Va. Biog., IV, 451.
Lesner—Bruce IV, 451.
Lester (*Lunenburg*)—Brock II, 739; Bruce VI, 488; Lester Family of Virginia, by Owen Bryant Lester (1897); MMV, IV, 253-254; Old Free State II, 299-311.
Lesuer—Douglas, 383.

Letcher—Brock I, 230-235; Bruce II, 486; VI, 13; Buford, 116-118; Crockett, 303; Hardesty, 383; Rockbridge, 261-262, 498; TD, Nov. 3, 1907; Trabue, 42-43; VM, XII, 200-201.
Letshaw—Rockbridge, 498.
Leverett—VM, XXI, 433.
Levert—WM, V, 9.
Levi (King George)—Lower Shenandoah, 712-713.
Levilain—Dupuy, 169-170, 360-365.
Le Villain—Huguenot Emigration, 154-155; Woodson, 48.
Levitt—Randolph Co., 358-359.
Lewelyn—Jones, 243.
Levy—Bruce IV, 65.
  (Richmond)—Tyler's X, 33-37.
Lewis—ARP, I, 129-140; Bruce V, 205, 238; BS, Jan. 22, June 4, Aug. 27, 1905; Burgess, 735-740; Carter Family Tree; Cyc. Va. Biog., I, 277-278; V, 576, 725-726; Gilmer's Georgians, 42-60, 105; Hayden, 377-394; Lewis, 394; Lewis Family Pioneers of Eastern Tenn. and Indiana; Munsell's V, 97; Old King William, 73-80; Rockbridge, 498; RS, II, 32; III, 23, 24, 38-40; IV, 1, 10, 14; St. Mark's, 184; TD, Oct. 11, Dec. 13, 1903; Aug. 27, Oct. 1, 15, 1905; May 20, 1906; July 21, 1907; Jan. 29, 1911; Nov. 8, 1914; Jan. 17, 1915; July 9, 1916; Va. His. Col. (Howe), 181-183; Va. His. Reg., V, 24, 184; Virkus II, 149; VSR, V (No. 2), 30; Welles' Washington Genealogy, 164, et seq; WM, IX, 200.
  (Albemarle)—Albemarle, 251-257; Draper Series, V, 196; King's Mountain, 456-458; VM, XVI, 171; XXVII, 72-73.
  (Albemarle, Col. Charles)—Burgess, 730-732.
  (Albemarle, John)—McAllister, 148-154.
  (Andrew)—SBN, XII, 92-94.
  (Augusta)—A Brief Narrative, by L. L. Lewis, Richmond, Va. 1915; Cabell, etc., 240-241; Convention 1788, II, 20-24; Dinwiddie Papers I, 113-114; Du Bellet II, 621-624, 635-650; Dunmore's War, 74-75, 272, 274, 312, 426-428; Green's Ky. Families, 4-6, 88-91, 105-107; History of Rockingham Co., 355-356; History of the Battle of Pt. Pleasant, 18-19; SHA, II, 158-159; Kanawha, 944-946; Lancaster, 473-475; Lewis, 5-13, 25-55, 394; Lomax, 24-25; Marshall, 162; McAllister, 178-188; McIlhany, 44-45; Meade II, 325-326; MMV, II, 247-250; Monroe Co., 370-371; Peyton, 25-31, 33-35, 112, 285-301, 333-342; Preston Family, 187-189; Rockingham, 355-356; RS, III, 16; Van Meter, 5-19; VM, XIII, 258-260; XIV, 22; XXVI, 366; WM 2d, VI, 55-56; WVM, IV, 81-94, 116-149.
  (Berkeley)—DAR, 53, p. 189-190.
  (Buckingham)—DAR, 76, p. 218.
  (Campbell)—Campbell Co., 455-456.
  (Clarke and Jefferson)—Cartmell, 456.
  (Fairfax)—Van Meter, 20-22, 28-30, 44, 102-106; WM, IX, 200.
  (Gloucester)—America Heraldica, 171; Boddie, 200-201: Bruce IV, 97; Buckners of Va., 201-205; Cartmell, 455-456; Cyc. Va. Biog., I, 140-150; Du Bellet II, 92, 624-633: IV, 25-26; Family Record of Lawrence Lewis and Nelly Parke Custis, from Martha Washington Bible, Philadelphia, 1890; Griffith-Meriwether, 86-87; Hayden, 81; Hening VII, 377-379; VIII, 59-61, 478-480: Lewis's Lewis Family, 14, 25-55; Mackenzie I, 231; II, 37-38: Marshall, 93-98; McAllister, 12-131; Meade II, 232-233, 325; Meriwethers, 10-11, 16-20, 31, 43-

Lillard—DAR, 83, p. 290; Virkus III, 101.
Lilly—Madison Co., Ohio, 898; Summers Co., W. Va., 462-472; TD, March 26, 1911; WM, I, 90.
Lincoln—Bruce VI, 182; History of the Lincoln Family, 193, et seq.; Mackenzie III, 296-299; Shenandoah, 648; Sangamon Co., Ill., 456-458; Strickler, 242-243; WM 2d, VI, 44-45.
  (Rockingham)—DAR, 45, p. 191; Virkus I, 689.
Lindawood—Bruce IV, 335.
Lindsay—Annual Report of the Lindsay Family Association; BS, April 14, 21, 28, May 5, 1907; Cyc. Va. Biog., I, 278; Garrard, 92-95; Mackenzie VI, 293; TD, Jan. 3, 31, March 6, 1904; Nov. 26, 1905; WM 2d, VI, 347-348.

  (Adam)—Francis Morgan, 120-124; Lindsay, 247; VM, X, 96-97, 203, 310-311; XI, 101-102, 216.
  (Albemarle)—Albemarle, 257.
  (Alexandria)—Lindsay, 228.
  (Bedford)—Hardesty, 422.
  (Berry's Ferry)—Lindsay, 231-232.
  (Berryville)—Lindsay, 229-231.
  (Caroline)—DAR, 78, p. 288; Virkus I, 689; II, 295.
  (Caroline and Albemarle)—Lindsay, 241-243.
  (David)—VM, XVIII, 90-92; WM, XI, 128-129; XVI, 136-138 (Lindsay); XX, 297-299.
  (Fauquier)—MMV, III, 213-214.
  (Northumberland)—ARP, II, 746; Browning, C. D., 3d, 303-304; Browning, R. D., 3d, 132-135; Du Bellet II, 186-188; Lindsay, 1-22; Magna Charta Barons, 139-140, 146; WM, XVI, 136-138; XX, 297-298.
  (Port Royal)—Lindsay, 232-240.
  (Rockbridge)—Lindsay, 243-245; Robertson - Taylor, 79, 150; Rockbridge, 499; Trabue, 44-47.
  (Westmoreland)—Browning, C. D., 3d, 303-304.
  (Williamsburg)—Lindsay, 240-241.
Lindsey *(Caroline)*—Arkansas, 269-276; Virkus I, 689.
  (Danville)—Lindsay, 245-246.
Lineberger (Lionberger)—Shenandoah, 615-616.
Lineweaver—Bruce IV, 207.
Link—Madison Co., O., 759.
Linkous—Tazewell II, 478-479.
Linn—Rockbridge, 499.
  (W. Va.)—Kanawha, 414-417.
Linthicum—Hampshire, 716.
Linton, Lyntone—Hayden, 166-167.
Lippitt—Kennedy I, 300-307; RS, II, 47; III, 37.
Lipscomb—Burgess, 768-776, 1059, 1223; Cooke-Booth, 138, 140-141; Old King William, 80-81; TD, Oct. 25, 1914; Tyler's X, 68; Virkus I, 955; III, 466; WM 2d, VI, 138-145; VII, 278.
Lipscombe—Bruce IV, 419.
Lister—Cyc. Va. Biog., I, 278; WM, III, 245-246; XXVI, 214.
Litchfield—Brock II, 739; Crockett, 304.
Little—Blair, etc., 171-176, 192-193; Rockbridge, 499; TD, June 16, 1912.
Littlepage—Culpeper, 48-50; Hayden, 395-420; Kanawha, 492; McAllister, 141; Old King William, 81-83; TD, June 2, 1907; May 21, 1916; VSR, IV (No. 2), 28; V (No. 2), 60; WM, V, 78.
Littler—Cartmell, 483; Madison Co., Ohio, 939.

Littleton—Bruce VI, 141; Cyc. Va. Biog., I, 110; N. E. His. and Gen. Reg., Vol. 42, pp. 364-368; TD, April 19, 1914; Virkus III, 404; VM, XVIII, 20-23; WM, VIII, 230-231; IX, 62-63.
Litton—Bruce VI, 304.
Litz—Bruce VI, 335; Tazewell II, 479-487.
Lively—Fayette Co., W. Va., 557-558; Kanawha, 435; TD, March 27, 1904.
Livesay—Bruce VI, 333.
Livingston—TD, Jan. 21, 1906; Aug. 8, 1909; March 12, 1911; WM, XX, 300-301; XXII, 68-69.
    (*Essex*)—WM, XIII, 262-263.
    (*King and Queen*)—Two Families, 116-117.
Llewellin—WM, VIII, 237-249.
Llewellyn—Cyc. Va. Biog., I, 279.
    (*Charles City*)—VM, IV, 6.
Lloyd—ARP, I, 354-355; Avery I, 64; Cyc. Va. Biog., I, 279.
    (*Culpeper*)—DAR, 48, p. 233.
    (*Lower Norfolk*)—VM, III, 187 [Loyd].
    (*Richmond Co.*)—VM, V, 160-161; XI, 76; WM, VIII, 18.
Locher—Rockbridge, 262-263.
Lockett—Dupuy, 260; SBN, XII, 106-108; Watkins, 24, 42.
Lockey—WM, III, 278; VIII, 202.
Lockhart—Bruce IV, 475; Cartmell, 442, 478; Dupuy, 260; Rockbridge, 499; Tazewell II, 487-491; WM 2d, VIII, 317.
    (*Augusta*)—VM, XXVII, 312.
Lockett—Dupuy, 260; SBN, XII, 106-108; Watkins, 24, 42.
Lockey—WM, III, 278; VIII, 202.
Lockridge—Bath Co., 196; Dunmore's War, 272-273; Highland Co., 314-315; Pocahontas Co., 207-210; Rockbridge, 499; Sangamon Co., Ill., 462.
Lodge—Lower Shenandoah, 778.
Lodwick—Adams Co., Ohio, 581-582.
Logan—Halifax, 228-229, 314-315; Kennedy II, 20-21, 587-588; Mackenzie IV, 7; Marshall, 278; McGavock Family, 134; Randolph Co., 357-358; RS, III, 39; Sangamon Co., Ill., 465; TD, June 15, 1905.
    (*Augusta*)—Dunmore's War, 82; Green's Ky. Families, 117-229; Irvins, Doaks and McCampbells of Va. and Ky., 198-205; Waddell's Annals of Augusta Co., 404-406; Walker-Wigton, 82-85, 90-94.
    (*From Pennsylvania*)—Browning, C. D., 344-345; Browning, R. D., 3d, 20-21.
    (*Rockbridge*)—DAR, 45, p. 119; Randolph Co., 357-358; Rockbridge, 499.
Logwood—Hardesty (Bedford), 422; TD, Sept. 10, 24, 1911 (misspelled "Ligwood").
Lohr—Madison Co., Ohio, 899-900, 1023.
Lomax—Cyc. Va. Biog., I, 280; De Bow's Review, XXVI; Genealogy of the Virginia Family of Lomax; Lindsay, 239; Meade I, 405; SBN, XII, 108-109; Southern Bivouac (1886), 649; TD, Aug. 8, 1915; VM, XIII, 145; XXXIII, 33-34; WM, VIII, 186; IX, 136.
Long—Bruce IV, 223; Hayden, 131; Pendleton Co., 250-251; Rockbridge, 499; TD, April 8, 1906.
    (*Culpeper*)—Culpeper, 108; Des Cognets, 76-77; MMV, V, 269-270; St. Mark's, 164, 179.
    (*Gabriel*)—DAR, 74, p. 54.

(Orange)—Bruce IV, 302-303.
(Page)—Bruce V, 390, 428; VI, 118; Cyc. Va. Biog., V, 901.
Longley—DAR, 43, p. 299.
Longworth—Fothergill, 88.
Looney—DAR, 45, p. 199; Miami Co., Ohio, 508.
Lord—Cyc. Va. Biog., I, 280; RC, II, 18; VM, I, 200-201; WM, XV,
189; XVI, 291; WM 2d, IX, 69.
(Westmoreland)—VM, XXXIV, 345; see also above.
Lorenz—Braxton Co., W. Va., 402; Monongahela III, 973-974.
Lorrimer—TD, June 13, 1909.
Lorton—Crockett, 205; TD, March 8, 1908; VSR, IV (No. 3), 19.
Loth—MMV, III, 221-222.
Lough—Pendleton Co., 251-252; Randolph Co., 359; Ritchie Co., 369-
371.
Lound—WM, XXVII, 192, 194.
Louthan—MMV, IV, 265-272.
Love—Brock II, 740; Bruce V, 295; Chappell, 187-190; Hayden, 646;
Kennedy I, 327-328; Lower Shenandoah, 728-729; Old Free
State II, 196-200; Rockbridge, 499; VM, XXVII, 353.
(Augusta)—DAR, 69, p. 112.
(Botetourt)—Dunmore's War, 273.
Lovelace—Cyc. Va. Biog., I, 280; Halifax, 229-230; VM, XVII,
288-293; XXIX, 110-124; VSR, IV (No. 3), 29; (No. 4),
30; (No. 2), 20.
Lovell—Cartmell, 501, 514; Fothergill, 83; Hayden, 646; Marshall,
17; MMV, V, 295-302.
Lovett—Cartmell, 477; TD, Nov. 21, 1915.
(Loudoun)—Adams Co., Ohio, 790-791.
Loving—Bruce IV, 567; Cyc. Va. Biog., I, 280; Maxwell, 158; Virkus
II, 241; WM, IX, 135.
(Nelson)—Hardesty *(Amherst)*, 442.
Low—DAR, 67, p. 251.
Lowder—Tazewell II, 414.
Lowe—Cyc. Va. Biog., V, 1018; DAR, 76, p. 74; Summers Co., 553-554.
Lowry—Hardesty *(Bedford)*, 422; MMV, V, 271; Rockbridge, 499;
Two Families, 151-152; TD, Feb. 26, May 14, Sept. 17,
1905; VM, IV, 171; WM, XVIII, 234-235.
(Elizabeth City)—WM, XVI, 236-237.
Lowther—Border Settlers, 252; Ritchie Co., 118, 154-155, 227-228;
Virkus I, 699-700.
Loyall—VM, XV, 155-156.
Lucado *(Buckingham)*—Brock II, 576; Cyc. Va. Biog., V, 617.
Lucas—Adams Co., Ohio, 275-276; Burgess, 874-876; Cyc. Va. Biog.,
I, 280; Kennedy I, 560-562; SBN, XII, 119; TD, Sept. 29,
1912.
(Lancaster)—Two Families. 98; VM, XI, 76-77.
(Valley of Va.)—Cartmell, 455; Lower Shenandoah, 597-602;
Shepherdstown, 331.
Luck—Bruce VI, 213; Hardesty (Bedford). 423.
(Pittsylvania)—Pittsylvania, 143; WM 2d, VIII, 312-316.
Luckess—Rockbridge, 499.
Luckett *(Loudoun)*—Burgess, 872-874.
Ludlow, Ludlowe—TD, June 9, Sept. 29, 1907.
Ludlow—America Heraldica, 172; Browning, C. D., 131-132; Brown-
ing, R. D., III, 733; Cyc. Va. Biog., I, 113, 280-281: Magna
Charta Barons, 133; N. E. His. and Gen. Reg. XXX, 42;
TD, June 9, 1907; VM, IV, 364; XII, 178-179; XXIX, 350-
354; XXX, 42; WM, I, 81-82; II, 3-5; III, 181.

Ludwell—ARP, II, 458-463; BHNC, VI, 342-348; Cyc. Va. Biog., I,
126-127, 145-146, 160; Funsten-Meade, 44-45; Keith, 49;
Lancaster, 59-60; Lee, 112, 127-130; Ludwell Genealogy
(1879); Meade I, 195; N. Eng. His. and Gen. Reg., 1893,
pp. 277-278; XXXIII, 220-222; XXXIV, 162; RS, I, 44;
Southern Bivouac (1886), 649; TD, Nov. 11, 1906; Dec.
13, 1908; Oct. 10, 1909; VHS Col. XI, 76-77; VM, I, 174-
178; III, 156; IV, 162; VII, 356-357; XVIII, 5-6; XIX,
288-289, 401; XXI, 395-416; XXXII, 288-289; VSR, I (No.
4), 48-49; IV (No. 2), 30; V (No. 2), 65; WM, I, 110-111;
II, 79; III, 167, 197-199; IV, 156; V, 281; VI, 58; X, 172;
XIX, 199-214.
Luke—Cyc. Va. Biog., I, 281; Lower Shenandoah, 684-685; Tyler's
X, 67; WM, VII, 235.
(*Westmoreland*)—VM, III, 167-168; XXVI, 280-282.
Luker—Yeardley, 16, 18.
Lumbar (*Eastern Shore*)—Burgess, 870-872.
Lumpkin—Bagby, 366; Bruce V, 260; Hampden-Sidney, 144; Rag-
land, 20, 27, 41; TD, July 16, 1905; Virkus II, 210; 348;
VM, VI, 389-396; Whitaker, 229.
Lundie—DAR, 76, p. 64.
Lunsford—De Bow's Review, XXVI; Lomax, 57-63; Southern Biv-
ouac (1886), 649; WM, III, 154; IX, 135.
(*Highland*)—Highland Co., 315.
(*Lancaster*)—WM, XVIII, 292-293.
(*Sir Thomas*)—Cyc. Va. Biog., I, 115-116; VM, XVII, 26-33;
WM, IV, 202; VIII, 183-186.
Lunt—Avery I, 99.
Lupo—TD, Oct. 19, 1913; VM, I, 194-195; XXVI, 119.
Lupton—Bruce IV, 304, 385; VI, 152; Cartmell, 286-288, 453-454;
Jolliffe, 126-127; Lower Shenandoah, 740-741; WM 2d, VI,
41, 43.
Lurty—Burgess, 1165; DAR, 49, p. 433; Munsell's III, 34; RS, IV,
15.
Lusk—Rockbridge, 263, 499.
Luttrell—Armstrong I, 126; Bruce VI, 270; Cyc. Va. Biog., IV, 400-
405; Fauquier Bulletin, 317; Fothergill, 76, 163; VM,
XXXIV, 80-81, 175-178; XXXVII, 57, 59; WM 2d, VIII,
60-61.
Luxford—Cauthorn, 20; Old King William, 140.
Lybrook—New River, 427-430.
Lyddall—RS, I, 44; WM, VII, 223; Valentine II, 779-786; IV, 2240-
2242.
Lyde—WM, VII, 4, 5.
(*King William*)—VM, XXXVII, 23.
Lyle—Armstrong I, 132-139; Green's Ky. Families, 44-45; RS, III, 2;
The Lyle Family; Virkus I, 119, 486.
(*Augusta*)—Munsell's VI, 132; VII, 205; The Ancestry and
Posterity of Matthew, John and Samuel Lyle, Pioneer Set-
tlers in Virginia, by O. K. Lyle, New York, 1912.
(*Manchester*)—Goode, 118-119, 161, 229, 294, 374-375.
(*Rockbridge*)—Cartmell, 415; Foote I, 548-554; II, 315-316, 403-
405; Mackenzie V, 275; Rockbridge, 500.
Lynch—Bell, 258-259; Campbell Co., 62-75, 456-458; Lynchburg, Va.,
Sketches, 9-23; Monroe Co., 372-373; TD, June 25, July 16,
1905; May 4, 1913; Virkus II, 362.
(*Albemarle*)—Cyc. Va. Biog., I, 281; V, 963, 965; Albemarle,
258-259.

Lynch-Blosse—TD, June 11, 1905.
Lyne—Bagby, 311, 345; Cyc. Va. Biog., I, 281; Du Bellet II, 442-443; Hayden, 443; Old King William, 83-84, 120-122; RS, III, 51; WM 2d, VIII, 308-309.
Lynn—Bruce VI, 217; MMV, III, 225-227.
Lyon—Rockbridge, 500; Sangamon Co., Ill., 469.
Lyons (*Richmond City*)—Meade; RS, II, 11, 13; III, 27; Virkus III, 366, 439.

M

Maben—Du Bellet II, 711.
Mabry—Burgess, 1189; DAR, 47, p. 317.
McAdam—Burgess, 649-650; TD, July 17, 1910; May 10, 1914; VM, XVII, 210-211; WM, XI, 280; XIII, 25-26; XX, 61.
McAdams—Rockbridge, 501.
McAdoo—Armstrong I, 140.
McAfee—Dunmore's War, 207; Woods-McAfee, 154-218, 247-260, 268, 275, 277.
McAllister—Bruce V, 283-286, 541; Jolliffe, 100; McAllister Family Records (Abraham A. McAllister), by J. Gray McAllister); Munsell's VIII, 64; Rockbridge, 501; Virkus I, 702-703; III, 313.
　　(*Amherst*)—McAllister, 233-236.
McAlpine—Norfolk, 541-544.
Macaulay—WM, VII, 42; XI, 180-181; XII, 29, 31-32.
McAvoy—Pendleton Co., 257-258.
McBride—Rockbridge, 501; Sangamon Co., Ill., 486.
McCabe—MMV, III, 233-240.
　　(*Bedford*)—Hardesty, 423.
　　(*Richmond*)—Cyc. Va. Biog., IV, 231; VM, XXVII, 180; XXVIII, 195-197, 205.
McCaleb—Rockbridge, 501.
McCalpin—Clemens' Wills, 56-57; Rockbridge, 501.
McCamant—Grayson Co., 59-61.
McCampbell—Irvins, Doaks, Logans and McCampbells, etc.; Madison Co., Ohio, 974; Miami Co., Ohio, 700; Rockbridge, 501-502.
McCandless—Rockbridge, 502.
McCann—DAR, 51, p. 375.
McCarthy—BS, Oct. 22, 1905; McCarthys in Early American History, by Michael J. O'Brian; VSR, III (No. 3), 26; WM, VII, 97;
McCarty—Alstons and Allstons, 411-412; ARP, II, 817-818; Bruce IV, 440; BS, April 16, 1905; Cyc. Va. Biog., I, 288; Fothergill, 11, 117; Hampshire, 719; Hayden, 84a-92, 129- 130; McCarthys in Early American History; Pocahontas Co., 404-408; Rockbridge, 502; RS, III, 44; Stubbs, 400-407; TD, Nov. 25, Dec. 30, 1906; VM, XXIII, 307; WM, XXII, 186-189; WM 2d, I, 295; II, 119-132, 167-179; III, 121.
　　(*Culpeper*)—Johnson Co., Ky., 325-327.
　　(*Fauquier*)—WM, XXII, 184-189.
McCaskey—Rockbridge, 502.
McCaslin—Johnson Co., Ind., 630-631.
McCausland—Crockett, 51.
McCaw—Brock II, 792; Major, 179-190; TD, Sept. 9, 1906; Dec. 25, 1910; VM, XXII, 169-170, 172; XXVII, 94, 97.
McChesney—McCormick, 95-104; Rockbridge, 502.
McClain—Rockbridge, 502.

McClanahan—Bruce VI, 376; Cabell, etc., 296; Dunmore's War, 160-161; Kith and Kin, 149-151; Montague, 139-140; Peyton, 287, 290; VM, XXII, 271; Waddell's Annals of ugusta, 233-234.
   (*Culpeper*)—Culpeper, part 2, p. 3; WM 2d, I, 209, 213.
   (*Fauquier*)—VM, XXV, 406-407.
   (*Westmoreland*)—Buford, 209; Marshall, 35-36, 88-89; VM, XIX, 308-309; WM 2d, I, 209-212.
McClarty—Green's Ky. Families; Hayden, 85-91.
McClaugherty—Monroe Co., 377; New River, 430-431.
McClaurine—Meade II, 33.
McCleary—Rockbridge, 502.
McClelland—Cabell, etc., 339-354; Rockbridge, 502; Sangamon Co., Ill., 493; Virkus II, 110.
McClenachan—Rockbridge, 502.
McClenahan—Alleghany, 207.
McClenny (*Nansemond*)—Montague, 145-146, 253-254.
McClintic—Alleghany, 208; Bruce VI, 115; Highland Co., 362; Kanawha, 369; Rockbridge, 503.
McClintock—Hardesty (*Bedford*), 423.
McCloud—Johnson Co., Ky., 327-328.
McCluer—Bruce V, 416.
McClung—Bruce V, 418, 420; VI, 77; Buford, 81; Campbell, Pilcher, etc.; Clemens' Wills, 57; Green's Ky. Families; Highland Co., 319; Kanawha, 663; Johnstons of Salisbury, 145-150, 166-170; Kennedy I, 74-76; Marshall, 75-76, 170-178, 280-282; Munsell's IV, 56; Rockbridge, 503; TD, March 1, 22, April 12, 1908; The McClung Genealogy; Walker-Wigton, 75-76.
McClure—Cyc. Va. Biog., IV, 302-303; Green's Ky. Families, 186-187; Rockbridge, 503-505; RS, III, 7; The McClure Family.
   (*Spotsylvania*)—Hayden. 386-388.
McClurg—DAR, 76, p. 295; Kennedy I, 74-76; WM, I, 164-165.
McCobb—Avery I, 100.
McCollam—Pocahontas Co., 229-234.
McCollem—Rockbridge, 505.
McColloch—Draper Series, V, 397; Panhandle, 133-135.
McCollough (*Augusta*)—Maxwell, 134-137, 141-143, 146-155, 366-276.
McCollum—Randolph Co., 361.
McComas—Bruce IV, 512-513; New River, 431-434; Sangamon Co., Ill., 494-495.
McComb—Rockbridge, 505.
McConkey—Rockbridge, 505.
McConnell—Bruce V, 459; Cyc. Va. Biog., V, 632; McConnell Marriage Genealogy.
McConnico—WM, V, 231.
McCool—Hampshire, 717.
McCorkle—Bruce VI, 289; Cyc. Va. Biog., IV, 173; McCormick, 110-119; Rockbridge, 278-292.
MacCorkle—DAR, 70, p. 140.
McCormack—Lower Shenandoah, 777.
McCormick—Cartmell, 448; His. Encyc. of Ill., 361; McCormick Family Records and Genealogy of the McCormick Family; Miami Co., Ind., 584; Munsell's XI, 232; SBN; XII, 132; Virkus I, 180-182.
   (*Frederick*)—WVM, I, Oct., 1901, p. 34.
   (*Clarke*)—Lower Shenandoah, 627-631; McIlhany, 153-156, 211, 214, 221, 227; MMV, III, 241-244; "Old Chapel", 55-56.
   (*Rockbridge*)—Bruce V, 317, 322; McCormick, 47-50, 205-213; Rockbridge, 307-329, 505; Virkus I, 705-706.

McCourt—Braxton Co., W. Va., 403.
McCown (*Rockbridge*)—Knox Co., Ill., 649; McClure, 199-200; Rockbridge, 515.
McCoy—Bruce V, 485; Highland Co., 319-320; Meade II, 160-161; Rockbridge, 506.
McCraw—Burgess, 31-32.
McCrea—Highland Co., 320; Hampden-Sidney, 230-231 [McRae]; Old Alexandria, 310-311.
McCreery—Alleghany, 208; Armistead, 142-143.
McCrory—Rockbridge, 506.
McCroskey—Rockbridge, 505-506.
McCue—Boogher, 310, 313; Peyton, 315-316; The McCues of the Old Dominion.
McCuen—Avery I, 169.
McCulloch—Cabell, etc., 174-175, 282, 291-300; Virkus I, 706-707; VSR, I (No. 1), 18 (Gen. Sec.)
McCullough—Adams Co., Ohio, 808-809; Rockbridge, 506; TD, July 7, 1907.
McCune—Rockbridge, 507.
McCurdey—Norfolk, 729-730.
McCurdy—TD, July 4, 1909.
McCutchan—Pocahontas Co., 359-362.
McCutchen—Alleghany, 209; Rockbridge, 506-507; Virkus III, 500.
McCutcheon—DAR, 81, p. 327.
McDannald—Bath Co., 198.
McDaniel (*Amherst*)—Life of George White McDaniel, D. D., 15-17; Virkus III, 164.
(*Pittsylvania*)—DAR, 83, p. 267.
McDearmon—TD, Oct. 1, 1905.
McDermont—WM, VII, 131.
MacDonald—Bruce VI, 180.
McDonald (*Valley of Virginia, etc.*)—Campbell, Pilcher, etc.; Dunmore's War. 152-153; Genealogy of the McDonald Family; Glengarry McDonalds; History of the Battle of Pt. Pleasant; Madison Co., Ohio, 668; New River, 436-439; Pendleton Co., 258-259; Rockbridge, 507; RS, IV, 3; Speed, 133-134; VM, XX, 83-84.
McDougal—Ritchie Co., 491-493.
McDowell—Brock I, 204-208; Buford, 78-91; Cyc. Va. Biog., I, 288; Dunmore's War, 25; Foote II, 92-95; Genealogy of the Cloyd, Basye, etc., Families of America, 33-34; Green's Ky. Families, 1-116; Hardesty, 378-380; Keith, 67-71; Kith and Kin, 88-95, 127-128; Letters of the McDowell Family; Lewis, 394; Mackenzie II, 420, 628-629; Marshall, 60-68; McDowells, Irwins and Connections; Monroe Co., 378-379; Peyton, 302-303; Preston, 183-185; Rockbridge, 263-266, 507; RS, II, 7; III, 2; TD, June 10, 17, 1906; The Lyle Family, etc., 33-34; Virkus I, 187; II, 185; III, 94; VM, XIII, 12; Waddell's Annals of Augusta Co., 121-122; Woods-McAfee, 40-52, 144-145, 294-297.
(*Augusta*)—VM, VII, 214-216.
McElheny—Rockbridge, 507.
McElroy—Rockbridge, 507; "The McElroys of Kentucky"; McCue, 12-13, 19-21, 81-86, 136-140, 171.
McElwee—Life of the Rev. William Smith; Old King William, 84; Rockbridge, 507.
McFadden—Rockbridge, 507.
MacFarland—Old Free State II, 310-311; Virkus I, 223.

McFarland—Bruce VI, 72; Hampden-Sidney, 193-194; Rockbridge, 507-508.
McFarlane—TD, June 19, 1910.
McFerrin—DAR, 51, p. 238.
McGannon (*Culpeper*)—DAR, 55, p. 95.
McGavock—Bruce IV, 7; Genealogy of the Cloyd, Basye, etc., Families, 71; "The McGavock Family, etc.", by the Rev. Robt. Gray (Richmond, 1903); Lewis, 140-142; McAllister, 373, 397-399; VM, XXVI, 375.
McGeach—Clemens 'Wills, 60.
McGee—Kanawha, 552; Millers of Millersburg, 39; Rockbridge, 508.
McGehee—Albemarle, 259-260; "Francis Morgan", 39-40, 67-80; Gilmer's Georgians, 163; Rockbridge, 508; RS, IV, 3; Stubbs, 448-454, 501-502, 519-528; Two Families, 159-161; Virkus III, 439.
  (*King William*)—WM, XXV, 275-288; XXVI, 50-58.
McGhee—Stubbs, 66-67.
  (*Bedford*)—Hardesty, 423.
McGill (*Petersburg*)—Cyc. Va. Biog., IV, 189.
McGinnis—Bruce V, 84; Miami Co., Ohio; Ritchie Co., W. Va., 151-153.
  (*Amherst*)—Hardesty, 442.
McGlaughlan—Highland Co., 320-321.
McGowen—Miami Co., Ohio, 747.
MacGregor—Virkus II, 311.
McGrew—Clemens' Wills, 60; Monongahela II, 717-718.
McGruder—Cartmell, 505.
McGuffin—Bruce VI, 222; Highland Co., 362; Rockbridge, 508.
McGuire—Brock II, 792; Bruce IV, 8, 165-166, 221-222; Cyc. Va. Biog., IV, 343-347; V, 585; Hayden, 39; Lower Shenandoah, 620-621; Mackenzie IV, 162; Marshall, 347-348; McAllister, 122-123; McGuire Family in Virginia, by W. J. Stanard; Meade II, 149-151; MMV, I, 247-249, 279-281; III, 245-246; V, 279-281; "Old Chapel", 40-41, 51-52, 55; RS, III, 11; Tazewell II, 505; The Glengarry McDonalds in Virginia, 51; Virkus I, 190; VM, II, 336-337.
Machen—TD, March 12, 1912.
McHenry—Rockbridge, 508.
Machir—Shenandoah, 616.
McIlhany—Burgess, 837-838; McIlhany, 133-175.
McIntosh—Bruce VI, 100; BS, Feb. 9, 1908; Buckners of Va., 121; RS, III, 50; VM, V, 150.
McIlvain—Rockbridge, 508.
McIlwaine—Bruce VI, 201; Mackenzie VI, 155-156; Memories of Three Score Years and Ten; MMV, I, 35-38, 263-265; Virkus II, 45; VSR, V (No. 1), 77.
McIlwee—Bruce V, 28-29.
McKamin—Rockbridge, 508.
McKay—Funsten-Meade, 46-50; Goode, 91-93; Rockbridge, 508.
McKee—Bruce VI, 173; Buford, 102-106; Waddell's Annals of Augusta, 210-212.
  (*Rockbridge*)—Clemens' Wills, 61; Dunmore's War, 348; Rockbridge, 348, 508; Virkus III, 301.
McKeever—Rockbridge, 508.
Mackemie—Cyc. Va. Biog., I, 282.
McKemy—Rockbridge, 508.
McKendree—Cisco, 280; His. Encyc. of Ill., 364.
McKeney—Rockbridge, 508.

McKennie—Albemarle, 260.
McKenry—Bruce V, 124; Rockbridge, 508.
McKensie—Cyc. Va. Biog., I, 288; WM, VIII, 16-17, 150.
Mackey—Berkeley, 169; Rockbridge, 500.
(*Winchester*)—McIlhany, 108-110.
McKie—DAR, 49, p. 97.
McKinley (*Culpeper*)—Green's Ky. Families, 226-227.
McKinne—Tyler's III, 166-173; WM, XXVII, 59-61.
McKinney—Barbour Co., W. Va., 428; Brock II, 628; Bruce VI,
    454; Dupuy, 192, 243-244; Huguenot Emigration, 159-161;
    Ritchie Co., 162-169; Rockbridge, 509.
    (*Loudoun*)—Ritchie Co., 607-609.
McKinsey—Rockbridge, 509.
McKnight—Goode, 300; Green's Ky. Families, 158-159, 161-168; LCJ,
    Sept. 20, 1914 (II, 2); RS, III, 7; Whitaker, 125-126.
McKown—Berkeley, 244; Cartmell, 474; Lower Shenandoah, 775.
McLaughlin—Braxton Co., W. Va., 404-405; Pocahontas Co., 315-
    327; Rockbridge, 509.
McLaurin, McLaren—TD, April 29, May 13, 1906.
McLean—Randolph Co., 364-365.
McLemore—Bruce VI, 557.
    (*Sussex*)—MMV, V, 284-285.
McLeod—VSR, I (No. 3), 42.
Maclin—Cyc. Va. Biog., I, 281; MMV, III, 249-250; Stubbs, 385; VM,
    XXXVII, 61-64; WM, VII, 108-109.
McManamy—Rockbridge, 509.
McMann—Monroe Co., 379-380.
McManaway—Bruce V, 399; Carolinians II, 402..
McMath—Rockbridge, 509.
McMellon—Hardesty (*Bedford*), 423.
McMillan—Armstrong I, 153-157; WM, VII, 127.
    (*Halifax*)—Hardesty (*Bedford*), 423.
McMillen—Rockbridge, 509.
McMorris—Coshocton Co., Ohio, 737.
McMorrow—Braxton Co., W. Va., 403-404.
McMullen—Hardesty (Bedford), 423; McCue, 226, 239; Pendleton Co.,
    322-323; Rockbridge, 509.
Macmurdo—Cabell, etc., 423; Hardy, 427; Meriwethers, 51; Six Cen-
    turies of the Moores of Fawley, 48-49, 55; St. Mark's, 183;
    Virkus II, 318.
McMurran—Cyc. Va. Biog., V, 942.
McMurray—Rockbridge, 509.
McMurry—Sangamon Co., Ill., 505-506.
McMurtry—Rockbridge, 509; Virkus III, 501.
McNabb—Coshocton Co., Ohio, 737; Rockbridge, 509.
MacNair—Virkus III, 264.
McNauton—Rockbridge, 509.
McNeel—Pocahontas Co., 135-144, 177, 381-386.
McNeer—Monroe Co., 380-381; Summers Co., 454.
McNeil—Pocahontas Co., 385-386.
McNeill—Virkus III, 124.
    (*Hardy*)—Van Meter, 173-182.
McNight—Rockbridge, 509.
McNulty—Bruce VI, 141; Cyc. Va. Biog., IV, 304; Highland Co.,
    321-322.
MacNutt—Virkus I, 526-527; II, 90.
McNutt—Bruce IV, 28; Mackenzie V, 378-380; McCormick, 38-42,
    53-133; McGavock Family, 23-24, 57-58; Rockbridge, 266-

267, 509; Waddell's Annals of Augusta Co., 228-231; Walker-Wigton, 162.

Macock—Cyc. Va. Biog., I, 94.

Macon—Albemarle, 260; Alstons and Allstons, 507-515; Boogher, 252-258; Bruton, 89; Culpeper, 72; Cyc. Va. Biog., I, 281-282; V, 894-895; Kennedy I, 141, 575-580; Mackenzie II. 505; Major, 50-53; RS, III, 46; IV, 3; St. Mark's, 147; VM, X, 412; XXV, 433-434; VSR, IV (No. 3), 27; WM, VI, 33-36; X, 276-278; XII, 33-35; XIV, 265-267.

McPhail—Du Bellet II, 84; VSR, I (No. 3), 54.

McPheeters—Foote II, 210-216; Green's Ky. Families, 51-52, 118; Rockbridge, 509-510; Walker-Wigton, 5, 65-68, 70-75, 79, 94, 101, 111.

McQuain—Highland Co., 362; Pendleton Co., 259.

McQueen—Braxton Co., W. Va., 405; Licking Co., Ohio; Rockbridge, 510.

McQuilkin—Bruce V, 471; Rockbridge, 510.

McQuiltin—Rockbridge, 510.

McQuown—Brock II, 741; Hardin Co., Ohio, 617.

Macrae—RS, III, 37.

McRae—Bruce V, 307; Meade; MMV, III, 247-248; RS, II, 36; III, 37; VM, VII, 14, 241.

McReynolds—Campbell Co., 458-460.

McRobert—Hampden-Sidney, 56-57.

McRoberts—VM, XX, 198, 432.

McSherry—Lower Shenandoah, 708-710.

McSpaden—Rockbridge, 510.

McTeer—Rockbridge, 510.

McVeigh—Bruce VI, 421; McIlhany, 144-146, 262-263.

McVey—Rockbridge, 510.

McVicar—Bruce IV, 506.

McWhorter—Border Settlers, 285; Kanawha, 387, 732; Ritchie Co., 566-570; WVM, I (July, 1901, 64-68; II, Jan., 1902, 68-72.

Maddox, Maddux—Douglas, 247; TD, July 3, Dec. 4, 1904; May 12, 1907.

Maddux—Virkus I, 178, 526-527.

Maddy—Monroe Co., 374-375.

Madeira—Shenandoah, 616-617.

Madison—BS, March 19, July 9, 1905; Culpeper, 71-72; Cyc. Va. Biog., I, 282; Draper Series, V, 167; Du Bellet IV, 372-379; Dunmore's War, 59, 280; Green's Ky. Families, 67-69; Hampden-Sidney, 35; Hayden, 255-259; SHA, II, 157; Lancaster, 385-389; Lewis, 392-402; Mackenzie V, 137-138; Marshall, 146-147; Meade II, 96-98; Munsell's II, 78; Notable Families, 52; Patrick Henry II, 640-643; Peyton, 290, 345-346; Preston Family, 182; SBN, XII, 145-148; TD, July 24, 1904; June 9, 1907; April 10, 1910; Dec. 1, 1912; VM, IV, 463-464; VI, 434-435; VII, 253; XXIX, 140-141; VSR, I, 79; V (No. 1), 74; Willis, 51, 53, 150-151; Winston, 221-234; WM, IV, 253; VI, 116, 180, 258; IX, 37-40, 268; WM 2d, II, 185-186.

Magill—Armstrong II, 231-238; Cartmell, 279, 450-452; Du Bellet IV, 282-300; Magill Family Record; TD, Sept. 30, 1906.
(*Augusta*)—Virkus I, 941.
(*Frederick*)—Lower Shenandoah, 801-804.
(*Winchester*)—Buckners of Va., 216; Virkus I, 301; III, 378.

Magruder—Albemarle, 260-262; Cartmell, 505; Magruder (McGregor) Clan Year Books; Minor, 29, 66-67; MMV, IV, 281-282;

Munsell's V, 164; TD, June 25, 1905.
(*Shenandoah*)—Bruce IV, 315.
Mahan—Kanawha, 756; RS, III, 14.
Mahone—SBN, XII, 152; TD, Feb. 18, 1906.
Maitland—VM, VIII, 324; WM, VI, 21; XXVII, 299-300.
Major—Bruce IV, 366; VI, 17; Cyc. Va. Biog., I, 282; Dupuy, 265-266, 273-274, 329-334; Halifax, 317; Hardesty (*Bedford*), 424; Huguenot Emigration, 167-169, 173; TD, April 3, 1910; July 30, 1916; The Majors and their Marriages, by James Branch Cabell.
Majors—DAR, 59, p. 57.
Makemie—WM, XXI, 278-279.
Malbone—McIntosh II, 238; VII, 348.
Malcomb—Highland Co., 315-317.
Maley—Ritchie Co., 24-26.
Mallicote—Barton II, 71-72.
Mallory—Cyc. Va. Biog., I, 282-283; Hayden, 13; TD, June 23, 1907; VM, XXVII, 181-183; VSR, I (No. 3), 42-43.
(*Culpeper*)—Culpeper, 54.
(*Elizabeth City*)—Armistead, 203; Brock II, 689; VM, III, 328, 344-345; VIII, 385; XII, 398-402; XIII, 216-219, 324-329, 441-445; XIV, 101-106, 215-222, 320-325, 431-436; XV, 99-102, 329-334.
(*Roger*)—VM, XXXIV, 376-377.
Mallow—Bath Co., 197; Pendleton Co., 252-254; WM 2d, VI, 152-153.
Malone—Halifax, 317; Kanawha, 811; Ritchie Co., 55-57.
Maloney—Hampshire, 720.
Maloy—Highland Co., 317.
Mallow—WM 2d, VI, 152-153.
Mandeville—Old Alexandria, 316.
Manear—Ritchie Co., 356.
Mangum—BHNC, VII, 380.
Mankin—Avery I, 170.
Manley—DAR, 44, p. 327.
Manlove—Maxwell, 401.
Mann—Alleghany, 209-210; Barbour Co., W. Va., 429; Bruce V, 37, 389; VI, 3; Cyc. Va. Biog., I, 283; Halifax, 316-317; Mackenzie VI, 155; Monroe Co., 375-376; Valentine II, 787-812.
(*Gloucester*)—WM, III, 36, 42-43; VI, 136.
Manning—Miami Co., Ohio, 533; Stubbs, 332.
(*Norfolk Co.*)—McIntosh II, 171.
Mansfield—Avery I, 102; DAR, 67, p. 52; TD, July 16, 1905; Dec. 1, 1907; Jan. 12, 1908.
Manson—Buckners of Va., 265-266; Buford, 282-283; WM, X, 115.
Maphis—Bruce IV, 317; V, 26-27; Shenandoah, 617.
Mapp—Bruce VI, 30.
Marable—Cyc. Va. Biog., I, 283; V, 620; Major, 113-118; TD, April 23, 1916; Virkus III, 488; WM, VI, 34; VII, 62; XII, 17.
Marbury—Cyc. Va. Biog., V, 604.
March—Virkus II, 316.
Marchant—Bruce VI, 62; MMV, I, 343-344.
Margrave—Rockbridge, 501.
Mark—WM, VI, 95.
(*Berkeley*)—Tyler's III, 48-49; Virkus III, 271; VSR, II (No. 1), 67.
Markell—Avery I, 171.
Markham (*Bedford*)—Hardesty, 425.
(*Chesterfield*)—VM, IV, 106; V, 205-206, 334-336, 439-440; VI, 80-82.

(*Henrico*)—VM, V, 343.
(*Westmoreland*)—Marshall, 16; VM, II, 428-429; WM, IV, 41.
Marks—Brock II, 651; Madison Co., Ohio, 758; RS, II, 24; SBN, XII, 106; Lower Shenandoah, 758-759.
(*Albemarle*)—Albemarle, 262-263; Munsell's IX, 54.
Marler—DAR, 83, p. 283.
Marlin (*Amherst*)—Clemens' Wills, 62.
Marlow—DAR, 69, p. 189.
Marmaduke—SBN, XII, 161-162.
Marnix—WM, XXII, 140.
Marot—Cyc. Va. Biog., I, 283; Tyler's II, 282; WM, V, 117; VI,
Marple—Braxton Co., W. Va., 405.
199; VII, 50, 151.
Marr—Blair, etc., 254-255; Hayden, 195; TD, June 6, 20, Aug. 29, 1909.
Marsden (*Norfolk*)—Antiquary II, 60.
Marsh—Ritchie Co., 133-136.
Marshall—ARP, II, 748-749; BS, April 9, 1905; Carter Family Tree; Coshocton Co., Ohio, 743; Cyc. Va. Biog., I, 283-284; V, 612-614, 760, 1035-1037; Du Bellet I, 49-51, 53, 81-87, 89-93, 104, 149-194, 230, 248-250, 257-258, 266-271; Lancaster, 142-143, 383-384; Lewis, 49; Mackenzie I, 355-360; II, 421; McAllister, 114-116; Md. Soc. Col. Wars, 4, 109; Norfolk, 954-957; TD, July 24, 1904; Oct. 22, 1905; Jan. 21, July 8, 1906; Feb. 2, March 8, 1908; Virkus II, 335; VSR, IV (No. 2), 38; V (No. 2), 52.
(*Amelia*)—Bruce V, 125, 163.
(*Bedford*)—Miami Co., Ind., 524.
(*Caroline*)—Hardy, 341-343.
(*Carroll, W. Va.*)—Kanawha, 582.
(*Charlotte*)—DAR, 72, p. 145.
(*Daniel, Westmoreland*)—Hardy, 362-365.
(*Gloucester and Northampton*)—Bruce V, 344.
(*Halifax*)—DAR, 72, p. 309.
(*Henry*)—Henry Co., 225-227.
(*Highland*)—Highland Co., 317-318.
(*Isle of Wight*)—WM, IV, 111.
(*King and Queen*)—Monograph of the Anderson, Clark, Marshall and McArthur Connection.
(*Mecklenburg*)—Genealogical Statement by Capt. C. T. Allen, 17-22.
(*Westmoreland*)—Beverage's Life of Marshall, I, 1-57; Cyc. Va. Biog., IV, 305; Du Bellet II, 458-484; Green's Ky. Families, 103-116, 168-170; Hardy, 343-362; Marshall Family, by W. M. Paxton, Cincinnati, 1885; McIlhany, 78; Meade II, 216, etc.; MMV, III, 251-252; SBN, XII, 162-167; Virkus 205-206, 640; VM, II, 343-344; XII, 328-331; XIX, 447; XXI, 328-333; XXVI, 410; XXVII, 93; Virkus I, 649; III, 413; Woods-McAfee, 50.
Marstiller—Randolph Co., 360-361.
Marston—Major, 133-134.
Martain—VM, XIX, 144.
Martener—Randolph Co., 359-360.
Martian—Armistead, 199; Cyc. Va. Biog., I, 284; TD, Aug. 29, 1909; July 5, 1914; Tyler's I, 52-57; VM. I, 425-426; IV, 206; XXI, 283; VSR, I (No. 4), 50; WM, II, 3; XIV, 123.
Martin—Cyc. Va. Biog., I, 284-285; IV, 79; Habersham Chap. II, 34-35, 140-141; Mackenzie VII, 282; Pendleton Co., 254; Rock-

bridge, 501; RS, III, 44; TD, April 23, May 7, 1905; Dec. 15, 22, 1912.

(*Abraham*)—Hughes, etc., 192-195; Tillman Genealogy (Nashville, 1905), 23-29.

(*Albemarle*)—Albemarle, 363-366; Hardy, 367-374; Hughes, etc., 123-146, 153-173, 177-192; Lewis, 359-378; Mackenzie I, 271-273; MMV, I, 161-164; Tazewell II, 493-495; Virkus I, 207; III, 97, 606, with arms.

(*Bedford*)—Brock II, 742.

(*Caroline*)—Caroline Co., 444-447; VM, XIII, 198-199; WM, X, 116-117; XI, 146; XVIII, 65.

(*Charlotte*)—DAR, 76, p. 212.

(*Fluvanna*)—DAR, 55, p. 26.

(*Goochland*)—Bruce V, 129; The Martin Family.

(*Halifax*)—Virkus I, 658.

(*Henry*)—Henry Co., 223-225.

(*Hudson*)—Meriwethers, 10-13.

(*Joseph*)—Annual Report Am. His. Asso., 409-415, 474-477; Dunmore's War, 235-236; Hughes, etc., 125-146, 173, 177, etc.; Gen. Joseph Martin; VM, VIII, 347-359.

(*King William*)—VM, XXI, 249, 372-373; WM, XVIII, 65.

(*Norfolk Co.*)—Bruce VI, 157; Cyc. Va. Biog., IV, 236; MMV, II, 270-271.

(*Pittsylvania*)—Pittsylvania, 143, 248.

(*Powhatan*)—VM, III, 193.

(*Rockingham and Berkeley*)—Monongahela III, 1041-1042.

(*West Va.*)—Harrison Co., 371-372; Ritchie Co., 204-205.

Martini—VSR, I (No. 2), 32.

Martz—Bruce IV, 282.

Marye—Culpeper, 62; Cyc. Va. Biog., I, 285; Huguenot Emigration, 183-191; Munsell's IX, 173; RS, II, 34; Shenandoah, 620; Strickler, 257; TD, March 31, 1907; VHS Col. V, 183-191; Virkus I, 207; VM, VIII, 322; XII, 379; WM 2d, I, 157, 168.

Mason—BS, March 5, April 9, Sept. 3, 10, 1905; Oct. 14, 1906; Cyc. Va. Biog., I, 285-286; Du Bellet I, 223, 267; TD, Aug. 4, 1907; Dec. 21, 1913; Virkus II, 123.

(*Alexandria*)—Avery I, 65-66.

(*Brunswick*)—Burgess, 40-42.

(*Enoch*)—Dinwiddie Papers I, XXVI; Life of George Mason I, 376-377.

(*Franklin*)—Kanawha, 823.

(*George*)—ARP, II, 805, 808-809; Du Bellet II, 581-599.

(*King George*)—Du Bellet III, 114-117; MMV, IV, 283-285.

(*Lower Norfolk*)—Du Bellet II, 614-619; McIntosh I, 182, 192; II, 9, 15-16, 38, 124-125; RC, III, 43; Virkus III, 113; VM, II, 385-386; XX, 41-42; VSR, IV (No. 4), 32.

(*Norfolk*)—ARP, II, 790; Ellis, 57; Mackenzie VII, 75; Major, 46-48; VM, II, 385-386; IV, 82-85; XXIX, 503-506; WM, IV, 172.

(*Stafford*)—Bruce V, 203; Campbell's History of Va., 648-650; Carter Family Tree; Convention 1788, II, 214-268; Cooke-Booth, 57; Cyc. Va. Biog., IV, 23; Du Bellet II, 609-614; Hardy, 375-380; Hayden, 109-110; SHA, VIII, 465; Kennedy I, 111, 481-485; Lancaster, 364-365, 377-382; Lee, 410-412; Life of George Mason I, 1-50, 373-376; Life of Stevens Thomas Mason, etc., 11-36; Mackenzie I, 363-364; II, 546-547; IV, 523; Meade II, 229; Public Life of John M. Mason, Carter, 332-334; Virkus III, 28; VM, XX, 4; XXVI, 406.

(*Surry*)—Goode, 236, 383; RC, III, 46; VM, XVI, 180; XXXIV, 212-215.
(*Sussex*)—VM, XVI, 180.
Massenburg—Bruce VI, 487; Burgess, 151-154; VM, XIX, 397-398; WM, V, 143 [Massenberg].
Massey—DAR, 82, p. 275; Kanawha, 446.
Massie—Adams Co., Ohio, 587-589; Albemarle, 266-267; Brock II, 794-796; Bruce IV, 329, 356, 361; Cabell, etc., 376-379; Cartmell, 444; Chaumiere Papers (edited by H. J. Peat, Chicago, 1883), 78, 80-81, 87-90; Cyc. Va. Biog., I, 286; IV, 143; V, 788-794; Goode, 238; Lancaster, 206-209; McGavock Family, 151; Meade II, 64, 429; MMV, III, 255-257; Nathaniel Massie, 11-22; Peyton, 301; RS, III, 8, 27, 31; Ruvigny, 519-520; Sangamon Co., Ill., 478; Tyler's I, 58-59; Virkus II, 278; VM, XXI, 184-192; XXVI, 406; Watkins, 29; Woods-McAfee, 106; WM, V, 140; XIII, 196-203, 301; XV, 125-129; XXVII, 244-246.
(*Goochland*)—Douglas, 34.
Masters—Highland Co., 318-319, 361; Pendleton Co., 255.
Mastin—Bruce IV, 89; WM, V, 8-9.
Matheny—Bruce V, 555-556; Highland Co., 318-319; His. Encyc. of Ill., 355; Sangamon Co., Ill., 479.
Mathew (*Northumberland*) Cyc. Va. Biog., I, 286-287; VM, I, 201-202.
Matthews, Mathews—TD, May 15, 29, 1904; Oct. 27, 1912; Aug. 17, 1913.
Mathews—BS, June 9, 16, 23, 30, July 14, 1907; Cyc. Va. Biog., I, 287; V, 834; Gilmer's Georgians, 73; Pocahontas Co., 497-500; Rockbridge, 501; Virkus II, 359; WM, VI, 91-93; XXV, 71-72.
(*Augusta*)—Mathews (Mathes) Family in America; Kanawha, 908-910; Peyton, 317; VM, XV, 214; WM, V, 277-278; see also "Matthews."
(*Buckingham*)—Kanawha, 845-846.
(*Norfolk*)—Convention 1788, I, 306-307.
(*Samuel*)—Du Bellet IV, 40-43; Tyler's V, 140-141; WM, II, 161 (note); V, 278; see also "Matthews."
(*Northumberland*)—WM, XXV, 71-72.
(*York*)—WM, XXV, 71.
Matthews (*Augusta*)—Convention 1788, II, 80-81; Dunmore's War, 160, 223; McCue, 27, 55, 100-101, 150-151; Stubbs, 216-217.
(*Henry*)—Henry Co., 221-223.
(*King George*)—VM, IX, 311.
(*Samuel*)—Du Bellet IV, 40-43; Tyler's V, 133-134, 140-141; VM, I, 91-92; WM, II, 151, 161; III, 173, 182.
(*Warwick*)—VM, I, 91-92;XV, 216; WM, V, 277.
(*Westmoreland*)—VM, XV, 216.
Maund—WM, IX, 26.
Maupin—Huguenot Emigration, 30; Norfolk, 603-607; RS, I, 24; II, 26; III, 27, 32; Virkus III, 163; VM, VIII, 216-218; XXX, 230.
(*Albemarle*)—Albemarle, 267-268.
(*Portsmouth*)—Brock II, 673.
Maury—Buford, 209-310; Cyc. Va. Biog., I, 287; V, 1035; Du Bellet III, 110-113; IV, 389-398; Fry Genealogy, 68; Goode, 216-218, 356-357, 363-364; Huguenot Emigration, 122-139; Kennedy I, 666-667; Lewis, 81-86, 299-300; Life of Matthew Fontaine Maury; Meade I, 465; II, 44; Notable Families, 94-95; Rockbridge, 263; Stubbs, 297-309, 316-318; TD, Jan.

24, 1904; Oct. 15, 22, 1905; April 3, 10, July 24, 1910; VHS
Col. V (1886), 123-135; Virkus II, 250; VM, XI, 449-450;
XVIII, 455-456; XIX, 292; XXVII, 375-376; WM, I, 220;
V, 208-209; X, 122-124.

Mauzy—Boogher, 364; Bruce IV, 270; Fishback Family, 125-126, 185-
188; Genealogical Record of the Descendants of Henry
Mauzy, etc., 1-143; Hayden, 451; Highland Co., 361-362;
Huguenot Emigration, XVII; Pendleton Co., 255-256.

Maxcy—Bruce V, 174, 461.

Maxey—Sangamon Co., Ill., 484.

Maxwell—Randolph Co., 363-364; Rockbridge, 501; Summers Co.,
432-438; Tazewell II, 374-380, 491-493; Tucker Co., 511-531.
(*Albemarle and Augusta*)—Maxwell, 22-642.
(*Norfolk*)—Antiquary II, 58; III, 24.
(*Washington Co.*)—DAR, 78, p. 266.

May—Bristol Parish, 187-194; Cyc. Va. Biog., IV, 307; TD, Feb. 15,
1905; Sept. 29, Dec. 29, 1907.
(*Bedford*)—Hardesty, 424; Kanawha, 845.
(*Lunenburg*)—Old Free State II, 312-319.
(*Tazewell*)—Tazewell II, 419-422.

Maybee—Halifax, 315.

Mayer—Brock II, 796.

Mayes (*Dinwiddie*)—Munsell's V, 189.

Mayhew—Bruce V, 472.

Maynard—Goode, 209-210, 349-352, 416-418.

Mayo—Albemarle, 269-270; Bruce V, 258; BS, June 11, Aug. 6, 1905;
Burwell, 28, 37-38; Cabell, etc., 168-171; Cyc. Va. Biog.,
I, 287-288; Goode, see index; John Wise, 237-238; Lancaster, 112-113; Mackenzie II, 503-510; Norfolk, 562; RS,
II, 46; SBN, XII, 180-181; TD, Feb. 15, June 5, 1905; Sept.
29, Dec. 29, 1907; Vestry Book of Henrico Parish, 163-165,
195-202; Virkus II, 71; VM, XXXII, 55-57; VSR, I (No.
1), 9-10 [Gen. Sec.], IV (No. 4), 31-32; WM, VII, 256.

Mays—Brock II, 577; Hardesty (*Amherst*), 442; Kanawha, 832; Rockbridge, 501; Tazewell II, 496-497.

Mayse (*Bath*)—Pocahontas Co., 561-563.

Meachum—WM, XII, 17.

Mead—Cyc. Va. Biog., I, 288; VSR, IV (No. 4), 25.
25.
(*Bedford*)—Cowles Family, 1125; DAR, 83, p. 20; WM, VIII,
275; X, 191-197, 242-245.

Meade, Mead—TD, Nov. 1, 29, 1903; Feb. 4, 11, 1906; Aug. 2, 1908:
Dec. 21, 1913.

Meade—Andrew Meade of England and America, by Hamilton R.
Baskervill (Richmond, Va., 1921), 1-62; Browning, R. D.,
III, 788-789; BS, Aug. 21, 1904; Feb. 4, 1906; March 24,
31, April 7, 1907; Cabell, etc., 431-433; Campbell's History
of Va., 690; Chaumiere Papers, etc.; Cyc. Va. Biog., I,
288-289; IV, 76-78, 177-178; Du Bellet IV, 315-317; Funsten-
Meade Genealogy (New York, 1926), 51-64; Genealogical
Statement of Capt. C. T. Allen; Goode, 477; Hampden-
Sidney, 57; Hardy, 101-102, 222-226; Hening VIII, 470-473;
SHA, II, 335-337; Kennedy I, 673; Magna Charta Barons,
143; Meade I, 292; "Old Chapel", 28, 40, 43, 51, 54, 57-59,
66, 69, 71-72; Ruvigny, Tables I, II, XVII, XXIII, pp. 518-
533; SBN, XII, 181-183; TD, Aug. 2, 1908; VM, VI, 306;
Virkus III, 371; VSR, V (No. 2), 50; WM, XIII, 37-45,
73-102.

(*Amelia*)—Bruce, IV, 482.
(*Brunswick*)—Old Free State II, 108-110.
(*Kentucky*)—Johnson Co., Ky., 338.
(*Loudoun and Russell*)—Bruce VI, 352.
Meador—Hardesty (*Bedford*), 425; Summers Co., 403-408; Virkus
    III, 273.
Meadows—Bruce VI, 71, 119; Highland Co., 383; New River, 434-
    436; Summers Co., 401-402.
Means—Auglaize Co., Ohio, 729-730.
    (*Accomac*)—Burgess, 653-654.
Meares—Cyc. Va. Biog., I, 289.
Mears—Bruce V, 477, 515.
Meaux—WM, XVI, 67-71.
Mebane—Bruce VI, 697; Crockett, 305; VSR, I (No. 2), 22; V (No.
    2), 55.
Medearis—DAR, 46, p. 71.
Medley—Halifax, 230, 318-320; VM, XXVIII, 78-79.
Meek—Rockbridge, 510; TD, May 26, 1912.
    (*Carroll*)—Adams Co., Ohio, 606-607.
Meekins—Barton I, R15, 92.
Meeks—Bruce IV, 383.
Meem—Bruce V, 98-99; Shenandoah, 620-621.
Meese—ARP, II, 448; Cyc. Va. Biog., I, 136; McIlhany, 101-104.
Meetze—Bruce VI, 269; Virkus III, 121.
Megginson—Burgess, 675-677; Cabell, etc., 227-228, 446-452; Goode,
    70, 132, 259-261; Robertson, 44.
Melson—Burgess, 1160.
Melvin—Madison Co., Ohio, 669.
Melton—Bruce V, 93; Cyc. Va. Biog., V, 722.
Menefee—Bruce IV, 302, 400, 423-424; V, 394; Buckners of Va., 226-
    227; McIlhany, 63-65; Mackenzie IV, 418-425.
Menifie—VM, I, 86-87.
Mennis—WM, VII, 18.
Menzies—DAR, 78, p. 70.
Mercer—Bruce IV, 182; Carter Family Tree; Cyc. Va. Biog., I, 289-
    290; Kennedy I, 499-505; "Life of Gen. Hugh Mercer";
    Meade II, 205; RS, I, 14, 28; II, 33, 35; SBN, XII, 187-
    188; TD, Nov. 14, 1909.
    (*Frederick*)—Cartmell, 481.
    (*Fredericksburg*)—Browning, C. D., 3d, 618; VM, XXVII, 97.
    (*Hugh*)—Burgess, 655; "Genealogy" (Clemens'), IX, 25-27; Life
        of Gen. Hugh Mercer; VM, XI, 449.
    (*John*)—Burgess, 655-650; Kennedy I, 112-113; RS, I, 14, 28;
        Warfield, 250-253.
    (*Marlborough*)—Genealogy of the Mercer-Garnett Family of
        Essex County; WM, XVII, 85-99, 204-223.
    (*Middlesex*)—Cyc. Va. Biog., IV, 113.
    (*Stafford*)—Dinwiddie Papers I, 110-111, 114-115; Mackenzie III,
        310-317; Md. His. Mag., II, 191-213; RC, III, 6 (Duplicated);
        VM, XIV, 232-235; XVII, 181, 325-328; XXX, 6; WM,
        XVII, 85-99, 204-223.
Merchant—Cyc. Va. Biog., V, 682.
Meredith—Bruce IV, 51, 568; Cabell, etc., 380-381, 454-462; Cyc. Va.
    Biog., I, 290; Du Bellet II, 423; Goode, 290; Kennedy II,
    399; King's Mountain, 460; Meade, 14; Old King William,
    127; Patrick Henry, II, 639-640; Ritchie Co., 350-351; RS,
    II, 31; St. Mark's, 188; TD, Oct. 14, Nov. 4, 1906; Virkus
    III, 131; VM, XVII, 382; WM, V, 184.

Meriwether—Albemarle, 270-274; Burgess, 656; Cabell, etc., 189; Crawfurdiana, 18, 20; Cyc. Va. Biog., I, 290-291; IV, 313; Douglas, 34, 76, 138; Gilmer's Georgians, 88; Hening V, 257-259; VI, 300-302, 405; VIII, 54-57; LCJ, Aug. 9, 1914; Mackenzie III, 318-321; V, 392-396; McAllister, 55, 61-62, 64, 136, 314-323; Merrywether-Meriwether and their Connections; Meriwether Genealogy, compiled in 1848, by G. W. Meriwether, published 1889, WM, IX; Morton Kin; Munsell's V, 164; VI, 50-51, 123-124; Notable Families, 82-85; Page (2d ed.), 178-179; Record of Nicholas Meriwether of Wales, etc.; Roger Jones, 149-153; RS, II, 5', 24, 27, 32, 39; III, 24, 32; TD, Oct. 18, 1903; Feb. 5, 1905; Feb. 18, 1906; Feb. 28, March 14, June 27, 1915; Virkus II, 90; VM, II, 306; V, 79, 197-198; XXXIV, 107-112; Watson, 245; WM ,VI, 100; IX, 202, 270; XVII, 65.
Merrick—Kanawha, 417.
Merrill—St. Mark's, 160; WM 2d, VII, 223-224.
Merritt—Bruce IV, 519.
Merry—Ellis, 44; VM, XX, 429-430.
Merryman—VM, V, 430.
  (*Lunenburg*)—WM 2d, VIII, 132-134.
Metcalf—ARP, II, 747.
  (*Stafford*)—Trabue, 38-41.
Metcalfe—Cyc. Va. Biog., I, 291.
  (*Fauquier*)—Hardy, 381-384; VM, XXIX, 360.
  (*King William*)—WM, V, 13-15.
  (*Richmond Co.*)—WM, IV, 165-166, 194; V, 10-13.
Mettauer—WM 2d, VIII, 95-99.
Metts—Hardesty (*Bedford*), 425.
Meyer (*Rockingham*)—WM, XXVI, 186-187.
Meyerhoeffer—Bruce IV, 296-297.
Meyers (*Richmond*)—Lancaster, 129-130.
Michael—ARP, I, 347-348; Harrison, Waples, etc., 128-129; Highland Co., 322; John Wise, 99-100; Rockbridge, 510; TD, Sept. 28, 1913; Yeardley, 6.
Michaux—Burgess, 656-663; Convention 1788, II, 370; Cyc. Va. Biog., IV, 125; de Graffenried, 197; Lancaster, 165-166; RC. II, 36; TD, Oct. 23, 1914; Virkus I, 186; VSR, I (No. 3), 41; Woodson, 34-35, 56, 69; WM, XXIV, 258-259.
Michie—Albemarle, 274-275; Bruce IV, 19, 30, 333; Dupuy, 192, 244-245; Huguenot Emigration, 123-124, 159, 162-163; Kanawha, 495; MMV, II, 278-279; VM, XXVII, 81; XXIX, 134-135.
Mick—Pendleton Co., 259.
Mickelborough—Hayden, 301; Montague, 94.
Micou—Burgess, 839-840; Culpeper, part 2, 75-79; Fry Genealogy, 17; Huguenot Emigration, XVII, XVIII; Lomax, 66; Meade I, 405; Virkus III, 319.
Middleton—Avery I, 104; Bruce V, 112; Fothergill, 136, 153, 191, etc.; Highland Co., 383; TD, May 17, 1908; VM, X, 315.
Miffleton—Avery I, 173.
Milburn—Burgess, 698.
Milby—Bruce VI, 14; WM, XVIII, 63-65.
Miles—Rockbridge, 510; RS, III, 2.
Miley—Pendleton Co., 259-260; Rockbridge, 510; Shenandoah, 621.
Mill (*King William*)—WM, XX, 208.
Millar (*Shenandoah*)—Bruce V, 212; Cyc. Va. Biog., V, 811; MMV, III, 260-262.
Millbourne—Bell, 39.

Miller—Barbour Co., W. Va., 426-427; Bruce V, 212; Fayette Co., 592; Pendleton Co., 260-261; Rockbridge, 510-511; TD, Oct. 2, 1904; June 4, 11, Sept. 10, 1905; Feb. 18, 1906; WVM, IV, 185-189.
  (*Albemarle*)—Woods-McAfee, 107-109.
  (*Alexandria*)—Old Alexandria, 318-319.
  (*Rev. Alexander*)—Rev. Alexander Miller of Virginia, etc.
  (*Augusta*)—McCue, 27, 54-55, 99-100, 148; Miami Co., Ind., 701; Summers Co., 386-400.
  (*Bath*)—Fayette Co., 595.
  (*Blandford*)—VM, X, 322-324.
  (*Campbell*)—Campbell Co., 460.
  (*Caroline*)—Virkus I, 111.
  (*Christian*)—DAR, 72, p. 13.
  (*Craig*)—Bruce IV, 508.
  (*Goochland*)—Bruce V, 120; Virkus II, 485; WM, XI, 208-209.
  (*Essex*)—Burgess, 1119.
  (*Halifax*)—Cabell, etc., 346-347.
  (*Highland*)—Highland Co., 383.
  (*Lancaster*)—Burgess, 1051.
  (*Loudoun*)—Sangamon Co., Ill., 520-521.
  (*New Kent*)—Cyc. Va. Biog., IV, 340.
  (*Powhatan*)—Mackenzie II, 414-415.
  (*Rockingham*)—Bruce IV, 267-268.
  (*Shenandoah*)—DAR, 45, p. 109; Kanawha, 746; Strickler, 54-55.
  (*Valley of Va.*)—Bruce IV, 383.
  (*Washington Co.*)—Brock II, 743.
  (*Woodstock*)—Ancestry and Descendants of Lieut. John Henderson, 19-21; Bruce VI, 519; Cartmell, 229-230; Thos. Carter, 190-191; VM, II, 38-43; WVM, II (April, 1902), 38-53; IV, 9-19, 172-178.
Milliken—Rockbridge, 511.
Mills—Du Bellet IV, 113-144; Rockbridge, 510-511; WM, VI, 192; VIII, 134.
  (*Albemarle*)—Albemarle, 276-277.
  (*Ambrose*)—King's Mountain, 481-482.
  (*Augusta*)—Munsell's XI, 207.
  (*Botetourt*)—Ewing Family.
  (*Eastern Shore*)—Researcher I; Virkus III, 495; WM, VIII, 275.
Milner—Cyc. Va. Biog., I, 291; TD, June 16, 1907; VM, IV, 168; VII, 355-356; WM, II, 140-141; IX, 128-129.
  (*Loudoun*)—Adams Co., Ohio, 190-191.
Milton—Bruce IV, 155; Mackenzie II, 518-522; McIlhany, 177-214.
Minge—Baskerville Family, 89, 97-99; Carter Family Tree; Cyc. Va. Biog., I, 291-292; Hardy, 153-156; Meade; RS, II, 32; TD, Oct. 28, 1906; Jan. 13, 1907; March 30, 1913; VSR, V (No. 2), 47; VM, III, 159-160; WM, XV, 280-282; XVI, 141; XVII, 228; XIX, 272-279; XXI, 31-33.
Minitree—RS, III, 40; VM, X, 105.
Minnegerode—Memoirs of a Poor Relation, by Mrs. (Minnegerode) Andrews (New York, 1927).
Minness—Pendleton Co., 323.
Miner—TD, April 9, 1905.
Minor—Bruce IV, 375; V, 43; BS, April 23, 1905; Culpeper, part 2, 141; Cyc. Va. Biog., V, 847-848; Goode, 272; Hayden, 371; Huguenot Emigration, 202-203; Kanawha, 480; Marshall, 335; McAllister, 117; Meriwethers, 46-51; Munsell's V,

162; TD, Jan. 1, Feb. 5, 26, April 9, July 9, 16, Aug. 6, 1905;
  Virkus III, 103; VM, I, 272; III, 295-297; IV, 5, 210-211;
  V, 441-442; XI, 207-209, 333-336, 443-444; XXX, 232; VSR,
  V (No. 2), 24; WM, VI, 127; VIII, 196-200; IX, 179-182.
(*Albemarle*)—Albemarle, 277-279; Bruce IV, 307, 309-310.
(*Doodes*)—Cyc. Va. Biog., I, 292.
(*Middlesex*)—Caroline Co., 447-453; Du Bellet I, 188-189, 273-
  274; II, 210-216, 407-409; Hardy, 119-120; Virkus I, 189;
  II, 250; VM, X, 97-98, 204, 311-312, 436-440; XXX, 232;
  WM, IX, 52-54.
(*Spotsylvania*)—VM, XI, 207-209, 335-336, 443-444; WM, VIII,
  250-251; IX, 55-60; XI, 207-209.
(*Westmoreland, etc.*)—Old Prince William I, 344-345; VM, I,
  272; XXXV, 296-297.
Minshall—Madison Co., Ohio, 910-911.
  (*Frederick*)—Miami Co., Ohio, 370.
Minter—Dupuy, 262, 269-284.
Mitchel—Goode, 370-371.
Mitchell—Burgess, 34-40; Cyc. Va. Biog., I, 292; Hardesty, 425;
  Pendleton Co., 261-263; Ritchie Co., 96-98; Rockbridge,
  511; TD, March 24, 1907; Feb. 16, 1913.
(*Augusta*)—McClure, 195-199.
(*Charlotte*)—DAR, 82, p. 131.
(*Hanover*)—Munsell's XI, 116.
(*Henry Co.*)—Henry Co., 219-221.
(*Highland*)—Highland Co., 363.
(*King George*)—DAR, 75, p. 131.
(*Pendleton*)—Virkus II, 173.
(*Prince George*)—Cyc. Va. Biog., V, 940.
(*Lewis*)—DAR, 51, p. 375.
(*Richmond*)—Bruce V, 433.
(*Rockingham*)—"Genealogy" (Weekes ed.), Vol. 4, pp. 126-127.
(*Stafford*)—Hayden, 392.
(*Sussex*)—WM, XXV, 107.
(*York*)—Burgess, 667-671; WM, XXVII, 299.
Mitchelson—Hayden, 150-151.
Mitchum—TD, March 12, 1912.
Moats—Highland Co., 363; Pendleton Co., 263.
Moberly (*Albemarle*)—Wallace, 104.
Mobley (*Lunenburg*)—N. C. His. Reg., I, 355.
Moffett—Bruce IV, 472; V, 409; Dunmore's War, 331; Green's Ky.
  Families, 15-16, 27; Miami Co., Ohio, 609; Munsell's IV,
  41; Peyton, 302; Rockbridge, 511; Sangamon Co., Ill., 527
  [Moffitt]; Shenandoah, 621-622; Woods-McAfee, 51-52.
(*Augusta*)—Kith and Kin, 127; Waddell's Annals of Augusta,
  176-177, 194.
(*Loudoun*)—WM 2d, V, 179-181.
Mohler—McCormick, 32b-32d; Rockbridge, 511-512.
Moler—Lower Shenandoah, 726.
Molesworth—Cyc. Va. Biog., I, 292-293; VM, XIX, 37.
Molloy—WM 2d, VII, 178.
Moncure—Bruce V, 302; VI, 109, 584; Caroline Co., 428-431; Cyc.
  Va. Biog., V, 623, 786-787; Du Bellet I, 65-67, 117-119, 125-
  130, 243-246; II, 426-457; Hardy, 17-18; Hayden, 421-458;
  Kennedy II, 410; Meade II, 198; Munsell's X, 21; Old
  King William, 85; TD, Aug. 1, 1909; Feb. 20, June 11,
  1916; Welles' Washington Genealogy, 249.
Moneymaker—Rockbridge, 512.

Monnett—Virkus III, 620.
Monro (*King and Queen*)—WM, II, 82.
Monroe—Albemarle, 279-281; Bruce V, 113; Cyc. Va. Biog., I, 293;
Hampshire, 718; Lancaster, 373-375; Life of James Monroe,
by George Morgan (Boston, 1921), 1-14; Roger Jones, 56;
TD, April 4, 1909; Oct. 6, 1912; VM, XXVI, 405; WM, VII,
265 [Monro]; XV, 192-195; XVI, 65-67; WM 2d, III, 173-
179; IV, 44-45.
(*Isle of Wight*)—WM, XV, 195.
(*Westmoreland*)—Tyler's VIII, 213-214; Virkus I, 31-32; WM,
IV, 39-40, 272-275; XV, 192-195; XVI, 65-67.
Montague—Brock II, 796-798; Bruce IV, 118; Cooke-Booth, 212-213;
Cyc. Va. Biog., I, 293; Montague, 9-48, etc.; MMV, I, 316-
319; IV, 292-294; Roger Jones, 98; TD, April 30, 1905; Virkus
I, 730; VM, III, 331-333; XV, 200; XXVII, 175; WM 2d,
VIII, 61-62.
Montford—WM 2d, VIII, 124.
Montgomery—Fayette Co., W. Va., 591-592; Rockbridge, 267, 512;
TD, March 22, April 5, 1908.
(*Valley of Va.*)—Green's Ky. Families, 141-143.
(*Western Va.*)—Crockett, 158-159; Dunmore's War, 225.
Montony—Pendleton Co., 263.
Moody—Cyc. Va. Biog., I, 293; Rockbridge, 512; TD, Nov. 3, 1907;
Virkus III, 352.
Mooklar—Cyc. Va. Biog., V, 625-626.
Moomaw—Shenandoah, 622.
Moon—Bruce VI, 158; Campbell Co., 96-97; Cyc. Va. Biog., I, 293;
MMV, III, 268-274; TD, June 25, 1911; WM, VII, 222;
XVII, 67.
(*Albemarle*)—Albemarle, 282-283; Bruce V, 247; TD, Feb. 6,
13, March 12, 1916.
Moone (Moon)—TD, June 25, 1911.
(*Isle of Wight*)—VM, IV, 76.
(*Lancaster*)—VM, V, 252-253.
Mooney—DAR, 42, p. 73.
Moore—BHNC, VIII, 355; BS, Feb. 19, 1905; May 27, 1906; Campbell's
Spotswood Family of Va., 20-23; Cyc. Va. Biog., I, 294;
Life of the Rev. William Smith (1880), II, 541-563; Mad-
ison Co., Ohio, 912; St. Mark's, 140, 165; TD, July 31, 1904;
Nov. 5, 19, Dec. 3, 1905; Feb. 18, April 22, 29, May 13, June
17, 1906; July 16, Sept. 17, 1916; Welles' Washington Gene-
alogy, 231.
(*Albemarle*)—Albemarle, 283-285; Family History Hughes, etc.,
110, et seq.; Lewis, 385-391.
(*Appomattox*)—Braxton Co., W. Va., 406.
(*Augusta*)—Convention 1788, II, 31-36; Green's Ky. Families,
231-233, 450; Walker-Wigton, 65-66, 68-70, 72-73, 130-146,
148-150, 174-176, 463-466; VM, XXIX, 29; Waddell's Annals
of Augusta Co., 51-54.
(*Bedford*)—De Graffenried, 192.
(*Bishop Moore*)—Memoir of the Life of the Rev. Richard Chan-
ning Moore, D. D.; Six Centuries of the Moores of Fawley.
(*Charlotte*)—Bruce VI, 334.
(*Chelsea*)—Beau Monde (weekly), Richmond, Va., April 14,
1894; Browning, C. D., 292-293; Browning, C. D., 3d, 245;
Browning, R. D., 3d, 112-114, 245; Browning, R. D., 3d,
112-114; Culpeper, 72-73; Du Bellet II, 704-715; Hening
VIII, 285-287, 476-478; Kennedy II, 309-315; Lindsay, 22;

RS, II, 35, 37, 40; III, 21, 36-38; IV, 1-2; Spotswood Letters I, XIV, XV; VM, XXV, 433-437; VSR, V (No. 2), 19; WM, XVI, 122-126; XVII, 49-53, 146; XIX, 177-179, 183.

(*Elizabeth City*)—Bruce IV, 14; Du Bellet II, 702-703; Kennedy II, 307-309; WM, II, 14; IX, 126-127.

(*Fairfax*)—Lindsay, 109-110; MMV, V, 307-310.

(*Fauquier*)—Van Meter, 124-131.

(*Henrico*)—Madison Co., Ohio, 373.

(*Highland*)—Highland Co., 383.

(*James City*)—Cyc. Va. Biog., IV, 341.

(*Kentucky*)—Burgess, 1013.

(*King William*)—Lancaster, 266-267.

(*Loudoun*)—Cyc. Va. Biog., V, 595.

(*Louisa*)—DAR, 78, p. 209.

(*Miscellaneous*)—"Genealogy" (Weekes ed.), Vol. 4, 1914, 63-64.

(*Northampton*)—Halifax Co., N. C., 188.

(*Orange*)—Culpeper, part 2, 138, 142-143.

(*Richmond*)—Cabell, etc., 423-424.

(*Rockbridge*)—Clemens' Wills, 67; Foote I, 505-524; Green's Ky. Families, 99-100; Kith and Kin, 140-143; Marshall, 67; Rockbridge, 267-268, 512-514; Tazewell II, 497-502; WVM, III, 83-85.

(*Shenandoah*)—Sangamon Co., Ill., 530.

(*Valley of Va.*)—Bruce IV, 249; Cartmell, 452-453.

(*West Va.*)—Pocahontas Co., 112-116 (Moses), 278-292, 355-359, 464-476.

Moores—DAR, 48, p. 446.

Moorman—Albemarle, 285-286; Campbell Co., 460-465; Clemens' Wills, 68-69; Goode, 49, 77; Pendleton Co., 264; TD, Sept. 30, 1906; June 22, 1913.

(*Bedford*)—Bell, 38, 79.

(*Louisa*)—Bell, 14, 37.

Moran—Rockbridge, 514.

Morancy—Old King William, 85-87.

Mordecai—VM, XXXI, 187-188.

Morecock—WM, VII, 54; XVI, 140.

Morehead—Coshocton Co., Ohio, 751; Family Record of the Moreheads (Los Angeles, n. d.); John Motley Morehead and the Development of N. C.; Mackenzie IV, 385; MMV, I, 206-207; Moreheads of Va. and N. C.; Rockbridge, 514; TD, March 29, 1908; June 16, 1912; April 26, 1914; Trabue, 39-41; VM, XXI, 429-430.

Moreland (*Campbell*)—Bell, 86.

Morelock—TD, March 29, 1908.

Morgan—Burgess, 679-680; Cyc. Va. Biog., 294; Hayden, 533; Meade II, 302; Rockbridge, 514; TD, July 31, Aug. 28, 1904; April 26, 1914.

(*Augusta*)—Marshall, 290-291.

(*Bedford*)—Bruce V, 422.

(*Campbell*)—Campbell Co., 465-466.

(*Daniel*)—Cartmell, 270-273; VM, XXXIV, 371-372; WVM, IV, 272-278.

(*Fauquier*)—DAR, 48, p. 258.

(*Frederick*)—Shepherdstown, 336-337.

(*Morgan Morgan*)—Cyc. Va. Biog., IV, 83, 452; Meade II, 302-304; Monongahela III, 949-959; Report of the Col. Morgan Morgan Monument Commission; Tyler's III, 52; Virkus II,

367; VSR, IV (No. 3), 18-19.
(*Pittsylvania*)—Pittsylvania, 152.
(*West Va.*)—Preston Co., 379, 455-456; Randolph Co., 361-362.
(*York*)—Francis Morgan, etc.
Morison (*Westmoreland*)—Bruce VI, 306, 458.
Morral—Pendleton Co., 264-265.
Morrell—Brock II, 723.
Morris—Burgess, 680-681; Cooke-Booth, 40; Life of Gen. Hugh
    Mercer, 132-133; Rockbridge, 133, 514-515; TD, June 19,
    Aug. 7, 21, 1904; Dec. 6, 1908; Sept. 15, 22, 1912; WM,
    VIII, 134.
(*Albemarle*)—Albemarle, 286-288; McIlhany, 26-27.
(*Brunswick*)—DAR, 43, p. 55.
(*Buckingham*)—Bruce IV, 337.
(*Goochland*)—Woodson, 85.
(*Hanover*)—Tyler's IV, 130-133.
(*Henry Co.*)—Henry Co., 216-218.
(*James City*)—Grafton Johnson, 160.
(*Kanawha Valley*)—WVM, I, 65-92.
(*Louisa*)—Lancaster, 213-214; Tyler's IV, 130-133.
(*New Kent*)—Two Families, 40-41; Tyler's IV, 130-133.
(*Northumberland*)—VM, XXV, 192-194.
(*Western Va.*)—Fayette Co., W. Va., 62-67; Shenandoah, 622;
    WVM, III, 189-190.
Morrison—History of the Morrison Settlers of Londonderry; Rock-
    bridge, 268, 515; Virkus II, 95; WM, IX, 122-123.
(*Frederick*)—Braxton Co., W. Va., 406-407; Monongahela III,
    1169.
Morriss—Bruce IV, 255.
(*Brunswick*)—DAR, 56, p. 7.
(*New Kent*)—RC, II, 50.
(*Washington Co.*)—Brock II, 744.
Morrissett—Bruce IV, 96.
Morrow—Carolinians II, 373; Shepherdstown, 245, 337; WVM, III,
    188.
Morse—VM, I, 468-469.
Morson—Cabell, etc., 331-332; Carolinians II, 420; Hardy, 457-459;
    Hayden, 653-654; Lancaster, 181; Marshall, 326; VM, XI,
    242; VSR, IV (No. 4), 35; WM, II, 87.
Morter—Rockbridge, 515.
Mortimer—VSR, V (No. 2), 28.
Morton—Buckners of Va., 89; Cabell, etc., 537-538; Hampden-Sidney,
    88, 120-121, 198; Hayden, 19-20, 323, 326-327; Meade II, 31;
    MMV, V, 318-319; Rockbridge, 515; RS, II, 20; III, 13;
    St. Mark's, 136, 173; TD, Dec. 18, 1904; Oct. 17, 1909; Feb.
    18, 1917; VM, XI, 205-207, 339-340, 451-453; XII, 96-99;
    XXVII, 177; Watkins, 18, 30-34.
(*Amelia*)—Crozier VII, 65-67.
(*Charlotte*)—Cyc. Va. Biog., V, 643, 1006; Halifax, 230-231;
    Life of Archibald Alexander. D. D., 179-182; Meade II,
    31; Morton Genealogy, by W. H. Morton; TD, Oct. 17,
    1909; WM 2d, I, 285-286.
(*Cumberland*)—Cyc. Va. Biog., IV, 335.
(*Henrico*)—Woodson, 33, 36, 57, 94, 96, 174, 275, 445.
(*Highland*)—Highland Co., 383-384.
(*John*)—The Mortons I; Morton Kin II (copy in Library of
    Congress), by Daniel Morton, M. D., St. Joseph, Mo.
(*Miscellaneous*)—VM, XXIX, 502-503.

(*Orange*)—MMV, IV, 295-296.
(*Pittsylvania*)—Pittsylvania, 144, 160.
(*Prince Edward*)—Burgess, 32-34; VM, XVII, 305.
(*Various Families*)—Morton Data; VM, XI, 205-207, 329; XVII, 311-316.
Moryson—Cyc. Va. Biog., I, 294; VM, XX, 70-71; WM, I, 194-195.
(*Francis*)—Tyler's IV, 446; VM, II, 383-385; WM, IX, 119-122.
Mosby—Burgess, 1285; Cabell, etc., 542-543; Goode, 219-225, 369-370; Hampden-Sidney, 30-31, 246-247; Huguenot Emigration, 141-142; Kennedy II, 376-377; RS, III, 14; TD, April 3, 17, May 1, 22, 1904; Valentine II, 813-904; IV, 2275-2283; VM, V, 103-104; XVII, 441-444; VSR, I (No. 3), 40; IV (No. 1), 40; Woodson, 388, 416.
Moseley—America Heraldica, 173; Cyc. Va. Biog., I, 294-295; TD, April 7, May 19, June 2, 16, Nov. 3, 1907; Sept. 26, 1909; Sept. 1, 29, 1912; March 22, Aug. 23, 1914; WM, II, 46; IV, 270-271.
(*Bedford*)—Thos. Carter, 126.
(*Goochland*)—Douglas, 256-257 (Mosely).
(*Henrico*)—Cabell, etc., 547; Genealogy of the Moseley Family of Bedford Co., by George C. Moseley (n. p.; n. d.); Hampden-Sidney, 95; Hardy, 280; McAllister, 150-152, 224-226; Montague, 134, 146-148, 219-220, 255-257, 360-362; TD, Aug. 6, 1911; VM, V, 207.
(*Lower Norfolk*)—Antiquary I, 64; II, 121-125; Carolinians II, 469-471; Habersham Chap. II, 571-572, 687-688; Hardy, 47; Lancaster, 42-45; Virkus III, 597; VM, V, 140-141, 327-334; XXXV, 49-54, 218-220.
(*Norfolk and Lower Norfolk*)—McIntosh I, 16, 183; II, 27, 299.
(*Princess Anne*)—Chart in VM, Vol. V; VM, XXXII, 58.
Moser—Pendleton Co., 323.
Moses—Brock II, 799; Montgomery Co., Ohio (TH), 419.
Moss—Burgess, 1286-1288; BS, April 30, 1905; Cabell, etc., 582; Hord (1898), 119-120, 122-123, 167; Tazewell II, 336-339; Virkus II, 71; VM, I, 468-469; VSR, II (No. 1), 63.
(*Fauquier*)—VSR, IV (No. 3), 19.
(*Goochland*)—Burgess, 18; Dupuy, 362-369; Van Meter, 45-46; Woodson, 150, 230, 545.
(*Miscellaneous*)—"Genealogy" (Clemens), VII, 101.
(*Westmoreland*)—Bruce IV, 202.
(*York*)—Tyler's VI, 48-52, 147.
Mossom—Burgess, 24-31; Cyc. Va. Biog., I, 295; WM, II, 206; V, 66-67, 77-78, 81, 204-206.
Mothershead—Fothergill, 111, 121, 128, 141; Morton Kin; TD, May 10, 1908.
Motley—Bagby, 366; Bruce V, 244; Caroline Co., 453-456; Cyc. Va. Biog., V, 809-811; The Morehead Family of North Carolina and Virginia, 102-105.
Mott—Essex, 36, 45; Price, 105.
Mottley (*Nottoway*)—McAllister, 292-294.
Mottrom—Cyc. Va. Biog., I, 295; WM, XVII, 53-56.
Mountfort—WM, VII, 266.
Mountjoy—Garrard, 103-107; Morton Kin; VM, XI, 206; WM, XVI, 291.
Mouring—WM, XII, 123-124.
Mouse—Pendleton Co., 323.
Mowrey—Pendleton Co., 265.
Mowry—Coshocton Co., Ohio, 252.

Mutterspaw—Rockbridge, 515.
Myers—Bruce IV, 306; Rockbridge, 515.
　　(*Frederick*)—Cartmell, 462.
　　(*Norfolk*)—Bruce IV, 433; Cyc. Va. Biog., IV, 526-527.
　　(*Richmond*)—Lancaster, 129-130.
　　(*Rockingham*)—Bruce IV, 209.
　　(*Shenandoah*)—Bruce IV, 259.
Myhill—Barton II, 161-162; Tyler's X, 138.

N

Naigley—Highland Co., 384.
Nalle—Culpeper, 53; part 2, 139-140; Dunmore's War, 405; Hayden,
　　730; Mackenzie II, 110; St. Mark's, 120; VM, XXVI, 406-
　　407; XXVII, 169-170.
Nalls—Avery I, 175.
Nance—A Nance Memorial; Halifax, 321; Hardesty (*Bedford*), 425;
　　Henry Co., 229-230; Major, 134-135; Researcher I, 257; TD,
　　Sept. 30, Oct. 28, 1906.
　　(*Charles City*)—Bruce IV, 370.
Nans—Hardin Co., Ohio, 962.
Napier—Habersham Chap. II, 126-127; Henry Co., 230-231; New River,
　　431-434; Virkus III, 29; VM, XXXIII, 45; Woodson, 29.
Nash—Cyc. Va. Biog., I, 206; IV, 430; McIntosh I, 118-119; II, 232-
　　233, 274-275; Virkus II, 170.
　　(*Fauquier*)—Brock II, 800.
　　(*Norfolk*)—MMV, II, 282-284; Norfolk, 523-525, 556, 597-598.
　　(*Prince Edward*)—DAR, 81, p. 203.
Naylor—BS, March 12, 1905; Glengarry McDonalds, 323-329.
Neal—Sangamon Co., Ill., 538; WM 2d, VIII, 132-133.
　　(*Pittsylvania*)—Brock II, 611.
Neale—BS, Aug. 6, 1905; Burgess, 4-5, 7-8; Cyc. Va. Biog., I, 296-
　　297; TD, Dec. 18, 1904; March 13, July 31, Nov. 6, 1910;
　　Feb. 7, 14, 1915.
　　(*Eastern Shore*)—RS, III, 37; VM, II, 309; V, 339; Yeardley, 29.
　　(*Fauquier*)—Thos. Carter, 345-346.
　　(*King William*)—Old King William, 88-92; WM 2d, VI, 328-330.
　　(*Northumberland*)—Hardy, 394-399; Mackenzie IV, 382-384; VM,
　　XXXV, 87.
Neavil (Neville)—Fauquier Bulletin, 318, 485; Old Prince William
　　II, 514-515.
Neblett—Hampden-Sidney, 160; Old Free State II, 319-327.
Neeb—Bruce IV, 255.
Needlar—RC, II, 12.
Needler—Cyc. Va. Biog., I, 297; Tyler's I, 69-70; VM, XIV, 26.
Neely—Rockbridge, 515.
Neff—Brock II, 745; MMV, IV, 308-309; Neff Genealogy (1896), 352
　　pages; Shenandoah, 624; Strickler, 57; WM 2d, VI, 39-40.
Neibel—Montgomery Co., Ohio (TH), 419.
Neil—Green's Ky. Families; Marshall, 276; Rockbridge, 515.
Neill—Jolliffe, 175-191; TD, June 21, 1912.
　　(*Frederick*)—McIlhany, 65-66.
　　(*Lee Co.*)—Hughes, etc., 73.
Neilson—Albemarle, 288.
Nelms—Hardy, 190-193.
Nelson—Albemarle, 288-289; Bruce IV, 58; V, 15; Campbell's His-
　　tory of Va., 653; Carter Family Tree; Cyc. Va. Biog., I,

70, 297; Funsten-Meade, 65-66; Goode, 277; Hardesty (*Bedford*), 426-427; Hayden, 446-447; Kennedy I, 543-544; Lancaster, 37-38, 458; Marshall, 109; Meade I, 205, 213-214; Nelson Family of Va.; "Old Chapel", 27, 35, 38-43, 47-48, 63, 65-66, 68, 72-73; Page (2d ed.), 155-194; Pendleton Co., 270-272; RC (1888); Rockbridge, 268, 516; SBN, XII, 226-228; TD, Dec. 13, 1903 (will of Thomas Nelson), Jan. 20, Feb. 24, 1907; July 6, 1913; Nov. 8, 1914; Welles' Washington Genealogy, 171-193.

(*Hanover*)—Virkus II, 51.
(*Highland*)—Highland Co., 363.
(*New Kent and Hanover*)—Armistead, 173-176.
(*Spotsylvania*)—VM, XXXIV, 157-158, 273.
(*Valley of Va.*)—VM, XVIII, 202-203.
(*York*)—Browning, C. D., 3d, 186, 437-439; Du Bellet II, 448-449; IV, 19-22; Kith and Kin, 57; Munsell's V, 31; RS, I, 40; II, 15; III, 4, 6, 9, 15, 32; Two Families, 41-42; VM, IX, 355-356; XIII, 402-403; XVI, 23-24; XVII, 187-188; XXVI, 411; XXXIII, 188-193; VSR, V (No. 2), 63-64; WM, IV, 134; V, 149-150.

Nesbett—Clemens' Wills, 71.
Nesbit—Rockbridge, 516.
Nesselrodt—Pendleton Co., 272-273.
Nestrick—Pendleton Co., 323.
Netherland—WM, V, 143.
Nethers—Licking Co., Ohio, 734.
Netherton—624-625.
Nevil—DAR, 81, p. 68; Virkus II, 241; III, 459.
Nevill—WM, XIX, 61.
  (*Amherst*)—Cabell, etc., 387.
  (*Fauquier*)—Old Prince William, II, 514-515; VM, XVI, 53-54, 53-54.
Neville—Hardin Co., Ohio, 848; Norfolk, 835-836; VM, XXVII, 123.
  (*Albemarle*)—WM, XIX, 123.
  (*Fauquier*)—Draper Series V, 333; VM, VI, 432; VII, 103-104; XVI, 53-54; see also Neavil.
  (*Frederick*)—Burgess, 1-2; Jolliffe, 74.
  (*Lancaster*)—Virkus III, 31.
New—ARP, I, 281-282; Cooke-Booth, 48-50; Descendants of John Stubbs, 113-114; WM, V, 259.
Newbill—Bruce V, 230; MMV, IV, 314-315.
Newce—Cyc. Va. Biog., I, 85-86, 91.
Newcomb—Bruce VI, 642; Descendants of John Stubbs.
Newcomer—Rockbridge, 516.
Newell—Rockbridge, 516.
  (*Frederick*)—King's Mountain, 408-409.
  (*Western Va.*)—Dunmore's War, 214-215.
Newman—Boogher, 237-282; Bruce IV, 551; Culpeper, part 2, 144-145; MMV, II, 287-288; Old King William, 92-94; Shenandoah, 625; St. Mark's, 120; TD, March 12, 1911; WM, VII, 249.
  (*Highland*)—Highland Co., 324.
  (*Roanoke*)—Adams Co., Ohio, 269-272.
  (*York*)—Tyler's VI, 277-279.
Newport (*Christopher*)—LCJ, Jan. 31, 1915 (III, 2).
Newsom—Sangamon Co., Ill., 542; VM, IV, 429-430.
Newsum—The Virginia Carys, 111-112.
Newton—BS, March 29, 1908; Cyc. Va. Biog., I, 297-298; Rockbridge,

516; TD, July 22, 1906; VM, I, 41; WM, I, 172; V, 68; IX, 28.

(*Lower Norfolk*)—WM, XX, 189.

(*Norfolk*)—Forrest's History of Norfolk, Va., 54; Kennedy I, 194; Marshall, 327-328; VM, XXIX, 516-519; XXX, 85-88, 307-309; Virkus III, 326; WM, II, 75; XX, 189.

(*Westmoreland*)—Arkansas, 190-195; Bruce IV, 288, 308; VI, 388; Fothergill, 158; Green's Ky. Families, 276; Kennedy I, 194; II, 483-500; Marshall, 107, 217; Meade II, 151-157; Virkus I, 951; VM, I, 269-270; XII, 92; XXXIII, 299-302, 393-395; XXXVII, 87-91; WM, IV, 279.

Nicely—Rockbridge, 516.

Nicholas—Albemarle, 289-291; Bolling Genealogy, 30; Brock I, 121-129; Browning, C. D., 133-134; Browning, R. D., III, 735-736; BS, April 2, 1905; Carter Family Tree; Convention 1788, II, 281-360; Cyc. Va. Biog., II, 314; Du Bellet I, 67-69, 117; II, 310-336; Fry Genealogy, 59; Goode (see index); Hardy, 18, 110; Kennedy I, 284; Mackenzie I, 50-52; Meade I, 184; RC, III, 50; Rockbridge, 516; RS, I, 39; III, 43; TD, Feb. 28, 1904; June 4, 1905; Tiernan, etc., 323-332; Van Meter, 69-72; VHS Col. VI, 92, 111; Virkus I, 507; VM, IX, 108, 358; XV, 151; VSR, I (No. 2), 16 [Gen. Sec.]; IV (No. 1), 35; (No. 2), 56; WM, I, 25; XXVII, 132-133.

(*George*)—VM, XXXIII, 43-44, 202-203.

(*Highland*)—Highland Co., 324-326.

Nichols—Bruce V, 414; VI, 555; Cyc. Va. Biog., IV, 409; Rockbridge, 268, 516.

(*Bedford*)—Hardesty, 426.

Nicholson, Nicolson—America Heraldica, 152; TD, Aug. 15, 1915; WM, I, 151; VI, 258.

Nickell—Monroe Co., 386-387.

Nickels—Bruce IV, 417, 489.

Nicklin—Mackenzie VI, 291; Tyler's XI, 38; WM 2d, IX, 61.

(*From Pa.*)—Mackenzie IV, 392-404.

Nicol—Cyc. Va. Biog., V, 669.

Nicolson (*York*)—Bruton, 95; Virkus I, 299; WM, XV, 63-64; see also Nicholson.

Nightingale—Burgess, 409-411.

Nimmo—Antiquary I, 89-90, 129; Cyc. Va. Biog., I, 298; Ellis, 32-41; Hampden-Sidney, 204-205; TD, July 5, 1908; WM, IV, 203; V, 134-137; VIII, 274-275; IX, 121-122, 134-135.

Nivison—Meade.

Nixon—Cyc. Va. Biog., V, 1076; "Francis Morgan", 142-151; Miami Co., Ohio, 535.

(*Loudoun*)—Adams Co., Ohio, 826-827.

Noble—"Francis Morgan", 182.

Noel—TD, April 21, 1907.

Noell (*Bedford*)—Bruce V, 439; Hardesty, 426; "Genealogy" (Clemens), IX, 9-11.

Noffsinger—Bruce VI, 349.

Noland—Mackenzie I, 343; Old Prince William II, 503-504; Tyler's II, 132-134; VM, XV, 204, 334-335; VSR, IV (No. 4), 40-41.

Nolande—Old Prince William II, 503-504.

Nolley—Bruce IV, 324.

Noltenius—VM, XXXV, 443.

Nolting—VM, I, 343.

Norfleet—Norfolk, 958; VM, XXXVII, 67.
Norman—Morehead Family of N. C. and Va., 108-110.
(*Fauquier*)—DAR, 82, p. 69.
Norris (*Fauquier*)—Ritchie Co., 115-116.
(*Lancaster*)—Bruce V, 167; DAR, 59, p. 234; VM, I, 468.
(*William, Coshocton Co., O.*)—Rejected Claim Papers, VSA.
Norsworthy (Nosworthy)—Cyc. Va. Biog., I, 298; WM, VII, 246; XX, 218.
North—Funsten-Meade, 77-79; VM, III, 82; Winston, 186-189.
(*Buckingham*)—Sangamon Co., Ill., 545-546.
Norton—Avery I, 68; Cyc. Va. Biog., I, 298; Du Bellet I, 41-47, 95-96, 177-178; Fry Genealogy, 61; Marshall, 212-213, 327-328; RS, I, 39; II, 47; Tyler's III, 287-298; VSR, V (No. 2), 50.
Norvell—Baskerville Family, 96-97; Campbell Co., 468-471; Cyc. Va. Biog., I, 299; Hord (1898), 66-67; Kanawha, 527; Lynchburg, Va., Sketches, 230-234; TD, July 1, Dec. 30, 1906; VM, XXIV, 203; VSR, V (No. 2), 47; WM, XX, 222; XXV, 71.
(*James City*)—WM, I, 209.
Norwood—Cyc. Va. Biog., I, 299; DAR, 44, p. 362; Throckmorton.
Nottingham—Bruce V, 475; Cyc. Va. Biog., I, 299; V, 827; Pocahontas Co., 526-529; John Wise, 86; Yeardley, 26.
Nourse—Du Bellet IV, 107-112; James Nourse and His Descendants; Mackenzie V, 404-407; Munsell's VII, 255; VM, VIII, 199-202; WVM, IV, 283-290.
Nowlin—Bruce IV, 404; The Nowlin-Stone Genealogy.
Nuchols, Nuckols—TD, May 5, 1907.
Nuckols—Bruce IV, 220; Cyc. Va. Biog., IV, 369.
Nuckolls—Grayson Co., 65-97; Sangamon Co., Ill., 547.
Null—DAR, 41, p. 37.
Nulton—Cartmell, 499.
Nunn (*King and Queen*)—Bagby, 366; Burgess, 406-408.
Nunnally—Habersham Chap. II, 19-20, 197, 304-305.
Nutt—Avery I, 175.
Nuttall—WM, XII, 177.
Nutter—Border Settlers, 260-262; Harrison Co., 372; Kanawha, 942-943; Ritchie Co., 160-162.

O

Oakes—Highland Co., 384.
Oates—Halifax, 321-322.
O'Bannon—Bruce VI, 442; Fauquier Bulletin, 205, 484 (Obanon); VM, XXXIV, 371-372.
Obenchain—Hardesty (*Bedford*), 420.
Obert (Hobert)—VM, V, 251-252.
O'Brien—Braxton Co., W. Va., 414; VM, IV, 363.
Ocheltree—Rockbridge, 516.
O'Daniel—Tyler's I, 164-166.
O'Donald—Brock II, 576.
O'Donovan—SBN, XII, 238.
O'Ferrall—Rockingham, 358-359; Thomas Carter, 72, 80.
Offner—Virkus II, 349.
Offley—ARP, I, 348-349; Harrison, Waples, etc., 135-138.
O'Friel—Rockbridge. 516.
Ogburn—Old Free State II, 261, 355-357.

Ogden—Cyc. Va. Biog., V, 813; Hardesty (*Amherst*), 443; Rockbridge, 516.
Ogilvie—Coshocton Co., Ohio, 760.
Ogle—His. Encyc. of Ill., 407; Rockbridge, 516.
Oglesby—Clemens' Wills, 72; Coshocton Co., Ohio, 525; Crockett, 141-142; TD, Aug. 7, 1904.
O'Hara—TD, Sept. 22, 1907.
Okeson—RS, III, 33.
Old—Bruce IV, 437; VI, 564; Norfolk, 985, 989; TD, Jan. 19, 1908.
　(*Albemarle and Lancaster*)—Albemarle, 291-292.
　(*Norfolk, etc.*)—The Olds Family, 322-333.
　(*Princess Anne*)—MMV, IV, 316-318.
Oldfield—Virkus III, 105.
Oldham—Albemarle, 292; Burgess, 1020; LEP, March 1, 1919; Maxwell, 454-456; Miami Co., Ind., 588; Shepherdstown, 339; TD, May 16, 1909; Virkus III, 425; VM, VII, 103-104; XXIII, 314; WM, XII, 195; XIX, 262-265.
Oldis—Cyc. Va. Biog., I, 299; VM, XI, 311-312.
Oliver—RS, IV, 23; Southside Va., 110, 171-172; Stubbs, 408-433, 519-520; WM, VII, 222.
　(*Fairfax*)—Bruce VI, 128.
　(*Mathews*)—Bruce IV, 453.
Omohundro—Bruce V, 262, 304; Fothergill, 23, 155, 200.
Omps—Cartmell, 482.
O'Neill—LCJ, June 13, 1915 (II, 9).
Opie—ARP, II, 745; Browning, C. D., 3d, 544-545; Bruce IV, 577-578; Cyc. Va. Biog., I, 299; Lindsay, 40-42; MMV, IV, 319-321; VM, XVIII, 90-92; XXVII, 75, 86, 363; WM, V, 12; XX, 288-289, 297-299.
Orbison—Rockbridge, 516.
Ord—Mathew Family, 31-32.
O'Rear—Woods-McAfee, 299.
Orgain—Cyc. Va. Biog., V, 638; WM, VIII, 112.
Orhenbaum—DAR, 78, p. 301.
Ornbaum—Rockbridge, 516.
Orndorff—Bruce V, 282-283.
Orr—Buckners of Va., 107; Tyler's IV, 47-53.
Orrick (*Maryland*)—Hardy, 402-408.
Osborne—Cyc. Va. Biog., I, 299-300; V, 724; Grayson Co., 171-173; Halifax, 324; Kanawha, 583; Monroe Co., 387; TD, Oct. 6, 1907.
　(*Charlotte*)—Bruce IV, 98.
　(*Chesterfield*)—Keith Addendum IV; TD, Aug. 27, Sept. 10, 1911; VM, IV, 247-248.
　(*Henrico*)—Habersham Chap. II, 438-439; VM, IV, 247-248; XVII, 432-433; XXIII, 131; WM, XXV, 113-114, 260.
　(*Loudoun*)—Adams Co., Ohio, 829-830.
Osbourne—Ritchie Co., W. Va., 92-93; TD, April 12, 1914.
Otey—Brock II, 580-583; Bruce IV, 572; V, 119; Buford, 133-136; Cabell, etc., 352; Campbell Co., 471-472; Floyd, 78; McGavock Family, 80, 130; Rockbridge, 516; Virkus III, 152.
Ott—Shenandoah, 625-626; Virkus III, 481.
Ould (*Cumberland*)—MMV, II, 295-296; The Olds Family, 320,334.
Overall—Cartmell, 447-448; Clemens' Wills, 103; Jolliffe, 104; Shenandoah, 626.
Overbey—Cabell, etc., 371-372; Cyc. Va. Biog., IV, 312.
Overby—Halifax, 323.
Overfield—Price, 138.

Overstreet—Bruce V, 276; Hardesty (*Bedford*), 427; Knox Co., Ill., 776; Sangamon Co., Ill., 551.

Overton—Andrew Meade, etc., 147-152; Dinwiddie Papers II, 157; Goode, 486; Hayden, 385-386; SBN, XII, 244; TD, April 10, 1904; July 1, 1906; Jan. 27, Feb. 10, 1907; Sept. 5, 12, 1915; Virkus III, 76; VM, XI, 305-307; XIII, 264; XXVI, 408-409; XXVII, 73; VSR, III (No. 1), 39; IV (No. 3), 28; Winston, 69-72.

Owen—RS, III, 28; TD, Oct. 15, 1911.
    (*Campbell*)—Campbell Co., 472-473.
    (*Goronwy*)—WM, II, 258-259; IX, 152-154.
    (*Halifax*)—Bruce IV, 509; Halifax, 231-233, 322-323.
    (*Henrico*)—Virkus II, 237.
    (*Mathews*)—Brock II, 800.
    (*Prince Edward*)—Dupuy, 336-342.

Owens—Rockbridge, 516; Sketches of Lynchburg, Va., 145-148.
Owsley—Bruce V, 398; Culpeper, part 2, 91; VM, XXX, 326-327.
Oyler—Rockbridge, 516.
Oxley—Kanawha, 862.
Ozlin—Bruce V, 57.

P

Pace—Brock II, 613; Cyc. Va. Biog., I, 300; Henry Co., 245-246; VM, I, 452; WM, IX, 212.
    (*Sussex*)—Cyc. Va. Biog., IV, 198.
Pack—Monroe Co., 388; New River, 439-441.
    (*Augusta*)—Summers Co., 447-452.

Packard—Hayden, 542.
Packe—WM, III, 267; VII, 11.
Padgett—Avery I, 176.
Page—American Family Antiquary, 125-170; Brock I, 95-97; Browning, C. D., 56-58, 134-135; Browning, C. D., 3d, 184-186, 333-337; Browning, R. D., III, 736-737; Bruce IV, 4, 321, 449; Bruton Church, 111-113; BS, July 31, 1904; Jan. 20, 27, Feb. 3, 10, 1907; Carter Family Tree; Cooke-Booth, 221-223; Cyc. Va. Biog., I, 114, 147, 156, 159, 164, 300; IV, 200; V, 976; Douglas; Genealogy of the Page Family of Virginia; Glenn's Some Colonial Mansions, 171-213; Hayden, 216; Hening V, 277-284; VII, 480-483; VIII, 445-447; Kennedy I, 113-120, 511-547; Lancaster, 185-186, 219-225, 279-281, 392, 460-461; Lee, 482-485; Meade I, 195-197, 334-335, 351-352; Mackenzie III, 364; MMV, II, 297-304; V, 333-336; Munsell's IV, 183; V, 98-99; Norfolk, 490, 492-493; Obituary Notices of Yale Graduates, 1921-22 (New Haven, 1922), 327-329; Old Chapel, 31-34, 38-39, 43, 51, 54, 57, 70, 74; RC (1888); RS, III, 4, 29, 37; Robertson; SBN, XII, 246-249; TD, Nov. 1, 1914; June 27, 1915; Virkus II, 21; III, 33; VM, I, 336; IV, 365; XV, 216; XIX, 154; XXVII, 73, 76; XXXII, 37-47, 290-291; XXXIII, 86-87; VSR, IV (No. 1), 32; V (No. 2), 61; Willis, 57-58; WM, I, 84; II, 149, 266; III, 153, 185-189; IV, 32, 250; VI, 62, 146; VII, 159.

    See also Bibliography.
    (*Albemarle*)—Albemarle, 293; Bruce IV, 277.
    (*Clarke*)—Bruce V, 185-186; Cartmell, 458; Lower Shenandoah, 570-571.

(*Nansemond*)—Cyc. Va. Biog., I, 301-302; Virkus I, 766; VM, XIX, 191-192.
(*Nansemond and Isle of Wight*)—VM, V, 446-447.
(*Northern Neck*)—Cyc. Va. Biog., I, 301.
(*Westmoreland*)—Cartmell, 457; Hardy, 410-413; Mackenzie I, 91; VM, VI, 86-88, 195-197, 301-303; XIX, 447.
Parkes—Armstrong III, 112.
Parks—Clemens' Wills, 73; Cyc. Va. Biog., I, 302; V, 759, 813; Ritchie Co., 211; Rockbridge, 516; VM, VIII, 324-325; Whitaker, 71-72; WM, VI, 128; VII, 11-12.
(*Prince Edward*)—VM, IX, 213-214.
Parkins—Bruce VI, 86; Cyc. Va. Biog., IV, 197.
Parnell—WM, VII, 244.
Parr—Bruce IV, 447; VI, 266; Burgess, 1022.
Parramore—VM, XV, 407.
Parrish—Bruce IV, 71, 146; Burgess. 303-306, 308; Coshocton Co., Ohio, 762; Cyc. Va. Biog., IV, 164.
(*Fluvanna*)—Bruce V, 13.
(*Nelson*)—Bruce V, 497.
(*Pittsylvania*)—Cyc. Va. Biog., IV, 195.
(*Portsmouth*)—Bruce VI, 194; Cyc. Va. Biog., IV, 324.
(*Richmond City*)—Bruce V, 364.
Parrott—Bruce VI, 407; DAR, 81, p. 288; Halifax, 324.
Parry—Jolliffe, 209-214; Rockbridge, 521.
Parsons—Rockbridge, 269, 516-517.
(*York*)—VSR, I (No. 3), 51; IV (No. 4), 22.
Partlow (*Spotsylvania*)—Researcher I, 256-257.
Pasteur—Burgess, 867; Cyc. Va. Biog., I, 302; Huguenot Emigration, 33; Valentine II, 918-948; IV, 2284-2288; VSR, II (No. 3), 33-34; WM, III, 274-275; V, 281.
Pate—Buford, 30-31; Chappell, 324-329; Cyc. Va. Biog., I, 131; TD, Dec. 18, 1910; March 19, 1911; June 22, 1913; VM, IV, 153; XIX, 255-257; XXIX, 435-436; WM, V, 279; XII, 119-120, 196-198.
Paten—RS, III, 33.
Patillo—TD, March 25, 1906; VM, VI, 432.
Patrick—Albemarle, 293-294.
(*Augusta*)—Cyc. Va. Biog., V, 914; MMV, I, 201-203.
Patteson—Cabell, etc., 173, 302-303; Convention 1788, II, 369-370; De Graffenreid, 256; Lancaster, 203-204; Major, 154-185; MMV, I, 290-291; III, 300-303; IV, 278; VM, V, 335; XI, 105; XXXV, 29-32; WM, IV, 278; VIII, 125.
(*New Kent*)—VSR, I, 20-21 (Gen. Sec.).
Patterson—Burgess, 386-389; Hayden, 393, 589-590; Rockbridge, 517; WM, XIII, 174-175.
(*Gloucester*)—WM, XIII, 174-175.
(*King William*)—Brock II, 801.
(*Lunenburg*)—Cyc. Va. Biog., IV, 519.
(*Pendleton*)—Adams Co., Ohio, 264-266; Pendleton Co., 323.
Pattillo—Hampden-Sidney, 63-64, 184-185.
Patton—Brock I, 194-196; Cartmell, 446; Cyc. Va. Biog., I, 302; IV, 194; LCJ, Oct. 25, 1914 (II, 5); Pendleton Co., 323; St. Mark's, 178.
(*Augusta*)—Dinwiddie Papers, I, 8-9; Hayden, 32-35; RS, III, 3; VM, XXX, 303-304.
(*Fredericksburg*)—Cartmell, 505; Hayden, 32-35; Killing of Adam Caperton, 50; Life of Gen. Hugh Mercer, 105, 107-

118; Mackenzie IV, 569-570; Munsell's X, 41; MMV, V, 340-343; VM, X, 203; XXVII, 75-76.

(*James*)—Foote II, 37; VM, XIII, 145; XVI, 24.

(*Robert*)—Culpeper, part 2, p. 15; Du Bellet IV, 427-429.

(*Rockbridge*)—Adams Co., Ohio, 608-610, 830-831, 836; Rockbridge, 517-518.

Paul—Cooke-Booth, 64-65; Monongahela II, 472-473; Mordecai Cooke, 23-24; Rockbridge, 269, 518; RS, II, 47; VM, XXXIII, 303-304.

(*Rockingham*)—History of Rockingham, 326-327.

Paulett, Pawlett—Cyc. Va. Biog., I, 112.

Paulett—Brock II, 629.

Pauling (*Botetourt*)—Dunmore's War, 187.

Paulitz—WM, XXVI, 187.

Paull—Kith and Kin, 108-109, 131.

Pawlett—VM, XXIII, 4; XXV, 38.

Paxon—Bell, 88.

Paxton—Bruce V, 201, 406; Burgess, 385; Clemens' Wills, 74; Cyc. Va. Biog., IV, 317; Green's Ky. Families, 52, 107-111; Hampden-Sidney, 169-170; Marshall, 149-161, 266-272, 366-369; McCormick, 33-34, 77-85; Munsell's III, 145, 205; Rockbridge, 269-270, 518-521; RS, III, 2; The Paxtons; Walker-Wigton, 587-588; WM, X, 207-209.

Payn—Licking Co., Ohio, 740.

Payne—Brock II, 584-585; Bruce IV, 534; Burgess, 389-393; Cyc. Va. Biog., I, 300-301; Hayden, 124; McGavock Family, 122, 150-151; Montague, 62; Pendleton Co., 273; TD, May 20, 1906; Aug. 18, Dec. 8, 1907; Feb. 9, 1908; Oct. 17, 1909; June 12, 1910; Virkus I, 404.

(*Bath Co., etc.*)—Cyc. Va. Biog., V, 592-594.

(*Campbell Co.*)—Kanawha, 589; VM, XXXIV, 79.

(*Fairfax*)—DAR, 82, p. 336.

(*Fauquier*)—Hardy, 10-11, 459-460; Hayden, 654-655, 729; Monongahela II, 720-722; Munsell's VII, 70; VM, XVII, 203; WM, II, 88-89.

(*George*)—Campbell Co., 476-479.

(*Goochland*)—Hampden-Sidney, 174-175; Life and Letters of Dolly Madison, 9-25; McGavock Family, 122, 150-151; Pittsylvania, 144; Thos. Carter, 108-109; Vestry Book of Henrico Parish, 203; VM, VI, 313-316, 427-428; VII, 79-82, 200, 441; XVII, 249; XIX, 201; XXIV, 200-201, 221-222, 315-317; XXV, 78-79; XXIX, 498-499; XXXI, 174; XXXVI, 372; Woodson, 40, 71, 134.

(*Goochland, etc.*)—Vestry Book of Henrico Parish, 203.

(*Lancaster*)—VM, XXIX, 499; WM, XVII, 63-64.

(*Northern Neck*)—Cooke-Booth, 102-103; Hayden, 123-124; Lineage Book, Order of Washington, 181-183; VM, V, 430-431; WM, XVII, 63-64.

(*Warrenton*)—Meade II, 164-166.

(*Westmoreland*)—Mackenzie I, 401-402; VM, XXIX, 498.

Paynter—Hayden, 455.

Peacemaker—Cartmell, 482; Hampshire, 722.

Peachey—Cyc. Va. Biog., I, 303; Du Bellet II, 107-112; VM, XX, 180; XXXIII, 38-41; XXXVII, 60-61; WM, III, 111-115; V, 277; VI, 192.

Peake—Glengarry McDonalds, 330-332; WM, XXIII, 294-295.

Pearce—Madison Co., Ohio, 917.

Penny (Penney)—McIntosh II, 180, 234.
Pennybacker—History of Rockingham Co., 354-355; McIlhany, 69-74; Pendleton Co., 274; Shenandoah, 627-628.
Pennypacker—DAR, 69, p. 4.
Pentecost—Dunmore's War, 101-102; VM, XVI, 41, 50; XVII, 161.
Pepper—Barbour Co., W. Va., 441; Dunmore's War, 65.
Percivall—Brock II, 654.
Perkins—Bruce V, 26; Cabell, etc., 455, 457; TD, March 18, 1906; Nov. 3, 17, 1907.
    (*Albemarle*)—Virkus III, 465.
    (*Buckingham*)—DAR, 82, p. 71.
    (*Cumberland*)—Bruce IV, 311.
    (*Goochland*)—DAR, 75, p. 211; Douglas, 39, 81.
    (*Henrico*)—Crawfurdiana, 100, 104, 110.
    (*Louisa*)—Bruce V, 53.
    (*Pittsylvania*)—Pittsylvania, 95; VM, XXIV, 188.
Perrin—Burgess, 382; Cooke-Booth, 30-36; Cyc. Va. Biog., I, 303; Morton Kin; TD, April 7, July 28, 1912; Welles' Washington Genealogy, 262; WM, III, 253-254; V, 70, 174.
    (*Bedford*)—DAR, 45, p. 374.
Perrot (Parrot)—Buford, 19-21.
Perrot—Hening VI, 402-404.
Perrott—Cyc. Va. Biog., I, 303-304; RS, IV, 25; TD, Nov. 6, 1910; VM, V, 165-167; WM, IV, 135; VI, 173.
Perrow—Bruce IV, 392; V, 18, 20; Burgess, 1337; Campbell Co., 479-482.
Perry—Albemarle, 294-295; BHNC, VIII, 425; Cyc. Va. Biog., I, 103; TD, Aug. 6, 1905; VM, I, 451-452.
    (*Charles City*)—Cyc. Va. Biog., I, 304; WM, IV, 144.
    (*Frederick Co.*)—Jolliffe, 97.
    (*Gloucester*)—Cooke-Booth, 245-246.
Persey—VM, XII, 177-178; XIII, 204-205.
Persinger—Bath Co., 199.
Person—BHNC, VII, 380.
Pescud—Burgess, 262; WM, XIV, 109-112, 114-116.
Peter (*Amherst*)—Sangamon Co., Ill., 564.
    (*Surry*)—VM, V, 189.
Peters—New River, 448-450; Reminiscences of Judge B. J. Peters; Rockbridge, 521; Summers Co., 504-506; Virkus III, 273.
    (*Bedford*)—Bruce VI, 60; MMV, V, 344-346.
    (*Portsmouth*)—Brock II, 675.
    (*Rockingham*)—Monroe Co., 392.
    (*Winchester*)—Virkus III, 55.
Peterson—Bristol Parish, 205-206; Keith Addendum V; Pendleton Co., 324; RS, II, 31; WM 2d, II, 1-19.
Petite—TD, Oct. 8, 1905.
Pettigrew—Burgess, 398-400; Rockbridge, 521.
Pettis—Virkus III, 161.
Pettit—Avery I, 177; Bruce IV, 351; MMV, III, 311-313; V, 347-349; Van Meter, 93-94; Virkus III, 29.
Petro (Pedro)—Randolph Co., W. Va., 368.
Pettus—Andrew Meade, 141-143; Armistead, 279; Burgess, 498-499; Cyc. Va. Biog., I, 304; Old Free State II, 200; TD, Oct. 8, 1905; March 5, 1916; Vestry Book of Henrico Parish, 172-173; Virginia Gazette, June 28, 1780; VM, III, 153-154; VI, 405; X, 316; WM, VI, 138.
    (*Louisa*)—DAR, 55, p. 90.
Pettway—WM, XII, 14, 16.

Pettyjohn—Bruce IV, 391.
Peyton—ARP, II, 526-527; Bruce IV, 224-225, 473; Burgess, 400-402; Cisco, 288-291; Cooke-Booth, 30; Cyc. Va. Biog., I, 304-395; IV, 318; Dupuy, 257; Hayden, 459-566; Huguenot Emigration, 202-203, 284-285; Meade II, 466; Memoir of John Howe Peyton; New Eng. His. and Gen. Register XXXV, 145; Old King William, 95; Peyton, 295-296, 320-322, 358-375; Roger Jones, 112; RS, II, 7; III, 10; Speed, 179-180; TD, July 3, 17, 24, Aug. 28, Oct. 23, 1904; Dec. 18, 1910; Aug. 11, 1912; Aug. 16, 1914; Thos. Carter, 350; VM, XXVII, 173-174.
    (*Gloucester*)—America Heraldica, 63, 175; Browning, C. D., 167-168; Browning, R. D., III, 728-729; BS, June 17, 24, July 1, 1906; Chester of Chicheley; Magna Charta Barons, 150; VSR, V (No. 2), 29, 54; WM, III, 205-206; VI, 64.
    (*Northern Neck*)—Albemarle, 295-296; Browning, C. D., 3d, 193-194.
    (*Stafford*)—Browning, R. D., III, IX; Munsell's III, 128.
Phares—Pendleton Co., 274-275; Randolph Co., W. Va., 367-368.
Phelps—Bruce V, 424; TD, Jan. 3, 1909; June 22, 1913; Sept. 13, 1914; Virkus I, 932; III, 370.
Phettiplace—Cyc. Va. Biog., I, 305.
Phifer—Madison Co., Ohio, 921.
Phillips—Albemarle, 296; Barbour Co., W. Va., 435; Hardesty (*Bedford*), 428; Meade II, 482; Rockbridge, 521; TD, April 1, 1906; VM, XXV, 401-403.
    (*Elizabeth City*)—Brock II, 693.
    (*Hanover*)—Burgess, 765-767.
    (*Norfolk Co.*)—McIntosh II, 42, 53, 90.
    (*Stafford*)—Dinwiddie Papers I, XXV, XXVI; Hayden, 158-159; Munsell's VI, 137; VHS Col. VI, 196.
Philpotts—Bruce VI, 36.
Phipps—Bruce V, 487; Grayson Co., 173-176.
    (*Botetourt*)—Tyler's IX, 273.
Phlegar—Bruce IV, 532; Grayson Co., 198-204; MMV, III, 320-322.
    (*Frederick*)—Adams Co., Ohio, 270-271.
Phripp—ARP, II, 789; McIntosh II, 106, etc.; VM, XV, 148; XVIII, 402-406; XIX, 194.
Piatt—Adams Co., Ohio, 336; DAR, 83, p. 75.
Pickens—Highland Co., 384; Virkus II, 312; VM, XXVI, 378.
Pickett—Alstons and Allstons, 142-145; Burgess, 622; Buckners of Va., 104-105; Cisco, 172-173, 176-177, 180; Du Bellet I, 61; Fauquier Bulletin, 207-215; Green's Ky. Families, 61; Habersham Chap. II, 81-82; Hardy, 414-438; Hayden, 645; Marshall, 54-58; TD, April 11, 18, 1909; Dec. 11, 1917; Virkus II, 96; III, 378; VM, XXIII, 437-438; XXIV, 99-100; VSR. II (No. 2), 71; IV (No. 4), 37; Walker-Wigton, 525-527; WM, I, 25; WM 2d, VIII, chart opposite p. 34.
Pickle—Pendleton Co., 324.
Pidgeon—Bell, 39, 88.
    (*Frederick*)—Adams Co., Ohio, 270-271.
Pierce—WM, IV, 41.
    (*Westmoreland*)—Mackenzie VII, 186; VM, III, 65, 188; WM, IX, 26-27.
Pierpont—Brock I, 235.
Piersey—Major, 118-125.
Piersol—Miami Co., Ohio, 757.

ertson); RS, II, 10, 12, 32, 36, 38; IV, 4, 20-21; TD, Nov.
1, 1908.
Pogue—LCJ, July 4, 1915 (II, 2); Virkus III, 569.
Poindexter—Bruce IV, 551-552; Cyc. Va. Biog., IV, 192-193; Douglas,
275; Du Bellet I, 260; Halifax, 327; Norfolk, 494; TD, Oct.
16, Nov. 20, 1904; May 12, 1907; June 23, 1912; Virkus I,
775; VM, XIX, 215-218, 326-329, 430-440; XX, 107-110, 218-
220, 329-331, 440-443; XXI, 87, 102-104, 214-218, 314, 333;
WM, II, 206.
Poince—Miami Co., Ohio, 858.
Poling—Barbour Co., W. Va., 437-440.
Polk—Virkus II, 192; WM, XXI, 21-22.
  (*Accomac*)—DAR, 81, p. 131.
Pollard—Avery I, 178; Bagby, 345-352; Bruce IV, 231; Burgess, 320,
593; Cabell, etc., 433-438; Coghill, 117; Cyc. Va. Biog., I,
306; IV, 86-88; Hampden-Sidney, 232; Kemper Family, 201;
Memoirs and Sketches, by Henry Robinson Pollard, 1-31;
20, 96, 184-193; Rives, 592-595; RS, II, 45; Sneads of Flu-
vanna, 50-57; TD, Dec. 25, 1904; Jan. 1, 15, 29, Feb. 5, 26,
March 5, April 16, Dec. 24, 1905; April 8, June 3, 1906;
Sept. 14, 28, Oct. 12, 1913; Tyler's III, 211-214; X, 58-60;
Virkus I, 562; WM, VIII, 127; X, 202; XV, 64-69; WM
2d, II, 162-166; VIII, 46-47.
Pollock—Hayden, 543; Rockbridge, 522.
Pomfret—Burgess, 879; TD, Sept. 18, 1904; May 31, 1908.
Ponsonby—VM, XXIII, 203.
Pool—Bruce V, 384.
Poole—Cyc. Va. Biog., I, 306; McIntosh II, 225; VM, I, 440; XX,
156-157.
Poor—Douglas, 82.
Poore—Kith and Kin, 39; TD, Nov. 25, 1906.
Pope—Burgess, 321-325; Cyc. Va. Biog., I, 306; His. Encyc. of Ill.,
428; LEP, March 8, 1919, pp. 6, 13; Louisville's First Fam-
ilies (Jennings), 69-80; Pendleton Co., 276; RS, II, 34; III,
35-36; TD, Dec. 30, 1906; May 2, 1909; Virkus II, 317;
Woodson, 225; WM, XII, 192-196; XIX, 293; XXVII, 61-64,
104-112.
  (*Highland*)—Highland Co., 363.
  (*Isle of Wight*)—WM, XXV, 208.
  (*Nansemond*)—WM, XXVII, 61-64, 104-112.
  (*Northumberland*)—Burgess, 323-325; Thos. Carter, 223-224;
WM, XIII, 280-286; XXII, 209-215.
  (*Westmoreland*)—ARP, II, 438; RS, III, 35, 36; Virkus I, 375;
VM, III, 422-425; Woodson, 225; WM, I, 187-189; IV, 37,
78-79; VII, 62; XII, 192-196, 250-253; XXIV, 194-198; XXV,
208-209.
Popeley—Cyc. Va. Biog., I, 306.
Popkins—Bruce IV, 454.
Porch—DAR, 59, p. 234.
Porten—McIntosh I, 56-57; II, 38 (Porteen).
Porter—Highland Co., 384; Rockbridge, 522; TD, Jan. 27, 1907; Aug.
22, 1909.
  (*Fauquier*)—DAR, 67, p. 187.
  (*King and Queen*)—Bagby, 352, 367; Cooke-Booth, 95-97.
  (*Louisa*)—Bruce V, 18.
  (*Lower Norfolk*)—Fenwick Allied Ancestry.
  (*Norfolk*)—Barton II, 93-94; McIntosh I, 45, 88; II, 68; Norfolk,

811, 891-900; TD, Aug. 22, 1909; Virkus III, 207; WM, XXIV, 287-288.
(*Orange*)—McCormick, 5-12; Virkus III, 307.
(*Pittsylvania*)—VM, XIX, 424.
(*Powhatan*)—Cyc. Va. Biog., IV, 98.
(*Prince Edward*)—VM, VII, 441.
(*Prince William*)—DAR, 51, p. 85.
Porterfield—SHA, VI, 113, 199, 295, 400; Lower Shenandoah, 607-609; McCue, 27, 54, 99, 148; McIlhany, 30-31; Munsell's IV, 24-25; Peyton, 317-318; SBN, 208-209; Shepherdstown, 341-342; Virkus III, 500; VM, IV, 439; IX, 144-152; Waddell's Annals of Augusta Co., 337.
Porteus—Cyc. Va. Biog., I, 152-153; Spotswood Letters II, 54; TD, April 23, 1911; VM, I, 397; XIII, 310-311; WM, III, 21, 28-29, 38-39; V, 149.
Portlock—Cyc. Va. Biog., I, 306; V, 742-744; McIntosh II, 42-43, 291, etc.; Norfolk, 555-556, 811.
Posey—Dunmore's War, 196; Goode, 264; His. Encyc. of Ill., 430; Munsell's VIII, 146; SBN, XII, 309; TD, Dec. 26, 1915; Jan. 2, 9, 16, 23, 30, Feb. 6, 1916; Waddell's Annals of Augusta Co., 290; WM, V, 141, 212-213; VI, 65.
Postlewaite—Licking Co., Ohio, 668.
Pott—Cyc. Va. Biog., I, 306-307; RC, II, 28; RS, IV, 7; The Potts Family; VM, I, 88-89, 198, 429; WM, XIV, 100.
Potter—Rockbridge, 523; VM, XXVII, 408-409.
(*Lancaster*)—VM, V, 429; XXV, 141.
Potts—Early Records of the Simpson Family, 345-346; Randolph Co., 365-367; RS, IV, 10; The Potts Family.
(*Loudoun*)—Clemens' Wills, 77.
Poulson—Norfolk, 718-719.
Poultney—Clemens' Wills, 77; TD, June 23, 1907.
Povall—Goode, 68-69, 127-128; RS, III, 17; TD, March 21, 1915; Valentine III, 1297-1316; IV, 2300-2301; WM, IX, 273.
Powell—Burgess, 326-332; Cyc. Va. Biog., I, 307; Hayden, 507-510; TD, April 28, May 19, Dec. 22, 29, 1907; Oct. 18, Nov. 1, 1908; Feb. 21, March 14, April 25, 1909; Oct. 12, Nov. 16, 1913; VM, II, 313; V, 258; WM, V, 127; VI, 128; VII, 247; VIII, 101.
(*Alexandria*)—Avery I, 69-70.
(*Amherst*)—Clemens' Wills, 78; Floyd, 99-102; TD, March 14, 1909; WM, IV, 277.
1909.
(*Brunswick*)—TD, Oct. 18, 1908.
(*Culpeper*)—BS, Oct. 2, 1904; St. Mark's, 193; VM, VI, 344-345.
(*Cumberland*)—Woodson, 196.
(*Eastern Shore*)—Yeardley, 9, 15-26.
(*Elizabeth City*)—VM, I, 192.
(*Franklin Co.*)—VM, XXXIV, 78-79.
(*Halifax*)—Halifax, 328.
(*Isle of Wight*)—Kilby, Tynes, etc., 20-22.
(*King William*)—Cyc. Va. Biog., IV, 319-320; Old King William, 185.
(*Lancaster*)—VM, V, 258-259; XXVI, 207-216.
(*Loudoun*)—Biographical Sketch of Col. Levin Powell; Cyc. Va. Biog., IV, 356; Draper Series V, 319; Hayden, 507-510; H. T. Harrison, 15-16, 20; Mackenzie I, 418-420; Meade II, 277; TD, March 21, 1915; Tyler's IV, 51-53; Virkus III, 378; VM, XV, 203-204; WM, XII, 221, 231-232.

(*Nelson*)—Burgess, 677.
(*Norfolk Co.*)—McIntosh I, 120, 132; II, 28, 43, 71, etc.
(*Nottoway*)—Cyc. Va. Biog., V, 617-625.
(*Southampton*)—Cyc. Va. Biog., V, 1021.
(*York*)—DAR, 83, p. 140; MMV, IV, 337-338.
Power—Cyc. Va. Biog., I, 307; TD, March 28, April 4, 1915; VM,
    XXXIII, 25-26; WM, VII, 129.
(*King William*)—VM, XV, 381-382.
(*York*)—WM, I, 144, 209-211.
Powers—Bruce V, 141; Du Bellet III, 96-97; Pendleton Co., 276-277;
    TD, March 17, 1912.
Poythress—Bristol Parish, 173; Cyc. Va. Biog., I, 307-308; Goode, 55;
    Lee, 289; Robertson, 30; VM, VII, 71-72, 190, 438-440; X,
    106; XIX, 428-429; XXVI, 385-386; XXXIII, 31-33; VSR,
    IV (No. 4), 33; V (No. 1), 71; WM, VI, 22.
Prather—Louisville's First Families, 35-44.
Pratt—Bruce VI, 94; Caroline Co., 459-461; TD, April 24, 1910.
Preeson—R. W. Johnson, 6-7.
Prentis—Brock II, 662; Cyc. Va. Biog., I, 308; IV, 445; MMV, I,
    351-354; VM, XXXII, 250-251; WM, VI, 125, 190; VII, 135.
Prescott—McIntosh II, 271, etc.
Presley—VM, XXVI, 87-88; XXXIV, 92-93, 187-192, 287-292; WM,
    IV, 179; VIII, 2; XXIII, 184-185.
Presly (*Northumberland*)—Cyc. Va. Biog., I, 308; Tyler's IX, 265-270.
Pressley—Bruce VI, 595.
Pressly—Rockbridge, 523.
Preston—Bell; Brock I, 129-134; II, 745-747; Bruce IV, 174; BS,
    Oct. 16, 1904; July 8, 15, 22, 1906; Cabell, etc., 399-401; Cyc.
    Va. Biog., I, 308-309; Dinwiddie Papers II, 153; Dunmore's
    War, 174, 430-431; Foote II, 37-38; Glenn's Some Colonial
    Mansions, II, 376-394; Hampden-Sidney, 248-249; Hardy,
    463-464; Johnstons of Salisbury, by W. P. Johnston (New
    Orleans, 1897), 193-201; Kennedy I, 637-654; Killing of
    Adam Caperton, 56-57; Lancaster, 468-470; LCJ, March
    7, 1915 (II, 3); Madison Co., Ohio, 812; Marshall, 71-73;
    Memoranda of the Preston Family; MMV, V, 357-360;
    Patrick Henry II, 641-642; Peyton, 303-307; Preston Gene-
    alogy; Preston Family in Great Britain, New England and
    Virginia; Randolph Family, 13 (MS., Va. State Library);
    RC, II, 7; Rockbridge, 270-271; RS, I, 12; II, 7, 40, 42-43;
    III, 20, 27; SBN, XII, 312-316; St. Mark's, 188; TD, April
    14, June 30, 1907; Oct. 18, 25, Nov. 1, 15, 1914; Thos. Carter,
    91-92; Virkus III, 381-382; VM, VII, 127-128; Walker-
    Wigton, 109-110; WM, II, 126; III, 139, 209; VIII, 226.
(*Augusta*)—VM, XXVI, 363-365; VSR, V (No. 2), 31; Wad-
    dell's Annals of Augusta Co., 117.
(*Campbell*)—Campbell Co., 482-484.
(*Kentucky*)—Johnson Co., Ky., 375.
(*Smithfield*)—DAR, 76, p. 297.
Pretlow—Bell, 65-66.
Prewitt—Campbell Co., 484-486; LCJ, Nov. 8, 1914 (II, 3); Van Meter,
    74-75; Virkus II, 118, 340.
Price—Albemarle, 298-299; Douglas, 278; Hayden, 394; Henry Co.,
    234-237; Rockbridge, 523; TD, April 15, 22, May 27, June
    10, 1906; Oct. 27, Dec. 8, 22, 1907; Jan. 12, Feb. 9, 1908;
    Virkus II, 346; RS, II, 12.
(*Alexandria*)—Avery I, 70.
(*Augusta and W. Va.*)—Pocahontas Co., 545-547.

Pullen—DAR, 51, p. 260; Bruce IV, 67.
Puller—Bruce IV, 61; Cyc. Va. Biog., IV, 323.
Pulley—Cyc. Va. Biog., IV, 189.
Pulliam—Bruce IV, 106; Kemper Family, 196; Sangamon Co., Ill., 584; TD, May 5, 1912.
Pullin—Highland Co., 326-329; Rockbridge, 523.
Pully—WM, XII, 198.
Purcell—Bruce IV, 289; Burgess, 380-381; Lower Shenandoah, 783-784.
 (*Alexandria*)—WM, IV, 136, 202.
 (*Frederick*)—Cartmell, 476-477.
 (*Henry*)—Henry Co., 246.
 (*Louisa*)—Bruce V, 84.
 (*Prince William*)—Montgomery Co., Ohio, 302.
 (*Richmond*)—Cyc. Va. Biog., IV, 97; VM, II, 331.
Purdie—Bruton Church, 96; Cyc. Va. Biog., I, 309; RS, III, 30; WM, I, 48, 149; VII, 266.
Purefoy—Cyc. Va. Biog., I, 100; Virkus II, 279; VSR, I (No. 3), 45; WM, VII, 47-48.
Purifoy—VM, I, 417-418; VII, 100-101; WM, XVI, 235-236.
Purinton—SBN, XII, 319.
Purkins—TD, April 18, May 30, 1915.
Purkinton—Burgess, 26, 200.
Purks—Bagby, 352, 369, 373.
Purnell—RS, III, 4.
Puryear (Preer)—DAR, 43, p. 68-69; Old King William, 122; WM, V, 140.
Pusey—Pittsylvania, 44.
Putnam—WM, IV, 67.
 (*Bath*)—VM, V, 354.
Putney—Bruce IV, 384; Kanawha, 859; TD, June 25, 1911.
Pye—Burgess, 21, 313, 652.
Pyland—Cyc. Va. Biog., I, 309.
Pyle—Ritchie Co., 201-202.
Pyles—Monroe Co., 393-394.

Q

Quarles—Albemarle, 299-300; Burgess, 332-335, 337, 340; Cabell, etc., 285; Cyc. Va. Biog., V, 685; Douglas, 280-281; McGavock Family, 152; MMV, II, 325-327; III, 330-333; IV, 343-344; Old King William, 153-157; Virkus II, 113, 271; VM, XXXIV, 173-174; Winston, 431-445; WM 2d, III, 91; VI, 72-73.
Quarrier—Cabell, etc., 547-548; Genealogical History and Table of the Quarrier Family in America (1890); Kanawha, 749, 919-927; Meade II, 345.
Queene—McIntosh I, 181.
Quenlin—Armistead, 226.
Quesinberry—Bruce VI, 515.
Quick—DAR, 75, p. 230; Kanawha, 469.
Quigley—Rockbridge, 523.
Quinlan—Burgess, 337.
Quinn (*Culpeper*)—Sangamon Co., Ill., 359.
Quisenberry—Fishback Family, 235-236, 315; Mackenzie I, 423-430; Genealogical Memorandum of the Quisenberry Family; Memorials of the Quisenberry Family in Germany, Eng-

land and America, by A. C. Quisenberry; Munsell's IX, 216-217; Quisenberry, 9-76; VM, X, 431-432; XI, 423.

R

Radcliffe (Ratcliffe)—WM 2d, VII, 221.
Rader—Miami Co., Ind., 438; Rockbridge, 523; Shenandoah, 630.
Radford, Redford—VM, XXXII, 58.
Radford—Hardesty (*Bedford*), 428; McGavock Family, 78-79; SBN, XII, 320.
Rager—Hardin Co., Ohio, 801.
Ragland—Cyc. Va. Biog., IV, 3; Du Bellet I, 261; Ellis, 30; Habersham Chap II, 305-307; Halifax, 240-244, 329-330; Maxwell, 552-555; Ragland, 6-26; RC, II, 26; TD, Jan. 19, 1908; Vestry Book of Henrico Parish, 187-188; Virkus II, 125; VM, XXXVII, 24.
Ragsdale—Buford, 275-276, 355-356; Throckmorton, 352; Virkus III, 388; WM, XXIV, 140-141; XXVI, 262-264.
Railey—Albemarle, 300; Ewing Genealogy, 139; VM, VII, 315; XX, 90; Woodson, 84-85, 151, 153-154, 234, 238, 353, 371, 377, 381.
Raine—De Graffenried, 192; TD, July 18, 1909.
Raines—Burgess, 5-6, 323-324; Pendleton Co., 282-283; Virkus III, 225; VM, XXI, 443-444.
Raleigh—TD, Sept. 3, Dec. 10, 1905.
Ralston—Bruce IV, 260-261; Sangamon Co., Ill., 591.
Rambo—Knox Co., Ill., 563.
Rambough—Hardin Co., Ohio, 594.
Ramey (*Valley of Va.*)—Bruce VI, 322; Cartmell, 441; Licking Co., Ohio, 753.
Ramsay—Bristol Parish, 210-212; Cyc. Va. Biog., I, 310; Rockbridge, 523.
   (*Albemarle*)—Albemarle, 300-301; DAR, 59, p. 274.
   (*Fairfax*)—Hayden, 88.
   (*Petersburg*)—VM, XIX, 96.
Ramsey—Keith, 72-82; Pittsylvania, 251.
Randle—DAR, 75, p. 16.
Randles—Coshocton Co., Ohio, 502, 769.
Randolph—America Heraldica, 65; Bristol Parish, 212-222; Brock I, 134-138; Bruce VI, 4-5, 360; Chaumiere Papers, 79, 86-87; Cyc. Va. Biog., I, 155, 160, 310-311; V, 620-622; Goode, 111-115; Habersham Chap. II, 127; Marshall, 26; Meade I, 138-140; Munsell's V, 32; Randall's Life of Jefferson, I, 7-10; RS, I, 23; II, 36; III, 6, 16, 26, 38; Ruvigny, 528-532; Sketches of Lynchburg, Va., 190-194; Southern Bivouac (1886), 730; Southside Va., 178-179; TD, Jan. 24, 31, March 13, May 29, 1904; Oct. 21, 1906; Feb. 10, 24, April 28, 1907; Aug. 23, Oct. 4, 1908; Feb. 7, 14, 28, March 21, July 4, 1909; June 19, 1910; Jan. 21, Nov. 3, 1912; June 28, July 12, 19, 26, Aug. 2, 9, Sept. 6, 1914; Valentine III, 1317-1479; Virkus II, 194; VSR, I, 15; IV (No. 1), 30, 43; V (No. 2), 21, 25, 37, 53, 65; WM, XVII, 267.
   (*Albemarle and Tuckahoe*)—Albemarle, 301.
   (*Brett*)—Robertson, 47; VM, XIX, 398-400.
   (*Clarke, from William*)—Avery II, 416, etc.; Brock II, 615; Bruce VI, 360; "Old Chapel."
   (*Goochland*)—Douglas, 282-283.
   (*Henry*)—RC, Sept. 3, 1888; TD, Aug. 20, 1911; Jan. 21, 1912;

Valentine III, 1317, et seq.; IV, 2303-2305; Virkus II, 327; VM, III, 261; XI, 58; XXXIII, 88-89; WM, I, 158-159; IV, 125-127.

(*Norfolk Co.*)—McIntosh II, 109; VM, VI, 429-430; WM, VIII, 75.

(*Peyton*)—VM, XIX, 87-88; WM, IV, 136.

(*Prince William*)—McClure, 218; VM, XXVI, 312-313; WM, IV, 136.

(*Sir John, will*)—VM, XXXVI, 376-381; Family Tree—Sir John Randolph, by Allan (Va. State Lib.)

(*Turkey Island*)—Alstons and Allstons, 145-146; Beau Monde (Weekly), March 16, 1894; Hayden, 133, 217; Lee, 406-408; Page (2d ed.), 251-272; Robertson, 32-33, 36-37, 46-49, 65, 70-73; Randolph Tombs; The Poems and Amyntas of Thomas Randolph, edited by J. J. Parry (Yale University Press, 1917), 1-30; Vestry Book of Henrico Parish, 182-183.

(*William*)—ARP, II, 750-751; Bland Papers (Petersburg, 1847); II, 119-120; Bristol Parish, 212-222; Browning, C. D., 180; Browning, C. D., 3d, 389-392, 447; Browning, R. D., III, 719-721, 729-731, 788; Bruce IV, 315; BS, March 19, 1905; Cabell, etc., 238-240; Campbell's History of Va., 629; Carter Family Tree; Cartmell, 452; Dinwiddie Papers I, 71-72; Du Bellet I, 202; II, 129-164; IV, 324-326; Fauquier Bulletin, 278-286; Foote II, 340-349; Goode, 111-116, 212, 218-219, 353-355, 418-423, 477; Lancaster, 105-106, 168-173, 395-396, 440-441; Mackenzie II, 136-137; V, 426-431; MMV, III, 336-337; V, 361-362; Munsell's XI, 176; Norfolk, 550; "Old Chapel", 26-27, 33, 8, 32; RS, II, 43; SBN, XII, 325-333; Thomas, 344-345; Virkus I, 17-18, 120; VM, III, 261-268, with chart; VII, 331-332; IX, 256-257; XIII, 99, 228-229; XIV, 225-227; XV, 149; XIX, 87-88, 398-400; XXII, 98, 441-446; XXIV, 193-194; XXV, 403, 407-411; XXVI, 321-324, 411; XXVIII, 363-364; XXXII, 136-141, 391-395; XXXIII, 395-398; XXXIV, 72-76, 162-163; WM, I, 7-8, 132, 158-159; II, 142, 175, 213; IV, 136-137; V, 112, 158; VI, 21; VII, 122-124, 195-197; VIII, 119-122, 263-265; IX, 182-183, 250-252; X, 34, 166; XII, 66-69; XVII, 267; XXI, 25-28.

Rangeley—Henry Co., 250-251.
Ransdell—Mackenzie I, 91-92.
Ransom, Ranson—Barton II, 333-334.
Ransom—Barton I, R11; WM, XIV, 129-130.
Ransome—Burgess, 62, 343-348.
Ranson, Ransone—TD, Feb. 25, March 4, 1906.
Ranson—ARP, I, 285; Barton I, R11; Kennedy I, 309-311; MMV, I, 372-374.
Ransone—Cyc. Va. Biog., I, 311-312; VM, VIII, 127-128; WM, X, 264-267.
Raper—Crockett, 45, 60-63.
Raphaels—WM, XII, 123.
Rapp—Rockbridge, 523.
Rarey—Hardin Co., Ohio, 802.
Rasnick—Bruce V, 484.
Ratcliff—Brock II, 747; TD, March 25, 1906.
Ratcliffe (Radcliffe)—Bruce IV, 475, 561; WM 2d, VII, 221.
Ratliff—Highland Co., 365; Pendleton Co., 283-284.
Rauhof—Bruce V, 542.
Raven—Hayden, 493-494.

Ravenscroft—Cyc. Va. Biog., I, 312; Meade I, 488; SBN, XII, 337; VM, IX, 242-243; WM, XVIII, 213-214.
Rawle—Glenn's Colonial Mansions II, 184-197.
Rawlings—Bruce VI, 242; Burgess, 353-357; Minor, 67.
Rawlins—Clemens' Wills, 79; TD, June 29, 1913.
Rawls—Bruce V, 489; Cyc. Va. Biog., V, 679, 739.
Ray—Burgess, 1291.
Rayburn—Madison Co., Ohio, 679; St. Louis, II, City, etc., 1260.
Rayfield—Brock II, 674.
Rea—Albemarle, 303-304; Bruce IV, 283-284; Madison Co., Ohio, 842, 929.
Reaburn—Monroe Co., 345-346.
Read—Hening VIII, 483-485; RS, IV, 25; TD, Oct. 14, 1906; Aug. 17, 31, 1913.
　(*Bedford*)—Boddie, 157-159.
　(*Brunswick*)—WM, VII, 109.
　(*Charlotte*)—Burgess, 357-358; Cabell, etc., 207-242, 562-564; Convention 1788, II, 369; Dinwiddie Papers II, 156; Foote II, 573-580; Hampden-Sidney, 60-61, 267, 276; Hardy, 301-304; Lancaster, 431-435; McAllister, 92-97, 165-167; Meade II, 28; Venables of Va., 75-89; VM, XVII, 100; Watson, 49-57, 85-86.
　(*Clement*)—Foote II, 573; Goode, 195; VSR, V (No. 1), 77.
　(*Gloucester*)—Hening V, 69.
　(*Hampden-Sidney*)—Venables of Va., 93-98.
Reade—BS, Nov. 29, 1904; Sept. 15, 22, 29, Oct. 6, 1907; Cyc. Va. Biog., I, 123; TD, Dec. 24, 1905; Jan. 22, 1911; Aug. 17, 1913.
　(*Clement*)—WM 2d, VI, 242-244.
　(*Gloucester*)—Armistead, 89; ARP, II, 440-441; Browning, C. D., 248-251; Cooke-Booth, 237; Cyc. Va. Biog., I, 123-124; Du Bellet IV, 1-12; Habersham Chap. II, 67-68; Hening V, 61; McAllister, 21-22, 163-165; Millers of Millersburg, 85; Notable Families, 73-77; Rootes of Rosewell, 7-11; Throckmorton, 332; VM, IV, 204-205; VI, 409; IX, 219-220, 270; XIX, 290; XXI, 326-327; XXVII, 303-306; XXXII, 289-290; VSR, IV (No. 4), 22; V (No. 1), 75-76; (No. 2), 58; Watson, 49-51, 78-80, 263-267; Willis, 155-156; WM, I, 90; II, 9-10, 133-134; III, 29-30, 40-41; IV, 51, 277; XIV, 117-125, 281-282; XV, 211.
　(*Thomas*)—WM, IX, 124.
　(*York*)—WM, XI, 264.
Reaguer—Bruce VI, 420.
Reamey—Henry Co., 248-249.
Reamy—Bruce V, 547.
Reany—Rockbridge, 523.
Reardon—Rockbridge, 523.
Rector—Arkansas, 106-107, 370-410; Burgess, 146, 162; Fauquier Bulletin, 483; Fishback Family, 83, 88-89; McIlhany, 235-237.
Redd—Caroline Co., 461-465; Halifax, 330; Henry Co., 247-248; Mackenzie II, 89-90; Norfolk, 773-774; TD, Oct. 1, 1911; WM, XXI, 70; XXV, 287-288; Virkus III, 343-345.
Redford-Radford—TD, Dec. 2, 1906; VM, XXXII, 58; Woodson, 169 (Redford).
Redman—TD, April 28, 1907.
Redmond—Highland Co., 384.
Redwood—Cyc. Va. Biog., IV, 376.

Reed—Monongahela II, 667-668; Rockbridge, 523-524.
  (*Botetourt*)—Miami Co., Ohio, 788.
  (*Fairfax*)—DAR, 51, p. 301.
  (*Fauquier*)—Coshocton Co., Ohio, 771.
  (*Pendleton Co.*)—Braxton Co., W. Va., 420.
  (*Portsmouth*)—Cyc. Va. Biog., IV, 450.
  (*Washington Co.*)—Brock II, 749.
  (*Westmoreland*)—VM, XXIII, 204-205.
Reeder—Clemens' Wills, 80; Miami Co., Ohio, 788.
Rees (Reese)—Cartmell, 484; Lower Shenandoah, 780; WM, XXIII, 145-146.
Reese—VM, XXXII, 90-91; WM, XXIII, 145-146.
  (*Prince William*)—Clemens' Wills, 81.
Reeve—Clemens' Wills, 180.
Reeves—Grayson Co., 176-178; TD, Sept. 22, 1912.
Reger—Border Settlers, 296-308.
Reid—Kith and Kin, 128; WM, VIII, 227.
  (*Augusta*)—Cabell, etc., 597-601; Green's Ky. Families, 99-100, 160-161; Marshall, 67-68.
  (*Botetourt*)—DAR, 78, p. 358.
  (*Campbell*)—Cyc. Va. Biog., IV, 328.
  (*Hampshire*)—Bruce V, 333.
  (*Norfolk*)—Antiquary III, 149-150; ARP, I, 141; Norfolk, 491.
  (*Rappahannock*)—Bruce VI, 48; Burgess, 879.
  (*Rockbridge*)—Kith and Kin, 128; Rockbridge, 271; Virkus III, 460; Woods-McAfee, 49-50, 106-107.
Renforth—Bruce IV, 549.
Renfro (*Bedford*)—Virkus II, 385.
Renick—SHA, III, 221-227; The Renick Family of Virginia, by E. I. Renick, 1889; Rockbridge, 524; VM, X, 92-93.
Renn—WM, XII, 13.
Rennolds—Cyc. Va. Biog., I, 312-313; IV, 255.
Reno—Shenandoah, 630.
Renshaw (*Clarke*)—Lower Shenandoah, 631.
Rentfro—Clemens' Wills, 81.
Repass—Bruce VI, 508.
Replogle—Rockbridge, 524.
Revell—ARP, II, 484; Cyc. Va. Biog., I, 313; VM, XXIII, 84-85, 428.
Revercomb—Cyc. Va. Biog., V, 985; Highland Co., 329.
Revere—TD, Sept. 22, 1907.
Revis—TD, Oct. 14, 1906; June 27, 1915.
Rexroad—Braxton Co., W. Va., 448; Pendleton Co., 284-286.
Rexrode—Highland Co., 365, 367.
Reyburn—Crockett, 52; Miami Co., Ind., 464.
Reynolds—Crockett, 135-137; Kanawha, 460; Rockbridge, 524; WM, VII, 221, et seq., 277.
  (*Highland*)—Highland Co., 329.
  (*Isle of Wight*)—VM, VI, 252-253.
  (*Patrick*)—Carolinians II, 550; MMV, IV, 347-348.
  (*York*)—WM, XII, 128-129.
Rhea—Armstrong II, 253, et seq.; Bath Co., 200; Buford, 82; Knox-ville, Tenn., Sentinel, about 1909; Rockbridge; Sangamon Co., Ill., 611; VM, XXIII, 423-424; XXVIII, 350.
Rhodes—Bruce IV, 265-266; V, 200; Licking Co., Ohio, 753; Rockbridge, 524.
  (*Frederick*)—Cartmell, 490; TD, Sept. 10, 1905.

Rice—Foote II, 78-87, 241-247, 444; Hampden-Sidney, 27-28, 97, 126-127, 239; Lower Shenandoah, 700; Rockbridge, 524; TD, March 27, 1904; Feb. 24, March 24, 1907; VM, VIII, 219-220.
(*Culpeper*)—Culpeper, part 2, 132-134.
(*Hanover*)—VM, XIII, 45.
(*Kentucky*)—Johnson Co., Ky., 446-451.
Richard—Cartmell, 495; Hayden, 92A, 92B.
Richards—ARP, I, 323-324; TD, Sept. 8, 1907.
(*Alexandria*)—Avery I, 333.
(*Franklin*)—DAR, 83, p. 326.
(*Frederick*)—Bruce IV, 395; VI, 39; Cartmell, 494-495.
(*King and Queen*)—Montague, 119-120, 191.
Richardson—Habersham Chap. II, 346-348, 494; Rockbridge, 524; TD, Dec. 25, 1904; April 9, 30, May 14, 28, Aug. 20, Sept. 3, 1905; July 29, 1906; Jan. 15, 1911; May 10, 1914; WM, VI, 121.
(*Alexandria*)—Avery I, 333.
(*Charlotte*)—VM, III, 303-304.
(*Cumberland*)—Woodson, 198.
(*Henrico*)—VSR, II (No. 2), 55.
(*James City*)—Old King William, 181.
(*Jamestown*)—DAR, 67, p. 92.
(*Montgomery*)—Auglaize Co., Ohio, 638-639.
(*New Kent*)—Cyc. Va. Biog., I, 313; MMV, V, 370-372; VM, XXXV, 414-415.
(*Valley of Va.*)—Shenandoah, 631-634.
Richeson—TD, May 5, 1907; WM, XXVI, 259-264; XXVII, 200-202; WM 2d, VI, 351.
Richey—Burgess, 363.
Richie—TD, Nov. 11, 1906.
Richmond—Bruce VI, 323; Summers Co., 409-414; TD, March 24, 1907.
(*Lee*)—Bruce VI, 227.
(*Princess Anne*)—Researcher II, 147-153.
Rickard—Sangamon Co., Ill., 613.
Rickett—Braxton Co., W. Va., 421.
Ricketts—Brock II, 749; Burgess, 358-359; Cyc. Va. Biog., I, 313.
Ricks—Bell, 16, 63-64; Caroline, 478-480; "Trezevant", 64; History of Ricks Family of Va. and N. C.
Riddel—Bruce IV, 329; Ritchie Co., 276-278.
Riddell (Riddle)—Riddell Genealogy (1850), 44 pp.; RS, I, 9.
(*Brunswick*)—Ridley, 341, etc.
(*Goochland*)—Ridley, 347.
(*Orange*)—Ridley, 374, etc.
(*Pittsylvania, etc.*)—Ridley, 343, etc.
Riddick—Alstons and Allstons, 146-147; Burgess, 868; Cyc. Va. Biog., I, 313; V, 891, 897, 987-988; Kilby, etc., 25-32; MMV, IV, 349-350; Norfolk, 650, 918; St. Louis, II, 1482; III, 1910-1911; Virkus III, 180; VM, VII, 212-213.
Riddle—Madison Co., Ohio, 930.
(*Accomac*)—Ridley, 350, etc.
(*Loudoun and Pittsylvania*)—Ridley, 346, etc.
(*Richmond*)—Kennedy I, 569-572.
(*Rockbridge*)—Rockbridge, 524.
Riddleberger—Shenandoah, 635.
Rider—Braxton Co., W. Va., 417; DAR, 75, p. 214.
Ridgeley—Munsell's X, 139.
Ridgeway—Sangamon Co., Ill., 617-618.
Ridgway (*Frederick Co.*)—Funsten-Meade, 67-70.

(*King William*)—Virkus III, 103.
(*Giles*)—Virkus II, 363.
(*Hampton*)—DAR, 45, p. 204.
(*King and Queen*)—Draper Series V, 126-127; Kith and Kin, 41-58; Robertson-Taylor, 205-224; Virkus I, 110; VM, V, 91.
(*Loudoun*)—McIlhany, 227-263.
(*New Kent*)—Tyler's X, 169-170.
(*Northumberland*)—ARP, II, 452.

Roley—Licking Co., Ohio, 752.
Rolfe—Baskerville Family, 153, 155-165; BS, Nov. 5, 1905; Cyc. Va. Biog., I, 82; Marshall, 35; Neill's Virginia Carolorum, 194; Robertson, 1-31; Rolfe Genealogy; RS, IV, 21; TD, Nov. 1, 1908; Sept. 4, 1913; VM, I, 445-447; X, 134-138; XIX, 203-204; XXI, 105-106, 208-211; XXII, 150-157; XXX, 295-298; VSR, IV (No. 1), 34; (No. 4), 39; V (No. 2), 49.

(*Mecklenburg*)—Tyler's III, 301.
Roller—Bruce V, 550; MMV, V, 379-381, 384-388; TD, Feb. 19, 1905.
Rollin—Rockbridge, 526.
Rollins—Bruce IV, 541; Miami Co., Ohio, 708; Ritchie Co., 206.
Romney—WM, XII, 265.
Ronald—Convention 1788, II, 380; Crockett, 288; Culpeper, part 2, 90-91; Ellis, 45.
Rookings—TD, April 19, 1914; VM, V, 96; WM, V, 191.
Rookins—Cyc. Va. Biog., I, 316; VM, V, 95-96; XI, 57.
Rooney—Berkeley, 237; Randolph Co., 371.
Roop—Bruce IV, 534.
Rootes—Browning, C. D., 248-249; Cyc. Va. Biog., I, 317; Du Bellet III, 11, 27-28, 55-56, 122-123; Rootes of Rosewell, by W. C. Torrence; TD, Dec. 17, 1916; VM, IV, 204-211, 332-333; WM, VII, 130, 202; XII, 270-271.
Roper—Bruce IV, 275; Cyc. Va. Biog., IV, 201, 333; WM, XX, 294-295.

(*Eastern Shore*)—Cyc. Va. Biog., I, 317.
Rorer—Cyc. Va. Biog., V, 999.
Roscoe (Roscow)—ARP, II, 782; Barton I, 109; TD, July 5, 1914; VM, XXXIV, 174-175.
Roscow—Cyc. Va. Biog., I, 316-317; Hening VIII, 301-303; Kennedy I, 266-267; RC, III, 39; VM, VII, 285-286; IX, 110; XVII, 155; Winston, 327-336; WM, XIV, 163-164.

Rose—Culpeper, 72; Huguenot Emigration, 145-146; Kennedy I, 676-677; Magna Charta Barons, 145; Meade I, 398; Munsell's X, 20; RS, II, 30; III, 10; IV, 1; St. Mark's, 147; TD, Sept. 2, 16, 1906; Feb. 17, Oct. 27, 1907; July 12, 1908; Watson, 79-81, 160-165, 312-314.

(*Botetourt*)—Braxton Co., W. Va., 417.
(*Essex*)—VHS Col. VI, 110.
(*Kilrabbock*)—Browning, C. D., 198-199, 328; Cabell, etc., 214-216.
(*Rev. Robert*)—Chart of the Ancestors and Descendants of Rev. Robert Rose, by W. J. Stanard (Richmond, 1895).

Roseberry—Madison Co., Ohio, 750.
Rosenberger—Cartmell, 440-441.
Ross—Kanawha, 370; Ritchie Co., 224; Rockbridge, 526; TD, April 23, 1911.

(*Alexander*)—Jolliffe, 70-73.
(*Culpeper*)—MMV, V, 389-392.
(*Fauquier*)—WM, X, 68-69.
(*Highland*)—Highland Co., 330.

Rosser—Bruce V, 162; VI, 131; Campbell Co., 488-489; Cyc. Va. Biog., III, 85; MMV, I, 387-390; SBN, XII, 359.
Roszel—Bruce VI, 245.
Rountree—DAR, 51, p. 196.
Rouse—DAR, 67, p. 266; Virkus II, 308.
Row (*Orange*)—VSR, IV (No. 4), 29.
Rowan—Monroe Co., 397-399; Randolph Co., 371-372; Rockbridge, 526; Virkus II, 199.
Rowe—Bruce V, 200; Cyc. Va. Biog., V, 826; TD, March 26, 1911.
Rowland—Henry Co., 252-254; Lewis, 239-256; RS, II, 34; Virkus III, 404.
    (*Hanover*)—DAR, 42, p. 87.
Rowlett—WM 2d, VIII, 59-60.
Rowley—Robertson-Taylor, 257-263.
Rowlinson—Rockbridge, 526.
Rowlston—Cyc. Va. Biog., I, 517.
Rowzie—Hayden, 498; Huguenot Emigration, 179-180; Two Families, 98-99; VM, XXXI, 165-166.
Roxbury—Avery I, 181-182.
Roy—Bagby, 354-356; Cooke-Booth, 227-228; Hayden, 159; Lancaster, 230-231; Meade I, 405; RS, II, 47; TD, April 17, June 5, 12, 1910; Feb. 20, 1916; VM, VIII, 331; XX, 214; WM, III, 116.
Royall—Bruce VI, 155; Cyc. Va. Biog., IV, 517-518; Dupuy, 254-255; Hampden-Sidney, 153, 268; Huguenot Emigration, 195, 199-200; John Price the Emigrant, etc., 45-46; Marshall, 293-295; Sketches of Lynchburg, Va., 254-257; Southside Va., 120, 181-182; TD, Sept. 3, 1905; Dec. 13, 1914; Virkus II, 330; VM, VIII, 75-76, 296-297; XXIV, 309; XXXII, 411-412; XXXIII, 103-107, 208-212, 322-327, 420-423.
Royle—Cyc. Va. Biog., I, 317; WM, VII, 14.
Royster—Carolinians II, 238-239; Kith and Kin, 38; "Old Chapel", 46; Researcher I, 188-191; TD, April 20, 1913; Virkus III, 404; Woods-McAfee, 316-318.
    (*Goochland*)—Watkins, 36-37.
Rozier—Cyc. Va. Biog., I, 317.
Rucker—Boddie, 169-179; Bruce IV, 180; Cyc. Va. Biog., IV, 347-353; Hardy, 269-270; MMV, V, 395-396; TD, Feb. 8, March 8, 1914; Virkus III, 260, 450; VM, XIX, 198; XXVIII, 77.
    (*Amherst and Goochland*)—Munsell's V, 75.
Ruckman—Highland Co., 384-385; Pocahontas Co., 159-164, 489-492.
Rudd—Avery I, 182, 335; Bruce IV, 76; TD, Aug. 23, 1914.
    (*Petersburg*)—"Genealogy" (Weekes ed.), Vol. 4, p. 52.
Ruddell—Shenandoah, 636-637.
    (*Roanoke*)—Ridley, 386, etc.
Ruddle—Pendleton Co., 287-288.
Ruebush—Bruce VI, 5.
Ruff—Rockbridge, 526.
Ruffin—Bagby, 312-315; Bristol Parish, 230; Browning, C. D., 3d, 301, 390; Bruce IV, 412; Convention 1788 II, 380; Cyc. Va. Biog., I, 318; Page (2d ed.), 261-262; Papers of Thos. Ruffin, N. C. Hist. Commission I, 19-22; RC, III, 5 (duplicated no.); RS, II, 31; Virkus II, 143; VM, V, 76; VSR, III (No. 3), 33; WM, XVIII, 251-258.
Ruffner—Kanawha, 508, 539, 572, 631, 635-640; MMV, I, 270-274; Rockbridge, 271-272; SBN, XII, 363-364; Shenandoah, 637-638; WVM, I, April, 1901, 31-38; July, 1901, 33-41; Oct.,

1901, 46-54; II, Jan., 1902, 45-53; April, 1902, 60-74; July, 1902, 36-44; Oct., 1902, 33-43.
Ruhl—Monongahela II, 690-694.
Ruleman—Highland Co., 367; Pendleton Co., 324-325.
Ruley—Rockbridge, 526.
Rumsey—Avery II, 468.
Rush—Bruce IV, 354; V, 265.
Rusmisell—Highland Co., 368.
Russell—Campbell, Pilcher, etc.; Cyc. Va. Biog., I, 318; Rockbridge, 526; RS, III, 40; TD, Dec. 4, 1904; March 12, 1905.
(*Andrew*)—Burgess, 376-377; Knoxville, Tenn., Sentinel, about 1909.
(*Campbell*)—Campbell Co., 489-491.
(*Loudoun*)—Burgess, 376-377.
(*Shenandoah*)—Lower Shenandoah, 646-647; Shenandoah, 638.
(*Western Va.*)—WVM, I (No. 4), Oct., 1901, p. 26.
(*Gen. William*)—King's Mountain, 406-407; LCJ, Aug. 2, 1914, p. 5.
(*William*)—Carter Henry Harrison; Dunmore's War, 6; VM, XIII, 283-284; XVII, 53; William Russell and His Descendants.
(*York*)—WM, XI, 264-265.
Rust—Avery II, 533; Bruce VI, 164, 364; Burgess, 377, 379-380; Cabell, etc., 436-537; Clemens' Wills, 85; Cyc. Va. Biog., V, 805-807; Fothergill, 29, 98, 132, 145, 173; Rockbridge, 526; Rust Family, by E. Marshall Rust, Washington, D. C.; TD, Oct. 15, Dec. 17, 1916; VM, XXIX, 360.
Rutherfoord—Brock I, 198-202; Hardesty, 376-377; Lancaster, 157-158, 183; Munsell's IV, 146; RS, II, 25-28; Vestry Book of Henrico Parish, 176-177.
Rutherford—ARP, I, 284; BS, Aug. 28, Sept. 18, 1904; Cyc. Va. Biog., I, 318; Ritchie Co., 173-174; RS, II, 22, 25, 26, 40; TD, Nov. 6, 1904; Virkus II, 201; III, 466; WVM, Oct., 1901, 54-61.
(*Berkeley Co.*)—Tyler's III, 50.
(*Frederick Co.*)—Winchester and its Beginnings, by Katherine Green, 364, 369-382.
Rutledge—Crockett, 26; Kanawha, 859; TD, July 5, 1908.
(*Prince Edward*)—Tyler's X, 289.
Ryan—Randolph Co., 371; Rockbridge, 526.
Ryder—Highland Co., 330-331.
Ryland—Bagby, 315, 356-357; LCJ, Sept. 13, 1914 (II, 2); Munsell's VII, 206, 279.
Rymer—Highland Co., 385; Pendleton Co., 288.

S

Sadler—Middlesex Par. Reg.; Millers of Millersburg, 163.
(*Mathews*)—Burgess, 864.
Safford—RS, III, 36.
Sale—Bruce IV, 11; V, 253; Norfolk, 812-813; Stubbs, 61-65; VCR, I; VM, XXXVI, 381.
Salford—Cyc. Va. Biog., I, 318.
Salle—Douglas, 289, 384; TD, July 11, 1909; Woodson, 47, 271-273, 626, 647.
Salling—Clemens' Wills, 85; Rockbridge, 271-273, 526.
Salmons—Henry Co., 254-255.

Salyer—Johnson Co., Ky., 511-523.
Samons—VCR, I.
Samsell—Bruce V, 152.
Samuel—St. Louis II, 1369.
Samuels—Shenandoah, 638.
Samples—Highland Co., 331-332.
Sampson—Albemarle, 310; Douglas, 290; Kith and Kin, 11-37, 40; RS, II, 35; Supplement to Kith and Kin; WM, VII, 245.
Sanders—Bruce IV, 503; V, 236; VCR, I, II, VI; Virkus III, 408.
(New Kent)—St. Peter's Par. Reg.
(Wythe)—Crockett, 454-456.
Sanderson—Burgess, 317, 493; Hardesty *(Bedford)*, 429.
Sandes—WM, II, 152.
Sandford—Cyc. Va. Biog., I, 318-319.
(Princess Anne)—VM, XVIII, 180-181; WM, IV, 15-17.
Sandidge, Sandridge—Burgess, 425-430; TD, Feb. 1, April 19, 1914.
Sands—TD, May 26, 1907.
(Williamsburg)—Cyc. Va. Biog., IV, 559.
Sandusky—DAR, 76, p. 101.
Sandys—America Heraldica, 48, 178; Essex Inst. Colls. XXIII, 232; Neill's Virginia Carolorum, 159; TD, June 16, 1907; VM, XXII, 227-243; WM, II, 152.
Sanford—Fothergill, 157, 178; WM, II, 272; Middlesex Par. Reg.; VCR, VI.

(Lancaster)—Cyc. Va. Biog., IV, 407.
(Loudoun)—Ellis, 31; VM, VII, 212; WM, II, 272.
(Pittsylvania)—Pittsylvania, 266.
(Westmoreland)—Bruce V, 173; Fothergill, 144-145.
Sanger—Bruce IV, 104; Fayette Co., W. Va., 542-543.
Sangster—Coshocton Co., Ohio, 781; Virkus I, 457.
Sankey—Hampden-Sidney, 70.
Santmiers—Bruce IV, 372.
Santos—WM 2d, VI, 349.
Sanxay—The Sanxay Family.
Sapsley—Burgess, 945.
Sargent—DAR, 71, p. 240, 253.
Satchell *(Accomac)*—Burgess, 265-266.
Satterwhite—TD, Jan. 14, 1911; Valentine III, 1479-1494; IV, 2213-2316.

Saul—Bruce VI, 401.

Saunders—Burgess, 256-260; Pendleton Co., 288; Rockbridge, 526; RS, II, 46; VCR, I, VI; Virkus II, 329; WM, VII, 155.
(Bedford)—Summers Co., 428-429; VSR, IV (No. 4), 27.
(Brunswick)—Des Cognets, 113-122.
(Buckingham)—Cyc. Va. Biog., IV, 552.
(Campbell)—Campbell Co., 530-531.
(Ceely)—Burgess, 256-257; Researcher I, 195.
(Caroline)—Bruce IV, 236; Buckners, 192-196.
(Cumberland, Rev. John)—Cyc. Va. Biog., I, 319.
(King and Queen)—Bagby, 367; Bruce IV, 121.
(Madison)—Pocahontas Co., 201-207.
(Miscellaneous)—Stubbs, 462-465.
(New Kent)—Bruce IV, 144.
(Norfolk)—Kennedy I, 135; VM, XXII, 327-328.
(Northumberland)—Stubbs, 7-32, 318-331, 337-364.
(Princess Anne)—Antiquary I, 63; Chart in VM, V; Cyc. Va. Biog., I, 319; VM, XI, 79; XXX, 373-375; XXXII, 92-96.

March 8, 22, 1908; Aug. 30, 1914; Valentine III, 1495-1578; VCR, I, II, V, VI; Virkus II, 59; Walker-Wigton, 296-298; WM 2d, VIII, 131.

(*Albemarle*)—Albemarle, 312-313.

(*Augusta*)—Cabell, etc., 350-351; Hayden, 322, 586-589; Waddell's Annals of Augusta Co., 39.

(*Buckingham*)—Cyc. Va. Biog., IV, 456-457.

(*Caroline*)—Burgess, 1167; Caroline Co., 465-466; "Francis Morgan", 59-66; Two Families, 159-164; Tyler's X, 213-214.

(*Cumberland*)—VHS, Col. VI, 94-95; VM, XXII, 427-428; WM, II, 133.

(*Dinwiddie*)—SBN, XII, 372-374.

(*Fauquier*)—Bruce IV, 308-309; Cyc. Va. Biog., I, 320-321; Hening VII, 630-634.

(*Gloucester*)—"Francis Morgan", 33-40, 50-194; Hampden-Sidney, 23-24; Stubbs, 442-443; Two Families, 153-164.

(*Goochland*)—Cyc. Va. Biog., I, 320-321; VM, XXXIII, 37-38.

(*Goochland, etc.*)—Campbell Co., 496-497.

(*Halifax*)—Boogher, 341-343; Halifax, 244-245, 334-336.

(*Hardy*)—DAR, 56, p. 131; Randolph Co., 381-382.

(*Rev. James*)—Meade II, 198, 208-211; VSR, IV (No. 4), 36.

(*Rev. John*)—Munsell's IX, 163.

(*Manchester*)—Goode, 119.

(*New Kent*)—St. Peter's Par. Reg.; WM, V, 282; XIV, 33.

(*Orange*)—Bruce IV, 166; Virkus I, 925-926; III, 470.

(*Prince Edward*)—DAR, 83, p. 141.

(*Prince George*)—VM, XXIX, 101.

(*Prince William*)—Hardy, 454-466; Munsell's IX, 163.

(*Rockbridge*)—Monroe Co., 400; Rockbridge, 527-528.

(*Stafford*)—Cyc. Va. Biog., I, 320; V, 1024.

(*West Va.*)—Randolph Co., 381-382.

(*Winfield*)—America Heraldica, 77; LCJ, Aug. 30, 1914 (II, 1); Life of Winfield Scott, by Edward D. Mansfield (1852); Meade II, 208; Researcher II, 63-64; SBN, XII, 372-374.

Screven—Hayden, 212-215.

Scrivener—Cartmell, 442.

Scrosby—Cooke-Booth, 39; VCR, III, 55.

Scruggs—Burgess, 276-277; Scruggs Genealogy; Stubbs, 332-333.

(*New Kent*)—St. Peter's Par. Reg.

Seacott—Rockbridge, 528.

Seager—VM, XXXII, 57-58.

Seal—Cyc. Va. Biog., IV, 276.

Sears—Middlesex Par. Reg.; Virkus II, 366; III, 370.

Seaton—Avery I, 113-114; RS, III, 30; TD, March 12, 1905; VCR, I.

(*Gloucester*)—VM, XXV, 431-432.

Seaward—Middlesex Par. Reg.; VCR, VI; WM, VII, 228, et seq.

Seawell—Cyc. Va. Biog., I, 321; TD, March 24, 1912.

(*Gloucester*)—WM, III, 278-279; IV, 173; VII, 194-195; VIII, 54, 62; XV, 135.

(*Lower Norfolk*)—Major, 48-49.

Seay—Bruce V, 45; VI, 204; Old Free State II, 286-287; VSR, IV (No. 4), 29.

Seayres—Burgess, 266-267.

Sebastean—TD, Feb. 13, 1916.

Sebrell—Bruce VI, 439; Cyc. Va. Biog., V, 778.

Seddon—Cabell, etc., 332-335, 395-396; Lancaster, 181; RS, II; VM, XI, 442-443.

Sedgwick—Cyc. Va. Biog., I, 321; VM, XII, 302 (Sedgwicke).

See—Pocahontas Co., 255-258; Randolph Co., 378-381.
Segar—Andrew Meade, etc., 133-135; Bruce V, 340; VI, 406; TD,
    Nov. 6, 1904 [Seger]; VM, V, 167-168; WM, II, 269.
Sehorn—Rockbridge, 528; Shenandoah, 640-641.
Seibert—Burgess, 750.
Seig—Highland Co., 385.
Seigle—DAR, 41, p. 161.
Seiper—Burgess, 286.
Seiver—Highland Co., 385.
Selden—Armistead, 269; Bruce VI, 611; Burgess, 267-269; Cyc. Va.
    Biog., I, 321; IV, 408; Du Bellet II, 65-66, 98-107; Goode,
    284, 485; Hayden, 62-63, 738; Kennedy I, 19-143; II, 571-
    572; Mackenzie I, 471-473; Meade I, 140; RS, II, 34;
    III, 23, 35, 37; Tyler's VIII, 214; X, 52-53; VM, IX, 109;
    WM, V, 60-62, 264-267; VI, 234-238; VII, 50-51; IX, 122;
    XII, 259.
Self—Fothergill, 97, 150, 191.
Semple—Bagby, 358, 378; Cyc. Va. Biog., I, 321-322; Robertson-
    Taylor, 34-38, 43-51, 65-70, 74-78, 80, 135-136; Tyler's VIII,
    142-143; VCR, I; Virkus III, 161.
Seneca—Antiquary.
Senseny—Cartmell, 486.
Servant—Burgess, 269-270; Cyc. Va. Biog., I, 322; Meade I, 236-238;
    WM, IX, 123-124.
Seton—Bullock and Allied Families, by J. G. Bullock.
Settle—Bruce VI, 413, 494; Fayette Co., W. Va., 577.
Sevier—Armistead, 170-173; Armstrong I, 180-202; IV, 17, et seq.;
    Dunmore's War, 271; History of Rockingham Co., 348-349,
    429; King's Mountain, 418-423; Shenandoah, 641-642; Vir-
    kus II, 50; III, 78; Waddell's Annals of Augusta Co., 325-
    327; Wheeler's Eminent North Carolinians, 462.
Seward—Cyc. Va. Biog., I, 322; Hening VII, 514-516; N. C. His. Reg.
    I, 163; RC, III, 11; VM, X, 406.
Sewell (*Lower Norfolk*)—WM, IV, 171-173.
    (*Norfolk*)—Warfield, 135-136.
Sexton—Cyc. Va. Biog., IV, 455; RS, II, 19, 23.
Seybert—Bruce VI, 79; Highland Co., 332.
Seymore—DAR, 75, p. 163.
Seymour—BS, March 5, 1905.
    (*Eastern Shore*)—Yeardley, 25-26.
Seymour—Licking Co., Ohio, 768; Old King William, 180-182.
Shackelford—Bagby, 376-378; Bruce IV, 39, 278; Burgess, 258, 580;
    Cooke-Booth, 128-129; Culpeper, 119; Cyc. Va. Biog., V,
    740-741; Des Cognets, 93; Du Bellet IV, 267-269; Middle-
    sex Par. Reg.; RS, III, 32; SBN, XII, 384-385, 450-452;
    St. Mark's, 156; Stubbs, 207-213; TD, May 7, 1905; June 2,
    1907; Aug. 16, 1914; VCR, I; Virkus I, 959.
Shacker—Barbour Co., W. Va., 485.
Shackleford—Culpeper, 100-101; Du Bellet IV, 267-269; MMV, I,
    147-149; TD, May 7, Aug. 6, 1905; Two Families, 122.
Shade—Cartmell, 482.
Shadley—Hardin Co., Ohio, 954.
Shadrach—Bruce IV, 316.
Shafer—Shenandoah, 642-643.
Shaffer—Bruce IV, 303.
    (*Loudoun*)—Preston Co., 465.
Shainor—Rockbridge, 528.

Shands—Burgess, 117-118; Cabell, etc., 226; Rives, 552, 637; VSR, I (No. 4), 53; WM, XII, 13.
Shank—Barbour Co., W. Va., 469; Montgomery Co., Ohio, 118, 350.
Shanklin—Burgess, 123; Crockett, 52; Kanawha, 628-629; Monroe Co., 401-402.
Shanks—Du Bellet II, 306.
Shannon—New River, 450-452; Tazewell II, 174, 176.
Shanton—Monroe Co., 402.
Shapleigh—VM, XXXII, 61-62.
Sharp—Burgess, 366, 624; Miami Co., Ohio, 710; Pocahontas Co., W. Va., 213-218, 518-522; Rockbridge, 528; RS, III, 6.
  (*Louisa*)—TD, Nov. 2, 1913.
  (*Norfolk*)—Brock II, 676-677; Cyc. Va. Biog., V, 895-896; Norfolk, 657-671.
Sharpe—Burgess, 366, 514, 621; Cyc. Va. Biog., I, 322.
Sharpnack—Ritchie Co., 184-187.
Shaull—Cartmell, 484.
Shaver—Braxton Co., W. Va., 436-438; Bruce IV, 299-300, 320, 497; Pendleton Co., 289; Rockbridge, 528; Strickler, 55-60.
Shaw—ARP, II, 657; Barbour Co., W. Va., 456-458; Monongahela II, 741-745; Pendleton Co., 289; Rockbridge, 528; VM, XXXIII, 405-407.
Shearer—The Shearer-Akers Family.
Shearman—Hayden, 75; WM, XII, 177, 179.
Sheets—Preston Co., 392, 466.
Sheffield—Henry Co., 243-258; TD, Sept. 29, 1907.
Sheffey—Peyton, 357-358.
Sheild—Cyc. Va. Biog., IV, 458-459; VCR, V; VM, II, 435; WM, III, 207-208, 268-271; IV, 59; V, 22-24.
  (*York*)—Armistead, 121; Cyc. Va. Biog., I, 322; Norfolk, 952-953; WM, XXIII, 130.
Shelbourne—MMV, III, 360-361; Tyler's X, 140.
Shelburne—WM 2d, VI, 245-246.
Shelby—Armstrong II, 305, et seq.
Sheldon—VM, XV, 266; XX, 91-92.
  (*York*)—WM, II, 7-8.
Shelor—DAR, 59, p. 82.
Sheltman—Rockbridge, 528.
Shelton—Albemarle, 313-314; Buford, 289; Burgess, 866; "Genealogy" (Weekes' ed.), Vol. 5, pp. 73-74; Henry Co., 259-262; Hord (1898), 74, 89-90; McAfee, 309; Md. Soc. Col. Wars, 106; Middlesex Par. Reg.; Old Free State II, 180; RS, III, 6; Sketches of Lynchburg, Va., 288; Stubbs, 457-458; TD, Feb. 26, 1905; March 23, 1913; VCR, V; VM, XIX, 423; Whittaker, 49, 131-134; WM 2d, X, 56.
  (*Pittsylvania*)—Bruce V, 444; Pittsylvania, 40.
Shenk (*Page*)—Hardesty (Bedford), 430.
Shepard—Virkus II, 345.
  (*Buckingham*)—WM 2d, VI, 148-154; VII, 174-180.
  (*Isle of Wight*)—Virkus I, 508.
Shephard, Shepherd (*James City*)—Cyc. Va. Biog., I, 323.
Shepherd—BHNC, VI, 420; Duke, etc.; Kanawha, 364; Lower Shenandoah, 641-644; Madison Co., Ohio, 799; VCR, I, II, IV.
  (*Elizabeth City*)—WM, XIII, 208.
  (*Nansemond*)—VM, XI, 423-424.
  (*Norfolk*)—VM, XXVII, 359.
  (*Prince Edward*)—Kanawha, 914.

(*Shepherdstown*)—Adams Co., Ohio, 257-260; Duke, etc., 141-254; Lee, 470-471; Lineage Book, Order of Washington, 207-209; WVM, II, April, 1902, 31-35; Oct., 1902, 28-33; III, 67-78, 190-209, 288-289; V, 33-35.
Sheppard—ARP, I, 355; VCR, I, VI; WM, VI, 233.
   (*Elizabeth City*)—Cyc. Va. Biog., I, 323.
   (*Orange*)—Virkus III, 502.
   (*Surry*)—VM, III, 275-276.
   (*Warren*)—Bruce V, 152.
Shermer—Cooke-Booth, 238-239, 242-244.
Sherman—Bruce V, 402.
   (*New Kent*)—Cyc. Va. Biog., I, 323; St. Peter's Par. Reg.; VCR, III, 52.
Sherrard—Browning, C. D., 3d, 669; Kith and Kin, 193.
Sherrill—TD, June 22, 1913.
Sherrod—Goode, 186; Stubbs, 233-235.
Sherwin—Southside Va., 121.
Sherwood—Burgess, 200; Cyc. Va. Biog., I, 323.
   (*Isle of Wight*)—Cyc. Va. Biog., IV, 205.
   (*James City*)—WM, V, 52-53.
   (*Princess Anne*)—Antiquary.
Shewmake—Bruce VI, 612.
Shield (*York*)—VSR, I (No. 3), 52; IV (No. 4), 23; see Sheild.
Shields—Cyc. Va. Biog., I, 323; Rockbridge, 528; RS, III, 27; TD, May 10, 1914.
   (*Gloucester*)—Brock II, 802.
   (*James City*)—WM, XX, 33, 36-38.
   (*Norfolk*)—Brock II, 677.
   (*Pittsylvania*)—Munsell's V, 69; Virkus I, 177; VM, XIX, 422; WM, XVII, 304.
   (*Rockingham*)—Armstrong I, 208; Cyc. Va. Biog., IV, 532.
   (*Valley of Va.*)—Bruce V, 140.
   (*York*)—Hardy, 467-471; WM, V, 117-120.
Shinn (*From Pa.*)—History of the Shinn Family in Europe and America; Munsell's V, 42.
   (*West Va.*)—Harrison Co., 385-386.
Shinneberger—Highland Co., 385.
Shipp—Antiquary; VSR, IV (No. 4), 35.
Shippey—VM, VI, 406.
Shires—Monroe Co., 402.
Shirk—Pendleton Co., 289-290.
Shirkey—Kanawha, 427.
Shirley—Bruce IV, 247; LCJ, Aug. 17, 1914, p. 5; Rockbridge, 528; VCR, I.
Shoemaker—Custer Family, 14; Douglas, 294.
   (*Loudoun*)—DAR, 51, p. 299.
Shoot (Shoots)—Virkus III, 166.
Shore—Dupuy, 241-242; VM, XXX, 65-66.
   (*Hanover*)—VM, XXXIII, 405-407.
Shores—DAR, 76, p. 302, 327; Clan McGregor Year Book (1926-1927), 56.
Short—Browning, C. D., 3d, 447; Green's Ky. Families, 269-270; Mackenzie V, 446-450; Rockbridge, 528; TD, May 17, 1908; Virkus I, 827; II, 112; WM, IV, 261-263.
   (*Nigart Valley*)—VM, XXXV, 294.
Shotwell—Carolinians II, 462.
Shoulders—Pendleton Co., 325.
Showalter—Bruce IV, 226; VI, 451; Funk, 207-212; Shenandoah, 643.

717; McIlhany, 259; MMV, V, 403-405; Old King William, 146; RS, III, 19; Shenandoah, 643-644; St. Mark's, 158-165; TD, March 18, 25, 1906; Feb. 3, Oct. 13, Nov. 3, 1907; Feb. 2, 1908; Feb. 20, 1910; Virkus II, 110; III, 190, 420, 426; VCR, I, II, V, VI; VM, III, 61-62; V, 283; VI, 323; XVII, 152; XXI, 306-310, 427-430, 440; XXII, 99-102, 208-211, 319-322; XXIII, 212-213; XXVII, 72, 367-369; XXX, 337; XXXI, 77-79.

Slaven (*Highland*)—Highland Co., 335-336; Pocahontas Co., 144-149.
Slavens (*Augusta*)—DAR, 83, p. 191.
Sledd—Hardesty (*Bedford*), 430.
Sleeth—Ritchie Co., 541-544.
Slemp—Cyc. Va. Biog., V, 812; MMV, II, 349-350.
Slicer—Hardesty (*Bedford*), 430.
Slingsby—Coghill, 163-193.
Sloan—Rockbridge, 529.
Sly—Rockbridge, 529.
Slyh—Madison Co., Ohio, 773.
Small—Cyc. Va. Biog., I, 325.
Smallridge—Highland Co., 386.
Smallwood—Bruce V, 320; Burgess, 279-280; VCR, I; WM, XII, 181.
Smart—ARP, I, 350; Harrison, Waples, etc., 126-127; WM, III, 30; VII, 108.
Smelt—Meade I, 401; TD, June 3, 17, July 29, Sept. 9, 1906; June 12, 1910.
Smiley—Rockbridge, 529.
Smith—Boogher, 330-372; BS, March 4, 11, 1906; Du Bellet IV, 79-102; Goode, 89, 164-169; Hampden-Sidney, 285-288; Hayden, 19-21, 32-35, 273; New River, 452-453; Pendleton Co., 298-299; Preston Genealogy (1870), 54-58; Rockbridge, 274, 529; RS, II, 2, 7, 47; III, 16, 24, 36; St. Mark's, 136, 178; TD, Oct. 2, 1904; Feb. 4, April 22, May 6, June 10, Oct. 21, 28, 1906; Oct. 20, 1907; July 4, Oct. 31, 1909; Feb. 4, April 14, 21, Sept. 1, 1912; Feb. 27, March 5, 26, April 9, 16, July 23, 1916; March 4, April 1, 1917; WM, IX, 42.
(*Abigail*)—Winston, 381-386.
(*Abingdon Parish, Gloucester*)—VM, VII, 400.
(*Albemarle*)—Albemarle, 316-317.
(*Alexandria*)—Avery I, 116-117; Du Bellet III, 25-26, 47-53.
(*Rev. Armistead*)—WM, III, 117-119; IV, 245.
(*Augusta*)—Waddell's Annals of Augusta Co., 39, 150-152.
(*Augusta and Rockingham*)—Boogher, 330-372; Bruce V, 545.
(*Augustine*)—TD, Oct. 31, 1909.
(*Austin, Hanover*)—Genealogy of the Cloyd, Basye, etc., Families, 251-254.
(*Back Creek, Frederick*)—Cartmell, 478-480.
(*Ballard*)—Draper Series V, 269; WM, X, 263-264.
(*Botetourt*)—Brock II, 753.
(*Brandon, Middlesex*)—VM, XXV, 268-269.
(*Caroline*)—Valentine IV, 2166-2169.
(*Charles, Berryville*)—Mackenzie IV, 188.
(*Charles City and Henrico*)—VSR, I (No. 3), 40.
(*Charles, Essex*)—Hening V, 287-292.
(*Chesterfield*)—Valentine IV, 2166-2169.
(*Christopher, Hanover*)—Tyler's IV, 150-151.
(*Cumberland*)—Bruce IV, 187; Montague, 91; Woodson, 212, 348, 510.
(*Daniel*)—Dunmore's War, 3-4.

(*Pittsylvania*)—Pittsylvania, 164, 223; VM, XXIII, 377.
(*Powhatan*)—Goode, 164-169; Valentine IV, 2189-2202.
(*Purton*)—Browning, C. D., 251-253; Cartmell, 296-297, 450;
    Cyc. Va. Biog., I, 326; Du Bellet IV, 27-34, 38-40, 94-102;
    III, 1-185; IV, 27-34, 38-40, 94-102; McIlhany, 108-109;
    Marshall, 141-142, 307-311; MMV, III, 372-374; "Old Chapel",
    44, 51, 64-65, 67, 73; Willis, 152-154; WM, IV, 46-52, 95-
    101, 183-185; V, 50-53; VI, 213; IX, 42.
(*Randolph Co., W. Va.*)—Randolph Co., 376-377.
(*Richmond Co.*)—Roger Jones, 44.
(*Rickahoc*)—Bagby, 73.
(*Gen. Robert*)—Cyc. Va. Biog., I, 128; VM, I, 432-433.
(*Robert, Port Royal*)—VM, III, 96-97.
(*Rockbridge*)—Rockbridge, 274, 529-530.
(*Rockingham*)—History of Rockingham Co. (Wayland), 352;
    Licking Co., Ohio, 757; Mackenzie V, 457-462; WM, XXVI,
    187-188.
(*Schmidt*)—WM, XXVI, 187-188.
(*Shenandoah*)—Shenandoah, 644.
(*Smithfield*)—Hening VI, 308-311.
(*Spotsylvania*)—Hening VI, 308-311; Valentine IV, 2202-2208.
(*Toby*)—Cyc. Va. Biog., I, 327; VM, V, 283-284, 432-433.
(*Valley of Va.*)—Bruce VI, 17 (Alphonso).
(*Westmoreland*)—Bruce V, 367.
(*West Va.*)—Monroe Co., 403-404; Pocahontas Co., 302-306;
    Randolph Co., 376-377; Ritchie Co., 61-62.
(*Gov. William*)—Brock I, 208-216; Hardesty, 378-380; Memoirs
    of Gov. William Smith, 2, et seq.
    (*York*)—Bruce VI, 481; Page (2d ed.), 79; Valentine IV, 2208.
Smithers—St. Peter's Par. Reg.; VCR, I.
Smithey—Cyc. Va. Biog., V, 705.
Smither—Old King William, 190.
Smithey (*Amelia*)—Munsell's V, 87.
Smithson—Monroe Co., 404.
Smoke—Cartmell, 484; Lower Shenandoah, 732-733.
Smoot—Avery I, 186-187; Monongahela II, 469-471; WVM, V, 410-411.
    (*Shenandoah*)—Bruce IV, 342.
Smyth—Bruce IV, 134, 432; Grayson Co., 179-182.
Snail—WM, XII, 103.
Snapp—Berkeley, 213-214; Cartmell, 469-470.
Snarr—Bruce IV, 281.
Snead—Bruce V, 116; BS, Aug. 2, 1908; Burgess, 310; Cyc. Va. Biog.,
    V, 974; VM, VI, 416.
    (*Eastern Shore*)—WM, X, 125-126.
    (*Fluvanna*)—Bruce IV, 26, 377; MMV, III, 386-387; IV, 372-
    373; The Sneads of Fluvanna, by Mrs. W. E. Hatcher, 1910,
    p. 37, et seq.
    (*Hanover*)—Virkus III, 192.
Snedicor—DAR, 75, p. 89.
Sneed—Bruce IV, 29.
    (*Albemarle*)—DAR, 45, p. 199; WM 2d, X, 90.
Snellings—TD, Jan. 23, 1910.
Snicker—Du Bellet III, 95.
Snickers—McIlhany, 107-108.
Snider—Pendleton Co., 299-300; Rockbridge, 530.
Snidow—Bruce VI, 501; New River, 453-455; Virkus III, 288.
Snoddy—Bruce IV, 255-256; Burgess, 107; VM, XXIII, 309; WM 2d,
    VIII, chart op. p. 33.

Snodgrass—Berkeley, 205-206; Clemens' Wills, 90; Kanawha, 907; Miami Co., Ohio, 517; Ritchie Co., W. Va., 98-100; Rockbridge, 530.
Snow—Campbell Co., 502-504.
Snowden—Avery I, 117.
Snyder—Highland Co., 336-337; Kanawha, 692; Lower Shenandoah, 655-656; Madison Co., Ohio, 1013; Randolph Co., 375-376. (*Rockingham*)—WM, XXVI, 188-189.
Soane—Cyc. Va. Biog., I, 327; TD, May 21, July 9, 1911; WM, IV, 127; V, 67.
Soblet—VH Col. V.
Solomon—Rockbridge, 530; Strickler, 206-213.
Somers—Shenandoah, 644.
Somersall—Zimmerman, 14-17.
Somerville—Cyc. Va. Biog., I, 327-328; Culpeper, part 2, 79.
Sommerville (Somerville)—Bruce VI, 642; Hayden, 14-17; LCJ, Aug. 30, 1914 (II, 1); Ritchie Co., 240, 248; WM, XII, 133.
Sorrell—VM, XXXV, 32; XXXVII, 159-160.
Sorsby—DAR, 48, p. 225.
Souder—Hardin Co., Ohio, 1030.
Sours—Shenandoah, 644.
Southall—Albemarle, 317-318; Armistead, 127; ARP, I, 282; Dupuy, 257-258; Goode, 333-334, 415; Huguenot Emigration, 201, 203-204; McGavock Family, 34; MMV, IV, 374-375; V, 412; Munsell's VII, 157; Patrick Henry II, 642-643; RS, II, 29, 42; III, 6, 8; TD, March 4, 18, 1906; Tyler's VIII, 133-136; Virkus I, 625; VM, IV, 436-437; Whitaker, 20; WM, IV, 374-375; VII, 112; XII, 29, 31; XIII, 143.
Southerland (*Albemarle*)—TD, Dec. 17, 1911.
(*Dinwiddie*)—N. C. His. Reg., I, 489.
(*King William, etc.*)—Land Office Book, 18, p. 279; Book 9, p. 494; Winston, 387-402.
Southern—Monongahela II, 578-579.
Southey—VM, XXV, 341; WM, VI, 231.
Southgate—Bagby, 88-91; Bruce VI, 530; Cyc. Va. Biog., V, 706.
Southwell—Kanawha, 585.
Soutter—RS, II, 47.
Sovain—Monroe Co., 404.
Soward—Marshall, 187; Monroe Co., 404-405.
Sowell—Albemarle, 318.
Sowers—Lower Shenandoah.
Spade—Monroe Co., 405.
Spaid—Bruce V, 333; Hampshire, 729.
Spain—Bristol Par. Reg.
Spalding—Edward Spalding of Va. and Mass. Bay and His Descendants, by C. W. Spalding, 1897.
Span—Cyc. Va. Biog., I, 328.
Spangler—Monroe Co., 405; WM, VII, 112.
Spann—Hayden, 245 (Span); WM, XII, 266.
Sparks—Bruce IV, 432; Tazewell II, 536-540; VCR, I.
Sparrow—Bruce V, 560; Cyc. Va. Biog., I, 328; TD, July 21, 1912; VCR, VI.
Speake—Burgess, 311-313.
Spearman—DAR, 59, p. 293.
Spears—TD, Feb. 16, 1908.
Speece—Hampden-Sidney, 106-107; History of Augusta Church, by Rev. J. N. Van Devanter (Staunton, Va.), 29-30.

Speed—Bruce VI, 193; Cyc. Va. Biog., I, 328; Fry Genealogy; LEP, March 15, 1919, p. 6; Mackenzie VI, 12-17; McCue, 21, 86, 141-142; Records and Memorials of the Speed Family, by Thos. W. Speed (1892); Stubbs, 382; Woods-McAfee, 228-231.
Speer—Rockbridge, 530.
Speiden—Cyc. Va. Biog., V, 1079.
Speight—Virkus III, 472.
Speke—Cyc. Va. Biog., I, 328; Hayden, 489-490; WM, II, 113-120; IV, 41.
Spelman (Spilman)—WM, XIV, 178-179.
Spence—Burgess, 238, 586; Cyc. Va. Biog., I, 328; Rockbridge, 530; TD, Dec. 21, 1913 (Spens); Thomas Carter, 314-315.
(*Westmoreland*)—WM, XXV, 43-45.
Spencer—Armistead, 276; Burgess, 315-319; Cyc. Va. Biog., I, 328-329; TD, Feb. 3, March 10, 1907; Tyler's X, 67; VCR, V, VI; WM, VI, 224; VII, 233; X, 173.
(*Buckingham*)—Bruce V, 26.
(*Charlotte*)—Hampden-Sidney, 85; Mackenzie VI, 425-427; Stubbs, 442; VM, II, 195; Watkins, 39.
(*Henry*)—Henry Co., 263-265; MMV, IV, 378-379.
(*New Kent*)—St. Peter's Par. Reg.
(*Nicholas*)—VM, II, 33-34.
(*Nomini*)—Hampden-Sidney, 85; Thomas Carter, 45-46; VM, II, 32-34; IV, 222-223, 451-452.
(*Westmoreland*)—VM, XVII, 215; WM, XVII, 56-57; WM 2d, III, 134-136.
Spengler—Bruce IV, 552-553; DAR, 48, p. 17; Shenandoah, 644-645.
Spense—TD, Nov. 25, 1906.
Sperry—Cartmell, 491; Cyc. Va. Biog., V, 931; Hardesty (*Bedford*), 430.
Spessard—Bruce IV, 232, 564; VM, XXVII, 357.
Spicer (*Richmond Co.*)—Cyc. Va. Biog., I, 329; Tyler's X, 163; VM, II, 122; XXVI, 388; WM, III, 133-134; VI, 173; XVII, 27.
Spiller—Bruce VI, 312; Cyc. Va. Biog., V, 747.
Spilltimber—WM, VII, 226.
Spilman—Bruce VI, 59; Cyc. Va. Biog., I, 329; Fishback Family, 101-102, 123-124, 178-179, 190-193, 270, 286-288; Kanawha, 513-514; McIlhany, 260-261; Virkus I, 582; II, 218; VM, I, 195-196; XXVII, 364.
(*Westmoreland*)—WM, IV, 41-42.
Spindle—Bruce VI, 315.
Spitler—Shenandoah, 645; Strickler, 227.
Spitzer—Bruce IV, 280; Shenandoah, 645.
Sponaugle—Highland Co., 368-369; Pendleton Co., 300-301.
Spotswood—America Heraldica, 100-101; Browning, C. D., 245, 290-290-293, 604-605; Browning, R. D., 3d, 111-114, 808-809 BS, Jan. 28, Feb. 4, 1906; Burgess, 420-423; Campbell's History of Va., 409; Culpeper, 1-3, 72-73, 119; Cyc. Va. Biog., I, 59, 329; Genealogy of the Spotswood Family in Scotland and America, by Charles Campbell; Goode, 115-118, 225-229, 371-372; Hening VII, 323-330, 445-452; VIII, 27-33; Kennedy II, 95-125; Lewis, 54; Lindsay, 22; Mackenzie I, 496-499; Magna Charta Barons, 147, 432-447; Meade I, 165-166; Norfolk, 493-494; RC, III, 6 (duplicate); Spotswood Letters I, VII-XVI; St. Mark's, 165-168; TD, Jan. 31, May 15, Oct. 30, 1904; June 11, July 2, 1905; Jan. 12, Dec. 20, 1908; Jan. 17, 1909; Virkus II, 220; VM, III,

Starke—ARP, I, 325; Cyc. Va. Biog., I, 330; Hening VIII, 289-291; Rockbridge, 531; TD, June 2, 1907; Virkus III, 379.
    (*Hanover*)—MMV, II, 361-363; RS, III, 3, 6; VSR, I, 55 (Gen. Sec.); WM, V, 256-259.
    (*Henrico*)—DAR, 72, p. 143.
    (*King and Queen*)—VCR, III, 53.
    (*New Kent*)—VM, XIV, 303-304.
    (*Norfolk*)—Brock II, 678-679; VM, XXVII, 96, 173.
    (*Stafford*)—Thos. Carter, 362-365; WM, V, 56-57, 255-256; VII, 109; XXI, 204-205, 294.
    (*York*)—VM, XXXIII, 27-29; WM, IV, 198-200, 270-272; XXI, 204-205.
Starkey—Bruce IV, 415; RS, II, 32; III, 33.
Starling—Green's Ky. Families, 82-93; Henry Co., 266-268; Marshall, 165-166; Munsell's VIII, 113.
    (*King William*)—DAR, 51, p. 136; Virkus III, 186-187.
Starr—Ritchie Co., 36-37.
Statham—Brock II, 587; Descent of the Family of Statham; TD, Aug. 22, 1909; WM 2d, II, 137.
Stauffer—Bruce VI, 495.
Staunton—Munsell's V, 173.
St. Clair—DAR, 48, p. 216; Tazewell II, 503-504.
Stearnes—Cyc. Va. Biog., IV, 39.
Stebbins—Brock II, 623-624; Halifax, 245-246.
Steck—Cartmell, 463.
Stedman—WM, VIII, 34.
Steed—Virkus III, 431.
Steele—Burgess, 457-459; McClure, 213-214; Virkus II, 165; Monongahela II, 722-723.
    (*Rockbridge*)—McCue, 174-233; Rockbridge, 531-532.
    (*Stephenburg*)—Cartmell, 489.
Steenberger (Steenbergen)—Shenandoah, 645-646.
Steger—Goode, 79, 278; Kennedy II, 271-272.
Stegg (Stagg)—VM, XVII, 279; VSR, V (No. 2), 66 [Stegge].
    (*Henrico*)—VM, VI, 300.
Stephen (*Adam*)—Berkeley Co., 225-227; Browning, C. D., 3d, 245; Cartmell, 456; Convention 1788, I, 300-302, 604-605; Dinwiddie Papers I, 112-113; Virkus III, 378.
    (*Berkeley*)—Dunmore's War, 191; Battle of Pt. Pleasant, 22; Kennedy II, 423-441; VM, XVI, 136-137.
Stephens—Cyc. Va. Biog., I, 230; TD, April 15, 1906.
    (*Frdeerick*)—DAR, 78, p. 158.
    (*Valley of Va.*)—Cartmell, 412-413.
    (*Warwick*)—Major, 122-128; VM, I, 82-83; VII, 345-346.
Stephenson—Kanawha, 420; Rockbridge, 532.
    (*Berkeley*)—DAR, 83, p. 60.
    (*Clarke*)—Mackenzie III, 109.
    (*Frederick*)—Cartmell, 482; Genealogical and Biographical Record of William Stephenson; Mackenzie III, 109.
    (*Highland*)—Highland Co., 337-340.
    (*Col. Hugh*)—Berkeley, 215; Burgess, 435-440.
    (*Orange*)—Virkus III, 556.
    (*Valley of Va.*)—Shepherdstown, 349.
Steptoe—BS, Oct. 15, 1905; Campbell Co., 207; Du Bellet II, 714-719; Hardy, 484-491; Hayden, 730; RS, III, 29; TD, April 9, May 14, 28, Nov. 19, 26, 1905; Jan. 28, 1906; VM, VIII.

212, 318-319; IX, 203; X, 95; XIX, 447; XXVI, 382; WM, XX, 297.
(*Bedford*)—Hardesty, 430.
Sterrett—Kanawha, 509; Miami Co., Ohio, 772; Rockbridge, 532; Virkus III, 266.
Stevens (*Culpeper*)—Culpeper, part 2, 5; St. Mark's, 128; WM 2d, I, 159-161.
(*Halifax*)—VM, XXX, 66-67.
(*Nelson*)—Bruce V, 52; Hardesty (*Amherst*), 414.
(*Orange*)—Montague, 87-88, 126-127, 210-211.
Stevenson—Albemarle, 319; Hardin Co., Ohio, 862; Hayden, 401; RC, II, 10; Rockbridge, 532.
(*Culpeper*)—DAR, 83, p. 231; St. Mark's, 168-169.
(*Rev. James*)—Culpeper, 73-74; VM, X, 200.
(*Rev. John*)—Browning, C. D., 184; St. Mark's, 168-169.
Stewart—BS, April 5, 1906.
(*Berkeley*)—Berkeley, 191; Hardin Co., Ohio, 1061.
(*Brooke Co.*)—DAR, 80, p. 118-119.
(*Brook Hill*)—Lancaster, 113; VSR, IV (No. 2), 27, 34.
(*Halifax*)—Halifax, 337.
(*Matthews*)—Burgess, 949.
(*Norfolk Co.*)—Burgess, 1211-1212; Cyc. Va. Biog., IV, 265-268; McIntosh II, 104, 223, 296-297; Minor, 67; Norfolk, 511-514, 615, 651-652; Stewarts of Beechwood (privately printed).
(*West Va.*)—Barbour Co., 463-647; Monongahela II, 552-553.
Stickley—Bruce V, 69-70, 83; Cartmell, 488; Lower Shenandoah, 769; Madison Co., Ohio, 1013; Shenandoah, 646-647.
Stiff—Bruce V, 396; Hardesty (*Bedford*), 430; VM, III, 317-319.
Stigleleather—Rockbridge, 532.
Stiles—WM, VII, 220.
Stinson—Bruce VI, 221.
Stinnett—Clemens' Wills, 9; Hardesty (*Amherst*), 444.
Stirewalt—Bruce IV, 349.
Stirling—TD, Aug. 18, 1912.
Stith—Armistead, 145-146; ARP, I, 326; Buckners of Va., 28-29, 206-209; Campbell Co., 504-506; Cyc. Va. Biog., V, 676; Goode, 210-212; Md. Soc. Col. Wars, 53; Meade I, 137; RC, III, 54, 56, 60-61; TD, April 17, 24, 1904; Sept. 17, 1905; Oct. 4, Nov. 1, 1908; June 29, 1913; July 23, 1916; Tyler's IV, 143-149; Va. His. Col., XI, 70-71; VM, III, 251; VII, 437-438; VIII, 95-96; WM, I, 28, 135-136; III, 204; IV, 250; V, 113; VI, 77, 125-126; VII, 57, 59; X, 195; XXI, 184-193, 269-278; XXII, 44-51, 131-133, 197-208, 273-275; XXIII, 221; WM 2d, II, 16-17; VI, 136-137; Cyc. Va. Biog., I, 330-331.
Stoakley—TD, Jan. 14, 1906.
Stockley—ARP, II, 485; Burgess, 452-453; County Court Note Book, VI, No. 4, 5; Md. Soc. Col. Wars, 22.
Stockton—Albemarle, 319-320; Ancestry of the Children of J. W. White, M. D., 126-129; Fayette Co., W. Va., 590; Glenn's Colonial Mansions, 91-93; TD, Sept. 6, 1903; May 10, 1914; WM, IX, 86.
Stoddert—Burgess, 280-282.
Stodghill—Monroe Co., 407.
Stoever—WM, IV, 62-63.
Stoffregen—Virkus III, 434.
Stokes—A Genealogical Study (1312-1903); Cyc. Va. Biog., I, 332; Halifax, 246-247, 338; TD, June 1, 8, 15, 1913; April 26,

1914; Thomas Carter, 83-84; VM, III, 184-185; VI, 95-99; WM, XIX, 191-192; WM 2d, VIII, 124-131.

(*Lunenburg*)—Bruce V, 49; Old Free State II, 328, et seq.

Stone—Armstrong I, 217; Goode, 210-212; Hayden, 175; Johnson Co., Ky., 523; Pendleton Co., 301-302; RC, III, 21; VM, X, 211-212; XII, 453-454; XX, 69; XXVII, 87.

(*Eastern Shore*)—VM, III, 272-273.

(*Essex*)—Barton II, 232-233.

(*Halifax*)—The Nowlin-Stone Genealogy, 395-471.

(*Highland*)—Highland Co., 369.

(*Miscellaneous*)—VM, XXVIII, 65-67.

(*Pittsylvania*)—Descendants of James Nowlin and George and James Hopkins Stone; Pittsylvania, 181.

Stonebraker—Miami Co., Ohio, 862.

Stoneburner—Cyc. Va. Biog., V, 1085.

Stoner—Rockbridge, 532; Shenandoah, 647-648; Virkus III, 436; VM, XXXIII, 36.

Stoops—Rockbridge, 532.

Storke—VM, II, 30; WM, IV, 80, 246; WM 2d, 61-62.

Storrs—Storrs Family, by Charles Storrs; TD, March 17, 1912; VSR, V (No. 1), 84; (No. 2), 37-38; Woodson, 645.

Story (*Southampton*)—Cyc. Va. Biog., I, 332; V, 1082.

Stott—Burgess, 450-452, 912, 1344.

Stovall—Clemens' Wills, 92; Henry Co., 268-269.

Stover—Boddie, 139-140, 142-143; Bruce VI, 193; Cyc. Va. Biog., I, 333; VM, XIV, 142, 157-167; XXIX, 183-184.

Strachan—TD, June 12, 26, 1904; VSR, IV (No. 3), 20.

Strachey—Cyc. Va. Biog., I, 333; TD, Oct. 5, 1913; Virkus I, 911-912; II, 203; VM, XVIII, 81; WM, II, 7; III, 143-144; IV, 192-194; V, 6-10; X, 168.

Strader—Randolph Co., 372-373.

Straley—New River, 456-459.

Strange—Campbell Co., 506-507; Minor, 67; Year Book of Clan Gregor (1911-1912), p. 58.

(*Fauquier*)—Border Settlers, 189.

Stras—Tazewell II, 531-536.

Stratham—TD, Sept. 9, 1906.

Stratton—Bell, 41, 94-95; Bruce IV, 553; Cyc. Va. Biog., I, 333; IV, 14; TD, Nov. 12, 1905; April 8, 15, May 6, 1906; VSR, V (No. 1), 69, etc.

(*Eastern Shore*)—A Book of Strattons, by Harriet B. Stratton (Grafton Press, 1908), I, 141-152.

(*Henrico*)—A Book of Strattons, I, 213-224; WM, XXIV, 274-277.

(*Joseph*)—A Book of Strattons.

Strayer—Bruce V, 392.

Street—Lower Shenandoah, 721; Old Free State II, 335-341; TD, June 1, 1913; WM 2d, VIII, 126-132.

(*Essex, King and Queen*)—Bagby, 368.

Stretchley—Cyc. Va. Biog., I, 333.

Stribling, Stribbling—Du Bellet I, 62, 108-111, 181-182; Hardy, 144-147; Marshall, 55, 214-215, 265-266, 362; McIlhany, 34-98; Thos. Carter, 344-345; WVM, V, 114-117.

Strickland—Rockbridge, 532.

Strickler—Barbour Co., W. Va., 467-469; Forerunner of a History or Genealogy of the Strickler Family; Ritchie Co., 536-539; Shenandoah, 650-651.

Strider—BS, Dec. 3, 1905.

Stringfellow—Culpeper, 87; Hardy, 474; St. Mark's, 158, 171; Willis, 50.

Strode—Shenandoah, 648.

Strong—Ragland, 57-58.

(*Hanover*)—DAR, 74, p. 270.

Strother—Berkeley, 215; BS, Nov. 26, 1905; Buckners, 220-240; Burgess, 162, 866; Cyc. Va. Biog., I, 333; Convention 1788, II, 370-371; Crozier's Va. County Records, VI, 296-298; Culpeper, 66, 79, 83-85; Du Bellet IV, 64-70; "Genealogy" (Weekes ed.), Vol. 4, p. 80; Gilmer's Georgians, 60; Green's Ky. Families, 87-90; Habersham, 120-121; Johnstons of Salisbury, by W. P. Johnston (New Orleans, 1897), 185-192, 202-204; Kennedy II, 138-142, 148, 185-192, 402; Mackenzie V, 477-498; Marshall, 146-147; Notable Families, 60-69; Reg. of the Ky. State His. Asso., Vol. XXV; Rockbridge, 532; Southern His. Asso., II, 149-173; St. Mark's, 149-173; TD, Nov. 27, 1904; Aug. 27, Sept. 24, 1905; Dec. 12, 1909; April 5, 1914; Dec. 12, 1915; Tyler's IX, 276; XI, 113-140; Virkus III, 284; VM, XXII, 321; William Strother of Va. and His Descendants (Owen); WM, VI, 113, 155; XII, 270; XXIII, 143.

Stroud—Cyc. Va. Biog., IV, 204.

(*Amherst*)—Clemens' Wills, 92.

Stuart—De Bow's Review, 126; Gilmer's Georgians, 50; RS, I, 12; WM, VI, 113-116, 155-158.

(*Alexandria*)—Avery I, 73.

(*Augusta*)—Battle of Pt. Pleasant, 47; Bruce V, 5-6; VI, 310; Convention 1788, II, 9-15, 25-30, 383-393; Cyc. Va. Biog., IV, 144; Foote II, 32, 36-37; Green's Ky. Families, 220-226; Pannill's Life of Gen. J. E. B. Stuart, 64-65; McClure, 63-64, 216; McGavock Family, 83, 133-134; MMV, I, 261-262; SBN, XII, 426-429; Thomas Carter, 247-250; Virkus III, 409; Walker-Wigton, 32-64, 286; WVM, IV, 91-92.

(*Floyd*)—Crockett, 303.

(*Greenbrier*)—Dunmore's War, 104; Peyton, 288, 292; WVM, V, 119, 127, 132.

(*King George*)—BS, July 29, Aug. 6, 12, Oct. 14, 1906; Convention 1788, II, 373; Hardy, 492-498; R. W. Johnson Chart, 22-23, 28-30, 33-34, 37-38, 40, 45-46.

(*Northern Neck*)—Macknezie I, 92.

(*Rockbridge*)—Rockbridge, 274, 532-533; Sangamon Co., Ill., 696; Virkus I, 325.

(*Wythe*)—Johnson Co., Ill., 660.

Stubblefield—Cooke-Booth, 263-264; DAR, 55, p. 311; Douglas, 300; Mackenzie IV, 557; Researcher I, 53-57; VCR, III, 56; VM, XX, 213.

Stubbs—Armistead, 281; Bruce V, 352; Buckners of Va., 165-166; Burgess, 23, 119; Cooke-Booth. 205-206; "Descendants of John Stubbs of Cappahosic", by Dr. William Carter Stubbs; Munsell's XI, 122; Sangamon Co., Ill., 699; SBN, XII, 429-430; TD, Jan. 1, 22, Feb. 19, 1911; Two Families, 134-137; WM, II, 234.

Stuckey—Berkeley, 208-210, 240; Knox Co., Ill., 677-678.

Stull—Bruce IV, 504; V, 400.

Stultz—Henry Co., 269-272.

Stump—Pendleton Co., 301-302; Braxton Co., W. Va., 426-427; Kanawha, 922.

Sturdevant—RS, III, 33; Thos. Hardaway, 32.

Sturdivant—Burgess, 449-450; Hardaway, 32; RS, III, 33; Tyler's X, 51.
Sturm—Barbour Co., W. Va., 458.
Sturman—WM, IV, 40.
Sublett—A Partial History of the French Huguenot, Etc.; Douglas, 300; Dupuy, 169, 263-264, 289-297; Huguenot Emigration, 77.
Suddarth—Albemarle, 321-322.
Sudduth—Bruce VI, 204.
Sudworth—Clemens' Wills, 93.
Sugg (Norfolk Co.)—McIntosh II, 159-160.
Sullenberger—Highland Co., 340.
Sullivan—DAR, 67, p. 16.
    (Culpeper)—Old King William, 163.
    (Nansemond)—Cyc. Va. Biog., I, 333; VM, XIX, 191.
Sullivant—A Genealogy and Family Memorial; Burgess, 316; Highland Co., 340; Marshall, 164-165.
Sully—Brock II, 656; Cyc. Va. Biog., I, 334.
Summerell—Carolinians II, 270-271.
Summerfield—Pendleton Co., 340.
Summerlin—DAR, 43, p. 63; Virkus III, 259.
Summers—Brock II, 754; Bruce V, 30; VI, 302; Highland Co., 386; MMV, III, 405-407; Ritchie Co., 339; Rockbridge, 533; Shenandoah, 651; WVM, III, 228-241.
    (Fairfax)—Avery I, 188; DAR, 42, p. 113.
Sumner—TD, Sept. 20, Nov. 8, 1914; VM, XI, 311; XXVII, 309.
Sumpter—VM, VII, 243-244.
Sumter—Albemarle, 322-323.
Surber—Alleghany, 211; Bruce IV, 381.
Surface—Bruce VI, 335.
Susong—Brock II, 754.
Suter—Bruce IV, 298; Burgess, 221.
Sutherland—Albemarle, 323-324; Brock II, 804; Bruce IV, 481; V, 495, 517-518; Burgess, 462; Douglas, 300.
Sutherlin—VM, I, 339-340.
    (Pittsylvania)—Brock II, 551; Pittsylvania, 243.
Summerfield—Pendleton Co., 302.
Sutphin—Bruce IV, 426.
Sutton—BS, Sept. 18, 1905; Caroline Co., 469; Fothergill, 122, 137; Rockbridge, 533; TD, March 11, 1906; Thos. Carter, 287-289, 293-294; WM, VIII, 126; XIX, 132-133.
    (Alexandria)—Braxton Co., W. Va., 421-424.
    (Westmoreland)—Burgess, 1346; Pocahontas Co., 485-486.
Swadley—Highland Co., 369; Pendleton Co., 303.
Swan—ARP, I, 330-331; Burgess, 446-449; RS, III, 36.
Swank—Bruce IV, 262, 283.
Swann—Carolinians II, 302-303; Cyc. Va. Biog., I, 124-125, 334; Hening VI, 446-448; Minor, 79; RC, III, 27; Roger Jones, 39, 341-345, 353-354; Virkus II, 291; VM, III, 154-156; Woodson, 335; WM, XII, 263; XVI, 234-235.
    (Loudoun)—Hayden, 182; Kennedy I, 530-533.
    (Surry)—VM, III, 154-156; XXVIII, 29-32; WM, IV, 113.
Swanson—Cyc. Va. Biog., V, 936-937; Pittsylvania, 259.
Swart (Fauquier)—McIlhany, 232, 235-236, 238-239, 242, 244.
Swearingen—Family Historical Register; Shepherdstown, 177-184, 232-233, 350-352; Tyler's III, 52.
Swecker—Highland Co., 340-341.
Sweeney (Swinny)—Cyc. Va. Biog., I, 334.
Sweeney (Elizabeth City)—WM, XVI, 237-239.

Sweeny (*Norfolk*)—McIntosh II, 129-130.
Sweet—Rockbridge, 533.
Swepson—TD, Sept. 12, 1909.
Swift (*Grayson Co.*)—98-103.
Swiger—Monongahela II, 509.
Swinley—Cartmell, 484.
Swisher—Hampshire, 727-729, 732; Hardesty (*Bedford*), 444; Rockbridge, 533; Tucker Co., 499.
Switzer—Barbour Co., W. Va., 462-463.
Swoope—Peyton, 298; Rockbridge, 533; Stubbs, 203-207, 360; Waddell, 337.
Swope—Highland Co., 369; Monroe Co., 408-409; Summers Co., 438-455; Swope Genealogy (1896).
Syders—Rockbridge, 533.
Sydnor—Bruce IV, 21; V, 437; Cartmell, 490-491; Halifax, 338; TD, Dec. 31, 1911; Tyler's III, 282-287; IV, 45-46; VM, XXX, 44.
Sykes—Stubbs, 257-260.
      (*Norfolk Co.*)—McIntosh I, 199 [Sikes].
Syler—Rockbridge, 533.
Syme—Bristol Parish, 40; Cabell, etc., 188-189; Cyc. Va. Biog., I, 334-335; Culpeper, 76-77; Du Bellet I, 262-264; II, 404-406; Kennedy II, 388-389; Patrick Henry II, 633-634; RS, II, 39, 40; III, 40; St. Mark's, 187; VM, XXXII, 396-397; WM, I, 211; IV, 67; VI, 62; XI, 77-78.
Symes—Hayden, 92A-92B.
Symington—TD, Sept. 9, 1906 (Under "A Romance in a Virginia Family").
Symmes—Keith, 83-84.
Symms—Monroe Co., 409.
Syms—Cyc. Va. Biog., I, 335.
Syne—Burgess, 214.

T

Tabb—Armistead, 104-106; Burgess, 262; Cyc. Va. Biog., I, 335; IV, 209, 283; Duke, etc., 225; Goode, 195; Hayden, 477; "Father Tabb", 1-10; Kennedy I, 55-56; Lancaster, 233-234, 236-237, 242-243; Lee, 382-383; Mackenzie I, 317, 343; Munsell's VI, 125; RS, III, 31, 43; Shepherdstown, 352; TD, Jan. 26, 1908; Feb. 5, 1911; Virkus II. 227; VM, XXII, 82; XXV, 314-315; VCR, IV, VI; VSR, I (No. 3), 43, 49; IV (No. 3), 22; (No. 4), 20-21, 29; WM, III, 117-120; V, 245; VII, 45-49; XIII, 121-128, 168-173, 270-278; XIV, 50-51, 150-154; XXII, 67; XXIV, 259; XXVI, 202-204.
      (*Amelia*)—Southside Va., 122, 183.
      (*Berkeley*)—DAR, 43, p. 32; Tyler's III, 50, 52.
      (*Norfolk Co.*)—McIntosh II, 129, 133.
Taberer—Cyc. Va. Biog., I, 335; VM, XXVII, 53-54; WM, VII, 212, et seq.
Taberner—VM, VI, 117-118.
Tabor—McIntosh I, 175-176; Tazewell II, 145, 156, 164-165, 182.
Taborer—VM, XXVII, 53-54.
Tackett—Monroe Co., 409.
Tait—DAR, 78, p. 141.
Talbert—Brock II, 755.

Talbot—Campbell Co., 508-510; Cyc. Va. Biog., I, 335-336; Du Bellet IV, 86; Habersham Chap. II, 54, 106-110, 146-147, 187, 228-230, 272-273; Virkus III, 83; WM, IX, 257-259; X, 61-62.
(*Bedford*)—Garrard, 82-86; VM, X, 108.
Talbott (Talbot)—VM, X, 108.
(*Fairfax*)—Barbour Co., W. Va., 473-479.
Talbott (Talbutt) (*Norfolk Co.*)—McIntosh II, 147.
Talcott—VSR, I (No. 3), 54.
Taliaferro—BS, July 30, Aug. 6, 1905; Buckners of Va., 106; Burgess, 421, 706-709; Campbell, Pilcher, etc.; Cooke-Booth, 216-218, 229-231; Crawfurdiana, 55-56, 70; Culpeper, part 2, 143; Cyc. Va. Biog., I, 336; IV, 9; Descendants of John Stubbs, 99-100; Du Bellet I, 150-153, 247-248; II, 731-742; Genealogy of the Mercer-Garnett Family; Hayden, 254, 448; Lewis, 15, 31, 160; Marshall, 83-86, 198-201, 313-315; McAllister, 115; McCormick, 162-164; McIlhany, 99; Munsell's IX, 88; Old King William, 100-101; RC, III, 10-12, 15, 17, 20, 22, 24; Roger Jones, 95; RS, II, 47; III, 31, 32, 35, 44, 50; IV, 1, 19, 23; Stubbs, 250-251, 499-501, 512-513; TD, Aug. 13, Sept. 10, Oct. 22, 1905; Oct. 31, Nov. 14, 1909; March 20, May 8, 15, 1910; Jan. 8, 1911; Sept. 14, 28, Oct. 12, 1913; Aug. 16, 1914; Thomas Carter, 294-302; Throckmorton, 342-344; Two Families, 15, 18, 38, 118-123; VHS, Col. VI, 112; VM, V, 74; X, 199, 443; XII, 104-107, 218-219, 321; XVI, 104-107; XXXVII, 171-175; VSR, V (No. 2), 20; Willis, 140-149; WM, III, 118; V, 176; VIII, 126; X, 51; XII, 124-125; XIX, 133-137; XX, 144, 210-214, 266-271; WM 2d, I, 145-166; II, 134-135; IV, 191-199; VII, 271-277; Zimmerman, 29-35.
(*Amherst*)—Gilmer's Georgians, 156-163.
Talley—Bruce IV, 75; Burgess, 710-711; Cyc. Va. Biog., IV, 101; Kennedy I, 653.
Tally (*Louisa*)—Douglas, 45.
Talman—WM, III, 101-104; Cyc. Va. Biog., I, 336.
Tallman—Pocahontas Co., 486-489; Randolph Co., 383-385.
Tandy—McAllister, 69, 74-75, 78-79, 81, 84-85; TD, April 12, 1908; April 27, 1913.
Tankard—DAR, 80, p. 187; MMV, III, 408-409.
Tankersley—Hardesty (*Bedford*), 430; Rockbridge, 533.
Tanner (*Henrico*)—VSR, I (No. 2), 29-30; WM, XXV, 87-95, 198-205.
Tanquary—Cartmell, 484.
Tapley—Rockbridge, 533.
Tapp—Genealogy of the Cloyd, Basye, etc., Families of America, 227-241.
Tapscott—ARP, I, 313; Bruce V, 161; Monroe Co., 409; Rockbridge, 523; WM, VI, 95; VIII, 209; XII, 176, 182.
Tarleton—Cyc. Va. Biog., I, 336.
Tarpley—Cyc. Va. Biog., I, 336; Morton Kin; VM, XXXVII, 60-61; WM, XVII, 153.
Tarrant—VCR, V.
Tarry (*Mecklenburg*)—Hamiltons of Burnside, N. C., 99-101.
Tart—McIntosh I, 180; II, 8, etc.
Tarver—TD, March 3, 1912; VM, XX, 431.
Tate—Crockett, 42-43; Goode, 78b, 142; McIlhany, 100-107; Monongahela II, 740-741; Rockbridge, 533.
(*Augusta*)—McClure, 186, 215-219; Peyton, 312-313; Waddell's Annals of Augusta Co., 311-312.
(*Campbell*)—Campbell Co., 510-511; Clemens' Wills, 93.

(Culpeper)—Culpeper, part 2, 155-156; St. Mark's, 148; Thomas, 92.
(Essex)—Thomas, 103-105.
(Gloucester)—Cyc. Va. Biog., IV, 287.
(High Knob)—Madison Co., Ohio, 798.
(Isle of Wight)—Crocker, 18-26.
(Loudoun)—Adams Co., Ohio, 221-222; Lower Shenandoah, 753.
(Miscellaneous)—Thomas, 589-594.
(Northumberland)—Burgess, 704.
(Orange)—Culpeper, part 2, 155-156; Proceedings of the His. Soc. of East and West Baton Rouge, Vol. II, 26-30.
(Rockingham)—Thomas, 132-133.
(Southampton)—Life of Major General George H. Thomas, 1-2; Thomas Genealogy.
(Surry)—Cyc. Va. Biog., I, 340.
(Vint, Smythe)—Brock II, 756-757.
(Westmoreland)—Boogher, 283-288.
(Wythe)—His. Encyc. of Ill., 522.
Thomasson—Burgess, 704.
Thompkins—Boogher, 329.
(Rappahannock)—Coshocton Co., Ohio, 804.
Thompson—Berkeley, 218-219; Browning. C. D., 38; BS, March 19, 19, 1905; Burgess, 272-273; Campbell Co., 514-515; Hardesty *(Bedford)*, 431; Pendleton Co., 306-307; Ragland, 59-60; Rockbridge, 536; Tazewell Co., II, 540-541; TD, Feb. 11, Aug. 26, Oct. 7, 1906; Feb. 2, 1908; June 30, 1912.
(Albemarle)—Albemarle, 328-330.
(Alexandria)—Old Alexandria, 317.
(Augusta)—Dunmore's War, 43.
(Campbell)—Clemens' Wills, 95.
(Chesterfield)—Stubbs, 474-481.
(Culpeper)—Browning, C. D., 249-250; Culpeper, 79-83, 88; part 2, 86-89; Hayden, 131-132; McIlhany, 50-52; Rootes of Rosewell, 33-34, 43-44, 52-53, 55-58; SBN, XII, 455-456; St. Mark's, 174-177.
(Dinwiddie)—Tyler's IX, 208-209.
(Elizabeth City)—VM, I, 188-190.
(Hanover)—Virkus I, 856; II, 292.
(Highland)—Highland Co., 386-387.
(Jefferson Co.)—Lower Shenandoah, 707.
(Kanawha Co.)—Burgess, 720-722.
(Rev. John)—Crockett, 194-202; LCJ, Dec. 20, 1912; Mackenzie V, 317-319; Munsell's VIII, 181; St. Mark's, 174-177.
(Miscellaneous)—Stubbs, 469-474.
(Nelson)—DAR, 82, p. 279.
(New Kent)—Browning, C. D., 65.
(Richmond)—Virkus III, 424.
(Stevens)—ARP, II, 807; WM, III, 154-162, 215-223.
(Summit Point)—"Old Chapel", 30-31, 35, etc.
(Surry)—VM, XIII, 193-195; WM, VII, 261.
(Waddy)—SHA, IX, 135.
(Warren)—Bruce V, 145.
(West Va.)—Monroe Co., 410.
(William, Culpeper)—Culpeper, part 2, 86-89.
Thomson—Cyc. Va. Biog., I, 339; Douglas, 89-90; Ragland, 61; RS, III, 68; TD, March 24, 1907; WM, III, 154, 215; X, 140.
(Summit Point)—McIlhany, 164-165.
(Waddy)—McAllister, 55-56, 317-318.

Thorburn—Buckners of Va., 120.
Thorn—Virkus III, 34.
Thornborough, Thornbury, Thornberry—VM, XXV, 113.
Thornburg (*Western Va.*)—WVM, I, Oct., 1901, 27.
Thornbury—Cyc. Va. Biog., I, 340; Virkus II, 318; WM, III, 71.
Thornhill—Bruce IV, 87, 449; De Bow's Review, XXXI, 128; Kanawha, 568.
Thornley—TD, Nov. 16, 1913.
Thornton—Buckners of Va., 280-282; Cabell, etc., 282-284; Cooke-Booth, 40-41, 89-91; Cyc. Va. Biog., I, 162, 340-341; Goode; Green's Ky. Families; Hampden-Sidney, 189-190; Hayden, 279; Hening IX, 573-576; His. Encyc. of Ill., 522; Lancaster, 297-300, 305, 307; Lomax, 51-54; Meriwethers, 62; Morton Kin; Notable Families, 96-98; Old King William, 105-106, 142; Rockbridge, 536; Rootes of Rosewell, 35-38; RS, II, 29, 31; III, 5, 21; Sangamon Co., Ill., 714; Sketch and Personal Reminiscences of Judge Anthony Thornton; St. Mark's, 174; TD, Oct. 23, Dec. 25, 1904; April 12, 1908; Nov. 28, 1909; Jan. 2, 1910; April 30, May 21, 1911; Jan. 14, 1912; Thos. Carter, 38-39; VCR, I, II, V-VII; Virkus III, 188, 297, 447-448; VM, V, 74; XXI, 204; XXII, 203-207; XXV, 297; Willis, 134-138; WM, II, 230; III, 71; IV, 89-93, 157-164, 280, 283; V, 58-60, 141-142, 197-200; VI, 53-57, 109-113, 238-244; VIII, 43, 57; X, 182; WM 2d, I, 166.
　(*Dumfries*)—Hayden, 337.
　(*Gloucester*)—Burgess, 627, 629; Cooke-Booth, 89-91; Hardy, 229, 233; Tyler's IV, 123-127; VM, XXVII, 370; WM, II, 80; IV, 89-93, 157-164, 280-281; V, 5-6, 58-60, 141-142; XIX, 111-113.
　(*Halifax*)—Halifax, 248-250.
　(*William*)—Blair, etc., 252. 255-256; Cabell, etc., 282-285; Caroline Co., 474-477; Du Bellet II, 725-730; Goode, 212-216, 356-358, 363; Notable Families, 96-98; TD, Dec. 25, 1904; VM, XXII, 203-207; WM, III, 71; VIII, 57-58; XIX, 111-113; XXIII, 131-132.
Thoroughgood (Thorowgood)—Antiquary I, 126; ARP, I, 347-348; II, 484; Cyc. Va. Biog., I, 341; Ellis, 39, 54; Harrison, Waples, etc., 130-133; Lancaster, 45-47; Mackenzie VII, 76; McIntosh I, 96-97; Norfolk, 488-489; RC, III, 2, 18; RS, IV, 13; TD, Nov. 3, 1907; July 5, 1908; VCR, V, VI, VII; VM, II, 414-418, with chart, 421-422; III, 91, 321-324; Chart in VM, Vol. V; XXVI, 414-416; XXVIII, 175; WM, IV, 170; Yeardley, 6-8.
Thorp—Rockbridge, 535; VHS Col. XI, 74.
　(*Bedford*)—"Genealogy" (Weekes, etc.), Vol. 4, p. 28; Meade I, 198.
　(*Highland*)—Highland Co., 386.
Thorpe—Campbell Co., 515-516; Cyc. Va. Biog., I, 341-342; VM, IV, 134-135; XII, 170-172; XXI, 136; Winston, 307; WM, III, 77, 153-154; IX, 209-211.
　(*George*)—VM, XVII, 398-399.
Threadgall—McIntosh II, 150-151.
Threlkeld—Blair, etc., 250-251; Hayden, 161-162; McIntosh II, 119-120.
Thrift—Burgess, 132; Tyler's, IX, 135.
Throckmorton—Browning, C. D., 38-39, 207; Bruce IV, 146; BS, Oct. 13, 20, 27, Nov. 3, 1907; Burgess, 710-712; Burke's Peerage

and Baronetage (1898), pp. 2262-2263 (Throckmorton of
Ellington and Virginia); Cooke-Booth, 26, 37-38, 40, 170-
177; Cyc. Va. Biog., I, 342; IV, 489; Hayden, 478; Mackenzie (Frazer), I, 523-526; Magna Charta Barons, 187, 189,
224; "Mordecai Cooke", 42-48; Munsell's X, 61; Nat. Cyc.
of Amer. Biog., II, 469; Throckmorton Family, by C.
Wickliffe Throckmorton (Richmond, Va., 1930); Two Families, 170, et seq.; Tyler's VI, 207-208; Virkus I, 858; II,
318-319; III, 207; VM, VI, 409; VIII, 83-89, 129, 309-312;
IX, 192-194; X, 320-321; XIV, 82-84, 204-205, 445-446; XV,
81-82; XIX, 430-431; VSR, V (No. 1), 75; Watson, 249-
259; Watkins, 38; Welles' Washington Genealogy, 170-172;
WM, II, 241-247; III, 46-52, 142-143, 192-195, 240-242, 280;
IV, 128-129, 202; V, 54-55; XIX, 104-107; XXI, 112-114;
XXII, 216; XXVI, 122-124.
    (*Henrico*)—VSR, IV (No. 4), 24-25.
Thruston—Buckners of Va., 210-216; Burgess, 722-727; Cooke-Booth,
    93-95, 263; Cyc. Va. Biog., I, 342; Du Bellet IV, 284-
    294; LEP, Feb. 22, March 19, 1910; Louisville's First
    Families; Lower Shenandoah, 797-800; Mackenzie IV, 530-
    535; McIntosh I, 96, etc.; Md. Soc. Col. Wars, 65; "Mor-
    decai Cooke", 40-41; TD, May 20, 1906; Sept. 27, Oct.
    11, 1908; Two Families, 44-45, 114-115; VCR, I, V, VI;
    Virkus I, 376; III, 55; VM, X, 379; XXIII, 433-434; WM,
    III, 169; IV, 23-28, 116-118, 180-183; V, 44-47, 120-122;
    VI, 13-18; VII, 130-131; VIII, 51-54, 115-119; X, 42-43.
Thuma—Bruce IV, 247.
Thurman—Albemarle, 330; Brock II, 589; Bruce VI, 182; Campbell
    Co., 516-518; N. C. His. Reg., I, 517.
Thurmon—Sketches of Lynchburg, 131-133.
Thweatt—Habersham Chap. II, 26; Rives, 225; Southside Va., 185;
    VM, VII, 354; XV, 213-214; VSR, III (No. 1), 37.
Tibbs—Ritchie Co., 94-96; RS, III, 51.
Tidball—Cartmell, 291-292.
Ticer—Avery I, 191.
Tidd—Rockbridge, 536.
Tiernan—Tiernan and Other Families (1899); TD, June 18, 1905;
    Feb. 1, 1914.
Tiffany—Monroe Co., 410.
    (*Loudoun*)—McIlhany, 239-242.
Tignor—TD, July 23, 1911.
Tilden—Bruce V, 32-33; Cyc. Va. Biog., IV, 465.
Tiller—Bruce IV, 203.
Tillett—Miami Co., Ind., 479, 580.
Tillman—Tillman Genealogy, Nashville, Tenn., 1905; Virkus III, 449;
    VM, XXXIV, 153.
Timberlake—Albemarle, 330-331; Bruce VI, 85; Burgess, 729; Cart-
    mell, 456-457; Lower Shenandoah, 635-636; Miami Co., Ind.,
    463, 480; Middlesex Co. Reg.; TD, Jan. 14, 1906; May 31,
    1908; Feb. 27, 1910; VM, XXVIII, 169-170; XXXIII, 404-
    405.
    (*King William*)—DAR, 45, p. 320.
Timson—Barton II, 85, 140-143; Cyc. Va. Biog., I, 342; TD, March
    19, 1911; Feb. 18, 1912; VCR, V; WM, II, 80, 220, 230;
    III, 208, 273-274; V, 3-6, 196-197; VII, 129.
Tindall (Tyndall)—Cyc. Va. Biog., I, 343; Gentry Family of Va.
Tingler—Pendleton Co., 307; Ritchie Co., 91-92.

Townes—Henry Co., 276-277; Kennedy II, 375; VM, XXI, 195-196.
Townley—RS, III, 23 (Feb. 5, 1881), 38; TD, July 21, 1907; VSR, II (No. 4), 48.
Townsend—McIntosh I, 144.
Townshend—Cyc. Va. Biog., I, 106; Hayden, 732; Highland Co., 342; VM, IX, 173-174; XI, 146-147; XXII, 313-314; XXIII, 124; XXX, 324; WM, XII, 245-246.
Towson—Hayden, 275.
Trabue—Buford, 255-257; Dupuy, 167-169, 259-260, 263-292, 301-324; Huguenot Emigration, 22-23, 167-171; Kith and Kin, 100-101; Meriwethers, 94; VHS, Col. V, 167; VM, IV, 452-453.
Tracy—English Ancestry of Gov. William Tracy of Va. (1620), by Dright Tracy (New Haven, Conn, 1908).
  (*Fauquier*)—Monroe Co., 411.
Trahorne—Cyc. Va| Biog., I, 344.
Trainor—Highland Co., 387.
Travers—ARP, II, 731-733; Cyc. Va. Biog., I, 344; IV, 530; Hayden, 297-301, 741; Lower Shenandoah, 681; Md. Soc. Col. Wars, 109; Meade II, 204; RC, II, 10; RS, III, 18; TD, June 7, 21, 1906; Sept. 8, 1912; WM, IV, 16, and chart, 27, 203.
Travis—Cyc. Va. Biog., I, 344; Hayden, 297; RS, II, 34; TD, Jan. 7, 21, 1906; Virkus III, 404; VM, VI, 192; WM, I, 28; V, 16-17; VI, 60; VII, 249; XIV, 67; XVIII, 141-144.
Traylor—Bristol Par. Reg.; Brock II, 805; Chappell, 346; Cyc. Va. Biog., IV, 277; Henry Co., 99, 277-280; TD, Aug. 20, Dec. 17, 1911; Virkus III, 96.
Treakle—TD, Nov. 8, 1914.
Tredway—Cyc. Va. Biog., IV, 531; V, 728; Hampden-Sidney, 281; Pittsylvania, 205.
Tree—Cyc. Va. Biog., I, 344.
Trenary—Bruce V, 36.
Trent—Cyc. Va. Biog., I, 344; Peyton, 291, 298; SBN, XII, 470-471; VCR, VI; VM, XXXIV, 367-368; XXXV, 440-442; Woodson, 51.
  (*Henrico*)—WM, XXV, 108, 110.
Trevethan—ARP, 789; VM, XXV, 380; XXVIII, 174.
Trevelyan—TD, Feb. 11, 1906.
Trevilian—Brock II, 699-700; Cyc. Va. Biog., IV, 102; Mackenzie II, 506; RS, II; TD, April 1, 1906.
Trevithan—WM, IV, 94.
Trevy—Rockbridge, 537.
Trezevant—TD, June 11, 1906; "Trezevant"; Virkus II, 368; VM, V, 449.
Tribble—Virkus III, 556.
Trice—Cyc. Va. Biog., IV, 501; Kith and Kin, 67-68; Minor, 70.
Trigg—Brock II, 757-760; Bruce VI, 645-648; Clemens' Wills, 97; Convention 1788, II, 367-368; Cyc. Va. Biog., I, 345; Draper Series, V, 212; Dunmore's War, 44; Floyd, 80; Green's Ky. Families, 185-186; Meriwethers, 13; Middlesex Par. Reg.; Montague, 97-98; VCR, I; Virkus III, 381; VM, VII, 252-253; XXVII, 164-165, 323-325.
Trimble—Autobiographical Correspondence of Allen Trimble, Governor of Ohio, with a Genealogy of the Family; Boogher, 309-310; Clemens' Wills, 97; Highland Co., 342-343; Old King William, 25-26; Rockbridge, 537; SBN, XII, 472-474; VCR, II; Waddell's Annals of Augusta Co.
Trindall (*Northampton*)—Harrison, Waples, etc., 87.
Trinkle—Bruce IV, 6; VI, 575.

Triplett—ARP, I, 322-323; Browning, C. D., 354; Bruce IV, 519-528; Cartmell, 444; County Court Note Book, VII, No. 2, p. 15; Cyc. Va. Biog., IV, 208; Fishback Family, 194-195 ,289; Hord (1898), 92-96; LCJ, Aug. 9, 1914; Lindsay, 98-100; Randolph Co., 382-383; VSR, II (No. 1), 62; WM, X, 136-137; XXI, 33-43, 115-134; XXII, 175-181.
Trolinger—Bruce V, 535.
Trollinger—Family of Hoge, 86-87.
Trotter—DAR, 83, p. 195; Habersham Chap. II. 334-338; Rockbridge, 537.
Trout—Cyc. Va. Biog., V, 658-659; Davis, 204; Hardesty (*Amherst*), 445; Licking Co., Ohio, 777; McIlhany, 112-132; Rockbridge, 537.
Trowbridge—Preston Co., 475-476.
Troxal—Rockbridge, 537.
True—VCR, I.
Trueheart—Goode. 220; TD, March 12, 1912.
Trueman—WM, XXV, 285-286.
Trumbo—Alleghany, 212; Custer, 10; Highland Co., 369; Pendleton Co., 307-309.
Truslow—Sketches of Lynchburg, Va., 272.
Trussell—Cyc. Va. Biog., I, 345; Lower Shenandoah, 698; VM, IV, 76.
Tubman—Avery I, 192.
Tuck—Old King William, 141; RS, III.
Tucker—Bristol Parish, 159; BS, Aug. 14, 1904; Hardesty (*Amherst*), 475; Ritchie Co., 141-142; Rockbridge, 276-277; Sketches of Lynchburg, Va., 172; St. Peter's Par. Reg.; TD, April 3, 1904; Sept. 30, 1906; VCR, III, V, VI, VII.
   (*Alexandria*)—SBN, XII, 479-480.
   (*Bermuda*)—Cyc. Va. Biog., I, 85. See also "St. George," below.
   (*Botetourt*)—Kanawha, 616.
   (*Brunswick*)—Carolinians II, 276; Goode, 66-67, 125-126, 243-244. 348.
   (*Elizabeth City*)—VM, I, 193.
   (*St. George*)—McAllister, 121, 125.
   (*Lunenburg*)—Virkus II, 234.
   (*Mecklenburg*)—Virkus I, 865.
   (*Norfolk*)—Cyc. Va. Biog., I, 345; Forrest's History of Norfolk, Va., 56; Hardy, 174; McIntosh II, 105-106, etc.; VCR, III, 57-58; VM, IV, 360-363.
   (*St. George*)—An Account of the Tucker Family of Bermuda, by T. A. Emmet (New York, 1898); Bolling Gen., by Robt. Bolling (1868); Browning, R. D., III, 722-724; Bruce V, 4; Cyc. Va. Biog., IV, 37-38; V, 861-862; Ellis, 47; Habersham Chap. II, 32-34; Hayden, 217; Kennedy II, 163-173; Life of Gen. Hugh Mercer, 135, 138; Mackenzie V, 509-513; MMV, I, 324-325; III, 418-419; V, 424, 427; RC, III, 1, 5; SBN, XII, 478-481; Tucker Family Tree, by Edward Tucker, Esq., of Bermuda; Virkus I, 863-864; VM, V, 350; IX, 63; Xl, 217-218; XV, 201; XVII, 394-397; XXVI, 311, 406; XXVII, 181; XXIX, 146, 153-154, 354-355; VSR, I (No. 1), 5 (Gen. Sec.); IV (No. 2), 26; Welles' Washington Genealogy; WM, V, 144-145; VI, 50; XVII, 267-268.
   (*Westmoreland*)—VM, I, 268-270.
   (*William*)—VM, XXII, 267-268.
Tuggle—Thos. Carter, 79-81; WM. XIX, 189-190.
Tuley—His. Encyc. of Ill., 529; LEP, April 19, 1919, p. 6.
Tully—McIntosh II, 17, 255.

Tunnell—Armstrong III, 127-129, 288-291; Burgess, 741-742; WM 2d, VIII, 63-64.
Tunstall—Bruce IV, 382, 459; Cyc. Va. Biog., I, 345; IV, 261, 329; V, 1121-1122; Halifax, 341-342; MMV, II, 385-386; Norfolk, 537, 945-947; Pittsylvania, 97; TD, Sept. 22, 1912; VCR, II, VI; VM, IX, 311; XIV, 124-125, 438-440, 444-445; VSR, IV (No. 4), 40.
    (*King and Queen*)—DAR, 55, p. 204.
Turberville (Turbeville)—Burgess, 743-744; Cyc. Va. Biog., I, 345; Fothergill, 112, 204; Hardy, 513-516; Lee, 93-96; Meade II, 146; TD, March 18, April 8, 15, Sept. 16, 1906; VCR, V; WM, IV, 254; V, 250, 281; VII, 95.
Tureman—VCR, I.
Turk—DAR, 59, p. 274; MMV, II, 389-391; Rockbridge, 537.
Turley—WM, XXII, 184-185; WM 2d, I, 295-296.
Turman—Bruce V, 500; Cyc. Va. Biog., IV, 544.
Turnbull—Bruce VI, 405; Burgess, 744-745; Cyc. Va. Biog., IV, 281, 393; Johnston's Old Va. Clerks; TD, June 20, 1909.
Turner—BS, Jan. 22, 1905; Aug. 25, Sept. 18, 1907; Bullock and Allied Families; Henry Co., 272-280; Pendleton Co., 309; Rockbridge, 537; RS, III, 5; IV, 1; St. Mark's, 179; St. Peter's Par. Reg.; TD, Oct. 23, 1904; April 29, 1906; Feb. 23, May 3, 1908; Dec. 26, 1909; April 3, 1910; May 19, June 2, 16, 1912; WM, I, 28; IX, 174; WM 2d, VI, 202.
    (*Albemarle*)—Albemarle, 333.
    (*Amherst*)—Virkus III, 190.
    (*Bedford*)—Foote II, 190-192.
    (*Dinwiddie*)—BHNC, VI, 451, 463.
    (*Essex*)—Cyc. Va. Biog., I, 346.
    (*Fauquier*)—Bruce VI, 246; Family Record of the Moreheads (Los Angeles), 33-35, 38-39.
    (*Henrico*)—N. C. His. Reg., I, 492.
    (*Isle of Wight and Southampton*)—Virkus II, 284.
    (*King George*)—Browning, R. D., III, 70-71; Bruce VI, 246; Cyc. Va. Biog., I, 345-346; Hayden, 637-638; Roger Jones, 181; Virkus III, 529; VM, XX, 438-440; XXI, 106-109, 211-212, 315-316, 421; XXII, 103.
    (*Prince Edward*)—Johnson Co., Ky., 556.
    (*Richmond Co.*)—Meade II, 186.
    (*Valley of Va.*)—Cartmell, 501-502.
    (*West Va.*)—Panhandle, 357.
Turnley—Armstrong I, 221-242; DAR, 76, p. 67.
Turpin—Bruce IV, 378; Bullington Chart, by Arthur B. Clarke (Va. State Library); Hampden-Sidney, 58-59; Lancaster, 163-164; Mackenzie II, 27; MMV, IV, 403-404; TD, April 26, May 3, 1908; VCR, VI; Virkus II, 183; WM, XXV, 108, 110-111.
    (*Bedford*)—Hardesty, 431-432; WM 2d, VIII, 317.
Tuthill—Keith, 85-86.
Tutt—ARP. II, 818; Burgess, 934, 1048; Culpeper, 100; Hayden, 108; Throckmorton, 373; VCR, I, II; Virkus II, 319; III, 399.
Tuttle—Burgess, 896; TD, July 17, 1904; Oct. 13, 1907.
Tutwiler—Cabell, etc., 354; Clan Gregor Year Book (1926-1927), 58; Virkus II, 111; III, 453.
Twiford—WM 2d, VIII, 40.
Twisdell—Burgess, 879-880.
Twyman—Albemarle, 333-334; Bruce IV, 215, 260; Buford, 23; TD, March 9, 1912; VCR, I; Virkus III, 224, 556.

Tyler—Bruce VI, 464; Campbell's His. of Va., 723; Goode, 121; RC (1888), I, 49; TD, Aug. 16, 1903; Nov. 6, 1904; Aug. 31, Sept. 7, 1913; The Tylers of Mass., Conn., R. I., Va. and N. J., by W. Tyler Brigham.
(*Caroline*)—Caroline Co., 212-215; Cyc. Va. Biog., IV, 284-285; MMV, I, 68-71.
(*Charles City*)—Brock II, 700; Bruce IV, 10; Tyler's X, 198-203.
(*Essex*)—Cyc. Va. Biog., I, 346-347; WM, XII, 120-121; XIX, 279-286.
(*Henry*)—Letters and Times of the Tylers (Richmond, 1884), I, 35-66, 194-195, 271-273.
(*Kentucky and Missouri*)—Tyler's X, 276-280.
(*Mecklenburg*)—WM, XXI, 71.
(*Prince William*)—Burgess, 745; Hayden, 166; WM, XVI, 66-67.
(*Stafford*)—WM, XVII, 68-69.
(*Westmoreland*)—Cyc. Va. Biog., I, 346; Tyler's V, 252-256; WM, XXI, 22-25.
(*York*)—Armistead, 234-238; Brock I, 103-108, 140-152; Bruce V, 61; Cyc. Va. Biog., V, 861; Lancaster, 73-75; MMV, I, 208-211, 357-362; Munsell's III, 145; Tyler's VIII, 144, 209-212; VHS Col. XI, 70, 78; Virkus I, 373; II, 225; WM, I, 103-104; III, 139-140; XVII, 68-69, 231-235.
(*York, etc.*)—Cyc. Va. Biog., I, 346.
Tynes—Tazewell Co., II, 542-543; Kilby, Tynes, etc., 15-19; Virkus III, 598.
Tyree—Brock II, 589; Campbell Co., 518-519.
Tyson—Thomas Book; Virkus III, 450.

U

Underhill—Burgess, 363, 813; TD, July 21, 1912; VCR, II, V, VI; VM, XVI, 94.
(*York*)—WM, II, 85.
Underwood—Cyc. Va. Biog., I, 347; Middlesex Par. Reg.; TD, Nov. 8, 1914; VCR, II, VI; VM, III, 65-66; WM, VII, 221; X, 275-276; Virkus III, 211.
(*Lancaster*)—Hayden, 161-162; Rockbridge, 537; SBN, IX, 490-491; Thos. Carter, 104; Two Families, 97.
Unrew—Rockbridge, 537.
Updike—Hardesty (*Bedford*), 432.
Upshaw—Cyc. Va. Biog., I, 347; Convention 1788, II, 372; TD, June 29, 1913.
Upshur (Upshaw)—Burgess, 812; TD, Nov. 12, 1905; March 5, 1911.
Upshur—ARP, II, 482; Cyc. Va. Biog., I, 347; IV, 35; Lancaster, 486-488; Md. Soc. Col. Wars, 21-22; MMV, V, 432-433; R. W. Johnson, 6-7; SBN, XII, 491-492; Wise's Eastern Shore, 279; WM, III, 256, 260; VII, 108; WM 2d, VIII, 39-40; Yeardley, 18-19, 29-30, 33.
Upshur-Nottingham—Brock II, 805-806; Bruce IV, 161-162.
Upton—Cyc. Va. Biog., I, 347; TD, Sept. 22, Oct. 13, 1907; Thomas Carter, 101; Two Families, 98; VCR, VI; VM, III, 60-66; VI, 36-38; XXIII, 10.
Urquhart—Bruce VI, 539; Goode, 181-182; Stubbs, 454-455.
Usher—Bath Co., 201.
Utie—Cyc. Va. Biog., I, 93-94; VM, XVII, 104; XIX, 374-375; XXVIII, 97; WM, IV, 52-58.
Utter—Rockbridge, 537.

Utterback—Barbour Co., W. Va., 487; Sangamon Co., Ill., 734.
Utz—WM, XXVI, 189-190.
Uzzell (*Isle of Wight*)—Maxwell, 335-352.

V

Vaden—Woodson, 649.
Vaiden (*New Kent*)—Old King William, 178-183.
Valentine—Burgess, 815-816; Cyc. Va. Biog., IV, 69; Huguenot Emigration, 142-143; Kennedy II, 377; MMV, I, 365-368; Valentine IV, 2059-2071, 2324-2368; VSR, IV (No. 1), 37.
   (*Norfolk*)—Burgess, 815-816; McIntosh I, 23, 169, 198; II, 186.
Vallandigham—Draper Series V, 58; WVM, IV, 36.
Van Bibber—WVM, II, 35; III, 213-225.
Van Buskirk—Shenandoah, 656.
Vance—Armstrong II, 331-335, 340, 346; Bath Co., 201; Cartmell, 411, 414; Hayden, 457-458; Highland Co., 370; King's Mountain, 474; Monongahela II, 731-732; III, 1281; Montgomery Co., Ohio (TH), 437; Pendleton Co., 309-310; Rockbridge, 537; Shenandoah, 656-657; TD, Oct. 10, 1909; VCR, II; VM, XII, 438.
Vancil—Sangamon Co., Ill., 735.
Vanderslice—Bruce IV, 544.
Vandervort—Monongahela II, 734-736.
Vandeventer, Van Deventer—Highland Co., 370; Mathews Family, 56; Pendleton Co., 310-311; Rockbridge, 537.
Vanhoose—Johnson Co., Ky., 562.
Van Mater (*Berkeley Co.*)—Tyler's VII, 50.
Van Meter—Berkeley Co., 207, 208; Cartmell, 10-15; Convention 1788; Lower Shenandoah, 697; Van Meter, 47-165; Van Meter Family of Va. and Ky., by B. F. Van Meter (1901); VM, XIII, 115-116, 119; WM 2d, VIII, 59; WVM, II, April, 1902, 5-18; IV, 224, 232.
Van Metre, Van Meter, Van Metear—Cyc. Va. Biog., I, 347; Duke, etc., 3-137, 399-403; Origin and Descent of the American Van Metre Family.
Vansandt—Rockingham, 537.
Van Swearingen—DAR, 59, p. 15.
Van Zandt—Burgess, 771; RS, III, 16.
Varner—Highland Co., 370-371; Pendleton Co., 311; Pocahontas Co., 327-331; Woods-McAfee, 321-325.
Vass—Carolinians II, 471-472; Huguenot Emigration, 126; Marshall, 190; Tyler's IX, 275; VCR, I; VM, XIV, 107-108.
Vasser—VM, VI, 247; WM, VII, 220.
Vaughan—Alston and Allstons, 168-170; Bristol Par. Reg.; Burgess, 657, 819-822; Douglas, 311; Goode, 247-249; Johnson Co., Ky., 571; Rives, 258; St. Peter's Par. Reg.; TD, March 26, 1905; Sept. 25, 1906; May 26, June 23, 1907; VCR, I, II, VI.
   (*Botetourt*)—Cooke-Booth, 91.
   (*Goochland*)—Griffith-Meriwether, 164-169.
   (*Orange*)—Monroe Co., 412.
Vause—Burgess, 42-43; Middlesex Par. Reg.
Vaux, Vaulx—Cyc. Va. Biog., I, 347; Fothergill, 142; WM, III, 153; IV, 42; XIV, 178.
Vawter—Ancestry and Descendants of Lieut. John Henderson, 24-28; Burgess, 819; Maxwell, 459-468; Monroe Co., 412-413; TD,

W

Waddill—Bruce IV, 31; Cabell, etc., 314-316; Cyc. Va. Biog., V, 750; Major, 135-137, 139-153, 186-188; TD, Oct. 1, 8, 1916; VM, XXVII, 80, 354.
Waddy—TD, Sept. 6, 1914; Valentine III, 1579-1592; VSR, II (No. 3), 33.
(*Northumberland*)—WM, XXV, 254-267.
Wade—Campbell Co., 521-523; Chappell, 285-295; Cyc. Va. Biog., I, 348; Halifax, 251-252, 343-344; Pittsylvania, 76; Rockbridge, 537; VSR, V (No. 2), 45.
(*Highland*)—Highland Co., 343-345.
(*Prince Edward*)—Hampden-Sidney, 97.
(*York*)—Armistead, 214; Hayden, 571; WM, I, 90-91.
Wagener—Cyc. Va. Biog., I, 348-349; Old Prince William II, 433-434; VM, XXXIII, 56.
(*Fairfax*)—VM, VIII, 60.
Wager—Cyc. Va. Biog., I, 349.
Waggaman—WM, II, 98, 135.
Waggy—Braxton Co., W. Va., 446; Highland Co., 371; Pendleton Co., 312-313.
Wagner—Bruce IV, 266; VI, 510.
Wagoner—Highland Co., 345-346; Pendleton Co., 313.
Waite (*Fauquier*)—Monroe Co., 413-414.
Wakefield—McIntosh I, 193, 196; II, 22.
Walcott—Madison Co., Ohio, 868.
Walden—Burgess, 207, 842; Campbell Co., 523-524; Pittsylvania, 140.
Waldo—Ritchie Co., 146-147.
Waldoe—VCR, V.
Waldrup—RS, II.
Walford—Bruce IV, 128.
Walke—Brock II, 682-683; Cyc. Va. Biog., IV, 295-296; McIntosh I, 147-148; II, 312; Norfolk, 619-620, 748-749; Robertson, 33, 38, 40, 50; RS, III, 50-52; VCR, III, V; VM, V, 89, 139-152; XXVI, 412-413; WM, II, 75-76.
(*Princess Anne*)—Chart in Vol. V, VM.
Walker—Bristol Par. Reg.; BS, March 3, 10, 17, 24, 1907; Burgess, 844-848; Cyc. Va. Biog., V, 694-695; Fry Genealogy; Lower Shenandoah, 605, etc.; Meade II, 43; Old King William; Pendleton Co., 313; RS, II, 47; III, 6, 29, 35; IV, 2; TD, April 10, 1904; April 21, 1907; April 5, 1908; Nov. 20, 1910; June 29, 1913; May 17, 1914; April 9, June 27, July 4, 11, 25, Aug. 1, 1915; Oct. 29, 1916; VCR, I-IV, VI-VII; WM, XXIII, 295.
(*Albemarle*)—Du Bellet II, 708; Watson, 92-98.
(*Albemarle and King and Queen*)—Albemarle, 334-336.
(*Augusta*)—Green's Ky. Families, 51-54.
(*Augusta—Walker of Wigton*)—Virkus I, 44; Walker-Wigton, VII-XXX, 1-722.
(*Botetourt*)—Woods-McAfee, 125-126, 319-320.
(*Charles City*)—Baskerville Family, 89, 95-97; Burgess, 845-846; WM, XVI, 139-140; XX, 33-35; XXI, 268-269.
(*Craig*)—Kanawha, 854.
(*Cumberland*)—DAR, 78, p. 148; Virkus III, 20.
(*Dinwiddie*)—ARP, I, 324; Bristol Parish, 232-233.
(*Elizabeth City*)—Cyc. Va. Biog., I, 349; Ruvigny, 532-533; VM, XVI, 79; WM, IX, 127-128; XVIII, 289-290.
(*Essex*)—Kanawha, 432.
(*Frederick*)—Bruce VI, 48.
(*George*)—VSR, V (No. 2), 55.

(*Giles*)—Bruce IV, 264; V, 279.
(*Goochland*)—Dupuy, 218-221.
(*Hanover*)—VM, XXXV, 191-193.
(*Henrico*)—Bullington Chart, by Arthur B. Clark (Va. State
    Library).
(*James City*)—WM, XX, 33-35.
(*John*)—John Walker of Wigton, Scotland and of Virginia, by
    Emma S. White (1902).
(*John, Rappahannock*)—WM, VI, 61-62.
(*Jaseph*)—WM, V, 65-66.
(*King and Queen*)—Bagby, 70, 72, 349, 360-363; Cabell, etc., 411-
    414; Cyc. Va. Biog., I, 349-350; Dinwiddie Papers I, 412;
    Green's Ky. Families, 154-158; Kennedy I, 469-475; Lancaster,
    396-402; Mackenzie VI, 15-16; Notable Families, 86-93; Old
    King William, 107; RS, III, 29; SBN, XII, 505; Virkus III,
    630-631; VM, IV, 357-359; X, 96; XIX, 187-188; XXVII,
    353; WM, II, 271; VI, 61; VIII, 17; XIX, 214-215.
(*King and Queen, etc.*)—Page (2d ed.), 199-234.
(*Mecklenburg*)—WM, XXIII, 295.
(*Middlesex*)—Middlesex Par. Reg.; Stubbs, 369; VM, I, 470-
    471; WM, VIII, 96, 133, 276; XVIII, 59.
(*New Kent*)—St. Peter's Par. Reg.
(*Norfolk Co.*)—Burgess, 846.
(*Northampton*)—Cyc. Va. Biog., I, 349.
(*Orange*)—Cyc. Va. Biog., I, 349.
(*Orange and Rockingham*)—Bruce VI, 592.
(*Petersburg*)—WM, XIV, 113.
(*Prince George*)—WM, XIV, 138.
(*Rockbridge*)—Monroe Co., 414; Rockbridge, 537-539; Virkus
    II, 70; Woods-McAfee, 325-326.

(*Rockingham*)—His. Encyc. of Ill., 548.
(*Sussex*)—Life of Gen. Hugh Mercer, 130-131.
(*Urbanna*)—WM, VIII, 133.
(*Warwick*)—Cyc. Va. Biog., I, 124.
(*Westmoreland*)—Bruce V, 158, 405.
Walkup—Houston Genealogy, 140; Rockbridge, 539.
Wall—Bristol Par. Reg.; VM, XXXIII, 183.
(*Winchester*)—Cartmell, 462.
Wallace—Genealogical Data Pertaining to the Descendants of Peter
    Wallace and Elizabeth Woods, His Wife, compiled by
    George Selden Wallace (Huntington, W. Va.); St. Mark's;
    Wallace of Virginia (1870), chart.
(*Albemarle*)—Kith and Kin, 95-96, 127; Wallace Family in
    America; Woods-McAfee, 3-9, 97, 109-110, 142, 322-323, 355-
    366.
(*Augusta*)—McClure, 220; Wallace, 773-778.
(*Bath*)—Bath Co., 202; Cyc. Va. Biog., IV, 466; Wallace IV, V.
(*Charlotte*)—Draper Series, V. 137; Green's Ky. Families, 147-148.
(*Elizabeth City*)—Armistead, 146; Cyc. Va. Biog., I, 351; Hay-
    den, 102; Kennedy I, 225-231; VM, VIII, 63-64; WM, III,
    168; IX, 130-131; XIII, 177-182.
(*Highland*)—Highland Co., 371.
(*King George*)—Hayden, 685-735; McAllister, 125.
(*Montgomery*)—Knox Co., Ill., 892.
(*Norfolk Co.*)—McIntosh I, 177, 190; II, 77, 308 (Wallis).
(*Rev. James*)—Cyc. Va. Biog., I, 350.

(*Rockbridge*)—Burgess, 1299; Clemens' Wills, 100; MMV, V, 436-437; Monroe Co., 414; Rockbridge, 277, 539-540.
(*Spotsylvania*)—Cyc. Va. Biog., I, 351.
Waller—ARP, II, 793-798; Bolling Family, by Robert Bolling (1868); Browning, C. D., 3d, 617; Bruce V, 204; Cyc. Va. Biog., I, 351; V, 736-737; Bruton Church; Middlesex Par. Reg.; Garrard, 46-48; Hayden, 382; Henry Co., 280-284; Kennedy I, 580; Mackenzie III, 369; Old King William, 108-109; TD, Dec. 18, 1904; April 16, June 18, 1905; Nov. 7, 28, Dec. 19, 1909; Jan. 9, Feb. 6, March 20, June 26, Aug. 21, Sept. 25, Oct. 23, 1910; Sept. 10, Oct. 29, Dec. 17, 1911; Jan. 21, 1912; Feb. 8, 15, Nov. 15, 22, 29, Dec. 6, 1914; Jan. 24, 31, 1915; VCR, I, II, V, VI; Virkus II, 95; III, 32-33; VM, XXVI, 32-35; XXXVI, 381-384.
(*John*)—Caroline Co., 480-485; RS, II, 34.
(*King William*)—WM, VIII, 79; IX, 63-64; X, 118-120, 278; XIII, 175-177.
(*Spotsylvania*)—Armistead, 177-179; Biography of William S. Waller, with family genealogy; Burgess, 1056; Cabell, etc.; Culpeper, 98; Hayden, 382-383; Kennedy II, 186; Lewis, 149-150; Life of Gen. Hugh Mercer, by J. T. Goolrick, 128, 131-132; Mackenzie II, 420-421; Marshall, 241-242; McAllister, 116; Munsell's XI, 143; RC, III ,26; RS, II, 34, 36, 40; III, 6; Two Families, 42-44; VM, VIII, 110; IX, 328; XXVI, 32-33, 275-276, 410; WM, X, 118-120, 278; VSR, V (No. 2), 60-61.
(*Stafford*)—Adams Co., Ohio, 276-277; Du Bellet I, 111-113; Hardy, 144-145; McIlhany, 79-81; Munsell's XI, 143.
Wallop—Hening V, 83-85.
Walpole—Tyler's VIII, 272-275.
Walters—DAR, 46, p. 250.
Walthall—SBN, XII, 510; Walthall Family; TD, Feb. 4, 1906; Aug. 20, Sept. 10, 24, 1911; May 30, June 6, 13, 27, 1915; VCR, VI; VM, X, 320.
Walthoe—Cyc. Va. Biog., I, 357.
Walton—BS, Nov. 20, 1904; BHNC, VIII, 123; Crozier's Va. County Records, VI, 261-263; Habersham Chap. II, 450, 494, 673-674; Hampden-Sidney, 190-191; Harris Genealogy, 101-104; Hughes, etc., 18-19, 77-109; John Price the Emigrant, etc., 40-41; Researcher II, 63; RS, I, 4, 88; II, 2, 6; III, 27; Stubbs, 217; TD, March 24, 1907; April 4, 1909; April 23, 1911; May 24, 1914; April 16, 1916; The Waltons of Va., Gulf State Hist. Mag., Vol. II, 1903 (Mrs. W. C. Stubbs); VCR, VI, VII; Woodson, 308, 324, 331, 483, 619.

(*Brunswick*)—Cyc. Va. Biog., I, 351.
(*Cumberland*)—Bruce IV, 13; WM, XV, 279-280; WM 2d, VI, 344-350.
(*Hanover*)—DAR, 72, p. 309.
(*New Kent*)—St. Peter's Par. Reg.
(*Louisa*)—Cyc. Va. Biog., IV, 295.
(*Prince Edward*)—N. C. His. Reg., II, 154.
(*Shenandoah*)—Shenandoah, 297, etc.
Wampler—Bruce IV, 314.
Wanless—Ritchie Co., 174-175.
Wanstaff—Monroe Co., 414; Pendleton Co., 325.
Waples—Harrison, Waples, etc., 76, et seq.
Warburton—WM, XVI, 237.

Ward—Cyc. Va. Biog., I, 351-352; Goode, 109-110, 203-209, 275, 343-
348, 416; Grayson Co., 73-75; Pendleton Co., 313-314, 325;
Rockbridge, 540; Tazewell Co., II, 544-546; TD, July 9,
1905; Aug. 18, Nov. 3, 17, 1907; June 26, 1910; May 10,
1914; WM 2d, IX, 148.
  (*Campbell*)—Campbell Co., 525-529; WM, XVI, 286-287.
  (*Culpeper*)—Cyc. Va. Biog., V, 754.
  (*Greenbrier*)—Dunmore's War, 276.
  (*Henrico*)—RC, II, 5; WM, XXVII, 185-189, 258-293.
  (*Norfolk*)—Antiquary; Cyc. Va. Biog., V, 899; McIntosh I, 29;
II, 35, 190, 241, etc.
  (*Pittsylvania*)—Cabell, etc., 546; VM, XXIV, 180.
  (*Sheffield*)—VM, II, 312-313.
  (*West Va.*)—Randolph Co., 401-403.
  (*William*)—VM, XV, 83.
Warden (*Augustine-Hardy*)—Bruce V, 187-188.
  (*Norfolk Co.*)—McIntosh I, 127; II, 98.
Warder—Family Record of the Moreheads (Los Angeles, n. d.), 45-
51, 64.
Wardlaw—Rockbridge, 540.
Ware—Bagby, 363; Barbour Co., W. Va., 512; Braxton Co., 447; BS,
Oct. 9, 1904; Cyc. Va. Biog., I, 352; Du Bellet III, 89-94,
157; Hardesty (*Amherst*), 445; Hayden, 23, 36, 39-42, 44;
McIlhany, 107-108; (Ware-Warr); Middlesex Par. Reg.;
TD, May 12, 1907; Aug. 3, 10, 1913; June 4, 1916; VCR, I,
VI; WM, V, 282.
Wareham—Cyc. Va. Biog., I, 352.
Warfield—Burgess, 848-849; RS, III, 28.
Waring—Bowies and Their Kin; Burgess, 850-852; Coshocton Co.,
Ohio, 899; Cyc. Va. Biog., I, 352; Hayden, 116; Old King
William, 77; Roger Jones, 135-137; TD, June 17, July 22,
29, Aug. 12, 19, 1906; June 12, Aug. 21, 1910; VM, V, 191-
192; X, 100-101; XI, 103-104, 209-210; XXXII, 63; Winston,
161.
Warman—Braxton Co., W. Va., 445-446.
Warner—ARP, II, 439-440; Browning, C. D., 251-255; BS, June 25,
1905; Cyc. Va. Biog., I, 124, 135; Du Bellet IV, 1-48;
Funsten-Meade, 71-72; Hening VIII, 484-485, 630-631; Lan-
caster, 247-249; McAllister, 22-23, 167-169; Notable Fam-
ilies, 69-71; Pendleton Co., 314-315, 325; RC, III, 4; RS,
III, 25, 38, 52; IV, 23; TD, Oct. 20, 1912; VCR, V, VI;
VM, II, 423; XXIII, 395; Watson, 57-58; Willis, 115-117;
WM, II, 226-227, 235; III, 165; IV, 51; IX, 264; VSR, V
(No. 1), 74.
  (*Fairfax*)—Madison Co., Ohio, 952-953.
Warren—Cyc. Va. Biog., 1, 352; Bruce VI, 484; RS, II, 47; VCR,
I, II, V-VII; VM, VI, 200-205.
  (*Essex*)—Virkus III, 344; VM, XVII, 444-445.
  (*New Kent*)—St. Peter's Par. Reg.
  (*Rockingham*)—Monroe Co., 414.
  (*Surry*)—Lancaster, 151-152; WM, VIII, 151-152.
Warrington—Burgess, 15-16; Meade I, 232; WM, XII, 198.
Warth—DAR, 53, p. 15.
Warthen—Randolph Co., 397.
Washbourn—Cyc. Va. Biog., 352.
Washburn—Harrison Co., 385.
Warvel—Montgomery Co., Ohio, 389.

Warwick—Buford, 23; Burgess, 368; Cyc. Va. Biog., IV, 216; Hampden-Sidney, 249-250; Randolph Co., 398-399; Rockbridge, 540; Sketches of Lynchburg, 235-238; TD, Jan. 14, Sept. 15, 1912.

(*Western Va.*)—WVM, II, July, 1902, 51-59.

(*William and Jacob*)—Bath Co., 202.

Washington—Burgess, 852-854; Cyc. Va. Biog., I, 352-353; RS, II, 5; TD, Feb. 21, May 15, Sept. 25, 1904; Aug. 27, Nov. 19, 1905; July 12, Dec. 13, 1908; March 28, Dec. 19, 1909; June 15, 22, 1913; March 19, June 25, 1916; VM, XX, 50; WM, X, 113-115.

(*Berkeley*)—Tyler's III, 51-52.

(*Caroline*)—Caroline Co., 485-486; WM, XX, 32-33.

(*Edward, Fairfax*)—VM, XXIV, 197.

(*Edward*)—McCue, 196-214; Old Prince William I, 275-276.

(*John*)—Munsell's VIII, 162.

(*John, Surry*)—Cyc. Va. Biog., I, 353.

(*Surry*)—Tyler's III, 142-143; VII, 45-49, 124-134; TD, March 19, 1916; VM, XXX, 306; WM, III, 71-74; XXIII, 178-180.

(*Westmoreland*)—An Examination of the English Ancestry of George Washington, etc. (Henry F. Waters, Boston); ARP, II, 407-408; Bolling Genealogy, 64; Browning, C. D., 253, 259; Buckners of Va., 150-152, 201; Campbell's History of Va., 456; Du Bellet II, 104-105; IV, 46-66; Ford's Washington Family Wills; Funsten-Meade, 73-76; Glenn's Some Colonial Mansions; Habersham Chap. II, 119-121; Hardy, 517-529; Harper's New Monthly Mag., March, 1879; Hayden, 79-82, 478, 517-522, 633-636; Heraldic Journal (1866), II, 66-74, 145-146; Kennedy I, 343-363; II, 52, 86-87; Lancaster, 356-362; Lee, 209-215; Lewis, 15-25; Lineage Book, Order of Washington, 228-251; McAllister, 169-174; Mackenzie I, 100, 561-564; II, 37-39, 52, 278, 740-746; IV, 368-369; Maternal Ancestry and Nearest of Kin of Washington, by N. R. Ball (Washington, 1885); Meade II, 166-169; Middlesex Par. Reg.; Munsell's IV, 243; V, 35; VIII, 162; New Eng. Hist. and Gen. Reg., Oct., 1889; Neill's Life of Washington, 1892; N. Y. Gen. and Biog. Record, XXXIII; "Old Chapel", 31; RS, II, 5; III, 37; SBN, 528-529; Southern Bivouac (1886); Sparks' Origin and Genealogy of the Washington Family (Boston, 1847); Thos. Carter, 288-289; Twing's Life of Washington, 1-7; Tyler's IV, 135, 315-380; VI, 61-64, 144-145; VII, 45-49, 124-134; VIII, 73-119, 217-241; IX, 34-38; XI, 93; VCR, I-VII; VM, XIV, 443; XV, 6; XXII, 211-214, 314, 328-330, 437-438; XXIII, 96-101, 203-205; XXVI, 311, 417-421; XXX, 18-20; XXXIII, 154-165; Washington Family in America, by Thornton F. Washington (1891); Watson, 169-170, 207-304; Welles' Washington Genealogy; WM, I, 183-189; II, 38-49, 137-138, 225-226, 235; III, 71-74; IV, 28-43, 75-89; V, 209-210; VI, 62-63; XIII, 145-148 (Will of John Washington); XV, 132-134, 204-205; XX, 32-33.

(*West Virginia*)—Kanawha, 618-619.

Waskey—Rockbridge, 540.

Wass—Ritchie Co., 98.

Wasson (*Rockbridge*)—Adams Co., Ohio, 633-634, 896-897, 910-911; Rockbridge, 540.

Waters—Cyc. Va. Biog., I, 353-354; TD, May 29, 1904 (Mary), Dec. 28, 1913; VCR, V, VII; Winston, 74-84.

Waugh—Cabell, etc., 291-292; Cyc. Va. Biog., I, 354; Grayson Co., 47-50; Hayden, 301; Pocahontas Co., 336-342; Price, 107-110; TD, April 21, 1907; VM, XXXVII, 161-162; WM, XV, 189-190; XVII, 69; XX, 154; WM 2d, I, 154.
Way—TD, Sept. 24, 1911.
Waybright—Highland Co., 346; Pendleton Co., 315.
Wayland—Bruce IV, 169, 328; WM, XXVI, 240-243.
Wayles—Cyc. Va. Biog., I, 354; WM, II, 273; VI, 63.
Wayne—RS, I, 40.
Wayt—Albemarle, 340; Peyton, 318.
Weakley—Halifax, 349.
Wear (*Augusta*)—Armstrong I, 16-19; II, 345-353.
Weaver—Cyc. Va. Biog., IV, 219; Miami Co., Ohio, 641; Montgomery Co., Ohio (TH), 391; Rockbridge, 541; VCR, IV, VI; WM, XVI, 237; XXVI, 243-245.
   (*New Kent*)—St. Peter's Par. Reg.
Webb—County Court Note Book (Ljungstedt), Vols. I, II, III; Miami Co., Ohio, 540; TD, March 5, 1905; VCR, I-III, V-VII; WM, VII, 256; WM 2d, VI, 63.
   (*Essex*)—Tyler's VII, 191-198, 269-277; VIII, 52-64; VM, XXIII, 91; WM, XXVI, 67.
   (*Gloucester*)—Cyc. Va. Biog., I, 355; Virkus III, 320.
   (*Henrico*)—VM, XXVI, 21.
   (*James City*)—Cyc. Va. Biog., I, 355.
   (*Middlesex*)—Middlesex Par. Reg.
   (*Miscellaneous*)—Stubbs, 363-364; Tyler's VII, 191-194.
   (*Nansemond*)—Cyc. Va. Biog., I, 354-355; Tyler's VII, 194.
   (*New Kent*)—Cyc. Va. Biog., I, 354-355; Lancaster, 261-264; St. Peter's Par. Reg.; Virkus III, 153; VM, XXV, 99-100, 210-212, 330-331; XXIX, 370; XXXV, 297-298; WM, V, 281; WM 2d, VIII, 117.
   (*Northumberland*)—Tyler's VII, 194.
   (*Orange*)—DAR, 81, p. 287.
   (*Richmond Co.*)—Hayden, 40-44; Tyler's VII, 194-198.
   (*Rockbridge*)—Ritchie Co., 306; Rockbridge, 541.
   (*Spotsylvania*)—WM 2d, V, 171-173, 178-179.
   (*Surry*)—VM, III, 57-58.
   (*West Va.*)—Pocahontas Co., 416-419.
Weber—Sangamon Co., Ill., 760-762.
Webster—Cyc. Va. Biog., I, 355; St. Peter's Par. Reg.; Virkus II, 88; III, 273; VM, XIX, 378.
Weddell—VSR, II (No. 4), 53.
Wedderburn—Avery I, 123; Rootes of Rosewell.
Weeden—VHS, Col. VI, 148-149.
Weedon—Bruce V, 549; VCR, II, VI, VII.
Weekes—Cyc. Va. Biog., I, 355; Middlesex Par. Reg.; VM, V, 168-169.
Weekly—Ritchie Co., 201-203.
Weeks—Rockbridge, 541.
Weems—Hayden, 339-340, 349-352; RS, III, III, 36.
Wees—Highland Co., 371.
Weese—Randolph Co., 389.
Weikel—Monroe Co., 415-416.
Weir—Cyc. Va. Biog., I, 355; Lower Shenandoah, 682-683; Rockbridge, 541; RS, III; VCR, I; VM, V, 434.
Weire—MHM, XVI, 27.
Weisiger—Cyc. Va. Biog., V, 775-776; Goode, 134; Major, 183, 185; Trabue, 53-55.
Welborn—Virkus II, 51; III, 642.

Welbourn—Cyc. Va. Biog., I, 355.
Welby—Carlyle, 30.
Welch—Boogher, 253; Bruce V, 246; Johnson Co., Ky., 594; Rockbridge, 541-542; VCR, II, VI, VII.
Weldon—Cyc. Va. Biog., I, 355; VM, IV, 357; XIII, 196; XXVI, 36-37; WM, I, 84; VI, 121.
Wellford—Brock II, 807-809; Bruce V, 449; Cyc. Va. Biog., I, 355; Lomax, 152; Marshall, 247-248; McIlhany, 251-252; Munsell's X, 23; RS, II, 29, 47; TD, Nov. 21, 1909; July 31, 1910; Virkus III, 223; WM, X, 139; XI, 1-2.
Wells—Bristol Par. Reg.; Bruton Church; Cyc. Va. Biog., I, 356; Henry Co., 284-285; Panhandle, 350; Stubbs, 481-485; VCR, VI.
Welsh—Winchester and Its Beginnings, by Katherine Green, 366.
(*Orange*)—Burgess, 755-756 (Welch).
Wence—Rockbridge, 542.
Wenger—Bruce IV, 374; History of the Descendants of Christian Wenger.
Wenlock—BS, Jan. 21, 1906.
Wentworth—TD, Sept. 2, 1906.
Wertenbaker—Albemarle, 341.
Wescott—Bruce IV, 580.
Wessley (*Norfolk Co.*)—McIntosh II, 23.
Wessels—Burgess, 756.
West—Bristol Par. Reg.; Burgess, 876-878; Cyc. Va. Biog., I, 356-357; Hardesty (*Bedford*), 433; Rockbridge, 542; RS, I, 49; II, 47; III, 37; Southern Bivouac (1886); TD, July 9, Aug. 6, 27, 1905; Jan. 20, March 3, 24, April 7, May 5, Aug. 11, 1907; Feb. 1, 8, 15, March 29, Sept. 6, 1914; VCR, I-II, V-VII.
(*Chesterfield*)—Bruce IV, 59; West Family, 410-412.
(*Eastern Shore*)—ARP, I, 289-290, 337; Border Settlers, 142; Bruce VI, 553; BS, Feb. 19, March 26, 1905; Cyc. Va. Biog., I, 356; IV, 214; Harrison, Waples, etc., 115-116; John Wise, 65; Mackenzie I, 23-25; Md. Soc. Col. Wars, 10,22; VM, II, 434; West Family, 59-106; WM, III, 259-262; WM 2d, I, 292-293; Yeardley, 9-10, 22, 26-36.
(*Elizabeth City*)—Brock II, 693.
(*Fairfax*)—Hayden, 342-343; West Family, 324-346.
(*Fairfax, etc.*)—Old Prince William, I, 138-140.
(*Greenbrier*)—West Family, 418.
(*Henrico*)—West Family, 412-414.
(*King William*)—Armistead, 114; Hening V, 297-299; VI, 321-324, 428; VII, 488-490; Magna Charta Barons, 321; Old King William; RC, I, 49; II, 21, 23, 38; Robertson, 35, 43; VM, VIII, 385; Winston, 268-283; WM, VI, 33; XXVI, 261.
(*Loudoun*)—West Family, 414-415.
(*Lord Delaware*)—Browning, C. D., 241-245, 476; Tyler's VI, 116-118; VM, I, 423; XXV, 101-103, 123; XXVII, 98; West (Lord Delaware) Chart (privately printed by George Gregory, Richmond, Va.); West Family, 29-58; WM, II, 152; III, 78; V, 139-140.
(*Norfolk Co.*)—Bruce VI, 522; Stewarts of Beechwood (privately printed); West Family, 378-381.
(*Stafford*)—RC, III, 47; WM, X, 65-66, 115, 132, 144.
(*Sussex*)—Bruce IV, 105, 557; MMV, I, 399-402; West Family, 415-417.

Whittle—Boogher, 345; Bristol Parish, 186, 203-204; Browning, C. D., 3d, 621; BS, July 7, 1907; Davis, 169-170; MMV, III, 437-439; RC, II, 47 (Aug. 4, 1889); Robertson, 40, 54, 74-76.
Wiatt—Tyler's X, 12-18; Sketches of Lynchburg, 226-229; see also Wyatt.
Wickens—Cyc. Va. Biog., IV, 238.
Wickham—Armistead, 73; Carter Family Tree; Cyc. Va. Biog., IV, 75, 141; Lancaster, 137-141, 276-278; Meade; MMV, I, 256-258; Virkus I, 886; III, 479; VM, XXX, 65-66, 294-295; Whitaker, 94.
Wickliffe—Cyc. Va. Biog., I, 359; Green's Ky. Families, 183-184; Throckmorton, 388-404; Tyler's X, 47; Virkus II, 263, 319; WM, X, 175-177; XV, 189-190.
Wickline—Monroe Co., 415.
Wier—VM, XIX, 425.
Wiggenson—Rockbridge, 542.
Wiggin—TD, Oct. 31, 1909.
Wiggins—WM 2d, VIII, 317.
   (*Nansemond*)—N. C. His. Reg. II, 451.
Wigginton—Cartmell, 439; Clemens' Wills, 103; Fothergill, 124; WM, 2d, VIII, 58.
Wigglesworth—McAllister, 67, 69-70.
Wight—Bruce IV, 226-227.
Wigner—Ritchie Co., 59.
Wikoff—Adams Co., Ohio, 227-228, 900-901.
Wilborn—Bruce V, 447.
Wilbourn—Halifax, 350.
Wilcox—Cabell, etc., 581; Dupuy, 365-366; Lancaster, 75-77; Meade; TD, Nov. 20, 1904; Jan. 8, 1905; VM, II, 78.
Wild (*York*)—WM, IV, 4.
Wiley—Bruce VI, 574; Crockett, 150; Highland Co., 348, 371-372; Rockbridge, 542.
Wilfong—Highland Co., 371-372; Pendleton Co., 315-316.
Wilford—Cyc. Va. Biog., I, 359.
Wilhelm—Rockbridge, 542.
Wilhoit (Wilhite)—Virkus III, 166; WM, XXVI, 245-248.
Wilhoite—DAR, 72, p. 88.
Wilkerson—Goode; VCR, I.
Wilkes—Hardesty (*Bedford*), 434.
Wilkins—Middlesex Par. Reg.; TD, Sept. 29, 1907.
   (*Eastern Shore*)—Burgess, 776; Cyc. Va. Biog., I, 359; Virkus III, 95; VM, XXV, 404.
   (*Norfolk*)—Antiquary; McIntosh I, 159; II, 208-209, 297-298.
Wilkinson—Cyc. Va. Biog., I, 359; His. Encyc. of Ill., 588; TD, April 22, 1906; VCR, I, III, VI.
   (*Albemarle*)—Albemarle, 344.
   (*Bedford*)—Kanawha, 642.
   (*Henrico and Chesterfield*)—WM, XXV, 112, 115-116.
   (*Nansemond*)—VCR, III, 60.
   (*New Kent*)—His. Encyc. of Ill., 589.
   (*Norfolk*)—Cyc. Va. Biog., IV, 220.
   (*Sussex*)—DAR, 56, p. 7.
Willard—Ritchie Co., 228-229.
   (*Loudoun*)—DAR, 56, p. 92.
Willcox—Bruce V, 527; Cyc. Va. Biog., I, 359-360; MMV, III, 440-441; WM, XI, 58-59; XVI, 141.
   (*Charles City*)—WM, XVI, 141.
   (*Prince George*)—Cyc. Va. Biog., IV, 326.

Willette (*Giles*)—Kanawha, 571.
Willey—Cartmell, 489; Licking Co., Ohio, 812.
    (*Norfolk Co.*)—Researcher I, 124.
Williams—County Court Note Book V, 4; VI, 4; McAllister, 92-93;
        Pendleton Co., 316-317; RS, III, 37; St. Mark's, 177; Rock-
        bridge, 542-543; TD, May 27, Oct. 7, Dec. 2, 1906; Sept.
        29, 1907; Virkus II, 327.
    (*Bedford*)—DAR, 80, p. 138.
    (*Blandford*)—WM, V, 238-240.
    (*Brunswick and Mecklenburg*)—DAR, 55, p. 435.
    (*Buckingham*)—Bruce IV, 256.
    (*Culpeper*)—Culpeper, 108-111; LEP, Aug. 23, 1914, p. 9; Lower
        Shenandoah, 602-607; Mackenzie IV, 554-572; Shenandoah,
        658-661; St. Mark's, 177-183; Virkus III, 484; VSR, I, 69.
    (*Danville*)—Hughes, etc., 152.
    (*Fairfax*)—Cyc. Va. Biog., IV, 508.
    (*Fauquier*)—Licking Co., Ohio, 799.
    (*General James*)—VM, XI, 329.
    (*Halifax*)—Halifax, 350-351.
    (*Hanover*)—Bruce VI, 122; King's Mountain, 465-467; VM, III,
        326-327.
    (*Henrico*)—VSR, IV (No. 4), 24.
    (*Isle of Wight*)—Cyc. Va. Biog., I, 360; Virkus III, 158.
    (*King and Queen*)—Bagby, 369.
    (*Loudoun*)—Jolliffe, 185.
    (*Middlesex*)—Middlesex Par. Reg.
    (*New Kent*)—St. Peter's Par. Reg.
    (*Norfolk Co.*)—Cyc. Va. Biog., IV, 468; McIntosh I, 72, etc.;
        VCR, III, 63-64.
    (*Orange*)—Cartmell, 138-258, 501-505; Culpeper, 56, 66; Du
        Bellet IV, 418-432; Hayden, 34-35, 132; MMV, IV, 432-433;
        Virkus I, 891; Willis, 82.
    (*Pittsylvania*)—Bruce IV, 537; Pittsylvania, 172.
    (*Prince George*)—DAR, 41, p. 55.
    (*Raleigh, born* 1754)—Van Meter, 95-97.
    (*Rappahannock*)—Bruce VI, 392.
    (*Richmond*)—Armistead, 270; Cyc. Va. Biog., V, 770; MMV,
        I, 410, 412, 416; VSR, I, 12.
    (*Scott*)—Johnson Co., Ky., 658.
    (*Stafford, etc.*)—Virkus III, 485.
    (*Tazewell*)—Tazewell II, 384-387.
    (*Westmoreland*)—DAR, 82, p. 300.
    (*West Va.*)—Monroe Co., 416-417.
Williamson—Caroline Co., 154-157; Rockbridge, 543; RS, III, 451;
        IV, 3; TD, April 19 ,1908; Feb. 27, 1916; VCR, I, VI;
        Virkus II, 267; WM, VII, 221, 237; IX, 37.
    (*Amelia*)—VSR, VII (No. 2), 63.
    (*Henrico*)—Lancaster, 113; TD, Feb. 20, 1916; VM, V, 151,
        433; chart in Vol. V; VI, 76-77; XXVI, 83; XXVII, 70;
        VSR, IV (No. 2), 27; VII (No. 2), 64-79.
    (*Isle of Wight*)—Habersham Chap. II, 317; VM, XXV, 377;
        VSR, VII (No. 2), 51-63.
    (*Jefferson*)—Bruce IV, 310.
    (*Lancaster*)—Cyc. Va. Biog., I, 360; Thos. Carter, 100-104; VM,
        V, 433.
    (*Middlesex*)—Middlesex Par. Reg.
    (*Lunenburg*)—Old Free State II, 375-380.
    (*Norfolk*)—McIntosh I, 147; II, 282.

(*Amelia*)—Cyc. Va. Biog., I, 361-362.
(*Fauquier*)—Virkus III, 225.
(*Hanover*)—Cooke-Booth, 113-116; Virkus III, 29.
(*Loudoun*)—WM 2d, VII, 220.
Winn, Wynne (*Loudoun*)—VM, VI, 203-205.
Winslow—VCR I; Virkus III, 32; VM, III, 391; XXXV, 33-34.
Winsot—Clemens' Wills, 185.
Winston—Bell, 22; Boddie, 55, 231; Bruce V, 193-194; Cabell, etc.,
    241-242; Campbell Co., 531-535; Culpeper, 75-79; Dupuy,
    284-285; Genealogy of Isaac Winston and Descendants;
    Griffith-Meriwether, 113-114; Hayden, 675, 729; Hughes,
    115-120; Huguenot Emigration, 141, 144; Garrard, 84; Ken-
    nedy II, 371-382, 392-394; King's Mountain, 454-456; MMV,
    III, 446-447; V, 459-461; VIII, 147; IX, 130; SBN, XII,
    566-567; Sketches of Lynchburg, Va., 220-225; St. Mark's,
    183-192; TD, Oct. 25, Nov. 1, 22, Dec. 6, 13, 20, 27, 1903;
    Jan. 3, Oct. 9, 30, 1904; March 5, 1905; March 24, 1907;
    March 25, 1917; Valentine III, 1604-1760; IV, 2369-2380;
    Vestry Book of Henrico Parish, 170-179, 191-192; Virkus
    II, 83-84; VM, V, 206-207, 442; XXIX, 357, 370; XXXI,
    350; XXXVII, 71; VSR, IV (No. 1), 40-41; Winston, 1-66,
    and supplement.
(*Buckingham*)—Cyc. Va. Biog., I, 362.
Winters—Rockbridge, 545.
(*Berkeley*)—Montgomery Co., Ohio, 252.
Wirt—TD, Oct. 7, 1906.
Wise—Brock I, 224-230; Cyc. Va. Biog., I, 362; Harrison, Waples,
    etc., 109-111; Hayden, 583-584; Norfolk, 798-801; Life of
    Henry A. Wise; Pendleton Co., 325; RC (1888); RS, IV,
    3; Rockbridge, 545; TD, Jan. 13, Oct. 13, 1907; VCR, V,
    VI; Wallace's Illustrated Weekly, Richmond, Va., May
    30, June 13, 20, 1891; Wise's Eastern Shore, 87-88; VM,
    XXVIII, 276; Yeardley, 19-20.
(*Eastern Shore*)—Col. John Wise of England and Virginia;
    Hardesty, 382; SBN, XII, 570-572; Virkus III, 141, 489;
    VM, XXVII, 78-79. See also above.
(*Highland*)—Highland Co., 387.
(*Norfolk*)—Virkus III, 105.
Wiseman—Summers Co., W. Va., 417-418.
Wishart (*King George*)—Hayden, 704.
(*Norfolk Co.*)—Antiquary; McIntosh I, 73, etc.; Va. Land Office,
    Book 8, p. 349.
Witcher—Bruce IV, 491; Pittsylvania, 242; Virkus III, 312; VM,
    VII, 11; XXIV, 273.
Witham—VCR, V; WM, II, 27.
Wither—VM, XV.
Witherford (*Charlotte*)—Burgess, 793-794.
Withers—Alexander Scott Withers, Author of Chronicles of Border
    Warfare. By Roy B. Cooke (n. p., 1921); Bristol Parish,
    234-236; Brock II, 763; Campbell Co., 535-536; Cyc. Va.
    Biog., I, 362; V, 965; Du Bellet II, 245-248; Garrard, 50-
    51; Hord (1896), 87-89, 113-114; MMV, II, 417; IV, 447-
    448; Monongahela III, 920-923; RS, II, 32; Stubbs, 515-517;
    VCR, V, VI; Virkus II, 330; VM, VI, 309-313, 425-427;
    VII, 87-91; WM 2d, VIII, 34.
(*Augusta*)—Virkus III, 490.
(*Dinwiddie*)—Dinwiddie Papers I, 441.
(*Fauquier*)—Virkus II, 278.

398; XXVI, 38, 40; XXVIII, 40; XXXVII, 56; WM, I,
203-206, 227-232; II, 262-264; V, 41-44.
(*York*)—WM, XII, 60.
Woodhall—Douglas, 323.
Wooding—Halifax, 352; Pittsylvania, 76, 199.
Woodleif—RC, III, 16.
Woodley—The Woodleys of Isle of Wight County, Va., by J. F.
Crocker (Crocker-Ancestors); WM, VII, 264, et seq.
Woodlief—Cyc. Va. Biog., I, 363; Robertson, 45; VM, III, 181.
Woodliffe—VM, XXVII, 142.
Woodroof—TD, Oct. 28, 1906; VCR, I; Virkus III, 244.
Woodrop—VCR, III.
Woodrough—DAR, 76, p. 326.
Woodrow—Hayden, 661.
Woodruff—TD, Oct. 28, 1906.
Woodrum—Kanawha, 607.
Woods—Highland Co., 351-352; MMV, II, 421-424; Rockbridge, 277,
546; RS, III, 32; TD, July 9, 1911; VCR, II.
(*Albemarle*)—Albemarle, 351-356; Bruce IV, 331; V, 251; Kith
and Kin, 81-131; Monroe Co., 418; Virkus II, 55; III, 255,
485; VM, 459-461; Woods-McAfee, 2-150, 290-294, 299, 307-
309, 318-321, 328-355, 389-404, 409-410, 420-421.
(*Albemarle and Roanoke Co.*)—Bruce VI, 505.
Woodsell—Rockbridge, 546.
Woodson—Albemarle, 356; Bruce IV, 386; Burgess, 18; Cabell, etc.,
270-272; Chaumiere Papers, 78-79, 81-83, 87, 90-93; Cyc. Va.
Biog., I, 363; De Graffenried, 183-203; Douglas, 95-96, 324;
Dupuy, 360-373; Green's Ky. Families, 43-44; Huguenot
Emigration, 155; Historical Genealogy of the Woodsons
and Their Connections; Le Grand and Lancaster Grants
and Marriages; Meade II, 31; RS, II, 20, 27, 34; III, 8, 14;
Ruvigny, 520; TD, Feb. 21, March 27, April 3, 1904; Jan.
22, 1905; Feb. 23, 1908; Aug. 25, Oct. 20, 1912; May 22,
Aug. 23, 1914; Valentine III, 1806-2069; IV, 2381-2382;
VCR, VI, VII; Virkus II, 113; III, 38; VSR, I (No. 2), 25;
IV (No. 1), 39; V (No. 2), 36; WM, VII, 55; IX, 254-256;
X, 44-48, 185-191; XI, 50-58; XVI, 285; XXIV, 280-283;
WM 2d, VIII, 310-312.
Woodville—Culpeper, 79; Meade II, 82; Monroe Co., 419; Peyton,
295; St. Mark's, 192-193.
Woodward—Bruce V, 41-43; VI, 82, 240; Coshocton Co., Ohio, 821;
Cyc. Va. Biog., I, 363; IV, 300; TD, April 16, 1905; VCR,
II, VI, VII; VM, V, 212; XXIX, 506; WM, VII, 213.
(*Isle of Wight*)—VM, XVIII, 297, 426.
Woody—Bruce V, 107.
Woofter—Ritchie Co., 254-255.
Wooldridge—Dupuy, 298-299; Goode, 333, 414; Huguenot Emigration,
167, 170-171, 174-175; TD, Aug. 27, 1911; Sept. 10, 1911.
Woolfolk—Caroline Co., 487-489; Marshall, 279-280; McAllister, 67-
80, 82-88; VCR, I, V; VM, IX, 111-112, 218; WM, XI,
118-119.
Woolwine—Bruce IV, 567; Fayette Co., W. Va., 467; Randolph Co.,
396-397.
Woory—Cyc. Va. Biog., I, 363.
Wooton—Kanawha, 762.
Wootton (Wotton)—Habersham Chap. II, 538-541, 644; Henry Co.,
286-288.

(*Westmoreland*)—Tyler's IV, 153-154.
(*West Va.*)—Monroe Co., 419.
Wroe—Fothergill, 175.
Wunder—Cyc. Va. Biog., V, 573.
Wyant—Bruce IV, 201; Rockbridge, 546.
Wyatt, Wiatt—Campbell Co., 536-538; Cyc. Va. Biog., I, 43, 364;
LCJ, Jan. 10, 1915 (II, 3); RC, III, 14; Roger Jones,
131; RS, II, 32-33; TD, Feb. 28, March 20, April 17, Sept.
25, 1904; Nov. 15, 1908; Sept. 8, 1912; VCR, I, V; WM, X,
59-61, 260-264; XII, 35-45, 111-116; XVII, 66; WM 2d,
VI, 352.
(*Caroline*)—Caroline Co., 490-495; VM, VII, 47-48.
(*Charles City*)—VM, III, 160.
(*Charlotte*)—Virkus III, 65-66; WM 2d, IV, 36-37.
(*Gloucester, Wyatt, Wiatt*)—Browning, C. D., 3d, 206-207; Cooke-
Booth, 267-268; Hardy, 539-544, 548-549; Two Families, 152-
153; Virkus III, 365; VM, II, 70-71; III, 177-180 (with
chart); VII, 46-48; VIII, 128; XVI, 204-205; XIX, 448;
WM, II, 152; III, 28, 35-38, 78.
(*Greenbrier*)—Braxton Co., W. Va., 447.
(*John*)—Hardy, 544-548.
(*New Kent, etc.*)—St. Peter's Par. Reg.; VM, III, 179; WM,
V, 257; XII, 273.
(*Prince George*)—VM, XXIX, 100, 102.
(*Royal Descent*)—VM, XXIII, 429-430.
(*Westmoreland*)—VM, XXIV, 196.
Wyche—Cyc. Va. Biog., I, 365; Rives, 93-94; Tyler's X, 289; VCR,
V; WM, XIII, 256-259; XIV, 59-62, 103-107; XV, 42-45;
XXVII, 43-44.
Wylie—Monroe Co., 419.
Wylly—Bulloch Family.
Wynkoop—Lower Shenandoah, 742-743.
Wynne, Wynn—Bristol Par. Reg.; Bruce VI, 245; Habersham Chap.
II, 250-252, 295-296; VCR, VI.
(*Charles City*)—Cyc. Va. Biog., I, 365; VM, VI, 203-205; XI,
59; XIV, 173-174.
Wyrick—Johnson Co., Ind., 679.
Wysong—Montgomery Co., Ohio, 395.
Wysor—Cyc. Va. Biog., III, 355; MMV, II, 431-433; V, 474-477.
Wythe—Campbell's His. of Va., 657; Cyc. Va. Biog., I, 365; VM,
IX, 357; WM, II, 69; XIII, 175.

Y

Yager—VM, XI, 231; XXVI, 190, 195.
Yancey—Albemarle, 357-358; Alstons and Allstons, 301-304; Boogher,
363-364; Bruce IV, 285, 448; V, 118; Cabell, etc., 301;
Crawfurdiana, 20a, 29-30, 33, 47-48, 52-53, 99, 128-131; Cyc.
Va. Biog., I, 365; IV, 224; Hardesty (*Bedford*), 435; MMV,
II, 436-438; Peyton, 289; TD, Sept. 27, Nov. 8, 1908; VCR,
I; Virkus I, 674; III, 163, 192; VM, XXIII, 306; WM,
XVII, 224-225; WM 2d, VII, 179.
Yarborough—DAR, 80, p. 354; Virkus III, 495-496.
Yarbrough—Middlesex Pra. Reg.; TD, Feb. 23, 1908.
Yardley—Cyc. Va. Biog., I, 111, 365; WM, IV, 170, 285; see also
"Yeardley".
Yarnell—Jolliffe, 93-94.